COLLINS
ILLUSTRATED CHECKLIST

BIRDS

OF SOUTHERN SOUTH AMERICA
AND ANTARCTICA

HarperCollins*Publishers* Ltd
77–85 Fulham Palace Road
London W6 8JB

First published 1998

1 3 5 7 9 10 8 6 4 2

98 00 01 99

ISBN 0 00 220077 5

Printed and bound by Rotolito Lombarda , Italy

COLLINS
ILLUSTRATED CHECKLIST

BIRDS

OF SOUTHERN SOUTH AMERICA
AND ANTARCTICA

MARTÍN R. DE LA PEÑA AND
MAURICE RUMBOLL

Illustrated by Gustavo Carrizo,
Aldo A. Chiappe, Luis Huber & Jorge R. Mata

Bird Songs by R. Straneck

HarperCollins*Publishers*

ACKNOWLEDGEMENTS

Al Dr Jorge Navas por permitirme la consulta de la colección ornitológica del Museo Argentino de Ciencias Naturales Bernardino Rivadavia, de Buenos Aires, y a la encargada de la sección Giovanna Crispo.

Al Lic. Carlos Virasoro, director del Museo de Ciéncias Naturales Florentino Ameghino, de Santa Fe, por ceder sin obstáculos las pieles y el lugar fisico para trabajar. A la Prof. Edelvita Fioramonti, por la voluntad puesta en la búsqueda de información, y a la Sra. Hilda B. de Cantarutti, por la preparación del material depositado en el museo.

Al ornitólogo Roberto Straneck, por el aporte de sus conocimientos sobre las voces de las aves.

Al Prof. Julio R. Contreras, por su predisposición para responder a las consultas y datos bibliográficos.

Al Dr Alejandro Gutierrez Márquez, con quien compartimos muchos días en el campo estudiando la vida de las aves.

Al dibujante Luis Huber, por todo su trabajo y esfuerzo para lograr lo mejor en cada lámina.

Al Elda Krüger, quien desde un principio, puso toda su voluntad para obtener la perfección en sus dibujos de nidos y ambientes incluidos en las primeras ediciones en español.

A los dibujantes Gustavo Carrizo, Aldo Chiappe y Jorge Rodríguez Mata, por el profesionalismo empleado y la perfección de sus trabajos.

A los amigos que me acompañaron en varias de las tareas de estudios en el campo, Sergio Galassi, Carlos Romero y Gustavo Marino.

Al ornitólogo Eduardo A. Casas, por realizar sus aportes sobre las aves de la región andino-patagónica.

A Oscar Pianetti, por los diversos trámites realizados.

A mi esposa, por el estímulo, apoyo y paciencia, brindada durante tantos años.

Martín R. de la Peña

PREFACE

This is an English language adaptation of the now classic work by Martín R. de la Peña, *Guia de las Aves Argentinas*, which is a basic text for students, for lovers of nature and for the growing number of birdwatchers.

The original Spanish language edition is in fact more of a manual as it includes nests, eggs and much more material which has had to be reduced here to make the book a pocket-sized volume. But it has also been expanded to include some 200 species of bird from neighbouring countries – Chile, Bolivia, Paraguay, southern Brazil and Uruguay.

The area covered by this book is enormous. Of the six countries involved, five speak a common language, but for all this the names of wildlife in general are far from standard. Add to this the many indigenous languages which were once spoken in the region (several of which are spoken today – one (Guarani) is still the official language of Paraguay, together with Spanish) one can grasp a little of the problem of standardizing names. Within some countries it has been attempted.

Some common or local names are given for the countries covered by this checklist but the variety of names for any one species of bird, even in a single country, makes it almost impossible to cover this aspect properly.

Maurice Rumboll

CONTENTS

INTRODUCTION

SOURCES OF INFORMATION

South America is to birds what Africa is to mammals; indeed about one third of the world's birds are found in this continent, and they are rather special. South America's long isolation has led to its having double the number of endemic families of birds as those of its closest rival continent.

With the awakening of birdwatchers and ornithologists to the great variety and the number of species, not to mention the peculiarities, a quantity of publications have been produced over the last fifteen to twenty years. There have been endeavours to cover all the birds of the continent but these are as yet incomplete. It is also unlikely that the volume of information can be reduced to any single tome – certainly not a field guide.

The area covered by this illustrated checklist is enormous, but with recourse to many works on the subject and our own observations, the ground has been covered completely. Historically in this continent there have been fewer resident birdwatchers and ornithologists per square kilometre than anywhere else on earth.

There are obviously gaps in the data for a continent where new species are yet to be discovered and a number of taxonomic conundra yet to be elucidated, and where opinions vary greatly between the experts.

Some of the basic sources consulted are listed in the bibliography at the end of the book, but this does not necessarily mean that the opinions versed therein are shared by these authors.

AREA AND SPECIES COVERED

In most atlases South America is shown on the penultimate page just before the Antarctic, and both these are shown on a scale which gives little idea of the enormous area involved. Six South American countries are covered here which, with nearby Antarctica, have an area equivalent in size to some other whole continents.

There is within this range a disparity of habitats from the torrid tropics to the frigid ice caps of the southern continent, from the wettest in southern Chile to the driest place on earth in the north of that same country, from the highest point outside the Himalayas at Aconcagua (nearly 7000 m above sea level) to the low spot at 50 m below sea-level near the Patagonian coast –and everything in between these extremes.

Because of this and the number of species involved and because of the uncertain taxonomic relationships, it was with certain trepidation that this work was undertaken at all. Further, our own experience and opinions (right or wrong) have been followed which may make it daring to put some of the birds in at all.

Bearing all this in mind, the work is presented to those who might journey to any place in the area covered, (accepting full well that it is unlikely that anyone will try to cover it all in a single trip), knowing that it will be of some use. It is the most up-to-date and comprehensive single volume on the subject with as much information as necessary – habitat, description, behaviour, voice, distribution and an illustration.

NOMENCLATURE

As far as scientific names go, there is constant revision of the taxonomic order; whole families appear or disappear; species are convalidated through 'lumping' or 'splitting'. New species are discovered, others scrapped, so over recent time these names have often changed.

In the local names there are complications from the national and even regional usages, from misnomers in the common names. All are in current use. Some efforts are being made to standardize names, at least within national borders. In English the names have been standard for years now and these names are accepted worldwide.

The abbreviations used for the countries covered in this book are as follows:

Arg – Argentina
Bol – Bolivia
Br – Brazil
Ch – Chile
Par – Paraguay
Uru – Uruguay

IDENTIFICATION

As a general rule one should first try to find the family to which any bird belongs. Frequent browsing through the pages of this book will acquaint the user with the families into which all birds are divided. Then on to the species.

Lengthy descriptions are not feasible here because of the number of birds to be included and because of the limitations to a useful portable size. So brief texts highlighting the salient characteristics, coupled with the illustrations of almost all species in most plumages, will suffice.

Habits, where particular, are given, as too a description of the habitat the species frequents. The size of all birds is given (bill to tail) and in some cases wingspan is also given, though this is difficult to gauge with no nearby references to the flying bird. Distribution maps and a description of the call or song should clinch the matter.

Appearance

Each species is illustrated as an adult male in breeding plumage. Many other plumages have also been added when different. The symbols and the abbreviations used in the text and on the plates are as follows:

SYMBOL	EXPLANATION
♂	male
♀	female
imm	immature
br	breeding (or summer)
n-br	non-breeding (or winter)
1st w	1st winter
ad	adult

Every bird that has not attained full adult plumage, including juveniles and sub-adults, is called an IMMATURE in this book. If there is more than one plumage for immatures, the one most likely to be seen in the field is depicted.

Different RACES are only illustrated when they are recognisable as such. Some species have several similar looking races, as well as one or more that is more distinct. Only the distinct races are mentioned.

The SIZE is given in centimetres. This is the total length between the tip of bill and end of tail (L).

Habits and Behaviour

All birds feed, nearly all fly, they lay eggs and nest, though some leave the nest upon hatching (precocial) while others stay in the nest till they fledge (altricial) and are brought food by the busy parents or parent. However, habits vary tremendously between families and from one species to another. Habits can be an important identification tool and are touched upon in the species text.

Habitat

Habitat is the home area of a free-living species where it finds its food, shelter and – in breeding condition – the circumstances in which to reproduce. A habitat can be described as a combination of climate, altitude (given in metres above sea level), earth surface-form, soil type, humidity, vegetation and human influence. The habitat each species is to be found in is usually specific and is described for all birds. The height frequented within multi-storied habitats is important and will be helpful in many cases.

Occurrence

Range, season and status determine the occurrence or possibility of seeing a species in a certain area. This information can be found on the DISTRIBUTION maps (after the plates). The shaded areas are the known RANGE of the species.

The seasons determine the presence or absence of migratory species, especially insectivores such as swallows. Snow-covered grass drives grazers to more temperate areas. However, migration in South America is not the massive exodus which takes place in northern climes. Since there are no extreme continental cold winters in Patagonia, because of the relative proximity of the oceans, there is an unremarkable drift northwards in some species, and many northern hemisphere migrants arrive to augment the southern bird faunas during our spring and summer. In this field there is much research yet to be done.

Voice

The calls or songs of birds, shown in italics, are important for identification since in many cases, where vegetation is dense, the voice is the first indication of the presence of a bird. Many poorly-seen birds, which bear a similarity to other species, are most easily determined by voice when taken in conjunction with habitat, habits and other indicators. In the vocalizations, no distinction has been made between calls and songs.

The transcription of sounds is often difficult and a certain amount of patience, training, determination and imagination is called for on the part of the user of this book. Accented vowels indicated that the stress falls on that syllable.

A special feature of the song and/or call of many species is that it is given in duet. This means that two birds (normally ♂ and ♀) produce sounds that might follow each other so closely or are inter-woven so harmoniously that the resulting song or call sounds as though it is from a single bird.

PARTS OF A BIRD

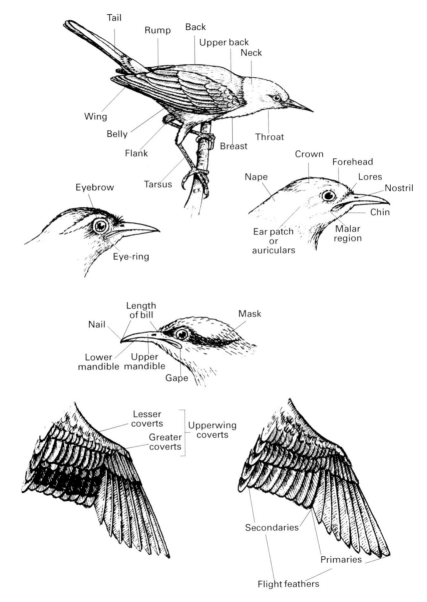

Tail
Rump
Back
Upper back
Neck
Wing
Belly
Flank
Tarsus
Throat
Breast

Eyebrow
Eye-ring

Crown
Forehead
Lores
Nostril
Nape
Chin
Ear patch
or
auriculars
Malar
region

Length
of bill
Mask
Nail
Lower
mandible
Upper
mandible
Gape

Lesser
coverts
Upperwing
coverts
Greater
coverts

Secondaries
Primaries
Flight feathers

10

Plate 1

RHEAS (FAMILY RHEIDAE)

1 GREATER RHEA *Rhea americana*
Ñandú (Arg, Uru), Ema (Br), Avestruz or
Piyo (Bol). L 180 cm. Habitat: the plains.
Huge grey birds with whitish bodies under
the enormous cape-like wings. ♂ has black
on the neck and chest. Nests can contain
over 40 eggs which are yellow for a day or
two but then turn white. In evasive action
birds 'throw' a wing one way and dodge the
other. Voice in breeding season is a deep,
ventriloqual 'boom'.

2 LESSER RHEA *Pterocnemia pennata* Ñandú Petizo, Choique or Suri (Arg, Bol), Ñandú (Ch).
L 98–110 cm. Habitat: Patagonian steppes and Andean *puna*. Large grey bird, body has a dumpy,
rounded appearance. White-tipped feathers. Feathering down onto the tarsi. Nests contain fewer eggs
than the Greater Rheas' – usually about a dozen but may be as many as 25. ♂'s 'gather' or steal broods
from neighbours, so often end up with vast broods of different ages.

Note: The Andean form in the *puna* region is considered by some to be a distinct species – the Puna Rhea,
Pterocnemia garleppi.

Plate 2

TINAMOUS (FAMILY TINAMIDAE)

1 **SOLITARY TINAMOU** *Tinamus solitarius* Macuco (Arg, Br). L 52 cm. Habitat: subtropical forests. Very large; slender neck with lateral longitudinal pale stripes. Large eyes. Back olive-brown with transverse blackish barring. At the rump the back drops off suddenly. Long legs. Greyish-brown chest, earth-brown and buff striped flanks, belly yellowish-grey with dark barring. Primary flight feathers are black. Voice: at dusk when going to roost on a horizontal branch at some height, it emits a series of usually three long, mournful whistles, descending half a tone on the last note.

2 **BROWN TINAMOU** *Crypturellus obsoletus* Tataupá rojizo (Arg), Inhambuguazu (Br), Tataupá grande (Bol). L 30 cm. Habitat: subtropical forests. Head and upper neck grey turning through earthy brown on the lower neck to reddish-brown on the back; chestnut underparts, paler on the belly and lower flanks which also have dark barring. Voice: a succession of strident whistles getting higher and faster, dimming until they become almost inaudible.

3 **UNDULATED TINAMOU** *Crypturellus undulatus* Tataupá listado (Arg), Jaó-verdadeiro (Br), Tataupá listado or Fonfón (Bol). L 30 cm. Habitat: woods and forests. Overall apperance reddish. Head and neck chestnut, darker on the crown; whitish throat. Some dark speckling turning to bars on the lower neck. Back chestnut with dark barring. Greyish breast and underparts with wavy barring, paler down the centre. Flanks barred with black, belly greyish-ochre. Wings with black and reddish speckled coverts, dark grey primaries.

4 **YELLOW-LEGGED TINAMOU** *Crypturellus noctivagus* Jaó-do-sul, Zabelé (Br). L 35 cm. Habitat: rainforest, woods and gallery forests. Legs yellow. Crown blackish, bordered by red. Back brownish-black. Lower back and rump chestnut, finely barred black. Sides of head dusky. Pale throat, grey neck. Rusty breast. Buffy belly. Lower belly and flanks barred darkish.

5 **SMALL-BILLED TINAMOU** *Crypturellus parvirostris* Tataupá chico (Arg), Inhambu-chororó (Br), Tataupá chico or Perdiz moradita (Bol), Ynambu chororo (Par). L 20 cm. Habitat: forest edges. Red bill and legs. Head, neck and breast brownish-grey. Back fairly uniform reddish-chestnut. Belly and flanks ochreous with black markings. Chestnut wings with greyish primaries. Seldom flies but runs from danger. Voice: starts with one single clear '*pip*' followed by another then accelerating, ending in a series of trilling ascending '*churr*'s almost running into each other and dimming to pianissimo.

6 **TATAUPA TINAMOU** *Crypturellus tataupa* Tataupá común (Arg), Inhambu-xinta (Br), Tataupá común (Bol), Ynambú tataupá (Par). L 23 cm. Habitat: woodland. Red bill, violet legs. Head and neck grey with dark crown, whitish throat. Back purple-brown; chest with a pinkish tinge. Black flank feathers edged with whitish-white. Whitish belly, and undertail speckled and streaked. Voice: a series of whistled '*preeeeps*', rising then descending in pitch and volume, accelerating towards the end.

7 **RED-WINGED TINAMOU** *Rhynchotus rufescens* Inambú colorado (Arg, Bol), Martineta (Uru), Perdiz or Perdigao (Br), Ynambú guasu (Par). L 40 cm. Habitat: tall grasslands. A large tinamou, long-legged and a good runner. In flight is noisy and shows red flight feathers. Yellow-ochre neck grading to grey breast. Back heavily barred and blotched with black, browns and sandy; flanks and belly barred black on grey-brown. Voice: a characteristic melodious whistle which seems to say '*to-wee-oo, who, you-two*'. Once extremely rare but recovering under protection.

8 **ORNATE TINAMOU** *Nothoprocta ornata* Inambú serrano grande (Arg), Pisaca (Bol), Perdiz cordillerana (Ch). L 35 cm. Habitat: grassy steppes between 2500 and 4000 m. Sides of the head, throat and neck whitish with black flecking. Back brownish-grey with black and ochre edging to feathers. Base of the neck and upper breast grey, lower breast and flanks reddish with faint ochreous wavy bars. Belly cinnamon. Voice: a sharp, short whistle which rises markedly in pitch, repeated occasionally.

9 **CHILEAN TINAMOU** *Nothoprocta perdicaria* Perdiz Chilena (Ch). L 30 cm. Habitat: cultivated fields and grasslands. Horn coloured bill with yellowish lower mandible. Yellow legs. Above greyish-brown barred cinnamon and buff, with black spots. Throat and belly whitish; lower neck and breast grey. Flanks barred whitish and cinnamon. Primaries grey, secondaries brownish.

10 **BRUSHLAND TINAMOU** *Nothoprocta cinerascens* Inambú montaraz (Arg, Bol). L 30 cm. Habitat: scrubland and open woods. Crown chestnut with black base to the feathers; when alarmed, these are raised to appear as a black top-knot. Pale face with brownish speckling, white throat. Back brownish-grey with irregular black barring and whitish bands. Breast grey with dark lines and white spots. Usually solitary, shy and flies noisily. Voice: a series of six to ten loud '*wheeew*'s, the first four rising in pitch, the rest evenly pitched.

Plate 2

Plate 3

TINAMOUS (FAMILY TINAMIDAE)

1 **ANDEAN TINAMOU** *Nothoprocta pentlandii* Inambú serrano chico (Arg, Bol), Perdiz cordillerana de Arica (Ch). L 25 cm. Habitat: grassland and scrubby areas on slopes up to 2500 m. Forehead, sides of neck and breast lead-grey, the last with small white speckles. Crown and nape black. Back brownish with black markings and white edging. Ochreous belly. Flanks greyish with dark and light markings. Voice: a sharp, loud, ascending whistle '*wheat*'; flocks of usually three ♀s keep contact with quiet, whispered '*coooop*'.

2 **WHITE-BELLIED NOTHURA** *Nothura boraquira* Codorna-do-nordeste (Br). L 23 cm. Habitat: savannahs, tall grass. Yellow legs. Above barred black and light tan, with whitish-buff streaks. Buff neck, streaked black. Buff breast with dark spotting; rest of underparts whitish. Voice: a long, thin '*peep*', descending at the end, every four or five seconds.

3 **DARWIN'S TINAMOU** *Nothura darwinii* Inambú chico pálido (Arg, Bol). L 19 cm. Habitat: dry grasslands and arid steppes. A small species. Head and upperparts light brown and grey with buff edging to the feathers (more uniform than Spotted Tinamou). Not heavily spotted and blotched. Voice: like the peeping of the Spotted (two per second) but without the coda or descending trill at the end, just fades out.

4 **SPOTTED TINAMOU** *Nothura maculosa* Inambú chico común (Arg, Bol), Perdiz común (Uru), Codorna-comum or Perdizinho (Br), Ynambu ñu (Par). L 20 cm. Habitat: short open grassland. A small species. Forehead and crown dark with lighter streaking, neck ochreous with dark streaks. White throat. Brown back boldly speckled with black, white and ochre (distinguishing it from Darwin's Tinamou). Breast cinnamon-buff with darker markings, barred flanks. Belly ochre. Voice: a series of more than ten peeps at the rate of two per second ending in a descending trill; or a long trill on an even high note.

5 **DWARF TINAMOU** *Taoniscus nanus* Inhambu-carapé (Br). L 13 cm. Habitat: grasslands, grassy clearings in forests. Tiny bird. Yellow legs. Crown black, feathers edged grey. Above greyish-brown with black spotting and wavy buff-grey markings. Throat and belly white. Breast buff, spotted dark. Flanks blackish, finely barred creamy-white. Flight feathers uniformly dark. Reluctant to fly.

6 **ELEGANT CRESTED TINAMOU** *Eudromia elegans* Martineta común (Arg) Perdiz copetona (Ch). L 38 cm. Habitat: dry grasslands, open woodland and steppes. A large, squat bird with slender, erect, black crest. Whitish facial stripes from above and below the eye go part way down the sides of the neck. Back finely mottled with ochre-grey and white, with black streaking. Breast greyish flecked with black, lower breast, flanks and belly ochre barred with black. Fast on the ground. Several forms are recognised. Voice: a three-note '*we we do*' descending one tone on the '*do*', or an aggressive, ascending, long and questioning '*wheeeeeet*,' repeated several times.

7 **QUEBRACHO CRESTED TINAMOU** *Eudromia formosa* Martineta grande (Arg). L 38 cm. Habitat: savannahs, woodlands and the transition zone. A large, short-legged tinamou with a long, slender crest. Crown and crest brown; sides of head and neck ochre-grey down the back and at the base of the neck. Two white stripes at the sides of the head and right down the sides of the neck, one from above the eye, the other from below. White throat. Back brownish with heavy black and ochre markings. Breast grey with black marks, creamy lower breast. Heavy black barring on flanks. Belly yellowish-brown.

8 **PUNA TINAMOU** *Tinamotis pentlandii* Quiula, Kiula (Arg, Bol), Perdiz de la puna (Ch). L 45 cm. Habitat: above 3500 m. Ochreous head with blackish streaks. Two whitish stripes from above and below the eye turn down on to the neck. White throat and white line down the back of the neck from the nape. Back bluish-grey with reddish marks. Lower back, rump and upper tail-coverts olivaceous with yellowish markings. Breast is ochre-cinnamon barred white and greyish-brown. Belly, flanks and under tail-coverts reddish-cinnamon. Flight feathers speckled greyish-brown with reddish marks.

9 **PATAGONIAN TINAMOU** *Tinamotis ingoufi* Inambú patagónico (Arg), Perdiz austral (Ch). L 39 cm. Habitat: Patagonian steppes. Brown head with white streaks, dark crown. Two whitish stripes down onto the neck. White throat with dark speckling, grey-ochre neck. Back grey with black and ochreous markings. Grey breast with black markings, lower breast whitish with irregular dark bands; reddish belly. Flight feathers reddish-cinnamon. Voice: birds call and answer each other in chorus – a series of unusually melodious notes, variations on '*tweee-oooh*'.

Plate 3

Plate 4

GREBES (FAMILY PODICIPEDIDAE)

1   **LEAST GREBE** *Tachybaptes dominicus* Macá chico (Arg, Bol), Mergulhao-pequeno (Br), Ype apa'i (Par). L 20 cm. Habitat: lagoons and marshes with dense (floating) vegetation and some small patches of open water. Brown-grey head with greenish-black on the crown and in a line down the back of the neck. Black throat, ash-grey neck. Back brownish-grey, underparts white with a grey wash. Dark wings with white secondary flight feathers, the white patch seen in flight. Alone or in pairs. Voice: a tiny, tinny trumpeting '*faaay, faaaay*'.

2   **PIED-BILLED GREBE** *Podylimbus podiceps* Macá de pico grueso (Arg, Uru, Bol), Mergulhao (Br), Picurio (Ch), Ype apa (Par). L 30 cm. Habitat: lakes, lagoons, marshes, wide roadside ditches and streams. Thick, cream-coloured bill with black band across it midway. Head blackish-brown with a dark line along the back of the neck. Neck ochre-brown, black throat. Back blackish-brown; underparts whitish with a yellow-grey tinge. Wings are brown with white on the inner webs of the secondaries. In n-br plumage the throat is whitish and the band across bill disappears. Generally in pairs, sometimes alone. Voice: a duetted '*diddle-diddle-diddle-diddle-diddle-diddle-did....*' lasting for several seconds in which one of the pair does the '*did-did-did-did*' while the other interposes the '*dle-dle-dle-dle*'.

3   **WHITE-TUFTED GREBE** *Podiceps rolland* Macá común (Arg, Uru, Bol), Patito pumpún (Bol), Mergulhao-de-cara-branca (Br), Pimpollo (Ch). L 26 cm. Habitat: lakes, streams and water holes. Head and throat black with a large white ear-patch or tuft, with a few black streaks. Black neck and back with some brownish flecking in some plumages. Cinnamon breast and silvery underparts, chestnut flanks. White secondaries show in the wing as a large white patch when flying. In n-br plumage the throat is white, the back brown flecked with red, brownish-grey around the neck, face and underparts. Singly, in pairs or groups. The Falkland (Malvinas) Islands form is larger and darker. In winter imm resembles Silvery Grebe but brownish on neck, whiter head and darker back. Voice: a soft '*eeoow, you*', repeated occasionally.

4   **SILVERY GREBE** *Podiceps occipitalis* Macá plateado (Arg, Bol), Blanquillo (Ch). L 28 cm. Habitat: open lagoons in Patagonia; the high Andes; sometimes at sea near the coast. Red eye. Grey-brown head with black nape extending in a line down along the back of the neck. Yellowish ear-tufts, grey throat, white fore-neck, brownish-grey hind-neck. Back dark brownish-grey, underparts white. Silvery-grey flanks. Wing when extended shows a white patch (secondaries). N-br plumage and imm lack the ear-tufts. Nests in colonies, usually out on the open water. Voice: contact call '*chook, chook*'; courtship call a piped whistle with trills, clear high notes.

5   **HOODED GREBE** *Podiceps gallardoi* Macá tobiano (Arg). L 35 cm. Habitat: open lagoons and lakes in the high Patagonian steppe in summer, rias on the Atlantic coast in winter. Pale blue bill, red eye, yellow eye-ring. Velvety-black hood down to throat, with white forehead grading into chestnut crest and ear-tufts. Neck white with a black line down the back joining the dark grey back. Underparts white with some grey flecking on the flanks. Wing-coverts grey, flight feathers white with dark brownish-black tips. Pairs within flocks during the breeding season. Voice: melodious piping whistles and trills which seem to say: '*who DIIIDyou?*' answered by '*WHOdidYOU?*'.

6   **GREAT GREBE** *Podiceps major* Macá grande (Arg, Uru, Bol), Huala (Arg, Ch), Mergulhao-grande, or Chorona (Br), Ypa apa guasu (Par). L 60 cm. Habitat: lakes, rivers, marshes and the sea, the last in winter and for non-breeders. Long bill, seems upturned. Slight crest. Head grey, crest and nape black, as is line down the back of the neck. Neck otherwise reddish-cinnamon. Back dark brown with a greenish tinge, underparts white with the sides of the breast cinnamon. Grey-brown flanks. 'Tail' chestnut-red. White proximal primaries and all secondaries show as a large white patch in the extended wing. In n-br plumage the throat, breast and part of the face are white, the crown and neck grey. Imm plumage is like the n-br. Alone or in pairs. Sleeps on the water with neck folded along the back. Voice: a long, mournfully wailed '*waaaaah*' which carries well over the water, sometimes preceded by two or three quiet '*tep*'s.

7   **SHORT-WINGED GREBE** *Centropelma micropterum* Macá alicorto (Bol). L 28 cm. Habitat: endemic to lakes Titicaca and Poopo (Bol). Blackish-rufous crown, bordered black. Chestnut nape and hind-neck. White throat, fore-neck and sides of head. Rest brownish.

Plate 4

N-br

Plate 5

ALBATROSSES (FAMILY DIOMEDEIDAE)

1 WANDERING ALBATROSS *Diomedea exulans* Albatros errante (Arg, Ch), Albatroz-gigante (Br). L 130 cm; wingspan 3.5–4 m. Habitat: open sea. Huge pink bill, pale pink feet. Adult ♂ white with dark upperwings, some white speckling and a white patch at the bend of the wing. Primaries and tips of secondaries black. ♀ similar but with a brown crown. Imm has whitish bill, brown body, white face, shiny white underwings with black primaries. White patch grows out along the wing with age. At rest on the surface of the sea when there is no wind. To take off they must run to gain some speed. Follows sailing vessels. So large that they appear to move in slow motion.

2 ROYAL ALBATROSS *Diomedea epomophora* Albatros real (Arg, Uru, Ch), Albatroz-real (Br). L 120 cm; wingspan 3.8 m. Habitat: open sea. Pale pink bill with black cutting-edge. Pale feet tinged with blue. All white but for flight feathers which are black. Does not follow ships. Very like some plumages of the Wandering Albatross but the black line along the bill (hard to see) may help to identify it.

3 BLACK-BROWED ALBATROSS *Diomedea melanophrys* Albatros ceja negra (Arg, Ch, Uru), Albatroz de sobrancelha (Br). L 80 cm; wingspan 2 m. Habitat: open sea, sometimes channels. Yellow bill with pinkish tip, pale ash-grey feet. White with black across the top of the wings and back, invading the underwing to leave a white stripe along the middle of the underside. Black eyebrow and blackish tail. Young birds have a dark bill and a greyish collar. This is the most common albatross in southern oceans around South America. Voice: sounds vary from a fast '*tack-a-tack*', a long drawn-out '*waaaaay*' with two notes on the vowel like a tinny trumpet, and a rapid '*kay kay kay kay kay*'; while chicks on the nest in self-defence warn the intruder with a series of '*clop*'s: beware, vomit follows.

4 BULLER'S ALBATROSS *Diomedea bulleri* Albatross de Buller (Ch). L 85 cm. Habitat: open sea. Blackish-grey bill with a broad yellow line along the top and another along lower mandible. Bluish-white legs. Head and hind-neck greyish, but crown and forehead white, grey throat and fore-neck. Blackish 'make-up' around eye and brow. Back and top of the wings blackish. On the underwing a narrow black border frames white all along. Dark grey tail. Rump and underparts white.

5 WHITE-CAPPED ALBATROSS *Diomedea cauta* Albatros corona blanca (Arg), Albatros de frente blanca (Ch). L 95 cm. Habitat: open sea. Grey bill with orange tip; pinkish feet with bluish knuckles. White, with grey on cheeks and upper neck, white crown. Blackish upperwings, browner across back. Black invades the underwing slightly from the edges. Young birds have dark grey bill. Rather like the Yellow-nosed Albatross but the bill colour differentiates it.

6 YELLOW-NOSED ALBATROSS *Diomedea chlororhynchos* Albatros pico fino (Arg), Albatroz-de-nariz-amarelo (Br). L 80 cm. Habitat: open sea. Black bill with a yellow stripe along the top and a reddish-orange tip. Pink feet. White crown; cheeks, nape and upper neck pale grey. Dark shadow over and behind the eye. Back greyish-brown and upperwings brownish-black. Tail blackish. Underwings with black invading from the edges, broader at the leading edge. Imm has a black bill. Breeding on Diego Alvarez and Tristan da Cunha, it visits waters off Brazil to Buenos Aires.

7 GREY-HEADED ALBATROSS *Diomedea chrysostoma* Albatross cabeza gris (Arg, Ch). L 80 cm. Habitat: open sea. Black bill with yellow line along the top, pinkish-brown at the tip, and another under the lower mandible. Pink feet. Head and neck grey, darker grey shadow with a white eyelid and white spot behind and below the eye. Back and upperwings dark brownish-black, tail dark grey. Rump and underparts white. Broad black leading edge of underwing displaces the white central stripe backwards against the narrow posterior edge. Imm has a black bill and almost totally dark underwing whitening with age.

8 SOOTY ALBATROSS *Phoebetria fusca* Albatros oscuro (Arg, Ch). L 82 cm. Habitat: open sea. Black bill with a pinky-yellow line all along the lower mandible. Pink feet. Overall a dark brownish-grey, darker on wings and head, lighter on the back and underparts. Small white crescent behind the eye. Wedge-tailed. Imm has lighter grey across the neck and shoulders, as do the young of the Light-mantled Sooty Albatross. Fast, agile swinging flight on half-cocked wings.

9 LIGHT-MANTLED SOOTY ALBATROSS *Phoebetria palpebrata* Albatros manto claro (Arg), Albatros obscuro de manto claro (Ch). L 73 cm. Habitat: open sea. Black bill with a pale blue line along the lower mandible. Pink feet. Head dark brownish-grey, body paler. Ashy-grey hind-neck, shoulders and upper back (mantle). Brownish-grey wings, flight and tail feathers darker, wedge-shaped tail. Imm indistinguishable from imm Sooty Albatross. Flight is characteristically fast and birds swing high on angular, bent wings.

Plate 5

1

Imm

2

Imm

5

Imm

4

3

Imm

6

9

7

Imm

Imm

8

Plate 6

PETRELS (FAMILY PROCELLARIIDAE)

1 **GIANT PETREL** *Macronectes giganteus* Petrel gigante común (Arg), Petrel gigante (Uru), Petrel gigante antártico (Ch), Pardelao-gigante (Br). L 90 cm. Massive pale yellowish bill with green tints, especially at the tip. Feet dark blackish-brown. Imm uniformly dark chocolate-brown, but with age get paler, especially around the head which eventually becomes ash-grey in old birds. Long wings have a slight notch between primaries and secondaries. There is another plumage in some individuals of the southern populations: white, with a few irregularly scattered and single brown feathers. Follows ships closely in hope of rubbish. Sailors called them 'stinkers'. Voice: a harsh growl in defence of the nest or when disputes arise with their kin over food.

2 **NORTHERN GIANT PETREL** *Macronectes halli* Petrel gigante oscuro (Arg), Petrel Gigante sub-antártico (Ch). L 90 cm. Massive pale yellowish bill with brownish-red tint especially at the tip. Plumages vary from the dark chocolate-brown of young birds to the predominantly grey of the old specimens, but these have a paler face and throat-patch slightly contrasting with the cap. There is no white phase in this species. Where the species overlap on nesting grounds (e.g. South Georgia) there is a marked discrepancy in timing, this species breeding long before the Giant Petrel. It does not follow ships.

3 **SOUTHERN FULMAR** *Fulmarus glacialoides* Petrel plateado (Arg, Ch), Petrel gris plateado (Uru), Pardelao-prateado (Br). L 45 cm. Pink bill, darker tip and bluish nostrils. Pink feet. Silvery-grey upperparts, white underparts and head. Slight eye shadow before the eye. Wing tip pattern blackish primaries with white at the base. Strikingly graceful and lovely.

4 **ANTARCTIC PETREL** *Thalassoica antarctica* Petrel antártico (Arg, Ch). L 43 cm. Black bill, yellowish feet. Brown and white in solid bold marking: brown head, back and upper wing-coverts. Paler brown on sides of head and throat. Inner primaries, secondaries, tail and its coverts, and undersides white; secondaries and tail tipped brown.

5 **CAPE (PINTADO) PETREL** *Daption capense* Petrel damero (Arg), Petrel moteado (Ch), Damero del cabo (Uru), Pomba-do-cabo (Br). L 42 cm. Bill and feet black. Plumage a chequered pattern of black and white. Head, leading edge of wing, trailing edge of wing and tip of tail blackish. Back, rump and wing-coverts speckled boldly blackish and white. Base of primaries and inner secondaries white forming 'windows' in the wing. White underparts; wing edges and tail black. Regularly follows ships, performing graceful pirouettes on agile wings.

Plate 6

Plate 7

PETRELS (FAMILY PROCELLARIIDAE)

1 **GREAT-WINGED PETREL** *Pterodroma macroptera* Petrel apizarrado (Arg), Fardela de alas grandes (Ch). L 40 cm. Stubby bill black. Bull-necked and stocky. Long narrow wings. Overall dark greyish-brown. Agile and frantic flight, swinging very high over the water. Like Kerguelen Petrel but brown.

2 **KERGUELEN PETREL** *Pterodroma brevirostris* Petrel pizarra (Arg), Petrel de Kerguelen (Uru), Fardela de Kerguelen (Ch). L 30 cm. Wholly slaty-grey with silver sheen especially on underwings in good light. Darker on wings and tail. Fast flier on long narrow wings, and performs high loops in flight.

3 **WHITE-HEADED PETREL** *Pterodroma lessonii* Petrel cabeza blanca (Arg), Fardela de frente blanca (Ch). L 40 cm. Stubby bill black. White head, tail and underparts. Dark wings; grey across back and neck.

4 **ATLANTIC PETREL** *Pterodroma incerta* Petrel cabeza parda (Arg). L 40 cm. Head, neck and upperparts brown, as are throat and under tail-coverts. Big white patch on lower chest and belly. Wings and tail darker blackish-brown. Dumpy body with long slender wings. Flies fast in high arcs.

5 **KERMADEK PETREL** *Pterodroma neglecta* Fardela negra de Juan Fernández (Ch). L 40 cm. Variable. Black bill; legs black or yellow. Dark form is overall blackish, pale at the base of the primaries. Light form: above brownish; head, neck and underparts white or greyish-white. There are intermediate plumages; in all morphs underwing is brown with white patch near the tip.

6 **HERALD PETREL** *Pterodroma arminjoniana* Fardela heráldica (Ch), Pardela-da-trinidade (Br). L 38 cm. Dark form: overall dark brown; underwing with a longitudinal white line. Pale form: above brownish-grey. White below. Brownish flanks. There are intermediate plumages.

7 **MOTTLED PETREL** *Pterodroma inexpectata* Fardela moteada (Ch). L 34 cm. Above grey, with a dark 'W' across wings and back. Crown and around eyes darker. Face, throat and breast white. Large grey patch on belly. Underwing boldly patterned: white with black leading edge and broad black stripe along tips of secondary coverts.

8 **SOFT-PLUMAGED PETREL** *Pterodroma mollis* Petrel collar gris (Arg). L 35 cm. Short bill black, feet pink. Crown, neck and back grey, face and throat white with a black mark behind the eye. Lighter grey collar. Rest of underparts white. Dark grey tail. Wings brown-grey above, paler and browner below.

9 **PHOENIX PETREL** *Pterodroma alba* Fardela de fénix (Ch). L 33 cm. Black bill. Pink or yellowish legs. Above dark brown, below white. Dark collar across upper breast. White throat. Underwing dark brown.

10 **WHITE-NECKED PETREL** *Pterodroma externa* Petrel cuello blanco (Arg), Fardela blanca de Juan Fernández (Ch). L 43 cm. Black bill, pinkish-yellow feet. Forehead and throat white, as is the complete collar and underparts. Crown and face brownish-black. Back grey, darker on the rump. Pale grey upper tail-coverts and tail. Upperwings grey, patterned darker on greater-coverts and outer primaries. Underwings with large white patch at base of the dark primaries. Underwing-coverts dark grey. There is a dark form with the same underwing pattern.

11 **COOK'S PETREL** *Pterodroma cooki* Fardela blanca de Masatierra (Ch). L 27 cm. Black bill. Legs with outer toe and webs black. Above pale grey with heavy dark 'W' across wings and back. Forehead and underparts white. Underwing white, leading edge with black line along it. Dark grey tail with white outer feathers.

12 **STEJNEGER'S PETREL** *Pterodroma longirostris* Fardela de Masafuera (Ch). L 28 cm. Black bill; blue legs. Forehead, brow, fore-neck and underparts white. Crown and hind-neck dark grey. Rest of upperparts dark brownish-grey. Upperwings brownish with a blackish 'W' right across. Underwing white with a short black line along leading edge at the bend only. Dark brown tail.

13 **BLUE PETREL** *Halobaena caerulea* Petrel azulado (Arg, Ch Uru). L 26 cm. Black bill with a blue-grey line along the lower mandible. Blue legs and digits with pink webs. White forehead with black edging to the feathers give a scaly appearance. Crown and hind-neck blackish, extending to form a dark half-collar. Upperparts blue-grey, underparts white. Outer primaries and greater wing-coverts dark brownish-grey making an extended 'W' pattern on the blue-grey base colour. Paler rump. Tail white-tipped with wide blackish sub-terminal band. Underwings all white.

14 **BROAD-BILLED PRION** *Pachyptila vittata* L 28 cm. Black bill. Dark crown. Dark line through the eye. Otherwise like all prions – blue-grey above, white below. Dark W across wings and back; blackish tip to the tail. Rarely found in the Atlantic.

15 **ANTARCTIC PRION** *Pachyptila desolata* Petrel azul de pico ancho (Uru), Pardela-de-bico-de-pato (Br), Petrel-paloma antártico (Ch), Prion pico grande (Arg). L 27 cm. Blue-grey bill some 38 mm long and 13–15 mm across at the base. Blue feet. Blue-grey upperparts. Black patch below and behind the eye, white eyebrow. Outer primaries, greater wing-coverts and tips of scapular feathers blackish forming a 'W' pattern across the wings and over the back. Blue-grey invades from the neck to form a half-collar. Underparts, including wings, are white. Wedge-shaped tail grey with black tip. Usually gregarious.

▶

Plate 7

16 SALVIN'S PRION *Pachyptila salvini* Not illustrated. L 28 cm. Like all prions, but bill is very broad and blue, filtering lamellae visible with the bill closed. Graceful and neat in appearance, the colour division being sharper. Found occasionally in the Atlantic.

Plate 8

PETRELS (FAMILY PROCELLARIIDAE)

1 FAIRY PRION *Pachyptila turtur* Prion pico corto (Arg), Petrel-paloma chico (Ch). L 24 cm. Feet and bill blue, the latter only 23 mm long, but relatively broad at the base (10 mm across). Bears the prion hallmarks of the dark 'W' on blue-grey back, white underparts and the wedge tail with black tip. However, the blue-grey is paler overall.

2 SLENDER-BILLED PRION *Pachyptila belcheri* Petrel paloma de pico delgado (Ch), Faigao (Br), Prion pico fino (Arg), Petrel azul de pico delgado (Uru). L 26 cm. Blue-grey bill 38 mm long and 8 mm across base. Pale blue feet. Blue-grey upperparts with dark 'W' across the back. Large white eyebrow, dark line below and behind eye almost on to neck. White underparts. Wedge tail grey with black tip. In huge loose flocks.

3 GREY PETREL *Procellaria cinerea* Petrel ceniciento (Arg), Pardela-cinza (Br), Petrel gris (Uru), Fardela gris (Ch). L 48 cm. Yellowish-green bill, pinkish-grey feet. Upperparts overall ash-grey with a brownish tinge, including face; darker on wings and tail, and darker still on forehead and lores. White underparts with grey under tail-coverts and underwings.

4 WHITE-CHINNED PETREL *Procellaria aequinoctialis* Petrel barba blanca (Arg), Pardela-preta (Br), Fardela negra grande (Ch), Petrel negro de barba blanca (Uru). L 55 cm. Ivory bill with black highlighting on nostrils and top, and along lower mandible. Black feet. Overall a dark blackish-brown. White chin spot, often small and very hard to see in some races, but extending onto the face or forming a 'gill' line up behind the ear patch in other forms.

5 WESTLAND PETREL *Procellaria westlandica* Not illustrated. L 51 cm. Overall blackish. Pale bill with black tip. No chin-spot. Very rarely found off Chile in the Pacific.

6 CORY'S SHEARWATER *Calonectris diomedea* Pardela grande (Arg), Bobo grande (Br), Petrel ceniciento (Uru). L 49 cm. Yellowish bill, pink feet. Dirty brown upperparts paler on head and neck, darker on wings and tail, lightly flecked with grey. Upper tail-coverts light-tipped, forming a line around lower rump. Face grey, lores dark. Underparts white. Primaries and wing edges dark, a faint brown line along under wing-coverts.

7 PINK-FOOTED SHEARWATER *Puffinus creatopus* Fardela blanca (Ch). L 48 cm. Pink feet. Bill pink with black tip. Dark greyish-brown upperparts. Below white with throat and flanks mottled grey. Under wing-coverts white, all tipped black producing lines of spots. Tail dark. Underparts sometimes grey.

8 FLESH-FOOTED SHEARWATER *Puffinus carneipes* Fardela negra de patas pálidas (Ch). L 50 cm. Overall evenly dark brown. Pale pink bill with dark tip. Underwing dark. Feet yellowish-pink. At sea around the Juan Fernández islands.

9 GREATER SHEARWATER *Puffinus gravis* Pardela cabeza negra (Arg), Petrel pardo (Uru), Fardela capirotada (Ch), Bobo-grande-de-sobre-branco (Br). L 46 cm. Bill blackish and feet pink with black outer side of tarsus. Upperparts earthy-brown with sharply demarcated blacker cap and tail; upper tail-coverts broadly white-tipped forming a noticeable white band around the lower rump. Underparts white with dark irregular flecking, thicker on belly. White invades upwards on the neck to form a collar. Dark edging around the white underwing; some darker patches in lines along the tips of the under wing-coverts.

10 GREY-BACKED SHEARWATER *Puffinus bulleri* Fardela de dorso gris (Ch). L 42 cm. Grey-blue bill; pink feet with outer toe black. Boldly patterned above: grey with a dark brown cap, a dark 'W' across from wing tip to wing tip, and dark tail. Below completely white.

11 SOOTY SHEARWATER *Puffinus griseus* Pardela oscura (Arg), Bobo-escuro (Br), Petrel oscuro (Uru), Fardela negra (Ch). L 42 cm. Slender bill blackish, feet bluish-black. Upperparts earthy-brown, underparts greyish-brown, lighter on the chin. Underwing silvery. Longish neck and short rounded tail. Loose flocks.

12 CHRISTMAS SHEARWATER *Puffinus nativitatis* Fardela de Pascua (Ch). L 38 cm. Dark bill and feet. Overall dark, even darker under the wing, which separates it from the Sooty Shearwater. Shortish rounded tail.

13 MANX SHEARWATER *Puffinus puffinus* Pardela boreal (Arg), Bobo-pequeno (Br), Petrel blanco y negro (Uru). L 34 cm. Black bill; pink feet with blue webs. Dark blackish-brown upperparts contrasting sharply with white underparts. Slight half-collar invades upwards from below, behind ear patch. Underwing white with black primaries and tips to secondaries, small irregular dark marks along outer leading edge. In loose flocks on the wintering grounds to Chubut, Argentina.

14 LITTLE SHEARWATER *Puffinus assimilis* Pardela chica (Arg), Fardela chica (Ch). L 27 cm. Very slender shortish bill and feet bluish-black. Upperparts dark blackish-brown, underparts white. Slight dark half-collar projects downwards from neck. Underwings slightly edged with blackish-brown.

▶

Plate 8

15 SNOW PETREL *Pagodroma nivea* Petrel blanco (Arg), Petrel de las nieves (Ch). L 30–35 cm. Grey feet, black bill and eye. Completely white.

Plate 9

STORM-PETRELS (FAMILY HYDROBATIDAE)

1 WILSON'S STORM-PETREL *Oceanites oceanicus* Paíño común (Arg), Golondrina de mar (Ch), Petrel chico de las tormentas (Uru), Alma-de-mestre (Br). L 17 cm. Black bill, black legs and toes, yellow webs. Dark chocolate-brown upperparts, blacker underparts, flight feathers and tail. Upperwing-coverts paler brown to beige. White rump spills over slightly on to the under tail-coverts. In flight, the legs are longer than the square tail.

2 ELLIOT'S STORM-PETREL *Oceanites gracilis* Golondrina de mar chica (Ch). L 14 cm. Black bill and legs, webs yellow. Mostly black, with white rump, lower flanks and lower belly. Large pale patch under wing.

3 GREY-BACKED STORM-PETREL *Garrodia nereis* Golondrina de mar subantártica (Ch), Paíño gris (Arg). L 17 cm. Bill and feet black. Head, neck, throat, upper breast and upper back dark grey, paler rump and basal half of tail. Square tail, tip broadly dark. Lower breast and belly white. Upperwing dark grey at the shoulder, paling towards the greater-coverts where light ash-grey. Flight feathers blackish. Underwing broadly edged black.

4 WHITE-FACED STORM-PETREL *Pelagodroma marina* Petrel de las tormentas de cara blanca (Uru), Paíño cara blanca (Arg). L 20 cm. Bill, legs and toes black, webs yellow. Greyish-brown crown, white face with a dark line through the eye and ear patch. Hind-neck and back grey, rump and upper tail-coverts ash-grey. Underparts white. Wings with brown coverts, whitish edge to greater coverts, black flight feathers. Black square tail.

5 WHITE-BELLIED STORM-PETREL *Fregetta grallaria* Golondrina de mar de vientre blanco (Ch), Paíño vientre blanco (Arg). L 18 cm. Bill and feet black. Head, neck, throat and upperparts black, greyer on the face. Greater upper wing-coverts grading to ashy. Rump, lower breast and belly white, under tail-coverts black. Square black tail. Legs barely pass the tail in flight.

6 BLACK-BELLIED STORM-PETREL *Fregata tropica* Golondrina de mar de vientre negro (Ch), Paíño vientre negro (Arg), Petrel de las tormentas de vientre negro (Uru). L 20 cm. Bill and feet black. Topside blackish but wing-coverts paler. Flanks and rump white. Chin and throat whitish. Breast and line down the centre of the belly black. Underwing-coverts white, under tail-coverts black. Square black tail.

7 WHITE-THROATED STORM-PETREL *Nesofregetta fuliginosa* Not illustrated. Golondrina de mar de garganta blanca (Ch). L 25 cm . Brown above. Narrow white rump. White throat followed by dark breast-band. White underparts. Bold underwing pattern: coverts black towards leading edge, white by the primaries, sharply demarcated. Slightly notched tail. Legs trail behind tail in flight.

8 GALAPAGOS STORM-PETREL *Oceanodroma tethys* Golondrina de mar peruana (Ch). L 17 cm. Black legs, including webs. All blackish but for broad triangular white rump spilling over on to sides of lower belly and reaching tail-notch. Upperwing-coverts paler. Paler patch under the wing.

9 SOOTY STORM-PETREL *Oceanodroma markhami* Golondrina de mar negra (Ch). L 23 cm. All blackish. Paler upper wing-coverts. Deeply forked tail.

10 RINGED STORM-PETREL *Oceanodroma hornbyi* Golondrina de mar de collar (Ch). L 21 cm. Above greyish, below white. Forehead white; darker hind-crown and nape. Grey collar from upper back around breast. White collar from throat around hind-neck. Wings dark brown, upper coverts grey. Darker grey tail forked.

DIVING-PETRELS (FAMILY PELECANOIDIDAE)

11 PERUVIAN DIVING-PETREL *Pelecanoides garnoti* Yunco (Ch). L 22 cm. Bill 18–23 mm long, 9–10 mm across the base. Legs and feet blue with black webs. Above black, some scapulars edged white. Black wings. Underparts white; grey flanks. The only species of diving-petrel in its range.

12 MAGELLANIC DIVING-PETREL *Pelecanoides magellani* Yunco ceja blanca (Arg), Yunco de Magallanes (Ch). L 20 cm. Black bill 15–18 mm long, 9–10 mm across the base. Legs and toes pale blue, webs black. Bluish-black upperparts, white underparts. Scapulars edged with white. A white 'gill' line curls up behind the ear patch from the throat. The gill line is diagnostic. Wings brownish-black. The dominant species around Fueguian waters.

13 COMMON DIVING-PETREL *Pelecanoides urinatrix* Yunco común (Arg), Yunco de los canales (Ch), Petrel zambullidor (Uru). L 19 cm. Black bill 13–18 mm long, 6–9 mm across the base. Feet pale blue with whitish webs. Grey flanks, sides of head and a touch on the sides of the breast, leaving the hint of a white 'gill' line. Upperparts bluish-black, underparts white. No white along the scapulars. The most likely species at sea.

14 GEORGIAN DIVING-PETREL *Pelecanoides georgicus* Yunco geórgico (Arg). L 20 cm. Black bill 13–15 mm long, 9–10 mm across the base. Feet pale blue with black webs. Bluish-black upperparts, white underparts. White along scapulars, and tips to secondary flight feathers. No 'gill' line. Shape of the nostrils differs from other species, but impossible to see in flight.

Plate 9

Plate 10

PENGUINS (FAMILY SPHENISCIDAE)

1 KING PENGUIN *Aptenodytes patagonica* Pingüino rey (Arg, Ch). L 95–100 cm. Long black bill with orange-red patch along the base of the lower mandible. Black feet. Head black with golden ear-patches, the gold extending forward and paling on to the upper breast. Back blue-grey. Underparts white. Narrow black line along the sides of the breast. Found in South Georgia and a few of the Falkland (Malvinas) Islands, and accidentally on the shores of Patagonia and Tierra del Fuego. Voice: tinny trumpeting.

2 EMPEROR PENGUIN *Aptenodytes forsteri* Pungüino emperador (Arg, Ch). L 120 cm. Long black bill, feathered at the base, with a red patch along the base of the lower mandible. Black feet. Black head with yellow ear-patches drooping on to neck. White chest and belly with black line along the sides of the breast. A truly Antarctic species but also seen as far as the South Shetlands, South Orkneys, occasionally on South Georgia, Falkland Islands, Tierra del Fuego and Santa Cruz province (Puerto Deseado), and at sea up to some 400 miles off the south shores of Buenos Aires province (40°30'S, 54°34'W).

3 GENTOO PENGUIN *Pygoscelis papua* Pingüino de vincha (Arg), Pingüino antártico (Ch). L 80 cm. Black tipped red bill; orange feet. Black head with a band of white over the crown from eyebrow to eyebrow. Back dark blue-grey, but brown when feathers old. White underparts, slate-grey flipper edged with white. The Antarctic form is dumpier with a shorter bill. Breeds in spring and summer. Northern populations probably not migratory. Voice: a series of '*brrrrray*'s. Also a contact call when at sea, '*hhhaaaaaa*'.

4 CHINSTRAP PENGUIN *Pygoscelis antarctica* Pingüino de barbijo (Arg), P. antártico (Ch). L 60 cm. Black bill; pink feet. Forehead, crown and nape black; throat, cheeks, sides of neck and underparts white. Fine black chinstrap from ear to ear. Back lead-grey, flippers with white trailing edge. Voice: at the breeding colony a hoarse, rapid laughing '*wayheyheyheyhey*' repeated three or four times.

5 ADELIE PENGUIN *Pygoscelis adeliae* Pingüino de ojo blanco (Arg), P. de adelia (Ch). L 65 cm. Slightly raised transverse crest-line between crown and nape. Bill black and short, feathered part way along. Feet pale pink. Black head and throat; white eye-ring. Back blue-black. White underparts. Flipper black with white trailing edge. Imm has white throat. Voice: on the breeding grounds call starts with a series of staccato '*kkk*' immediately followed by '*kekekekek*' ending on a prolonged, harsh '*air*'.

6 ROCKHOPPER PENGUIN *Eudyptes crestatus* Pingüino de penacho amarillo (Arg, Ch). L 60 cm. Red bill and pink feet. Head, throat, neck, back and flippers slaty-black with darker crown. Thin yellow eyebrow starting at the base of the bill extends with age and in the adult ends in a rigid drooping tuft. White underparts. Imm lacks black throat. Nest at the top of cliffs. Voice: a series of '*mc-ray*'s, lengthening, and with more rolling rrrs as they proceed.

7 MACARONI PENGUIN *Eudyptes chrysolophus* Pingüino frente dorada (Arg), Pingüino macaroni (Ch). L 70 cm. Bill red with a bright pink gape; pink feet. Head, throat and neck black. From the middle of the forehead back along the sides of the head a fairly wide streak of golden-orange ending in a floppy tuft. Black back, white underparts. Dark blue-grey flipper with white trailing edge. Nests on South Georgia, South Shetlands, South Orkneys, South Sandwich and the extreme south of the Fueguian archipelago, southern Chile and occasionally on the Falkland Islands. Voice: a series of loud '*rrrow*'s with very rolling rrrrs.

8 ERECT-CRESTED PENGUIN *Eudyptes sclateri* No local names. L 65 cm. Black head and back. Pale yellow brow from bill sweeps back and up in brush-like crest. Below, from lower throat, white. Black margins on under-flipper broad. Accidentally, from New Zealand waters.

9 PERUVIAN PENGUIN *Spheniscus humboldti* Pingüino de Humboldt (Ch). L 70 cm. Blackish bill and feet. Above dark slate-grey. Throat and face black. A narrow white brow from the base of the bill, over the eyes, broader down the sides of the head, to lower throat, joining that from the other side. Underparts white. A black band across breast and down the sides of the body to the legs.

10 MAGELLANIC PENGUIN *Spheniscus magellanicus* Pingüino patagónico (Arg), Pingüino de Magallanes (Ch) Pingüim-de-magalhaes (Br). L 70 cm. Bill black with a transverse pale stripe near the tip, feet blackish with speckling. Stripe and speckling become pink under heat stress, for thermo-regulation. Upperparts, head and throat black with a white band from the base of the bill, over the eye, down the face and forward to join the one from the opposite side. Underparts white. Wide black collar across the lower neck. Below this and on the white of the underparts, another black band but narrower, crossing the upper breast and descending down the flanks, thus forming two thick black bands across the upper breast but below the black throat. Nests southwards from Chubut to the Falkland Islands and Tierra del Fuego, migrating at sea as far as Cabo Frío north and east of Rio do Janeiro in winter, apparently following the migration of *Sardinops*, a small whitebait fish. Voice: during courtship and breeding call is similar to a donkey's bray; almost explosive '*ha - ha - ha - ha*' growing faster till they join into a long, drawn-out '*hhhaaaaaaa, hhaaaaaa*', ending with two or three short '*ha - ha*'s.

▶

Plate 10

11 BLACK-FOOTED PENGUIN *Spheniscus demersus* Pingüino del Cabo (Arg). L 65 cm. Black bill with a grey band across it. Black feet. Forehead, face, throat and upperparts black. A broad white brow turns down around behind the eye to lower throat. Underparts white with very few scattered black feathers. One black band across upper breast and down flanks. From Cape of Good Hope area. Recorded once on the coast of Patagonia, with Magellanic Penguins.

Plate 11

TROPICBIRDS (FAMILY PHAETONTIDAE)

1 WHITE-TAILED TROPICBIRD *Phaethon lepturus* Ave del trópico de cola blanca (Ch). L 40 cm; tail 40 cm. Yellow-orange bill. Greyish-white feet with black webs. White with black line before the eye. Another line along greater wing-coverts and a third on the outer primaries to the tip of the wing. The long tail-feathers are white. Imm are finely barred black and white above and lack the long tail feathers.

2 RED-BILLED TROPICBIRD *Phaethon aethereus* Ave del trópico de pico rojo (Ch), Rabo-de-palha (Br). L 60 cm; tail 40 cm. Red bill. Yellow feet with black webs. White, with a long black line over the eye to nape. Upperparts and coverts barred black and white. Primaries black. Two long tail-feathers white. Imm are barred black and white above, have yellow bills, lack the tail feathers (or these are short). Black markings on head.

3 RED-TAILED TROPICBIRD *Phaethon rubricauda* Ave del trópico de cola roja (Ch). L 45 cm; tail up to 45 cm. Red bill. Dark feet. White, sometimes with a pinkish wash. Black line from bill to eye and beyond. Long tail feathers red.

BOOBIES (FAMILY SULIDAE)

4 MASKED BOOBY *Sula dactylatra* Piquero blanco (Ch), Atobá-grande (Br). L 86 cm. Pale yellow bill. Bare face black. All white but for black flight feathers and tail. Imm brown above; white underparts and collar. Tail and wings dark.

5 BLUE-FOOTED BOOBY *Sula nebouxii* Not illustrated. Piquero de patas azules (Ch). L 80 cm. Blue feet. Brown back, wings and tail. Head streaked and freckled white and black. White below. Dark underwings with white axillaries. Occasional in northern Chile.

6 PERUVIAN BOOBY *Sula variegata* Piquero (Ch). L 74 cm. Blue bill. Blackish-blue feet. Head and neck white. Lower back, flanks and tail mottled brown and white. Underparts white. Wings dark brown with white-tipped coverts above, forming fine lines or bars.

7 BROWN BOOBY *Sula leucogaster* Piquero pardo (Arg, Uru), Atobá or Alcatraz (Br), Piquero café (Ch). L 70 cm. Yellowish bill (Atlantic) or grey (Pacific); greenish feet. Bare skin on face of ♂ blue, in ♀ yellowish. Overall brown with white lower breast, belly and under tail-coverts. White-tipped coverts under the wing form a thin line, a patch at the axillaries. Imm have brown-mottled belly and white patch under the wing.

PELICANS (FAMILY PELECANIDAE)

8 PERUVIAN PELICAN *Pelecanus thagus* Pelícano (Ch). L 125 cm. Huge yellowish-pink bill with reddish sides and tip. The bag below is blackish with blue stripes. Slate-coloured feet. Forehead and sides of neck white. Hind-neck dark brown. Yellow tuft on head and base of neck. Above grey, streaked whitish; below dark brownish. Wings have blackish flight feathers, grey coverts. Brown tail.

Plate 11

Plate 12

CORMORANTS (FAMILY PHALACROCORACIDAE)

1 **OLIVACEOUS CORMORANT** *Phalacrocorax olivaceus* Biguá (Arg, Br, Bol), Yeco (Ch), Viguá común (Uru), Pato cuervo (Bol), Mbigua (Par). L 73cm. Habitat: rivers and streams, roadside ditches, lakes, lagoons and marshes, estuaries and coasts. Brownish bill. Bare skin around eye and throat yellowish. Black feet. Overall shiny black and in br plumage some white around the gape and tufts on the sides of the head. Imm brownish, paler on the undersides. Swims with body half submerged. Perches on posts or branches with wings out to dry. Voice: a series of belches and grunts rather like a pig.

2 **ROCK CORMORANT** *Phalacrocorax magellanicus* Cormorán cuello negro (Arg), Cormorán de las rocas (Ch). L 68 cm. Black bill, bare face red, feet pink. Iris colour varies enormously. Head, neck and upper breast black. Back and wings black with a greenish sheen. Lower breast and belly white. In br plumage there are some white flecks around the ear-coverts, sometimes extending onto the face and throat. Imm are entirely black, the white coming into lower parts slowly giving a silvery-grey appearance. Fishes singly near the shore in the kelp beds.

3 **GUANAY CORMORANT** *Phalacrocorax bougainvillii* Guanay (Arg, Ch). L 78 cm. Habitat: marine islands and seashores. Bill greyish with a touch of red at the base. Bare face red, green eye-ring. Pink feet. Head, neck and back shiny black; bold throat patch, breast and belly white. In br plumage has a few white feathers on the sides of the head and neck.

4 **RED-LEGGED CORMORANT** *Phalacrocorax gaimardi* Cormorán gris (Arg), Lile (Ch). L 70 cm. Habitat: islands, sea coasts and rivers. Bright yellow bill, reddish-orange at the base. Scarlet legs. Bare face red. Head, neck, back, flight feathers and tail grey. Long white patch on side of neck. Paler grey underparts. Wing-coverts grey with white spotting. Feeds in riptide in estuaries and rias or between islands.

5 **BLUE-EYED CORMORANT** *Phalacrocorax atriceps* Cormorán imperial (Arg, Ch). L 75 cm. Dark brownish-grey bill with yellow (desalination glands) at the base of the upper mandible. Blue eye-ring. Pink feet with darker webs. Top of the head, back of the neck, back, wings and tail all shiny black. Throat, high on the cheeks, sides and front of neck and rest of underparts all white. Lesser wing-coverts edged white forming a wing-bar. In br plumage sometimes a small white tuft back from the eye, a black curly crest on the top of the head (soon worn down), and a white patch in the middle of the back. Imm and old-plumaged adults are greyish or brownish where normally black.

6 **KING CORMORANT** *Phalacrocorax albiventer* Cormorán real (Arg), Cormorán de las Malvinas (Ch), Viguá de vientre blanco (Uru). L 74 cm. Habitat: islands and sea coasts. Dark brownish-grey bill with yellow desalination glands at the base of the upper mandible. Blue eye-ring, pink feet. Shiny black topside, (black low on cheeks and half or more of the neck), white underparts, and on lesser wing-coverts forming a bar. No white back-patch. Long black curly crest in fresh br plumage soon wears down. Imm and old plumages brown where otherwise black.

Note: **5** and **6** are considered by some to be the same, but we believe that further research will confirm this separation.

ANHINGA (FAMILY ANHINGIDAE)

7 **AMERICAN ANHINGA** *Anhinga anhinga* Aninga (Arg), Biguatinga (Br), Viguá víbora (Uru), Mbigua mbói (Par). L 84 cm. Long, sharp bill yellow; yellowish feet. ♂ bluish-black with white feathers on the back, greyish-white wing-coverts and an ochreous band at the tip of the big black fan tail. ♀ head and hind-neck grey, crown darker; reddish throat. Dark back with long white plumes. Fore-neck and breast ochre-white. Reddish band separates the breast from the belly which is black. Wings bluish-black with greyish-white coverts, tail with ochre band at tip.

FRIGATEBIRDS (FAMILY FREGATIDAE)

8 **GREAT FRIGATEBIRD** *Fregata minor* Not illustrated. Ave fragata grande (Ch). L 93 cm. Pale bill. ♂ is black with purplish-green metallic sheen. Red legs. ♀ is black with white breast, grey throat and fine grey collar.

9 **MAGNIFICENT FRIGATEBIRD** *Fregata magnificens* Ave fragata (Arg, Ch), Fragata (Uru), Tesourao or Rabo-forcado (Br). L 110 cm. ♂ has bluish bill, black feet. Overall black with green sheen. Bare red gullet pouch hugely inflated during courtship. ♀ has greyish bill, red feet. Overall black, with white around neck, on to breast. Black throat.

Plate 12

Plate 13

HERONS AND BITTERNS (FAMILY ARDEIDAE)

1 PINNATED BITTERN *Botaurus pinnatus* Mirasol grande (Arg, Bol, Uru), Socó-boi-baio (Br), Hoko vaca (Par). L 60 cm. Habitat: dense reedbeds, flooded tall grassland. Neck ochre with brown barring, breast streaked reddish. Back ochre with reddish-brown markings, belly buff. Voice: deep and hollow.

2 STRIPE BACKED BITTERN *Ixobrychus involucris* Mirasol común (Arg, Bol), Huairavillo (Ch), Socoí-amarelo (Br), Mirasol chico (Uru). L 30 cm. Habitat: thickest reedbeds. Neck and breast whitish streaked with cinnamon. Back streaked black, ochre and cinnamon. Reluctant flier. Points bill skyward for camouflage. Voice: a series of low, deep 'woks', ending in a guttural rattle-rolled 'brrrrrrrrrrrok'.

3 LEAST BITTERN *Ixobrychus exilis* Mirasol chico (Arg, Bol), Socoí-vermelho (Br). L 25 cm. Habitat: densely vegetated marshes. Crown, nape and back black, ♀ with chestnut back. Neck and breast chestnut. White stripes along scapulars. Solitary.

4 RUFESCENT TIGER-HERON *Tigrisoma lineatum* Hocó colorado (Arg, Bol), Socó-boi (Br), Garza colorada (Uru), Hoko para (Par). L 76 cm. Habitat: dense reedbeds and swamps with emergent trees. Head and neck chestnut red. Fore-neck with black and white lines to the breast. Imm barred and speckled brown and ochre. Slow-moving and solitary. Voice: a series of 'kwock's.

5 FASCIATED TIGER-HERON *Tigrisoma fasciatum* Hocó oscuro (Arg, Bol). L 70 cm. Habitat: marshes and lakes with dense vegetation, shores of mountain rivers through forest up to 2000 m. Sides of head finely barred yellowish. Cinnamon stripe from throat to lower breast. Imm redder than Rufescent Tiger-heron. Voice: a series of 'gwock's.

6 WHISTLING HERON *Syrigma sibilatrix* Chiflón (Arg, Bol), Garza silbadora (Bol, Uru), Maria-faceira (Br), Kuarahy mimby (Par). L 50 cm. Habitat: puddles, ditches and marshes in open country and wooded areas. Crown bluish-grey, ear patch cinnamon. Plumes blue-grey with yellowish tip. Back dove-grey, rump creamy. Yellowish neck and breast. Flies with neck extended and wings below the horizontal. Voice: four or five long high-pitched whistles, all on the same note.

7 WHITE-NECKED HERON *Ardea cocoi* Garza mora (Arg, Bol, Uru), Garza cuca (Ch), Socó-grande (Br), Hoko guasu (Par). L 125 cm. Top of the head black; neck white. Blackish sides extending down onto belly. Thighs white. Grey back. Solitary and shy. Voice: a deep, rough 'oh-aaarrrk'.

8 GREAT EGRET *Egretta alba* Garza blanca (Arg, Bol), Garça-branca-grande (Br), Garza grande (Ch), Garza blanca grande (Uru), Guyratî (Par). L 85 cm. Habitat: roadside ditches and puddles, marshes, swamps, rivers and streams, lakes. Bill yellow, legs dark grey. Entirely white; in br plumage grows plumes on back. In winter plumage legs pale to greenish-grey. Flies with neck folded in a tight 'S' and legs trailing. Voice: in flight, and as an alarm call, emits a hoarse 'aaarrkk'.

9 SNOWY EGRET *Egretta thula* Garcita blanca (Arg, Bol), Garza chica (Ch), Garza blanca chica (Uru), Garça-branca-pequena (Br), Itaipyte (Par). L 50 cm. Habitat: in or near shallow water of puddles, marshes, lakes and streams. Slender black bill; legs black with yellow feet. Completely white. In br plumage long plumes on breast and back. Voice: a guttural 'goo-or, go- cor, goo-or-cor'.

10 LITTLE BLUE HERON *Egretta caerulea* Garza azul (Uru, Ch), Garça-azul (Br). L 60 cm. Habitat: riversides, pastures, ponds, and seashores (in Chile). Bill grey-blue with black tip. Head and neck purplish-brown. The rest greyish-blue. Imm white, tips of flight feathers black.

11 CATTLE EGRET *Bubulcus ibis* Garcita bueyera (Arg, Bol), Garça-vaqueira (Br), Garza boyera (Ch), Garza bueyera (Uru), Hoko'i vaka (Par). L 51 cm. Habitat: roosts on islands in lakes, marshes. Bill and legs yellow. White but in br plumage crown, and breast pale cinnamon. Non-breeders distinguished from Snowy Egret by thicker and yellow bill. Flocks on dry ground around cattle.

12 STRIATED HERON *Butorides striatus* Garcita azulada (Arg, Ch, Uru), Socozinho (Br), Garcita cuello gris (Bol), Hoko'i (Par). L 35 cm. Habitat: marshes, lakes, swamps, rivers and streams. Crown black; white stripes down front of neck and centre of breast. Back and flanks all grey. Wing-coverts grey with whitish edges. Characteristic tail movement. Voice: a harsh 'kyak'.

13 CAPPED HERON *Pilherodius pileatus* Garça-real (Br), Garcita real (Bol). L 56 cm. Habitat: riversides, tangled marsh edges, shallow streams. Bare face blue. All white except black crown. Two or three long white feathers on neck. In br plumage head, neck and breast buff-yellow.

14 BLACK-CROWNED NIGHT-HERON *Nycticorax nycticorax* Garza bruja (Arg, Uru), Cuajo nocturno (Bol), Huairavo (Ch), Savacu (Br). L 57 cm. Habitat: marshes, lagoons, gallery forests, rivers, seashores and islands. Plumages all variations on black crown and back, grey wings, creamy underparts. In br plumage two long plumes. Some forms darker. Imm all mottled light brown. Active at dusk; solitary, except at the day-roost. Voice: a harsh guttural yelp or when disturbed – 'quark' or 'bock'.

15 YELLOW-CROWNED NIGHT-HERON *Nycticorax violacea* Savacu-de-coroa (Br). L 60 cm. Habitat: salt and fresh water, mangroves, swampy woods, streams. Black head; yellowish crown and stripe below eye. Body blue-grey, back streaked black. Imm like **14** above but squatter and darker.

▶

Plate 13

16 BOAT-BILLED HERON *Cochlearius cochlearius* Garza cucharona (Arg, Bol), Arapapá (Br). L 55 cm. Habitat: densely vegetated marshes. Characteristic bill. Crown black. Back grey; breast whitish, reddish belly. Black flanks. Solitary or in pairs; crepuscular or nocturnal. Voice: loud, hoarse call.

Plate 14

IBIS (FAMILY THRESKIORNITHIDAE)

1 BARE-FACED IBIS *Phimosus infuscatus* Cuervillo cara pelada (Arg), Tapicuru-de-cara-pelada (Br), Cuervillo de cara roja (Bol), Cuervillo de cara afeitada (Uru), Karâu'i (Par). L 54 cm. Habitat: open fields, marshes, swampy areas, puddles, roadside ditches. Bill and legs pink; bare face red. Blackish with green and purple gloss. Gregarious. In flight the legs do not protrude beyond the end of the tail.

2 WHITE-FACED IBIS *Plegadis chihi* Cuervo de pantano (Ch), Cuervillo común (Uru), Cuervillo de cañada (Arg, Bol), Caraúna or Tapicuru (Br). L 56 cm. Habitat: marshes, shallow flooded areas and open fields. Adult glossy brown with purple sheen; green sheen on the tail and wings. N-br plumage all dirty brownish-black. Imm dirty blackish-brown flecked white on head and neck. Flies in long strings. Legs trail in flight. Voice: a nasal 'wek-oowek'.

3 PUNA IBIS *Plegadis ridgwayi* Cuervillo puneño (Arg, Bol), Yanavico (Bol), Cuervillo de pantano de la puna (Ch). L 56 cm. Habitat: wet areas and lakes in the high Andes. Generally dark chestnut, violet on flanks. Black back and flight feathers with green sheen, red sheen on wing-coverts.

4 GREEN IBIS *Mesembrinibis cayennensis* Tapicurú (Arg, Bol), Bandurria (Bol), Corocoró (Br), Kurukâu (Par). L 70 cm. Habitat: tree-lined marshes, lakes, streams and rivers in forests. Shiny black with green gloss. Voice: usually a duet and sounds remarkably like loud human chatter.

5 PLUMBEOUS IBIS *Harpiprion caerulescens* Bandurria mora (Arg, Bol), Maçarico-real (Br). L 73 cm. Habitat: woods interspersed with marshes. All grey but flight feathers and tail blackish with metallic sheen. Large crest hangs down at nape. Small white patch on forehead. Usually in pairs.

6 BLACK-FACED IBIS *Theristicus melanopis* Not illustrated. Bandurria común (Arg), Bandurria (Ch). L 73 cm. Habitat: dry woods, low islands in lakes, cliffs, reedbeds. Head, neck and breast ochre-yellow, with a grey band crossing the breast. Above and wing-coverts silvery-grey. Flight feathers, flanks, belly and tail all black. Voice: when alarmed or in flight a loud metallic honking; amongst themselves a loud 'chatter chatter CHATTER chatter chatter'.

7 BUFF-NECKED IBIS *Theristicus caudatus* Bandurria común (Arg, Bol), Tutachi (Bol), Curicaca (Br), Bandurria amarilla (Uru). L 74 cm. Elongated version of Black-faced Ibis but less vibrant in coloration and tone. Lacks grey band across the breast and has paler undersides.

Note: Certain authorities still consider **6** and **7** to be races of one species.

8 ROSEATE SPOONBILL *Ajaia ajaja* Espátula rosada (Arg, Uru), Espátula (Bol, Ch), Colhereiro or Ajajá (Br). L 85 cm. Habitat: shallow water of marshes and puddles. Wide, flat, broad-tipped bill. Bare head. Pink, stronger on underparts and rump. Brilliant carmine on chest and wing-coverts. Solitary or small flocks. 'Scythes' water when feeding. Voice: a cackled 'cococococococococococococ'.

STORKS (FAMILY CICONIIDAE)

9 WOOD STORK *Mycteria americana* Tuyuyú (Arg, Bol), Cabeca-seca or Passarao (Br), Cigüeña de cabeza pelada (Ch, Uru), Bato cabeza seca (Bol). L 95 cm. Habitat: wetlands, often perches in trees. Down-curved bill. Overall white with black tail and flight feathers. Bare neck and head are dirty brownish-black. Gregarious.

10 MAGUARI STORK *Ciconia maguari* Cigüeña americana (Arg, Bol), Cigüeña común (Uru), Pillo (Ch), Maguari or Joao grande (Br). L 127 cm. Habitat: open fields, flooded areas and marshes. White. Flight feathers, tail and lower back black. Imm black with upper tail-coverts and tail white. Singly or in small groups. Takes short run to take off. Soars high on thermals.

11 JABIRU *Jabiru mycteria* Yabirú (Arg, Bol), Jabiru (Br), Bato grande (Bol), Juan grande (Uru). L 140 cm. Habitat: marshes and swampy areas, and puddles when drying up. Huge upturned bill. All white, bare head and neck black; bare red collar at base of neck. Solitary or in pairs, occasionally in small groups.

FLAMINGOS (FAMILY PHOENICOPTERIDAE)

12 CHILEAN FLAMINGO *Phoenicopterus chilensis* Flamenco austral (Arg), Flamenco común (Uru), Flamenco chileno (Ch), Pariguana rosada (Bol), Flamingo (Br). L 100 cm. Habitat: shallow saline lakes, occasionally the sea. Bill black-tipped (for half its length). Legs bluish-grey with red joints. Overall pink with black flight feathers. Imm whitish-grey. Gregarious. Voice: guttural and nasal.

13 ANDEAN FLAMINGO *Phoenicoparrus andinus* Parina grande (Arg, Ch, Bol), Pariguana andina (Bol). L 115 cm. Bill black-tipped (for more than half its length); bright yellow legs. Head, neck and wing-coverts bright pink, body pale pink with brighter flecking. Flight feathers black. Often in mixed flocks with the Chilean Flamingo high in the Andes, but in winter some birds descend to the plains.

▶

Plate 14

14 PUNA FLAMINGO *Phoenicoparrus jamesi* Parina chica (Arg, Ch, Bol), Paruguana chica (Bol). L 90 cm. Habitat: high Andean lakes, often with the other two species. Yellow bill with small black tip, red on the face, red legs. Overall whitish-pink, brighter on the head. Long pink plumes flecking the breast and shoulders. Red scapulars. Flight feathers black.

SCREAMERS (FAMILY ANHIMIDAE)

15 HORNED SCREAMER *Anhima cornuta* Tapacaré cornudo or Gritón aruco (Bol), Anhuma (Br), Añuma (Par). L 88 cm. Habitat: wet savannahs and marsh edges, forest lagoons. Overall dark grey. Head and neck mottled white. Forward-curling 'horn' from forehead. Carpal spurs on the wings.

16 SOUTHERN SCREAMER *Chauna torquata* Chajá (Arg, Uru, Bol), Tapacaré (Bol), Tachá (Br), Chahâ (Par). L 90 cm. Habitat: marshes and edges of lakes. Large red feet. Head and crest grey. Black velvet collar with white ring above it. Grey back and paler breast. In flight, white under wing-coverts prominent. Walk slow and sedate. Voice: calls are solo or duets, while one says '*aha*' the mate interjects a soprano '*oglik*'. Another call sounds like a very loud '*chew-wheel, rrreap*', repeated over and over again.

Plate 15

SWANS, GEESE AND DUCKS (FAMILY ANATIDAE)

1 FULVOUS TREE-DUCK *Dendrocygna bicolor* Sirirí colorado (Arg), Pato silbón rojizo (Uru), Bichichí común (Bol), Marreca-caneleira (Br), Pato silbón (Ch). L 42 cm. Habitat: large marshes. Blue-grey bill and feet. Head, breast and belly reddish-brown, darker on the crown and nape, and almost black down the back of the neck; paler face. White streaking on the sides of the neck. Black back, feathers tipped reddish-cinnamon forming broad bars. Whitish rump, ochre streaks on flanks. Wing-coverts chestnut, flight feathers blackish, as is the tail. Often in large flocks. Long-legged and often terrestrial, standing upright, though dives well. Voice: whistled '*who TEE you*' or '*whee wheel*'.

2 WHITE-FACED TREE-DUCK *Dendrocygna viduata* Sirirí pampa (Arg), Pato de cara blanca (Uru), Pato silbón (or Bichichí) cara blanca (Bol), Irere (Br), Ype suirirí (Par). L 44 cm. Habitat: lakes and marshes. Black bill with a blue or grey band across near the tip, grey legs and feet. Black head and upper neck, with white face and throat spot. Chestnut lower neck and breast. Back dark brown with sandy edges to feathers. Sides of breast and flanks finely barred black and white. Rest of underparts, wings and tail black. In flocks from a few to many hundreds of individuals. Flies at night. Stands upright. Voice: a tri-syllabic, high-pitched, clear whistle '*see wee wee*', slightly descending in pitch.

3 BLACK-BELLIED TREE-DUCK *Dendrocygna autumnalis* Sirirí vientre negro (Arg), Asa-branca (Br), Pato silbón vientre negro (Bol). L 42 cm. Bill and feet pink. Crown, nape, neck and back reddish-brown. Head, throat, upper neck and breast grey-brown. Belly, flanks and tail black. Rump white, spotted black. Flight feathers black; lesser wing-coverts yellowish-brown, greaters white, form a big white patch seen in flight. Stands upright. Mostly in large flocks. Voice: a high, four-syllable whistle '*hayyy heeheehee*'.

4 COSCOROBA *Coscoroba coscoroba* Coscoroba (Arg), Ganso blanco (Uru), Capororoca (Br), Cisne coscoroba (Ch). L 112 cm. Habitat: open lakes in south, clearings in reedy marshes in north. Bill and feet cerise. All white except black tips to the primaries seen in flight. Patters across the water to take off. Voice: a trumpeted '*hon-carrar*', descending on the last syllable, and somewhat onomatopoeic '*cós-coró*'.

5 BLACK-NECKED SWAN *Cygnus melancoryphus* Cisne de cuello negro (Arg, Ch, Uru), Cisne-de-pescoço-preto (Br), L 122 cm. Habitat: lakes, marshes with clearings among the reeds, seashores on migration. Bill blue-grey with red caruncles at base, pale pink feet. White body and wings, black head and neck, narrow white eye-line to the nape. Pairs or flocks. Patters over the water to take flight. Voice: alarm call a quiet '*whip whip*'; '*wheeoo..*' in flight.

6 ANDEAN GOOSE *Chloephaga melanoptera* Guayata (Arg), Piuquén (Ch), Cauquén guayata or Ganso andino (Bol). L 75 cm. Habitat: high Andes 3–4000 m. Orange-red bill and feet. Head, breast and underparts white, upper back flecked with black. Greater wing-coverts dark green with purple metallic sheen. Primaries and tail black, secondaries white. Pairs or small (family?) flocks graze. Voice: ♂ a high whistled '*weep weep*'; ♀ a barked '*pair pair*'.

7 ASHY-HEADED GOOSE *Chloephaga poliocephala* Cauquén real (Arg), Canquén (Ch). L 55–60 cm. Habitat: near woods and water during nesting season. Bill black, legs mostly black on feet and outer tarsus, orange on inside. Ash-grey head, chestnut breast and upper back. Back dirty grey, rump and tail black. White flanks barred black. Wings white with blackish primaries and glossy speculum. In pairs and flocks. Voice: ♂ a series of strong whistled '*wheels*'; ♀ a honky '*crock crock*'.

8 RUDDY-HEADED GOOSE *Chloephaga rubidiceps* Cauquén colorado (Arg) Canquén colorado (Ch). L 50–55 cm. Habitat: open grasslands. Black bill, yellow legs, black on the outer tarsus and webs. Head and upper neck reddish-brown, lower neck, breast and flanks finely barred, giving silvery-grey effect. Back dirty grey, tail black, under tail-coverts chestnut. Wings white though primaries black and speculum shot metallic green. Now very rare on the continent. Often mixed in with Ashy-headed and Upland Geese.

▶

Plate 15

9 **UPLAND GOOSE** *Chloephaga picta* Cauquén común (Arg), Caiquén (Ch). L 65 cm. Habitat: green valley bottoms, around lakes, along rivers. Black bill. ♂ black legs, ♀ yellow. There are two forms. ♂ head, breast and underparts white, or lower neck, breast and underparts barred black and white. Flanks barred in both forms. Back grey, rump white. Primaries black, speculum greeny-bronze. Rest of wing white. Tail black or black and white. There are intermediate specimens, more or less barred. ♀ has sandy to dark brick-red head; breast barred brown and black, barred white and black on the flanks. Grey back and black rump and tail. Wing as in ♂. In pairs or flocks. Feeds on grasses. Migratory. Voice: ♂ a series of '*whee wheee*'s; ♀ honks loud '*har har harrrr*'s with rolling 'r's at the end.

Plate 16

SWANS, GEESE AND DUCKS (FAMILY ANATIDAE)

1 **KELP GOOSE** *Chloephaga hybrida* Caranca (Arg, Ch,). L 60 cm. Habitat: never far from the sea where they feed on seaweeds exposed at low tide. Bill black in ♂ with white spot at the nostrils, pink in ♀. Legs yellow in both sexes. ♂ entirely white; imm ♂ plumage some dirty brown feathers scattered unevenly over all. ♀ crown and nape brownish-grey, rest of head and neck blackish with a white eye-ring. Brownish-black back, lower back and belly, rump and tail white. Lower neck, breast and flanks boldly barred black and white. Wings with black primaries and glossy green speculum, rest white. Usually in pairs.

2 **ORINOCO GOOSE** *Neochen jubata* Ganso de monte (Arg), Pato roncador (Bol), Pato-corredor (Br). L 55 cm. Habitat: rivers and lagoons in forests. Black bill, reddish-orange legs. Head, neck and breast whitish-buff with reddish flecking, crown and hind-neck darker. Back reddish-brown. Belly and flanks reddish-brown, lower belly black. Under tail-coverts and rump white, tail black. Wings black with green sheen, white speculum. Perches in trees. Seen in pairs.

3 **CRESTED DUCK** *Anas specularioides* Pato crestón (Arg, Bol), Pato juarjual (Ch), Pato cordillerano (Bol). L 60 cm. Habitat: lakes, rivers and seashores. Dark grey upper mandible, pink lower; dark grey legs. Top of head to eye dark grey-brown. Floppy crest not always evident. Light brown-grey lores, across the face and ear-patch, throat, neck, breast and belly, all slightly mottled. Light grey-brown upper back, darker lower, grey rump, black tail. Dark wings with bronze-purple speculum and white secondaries. Flocks or pairs. Voice: ♂ repeatedly calls '*jzooéeooo*'.

4 **FLIGHTLESS STEAMER-DUCK** *Tachyeres pteneres* Quetro austral (Arg) Quetro no volador (Ch). L 83 cm. Habitat: seashores and fjords. Both sexes have orange bills with black nail. Legs yellow. ♂ has lighter head. Both all grey with white post-ocular streak, darker edgings to the feathers giving the effect of scales. Belly and under tail-coverts white. Wings grey with white speculum. Wings barely reach the rump. Cannot fly but 'steams' across water. Usually in pairs, sometimes flocks.

5 **FLYING STEAMER-DUCK** *Tachyeres patachonicus* Quetro volador (Arg, Ch). L 68 cm. Habitat: inland waters and sea coast. ♂ bill orange-yellow at base, blue-green at tip; ♀ blue-grey; big black nail on both. Legs yellow. ♂ head pale grey with white post-ocular stripe, ♀ darker. Back, breast and flanks of both grey with darker edges to feathers giving a scaly appearance. Belly and under tail-coverts white. Wing grey with white speculum; tail grey. Wings reach the base of the tail. In pairs or small flocks. Voice: ♂ a '*tishu tishu*': ♀ a deep '*ark ark*'.

6 **FALKLAND STEAMER-DUCK** *Tachyeres brachypterus* Quetro malvinero (Arg). L 80 cm. Yellowish bill in ♂, greenish in ♀; legs yellowish. Big grey flightless bird. ♂ lighter on the head with age, to quite white. White post-ocular streak. Reddish or rusty-yellow tinge to coloration. Breast, back and flank feathers edged darker, giving scaly appearance. Belly and under tail-coverts white. Short wings barely reaching rump show a white speculum. Usually in pairs but on certain coasts flocks form of non-territorial adults and juveniles. Voice: ♂ a sneezy '*tissue, tissue*': ♀ rattles a deep '*krok krok*'.

Note: There is a very similar bird on the coasts of Chubut which some consider a separate species, the White-headed Steamer-duck, *Tachyeres leucocephalus*.

Plate 16

Plate 17

SWANS, GEESE AND DUCKS (FAMILY ANATIDAE)

1 **SPECTACLED DUCK** *Anas specularis* Pato de anteojos (Arg), Pato anteojillo (Ch). L 55 cm. Habitat: high corrie lakes in summer, rivers and lake shores, ponds. Dark brown head and hind-neck with sharp white oval patch before the eye, and white crescent from throat, via neck, curling up to behind the ear. Breast brown, flanks lighter with dark tips to the feathers, appearing like large scales. Wings dark with lighter coverts and a bronzy-purple speculum edged white before and black and white behind. Dark tail. Pairs or small flocks. Voice: a short sharp bark.

2 **SPECKLED TEAL** *Anas flavirostris* Pato barcino (Arg, Uru, Bol), Pato piojoso (Bol), Pato jergón chico (Ch), Marreca-pardinha (Br). L 40–43 cm. Habitat: lakes, marshes, streams, rivers. Bill yellow with black line along the top, bluish-grey legs. Grey-brown head. Back blackish with ochre edges to the feathers; lower back and rump brown. Breast pale brown with blackish spots; flanks, belly and tail pale brown (flanks creamy in the high-Andean form). Wings brownish with a green speculum, bordered rich brown and cream. Voice: ♂ calls with a high whistle '*pireep*' or '*piripeep*', ♀ a quiet '*jziiiu*'.

Note: Some consider the Andean form a distinct species, the Sharp-winged Teal, *Anas oxypterum*.

3 **SOUTHERN WIGEON** *Anas sibilatrix* Pato overo (Arg, Bol, Uru), Marreca-oveira (Br), Pato real (Ch). L 51 cm. Habitat: shores of marshes, lakes and rivers. Sexes similar: white face, black head and neck with greenish or purple sheen in the ♂. Whitish patch on ear-coverts. Black back with sharply contrasting white edges to the feathers. Breast barred blackish and white. Cinnamon flanks and under tail-coverts brighter in ♂; white rump and belly, black tail. ♀s are duller. Dark wings with large white flash on coverts; underwing white. Voice: ♂'s call a strong whistled '*whooooeeeteeeooo*', louder and higher in the middle.

4 **WHITE-CHEEKED PINTAIL** *Anas bahamensis* Pato gargantilla (Arg, Bol, Uru, Ch), Marreca-toicinho (Br). L 48 cm. Bill blue-grey with red at the basal sides of the upper mandible, feet brown. Top of the head, nape and back of the neck brown. Face, throat and upper neck sharply white. Breast and flanks rich buff, spotted with brown. Tail creamy and pale, noticeable in flight at a distance. Dark brown wings with metallic green speculum bordered by wide cinnamon bands.

5 **BROWN PINTAIL** *Anas georgica* Pato maicero (Arg, Bol), Pato cola aguda (Bol), Pato pardo (Uru), Marreca-parda (Br), Pato jergón grande (Ch). L 45–52 cm. Habitat: lakes, streams, marshes, puddles. Crown chestnut-brown with black streaking; face and neck pale brown with darker flecking. Back dark brown, feathers edged ochre. Whitish throat. Lower neck, breast and flanks mid-brown slightly marked darker. Belly buff. Tail brownish. Wings brown with dark speculum bordered buff above and below. Overall impression is brown. Voice: a triple whistled '*piripip*'.

6 **SILVER TEAL** *Anas versicolor* Pato capuchino (Arg, Ch, Uru, Bol), Marecca-cricri (Br). L 40 cm. Bill blue, yellow at the base. Top half of the head and the nape blackish; lower half of the head, throat and upper neck creamy. Back blackish, upper back feathers edged buff. Rump and tail very finely barred black and white, looking silver, as also the lower sides of the body and undertail, though here paler. Lower neck and breast creamy buff speckled with dark brown, grading gently to flanks boldly barred black and white. Voice: ♂ calls a quiet non-vocal '*rrrrrrr*'.

7 **PUNA TEAL** *Anas puna* Pato puneño (Arg), Pato Puna (Bol, Ch). L 46 cm. Habitat: lakes, puddles or streams 3–4000 m in Andes. Bill blue with black line along the straight 'Grecian' culmen. Top half of head, and nape black; lower half of head, throat and upper neck pale cream. Rump, tail, undertail and sides of lower body finely barred brown and cream, looking dirty buff. Lower neck and breast ochre-buff speckled lightly brown. Flanks barred brown and cream.

8 **BLUE-WINGED TEAL** *Anas discors* Pato media luna (Arg, Bol), Pato aliazul (Bol), Pato de alas azules (Ch), Pato de ala azul (Uru), Marreca-de-asa-azul (Br). L 44 cm. Habitat: lakes and marshes. ♂: head dark blue-grey, large white crescent between eye and bill. Underparts reddish-brown, speckled. Wing-coverts blue, greaters tipped white; secondaries green. ♀: (very like ♀ Cinnamon Teal), brown head with eyebrow, face and throat pale; duller underparts than ♂. Singly or in mixed flocks.

9 **CINNAMON TEAL** *Anas cyanoptera* Pato colorado (Arg, Bol, Uru, Ch), Marreca-colorada (Br). L 42 cm. Habitat: lakes, marshes. ♂ overall deep chestnut-red, darker crown. Wing-coverts sky-blue, green speculum. ♀: blackish crown, pale throat. Buff face and neck speckled brownish. Back brownish, feathers edged buff. Breast cinnamon, spotted dark brown. Wings as in ♂ but duller. Often with other species.

Plate 17

Plate 18

SWANS, GEESE AND DUCKS (FAMILY ANATIDAE)

1 **RED SHOVELER** *Anas platalea* Pato cuchara (Arg, Bol, Ch), Marreca-colheira (Br), Pato espátula (Uru). L 51 cm. Habitat: lakes, marshes. ♂ has whitish head. Breast, belly, flanks and shoulders red-brown with dark spotting. Tail blackish. Wing-coverts blue. ♀ sandy brown. Darker back feathers pale-edged. Darker markings on breast. Flank feathers edged darker. Tail whitish. Wings have pale blue coverts and no speculum.

2 **RINGED TEAL** *Anas leucophrys* Pato de collar (Arg, Uru, Bol), Marreca-de-coleira (Br). L 33 cm. Habitat: marshes, lagoons and puddles surrounded by woods. ♂ has black crown and down back of the neck, forming an incomplete collar at the base. Back dark red-olive. Breast pink with black dots. Flanks silvery. Black undertail with a white patch. Wings dark with metallic green secondaries, white spot on greater secondary coverts. ♀: face brown, white eyebrow. Perches on trees or posts. Voice: a reedy long '*whoowaaaaay*'.

3 **TORRENT DUCK** *Merganetta armata* Pato de los torrentes (Arg), Pato corta corriente (Bol, Ch). L 40 cm. Habitat: white-water rivers and streams. Red bill. ♂ has white head with black line on crown and hind-neck; black post-ocular; black upper breast. Body black with white-edged feathers (brown-edged on underparts of southern form). ♀ has grey head with cinnamon-brown cheek (fore-neck in southern form). Cinnamon underparts. Black back streaked white. Voice high, whistled '*prreeeps*'.

4 **ROSY-BILLED POCHARD** *Netta peposaca* Pato picazo (Arg, Bol, Uru), Marrecão (Br), Pato negro (Ch). L 55 cm. Habitat: lakes, marshes. ♂ bill bright pink with red caruncles; ♀ bill bluish. ♂ black above with purple gloss. Finely barred 'silver' flanks. White bar in extended wing. ♀ overall brown, whitish underparts. Wings patterned like ♂. Voice: a growly '*aaark*'.

5 **SOUTHERN POCHARD** *Netta erythrophthalma* Pato castaño (Arg, Ch, Bol), Paturi-preta (Br). L 49 cm. Habitat: lakes, rivers and streams, coastal lagoons, marshes. ♂ has head, neck and breast black with purple sheen, dark back. Belly brownish. Wings dark with a conspicuous white line along base of the flight feathers. ♀ is brownish overall, darker on the back, with white patch at the base of the bill. Rarely seen.

6 **BRAZILIAN DUCK** *Amazonetta brasiliensis* Pato cutirí (Arg, Bol), Pato de ala verde (Uru), Pato brasileño (Bol), Pé-vermelho or Ananaí (Br), Ype'i vera (Par). L 42 cm. Habitat: lakes, marshes. ♂ bill red; feet scarlet. Crown brown with black flecking, black continuing down neck. Reddish-brown breast, light brown belly and flanks, with round black spots. Tail black. Wings velvety black, green sheen. Secondaries form white triangle at inner trailing edge. ♀ has white spot on the lores and above and in front of the eye, dark blue-grey bill. Voice: ♂ calls a high whistled '*whoweeeyou*'.

7 **COMB DUCK** *Sarkidiornis melanotos* Pato crestudo (Arg, Bol), Putriao (Br). L 80 cm (♂). Habitat: rivers, marshes and lagoons with wooded banks. ♂ has disk-shaped knob on bill. Head and neck white with blackish flecking. Breast and belly white, flanks blackish. Back black with metallic sheen. In pairs or flocks; perch in trees.

8 **MUSCOVY DUCK** *Cairina moschata* Pato real (Arg, Bol), Pato-do-mato (Br), Pato criollo (Ch, Uru), Ype guasu (Par). L 65–80 cm. Habitat: rivers, lagoons and marshes in wooded areas. Black with metallic sheen. Wing-coverts white. Imm brownish-black without white in wing. Perch in trees.

9 **BRAZILIAN MERGANSER** *Mergus octosetaceus* Pato serrucho (Arg), Pato-mergulhao (Br). L 55 cm. Habitat: streams and rivers in sub-tropical forests. Narrow bill. Head, neck and long crest black with green sheen. Back blackish; breast, flanks and belly finely barred dark and light grey. Wings blackish with white secondaries and a white line through wing-coverts. Extremely rare. .

10 **RUDDY DUCK** *Oxyura jamaicensis* Pato zambullidor grande (Arg), Pato malvasia (Bol), Pato rana de pico ancho (Ch) . L 48 cm. Habitat: open water on lakes and marshes. Bill blue in ♂, blackish in ♀. ♂ has a black head, rest of body is rich dark chestnut; cut off from chin to shoulder. ♀ dark chocolate-brown, lighter throat. Faint line below the eye. Voice: ♂ courtship call a hollow drumming rapid '*doodoodoo*' followed immediately by '*con your*'.

Note: Some still consider this race a separate species, the Andean Ruddy Duck, *Oxyura ferruginea*.

11 **LAKE DUCK** *Oxyura vittata* Pato zambullidor chico (Arg), Pato zambullidor (Uru), Pato rana de pico delgado (Ch), Marreca-pé-na-bunda (Br). L 39 cm. Habitat: open water of lakes and marshes. ♂ has blue bill, black head, chestnut body; cut-off between the colours straight across neck. ♀ is brownish-grey with a whitish line across face. Whitish throat. Grey-brown back with barred appearance. Tail held straight up, or flat when diving. Voice: ♂'s display call '*poor poor poor*' followed by a guttural '*wooork, wooork, woork work*'.

12 **MASKED DUCK** *Oxyura dominica* Pato fierro (Arg, Bol), Bico-roxo (Br), Pato sapo (Uru), Pato enmascarado (Bol). L 32 cm. ♂ has bright blue bill, face and crown black; nape, neck, breast, flanks and back all rich red-brown, back black streaks, flanks with black spotting. Wings with a round white spot seen in flight. ♀: blackish crown, two ochre face-stripes, above and below the eye. Dark line through eye and another across lower face. Back blackish with ochre wavy lines across. Stiff blackish tail.

▶

Plate 18

13 BLACK-HEADED DUCK *Heteronetta atricapilla* Pato cabeza negra (Arg, Bol, Uru), Pato rinconero (Ch), Marreca-de-cabeça-preta (Br). L 42 cm. Habitat: lakes and marshes. Bill blackish, red spot (♂), dark greyish (♀). ♂ has black head, blackish back, breast and flanks brown, lighter belly. Under tail-coverts cinnamon. ♀ has brown head, slight eyebrow and throat lighter; undertail white. Both have broadly white-tipped secondaries, visible as flash in flight.

Plate 19

NEW-WORLD VULTURES (FAMILY CATHARTIDAE)

1 BLACK VULTURE *Coragyps atratus* Jote cabeza negra (Arg, Ch), Urubu-de-cabeça-preta (Br), Buitre de cabeza negra (Uru), Zamuro negro or Gallinazo de cabeza negra (Bol), Yryvu (Par). L 56–65 cm, wingspan 1.4 m. Longish, slender bill grey, red iris, grey legs and feet, sometimes whitened. Head and upper neck bare and black. Rest overall dull black. Whitish patch at the base of the primaries seen in flight from below. Short tail about as long as the legs (in flight) or the folded wings when perched. (See Plate A for bird in flight).

2 TURKEY VULTURE *Cathartes aura* Jote cabeza colorada (Arg, Ch), Zamuro cabecirojo, Peroquí (Bol), Buitre de cabeza roja (Uru) Urubu-de-cabeça-vermelha (Br), Yryvu (Par). L 65–75 cm, wingspan 1.8 m. Habitat: over woodlands, open woods and mountainous terrain. Whitish beak, red iris, pink legs and feet. Bare head red with a small white spot on the nape. Overall dull blackish. Flight feathers on underside greyish giving a silvery look to this part of the underwing when in flight. Long rectangular tail. Hardly ever flaps. When perched the wings are not longer than the tail. (See Plate A for bird in flight).

3 LESSER YELLOW-HEADED VULTURE *Cathartes burrovianus* Jote cabeza amarilla (Arg), Urubu-de-cabeça-amarela (Br), Buitre de cabeza amarilla (Uru), Zamuro cabeciamarilla menor (Bol), Yryvu akâ sa'yju (Par). L 62–69 cm. Habitat: glides low over grasslands. Whitish beak, reddish iris, whitish legs and feet. Yellowish-orange head with blue on the crown. Overall dull blackish with silver under all flight feathers as in the Turkey Vulture, from which it is hard to tell apart. The shafts of the primaries are white and show on the upperside of the wing. (See Plate A for bird in flight).

4 ANDEAN CONDOR *Vultur gryphus* Cóndor (Arg, Ch), Condor-dos-andes (Br), Cóndor de los Andes (Bol). L 120 cm, wingspan 3 m +. Habitat: mountains. Creamy-tipped black beak. ♂ has brown iris, ♀ red. Grey legs and feet. Bare wattled and caranculated head dirty fleshy pink (blacker in southern latitudes). ♂ has a large bare crest on the forehead. White 'ermine' collar. Body, tail and wings all black, but greater upper wing-coverts and black-tipped secondaries white, forming a large white patch on the upperwing seen from above or when the bird banks. Imm dark brown with black flight feathers and tail, (no collar, no white on the upperwing). Primaries splayed finger-like. Outline very rectangular (long, squarish-tipped wings). Excellent glider and soarer. (See Plate A for bird in flight).

5 KING VULTURE *Sarcoramphus papa* Jote real (Arg), Cóndor blanco or real (Bol), Urubu-rei (Br). L 76 cm. Habitat: over woods and forests up to 2700 m. Beak and cere reddish-orange, white iris, legs blackish-grey. Bare head black with crown, nape and eye-ring red-orange. Bare orange neck. Downy velvet collar blue-grey. White back; rump and short tail black. Underparts white. Wings with white lesser coverts, black flight feathers and greater coverts. Imm all blackish (like the Black Vulture) but with the grey down collar. (See Plate A for bird in flight).

OSPREY (FAMILY ACCIPITRIDAE)

6 OSPREY *Pandion haliaetus* Aguila pescadora (Arg, Ch, Uru, Bol), Aguia-pescadora (Br), Taguato rye morotî (Par). L ♂ 56, ♀ 63 cm; wingspan 150–180 cm. Grey bill, yellow iris, bluish-grey legs and feet. Head white, crested from the nape. Crown and a line through the eye continuing down the side of the neck to the back, dark brownish. Back dark brown. Underparts whitish with brown flecking at the sides of the lower neck and breast. Wings long, narrow and angular, dark brown, secondaries finely edged whitish. Underwing with dark patch at bend; dark-tipped rows of coverts give a banded effect. Tail banded brown and ochre. Imm with light tips to all brown feathers of upperparts, so wings and neck look mottled. Solitary, perches in trees by the water. (See Plate A for bird in flight).

Plate 19

Plate 20

KITES, HARRIERS, HAWKS AND EAGLES (FAMILY ACCIPITRIDAE)

1 **GREY-HEADED KITE** *Leptodon cayanensis* Milano cabeza gris (Arg), Gaviao-de-cabeça-cinza (Br), Gavilán palomero (Bol). L ♂ 50, ♀ 55 cm. Habitat: sub-tropical forests and adjacent clearings. Black beak, brownish iris. Legs and cere pale bluish. Grey head, blackish back, white underparts. Broad rounded wings which from below show black under wing-coverts and flight feathers concentrically barred. Long blackish tail with three white bands; narrow white tip. Imm dark, dark head, brown back, light undersides streaked brown and barred tail. Light form: crown black, white cheeks, yellow lores. White from forehead through eyebrow and continuing to form a ring around nape. Voice: a cat-like mew. (See Plate A for bird in flight).

2 **HOOK-BILLED KITE** *Chondrohierax uncinatus* Milano pico garfio (Arg), Gavilán garfío (Bol), Caracoleiro (Br). L ♂ 38–40, ♀ 43–46 cm. Habitat: sub-tropical and cloud forest. Hooked beak dark grey; iris ivory; cere, lores and short legs yellow. ♂: head and back dark grey, undersides evenly barred grey and whitish right across. Top of the rounded, broad wings dark grey with barred primaries. Underwing whitish-grey, concentrically barred darker. Long dark tail with two bands and tip grey. ♀ is a brown version of the ♂, dark on back, redder on neck and undersides (similarly barred). A dark form occurs in which both sexes are all blackish-brown with a broad white band on the tail. Imm pale phase: head and back all blackish, undersides white with irregular brown marks, complete white collar and barred tail; dark phase imm: all blackish-brown. Imm lacks ivory iris. (See Plate A for bird in flight).

3 **SWALLOW-TAILED KITE** *Elanoides forficatus* Milano tijereta (Arg), Gaviao-tesoura (Br), Gavilán tijereta (Bol), Taguato jetapa (Par). L ♂ 55, ♀ 60 cm; wingspan 1.2 m. Small beak dark grey, cere lighter; iris reddish-brown; legs yellowish. Head, neck, rump and underparts white. Back blue-black with metallic sheen, wings blue-black, shoulders black. Flight feathers black, under wing-coverts white. Very long, deeply forked tail black. Flies superbly. Imm speckled. Call: a whistled '*he he wheee hewheee*'. (See Plate A for bird in flight).

4 **PEARL KITE** *Gampsonyx swainsoni* Milano chico (Arg), Milanito blanco (Bol), Gaviaozinho (Br). L ♂ 20, ♀ 22 cm. Habitat: savannas, palm groves and open country with some trees. Grey beak, brown iris; feet and cere yellow. Slate-grey head, forehead and cheeks orange. Slate-grey back and tail. White collar and underparts. Flanks and thighs reddish-brown. Long, narrow slate-grey wings, tip of secondaries white. White underwing. Imm has browner back and yellowish-brown underparts. (See Plate A for bird in flight).

5 **WHITE-TAILED KITE** *Elanus leucurus* Milano blanco (Arg), Peneira (Br), Bailarín (Ch), Halcón blanco (Uru), Gavilán blanco (Bol), Taguato morotî (Par). L ♂ 35, ♀ 37 cm. Habitat: open grassland and savannahs, steppes, agricultural areas (with trees). Black beak, red iris; yellow cere and feet. Head white, dark around eye. Grey back and wings, black shoulders. Underparts and tail white, slightly greyer central feathers. Small black spot under the bend in the wing. Imm: greyish on crown and hind-neck, brown flecking on breast, greyish sub-terminal band on tail, feathers on upperwing edged or tipped white. Voice: contact call an occasional whistled '*hee-op*' or '*heep*'. (See Plate B for bird in flight).

6 **SNAIL KITE** *Rostrhamus sociabilis* Caracolero (Arg, Par), Caramujeiro (Br), Aguila caracolera (Uru), Caracolero común (Bol). L ♂ 41, ♀ 43 cm. Habitat: marshes, swamps, roadside ditches (always near water). Slender, curved snail-picking beak; iris, cere and legs red. ♂: head and back slaty-black, dark lead-grey breast and belly, under tail-coverts white. Broad and rounded wings black. Tail black with white base and narrow white tip. ♀: brownish head with whitish forehead and eyebrow, dark brown back. Whitish throat, ochreous underparts with broad brownish streaking. White undertail. Dark primaries, paler wing-coverts and secondaries, these with ochre-cinnamon tip. Under wing-coverts cinnamon, ochre and dark grey; flight feathers grey and whitish from below. Tail as in the ♂ but brown. Imm like ♀ but stronger eyebrow and heavier streaking on underside. Voice: a rapid '*heckeckeckeckeckeck*' and a rattle. (See Plate B for bird in flight).

7 **RUFOUS-THIGHED KITE** *Harpagus diodon* Milano de corbata (Arg), Gaviao-bombachinha (Br), Gavilán pecho rojo (Bol). L ♂ 30, ♀ 36 cm. Habitat: sub-tropical woods and forests. Beak black; iris, cere and legs yellow. Head and back dark brownish-grey, underparts pale grey. Whitish throat with a brown mid-line. Thighs rufous. Short, wide wings. Underwing flight feathers concentrically barred, coverts rusty. Under tail-coverts whitish; long, broad tail dark with three or four greyish bands. Imm pale breast with brown streaks. No rufous on underwing. (See Plate B for bird in flight).

8 **PLUMBEOUS KITE** *Ictinia plumbea* Milano plomizo (Arg), Sovi (Br), Gavilán azulado grande (Bol). L ♂ 35, ♀ 37 cm. Beak black, cere grey; iris red, short legs yellow-orange. Head grey, back slate-grey and underparts light grey. Long, sharp-pointed narrow wings dark grey with black and rufous primaries. Underwing grey with rufous primaries. Tail from above blue-black with white bars on the outer feathers; from below and in flight black with three white bands. Imm streaked brown on head and underparts, white eyebrow, reddish-brown back and no rufous in the wings. Agile in flight. Voice: a high double whistle '*see see-ay*'. (See Plate B for bird in flight).

►

Plate 20

9 MISSISSIPPI KITE *Ictinia mississippiensis* Milano boreal (Arg), Gavilán azulado chico (Bol). L ♂ 35, ♀ 37 cm. Beak black, cere grey; iris red and legs orange. Ash-grey head, slate-grey back, pale grey underparts. Long, narrow, sharp-pointed wings grey with white on the secondaries. Underwing seen in flight shows ochreous coverts, whitish secondaries, dark primaries. Tail uniform blackish. (See Plate B for bird in flight).

Plate 21

KITES, HARRIERS, HAWKS AND EAGLES (FAMILY ACCIPITRIDAE)

1 CINEREOUS HARRIER *Circus cinereus* Gavilán ceniciento (Arg, Uru, Bol), Vari (Ch). L ♂ 40, ♀ 50 cm. Habitat: upland grass and scrub. Black beak; iris, cere and legs yellow. ♂: ash-grey head and breast, pale grey back. Underparts barred cinnamon and white. Wing-coverts and secondaries grey, primaries blackish. Under wing-coverts white, blackish primaries. Tail: broad dark brown bar near white tip. ♀: dark brown, white rump. Breast with streaks, underparts barred brown and white. Under wing-coverts barred cinnamon and white. Imm like ♀ but underparts streaked brown on light grey. (See Plate B for bird in flight).

2 LONG-WINGED HARRIER *Circus buffoni* Gavilán planeador (Arg), Gavilán de alas largas (Bol, Uru), Gaviao-do-mangue (Br), Vari huevetero (Ch). L ♂ 52, ♀ 56 cm. Habitat: marshes and wet grasslands. Black beak; reddish-brown iris, yellow cere and orange legs. Light phase ♂: head, breast and back black; eyebrow, rump, and underparts white. White ring around face. Long wings with grey barring. Long tail grey with five black bands and white tip. Light phase ♀: head and back dark brown, cream eyebrow and faint cream line framing the face. Breast streaked dark brown, belly and flanks ochreous. Imm darker than ♀ and heavily streaked and mottled. Dark phase – ♂ and ♀ alike: head and back black. Dark chestnut underparts. In flight wings in a shallow 'v' and primaries spread. Voice: during courtship a series of ascending '*feeay feeaaay feeaay*'. (See Plate B for bird in flight).

3 GREY-BELLIED HAWK *Accipiter poliogaster* Esparvero grande (Arg, Bol), Tauató-pintado (Br). L ♂ 48, ♀ 61 cm. Habitat: forests. Beak grey, iris orange; cere and legs yellow. Head and back dark grey, crown black. Underparts and thighs pale grey, under tail-coverts white. Rounded wings dark grey; under wing-coverts white with black dots. Flight feathers grey and white with dark bands. Long tail dark grey with four black bars and narrow white tip. Underside of tail with five dark bars. Imm: crown and malar stripe black, white chin and throat. Cheeks and sides of neck bright chestnut. Back dark brown. Underparts barred whitish and blackish. Wings brown with faint blackish bars; under wing-coverts white with black dots. Flight feathers ochre-grey with dark grey bands. Tail brownish with four black bands. Yellow iris. (See Plate B for bird in flight).

4 TINY HAWK *Accipiter superciliosus* Esparvero chico (Arg), Gaviao-miudinho (Br), Esparvero gris (Bol). L ♂ 22, ♀ 26 cm. Habitat: sub-tropical forests. Grey beak, brown iris; cere and legs yellow. Grey head with blackish crown and nape, lighter grey eyebrow. Dark grey back. White throat, chest and belly finely barred with grey. Short, rounded wings dark grey with brownish tip; long tail brown with three greyish bands. There is a reddish phase which is the same but with reddish-brown instead of grey. Imm is like the reddish form, but cinnamon thighs and yellow iris. (See Plate B for bird in flight).

5 SHARP-SHINNED HAWK *Accipiter striatus* Esparvero común (Arg), Esparvero chico (Bol), Gaviaozinho (Br). L ♂ 23, ♀ 29 cm. Habitat: savannahs, woods and transition forests up to 2000 m. Grey beak, red iris; cere and legs yellow. Grey head with blackish crown, whitish throat; brownish-grey back. Under tail-coverts white, thighs rusty, or barred rusty and cream. Underparts barred rusty and cream. Short, rounded wings. The underwing is pale with darker concentric bands. Long tail brownish-grey with four dark bands. Undertail whitish with dark barring. Imm: streaked crown, browner back, and underparts streaked instead of barred. Pale phase has hardly any markings on the breast and belly; dark form has breast, belly and under wing-coverts rich cinnamon. Voice: one call is a quiet '*syesyesyesyes*'. (See Plate B for bird in flight).

6 BICOLOURED HAWK *Accipiter bicolor* Esparvero variado (Arg), Peuquito (Ch), Esparvero común (Bol), Gaviao-bombachinha-grande (Br), Gavilán pardo (Uru). L ♂ 30, ♀ 43 cm. Habitat: woods and forests. Grey beak, orange iris, yellow cere and legs. Two races differ somewhat in plumage. Typical (northern) form dark grey head and dark lead-grey back. Underparts pale grey (or barred brown and white), with whitish under tail-coverts and throat. Reddish-brown thighs. Short, rounded wings brownish with faint darker barring; under wing-coverts reddish and flight feathers barred concentrically grey and whitish. Long tail brown with four dark bands in the ♂, five in the ♀. Seen from below the tail is greyish with four dark grey bands. Imm is ventrally ochreous flecked with dark brown, otherwise like the adult. (See Plate C for bird in flight).

►

Plate 21

7 **CRANE HAWK** *Geranospiza caerulescens* Gavilán patas largas (Arg), Gavilán patilargo (Bol), Gaviao-pernilongo (Br). L ♂ 43, ♀ 53 cm. Habitat: by water in savannahs, woods and sub-tropical forests. Slate-grey beak, red iris; cere and long legs orange. Head and back bluish-grey, underparts and wing-coverts barred grey and white. Broad wings. Primaries blackish spotted white halfway along, secondaries grey. When seen from below in flight, coverts are barred grey and white, secondaries are white-tipped and the primaries have a white spot halfway down each primary feather forming a white crescent. Outer tail feathers cinnamon with two broad black bands and white tip. Central tail feathers are also white-tipped but have three black bands, two grey and one white. Imm generally greyish-brown, underparts barred grey and white. Broad white bars on tail. A black phase has been reported in Mexico which is all black with orange iris and legs, and the white crescent of spots on the primaries, but may not be present in southern South America. Voice: a harsh whistled 'fee-aaay'. (See Plate C for bird in flight).

Plate 22
KITES, HARRIERS, HAWKS AND EAGLES (FAMILY ACCIPITRIDAE)

1 **MANTLED HAWK** *Leucopternis polionota* Aguilucho blanco (Arg), Gaviao-pombo-grande (Br). L ♂ 55, ♀ 60 cm. Habitat: sub-tropical forests. Grey beak, brown iris, yellow cere and legs. Head, neck and underparts white; back black. Broad, rounded wings black above with white tips to secondaries. Underwing white with black trailing edge. Short tail white, black at the base and subterminally. Imm: whitish-ochre, flecked and mottled with dark brown. Tail with several blackish and whitish bands. (See Plate C for bird in flight).

2 **GREY HAWK** *Asturina nitida* Aguilucho gris (Arg, Bol), Gaviao-perdrez (Br). L ♂ 40, ♀ 45 cm. Habitat: woods and forests. Grey beak; yellow iris, cere and legs. Grey head, pale grey back. Underparts barred grey and white. Top of the wings grey with light-tipped secondaries, darker-tipped primaries. Under wing-coverts and underparts barred, flight feathers also barred though dark tip to the primaries shows through. Tail evenly barred with black and white (three bands of each). Imm: dark brown back flecked with white and ochre. Underparts ochreous with dark brown streaking. Wings show a paler patch. Tail with several dark bands. (See Plate C for bird in flight).

3 **GREAT BLACK HAWK** *Buteogallus urubitinga* Aguila negra (Arg, Uru, Bol), Gaviao-preto (Br), Yryvytîngâ (Par). L ♂ 57, ♀ 63 cm. Habitat: around water. Beak black, iris brown, cere and legs yellow. All black with white on the rump and at the base of the short tail. The tail also has a white tip. Wings are huge. Imm whitish-ochre streaked and marked with dark brown, tail with several whitish and blackish bands. Fish-eater. Voice: is an occasional, harsh, high-pitched 'geeaaaaayip'. (See Plate C for bird in flight).

4 **SAVANNAH HAWK** *Heterospizias meridionalis* Aguilucho colorado (Arg), Gaviao-caboclo (Br), Aguila colorada (Bol, Uru), Chuví (Bol). L ♂ 53, ♀ 58 cm. Habitat: open country with scattered trees, savannahs, woodland edge, often near water. Grey beak, brown iris. Yellow cere and yellowish-orange legs. Head and neck reddish-brown, brown back, black rump. Breast and belly reddish-brown with fine darker brown barring. Wing-coverts and flight feathers bright reddish-brown with the outer third black. Under wing-coverts cinnamon. Tail black with white tip and white band right across half way along. Imm: head and underparts ochreous streaked brown, barred tail. (See Plate C for bird in flight).

5 **BAY-WINGED HAWK** *Parabuteo unicinctus* Gavilán mixto (Arg, Uru, Bol), Gaviao-asa-de-telha (Br), Peuco (Ch). L ♂ 49, ♀ 53 cm. Habitat: woodlands, savannahs and clearings. Grey beak, brown iris, yellow cere and legs. Head, back, breast and belly brownish-black. Upper and lower tail-coverts white. Thighs and wing-coverts (upper and lower) dark cinnamon. Flight feathers brownish-black. Large tail black, base and tip white. Imm: head and hind-neck reddish-ochre, streaked blackish; pale breast and belly heavily streaked blackish. Cinnamon on upper back and thighs less strong. Tail brown banded with blackish. Voice: loud harsh call. (See Plate C for bird in flight).

6 **BLACK-COLLARED HAWK** *Busarellus nigricollis* Aguilucho pampa (Arg, Bol), Gaviao-belo (Br), Taguato akatî (Par). L ♂ 50, ♀ 56 cm. Habitat: near water. Grey beak and cere, brown iris, yellowish-white legs. Head creamy-white with very fine brown streaks. White throat and a black half-collar below it, separating throat from breast. Back, breast, belly, flanks and undertail all reddish-cinnamon. Wings broad and long. Upper and under wing-coverts reddish-cinnamon, flight feathers black. Short tail reddish at the base barred black, then a broad black band, ending in a narrow white tip. Imm has the same collar and general pattern but is mostly pale with darker streaks. (See Plate C for bird in flight).

7 **BLACK-CHESTED BUZZARD-EAGLE** *Geranoaetus melanoleucus* Aguila mora (Arg, Uru, Bol), Aguia-chilena (Br), Aguila (Ch). L ♂ 70, ♀ 90 cm. Habitat: open steppes, mountains, woodland with clearings, up to 3000 m. Beak grey; cere, iris and legs yellow. Head and back lead grey, chest with a dark grey bib. Underparts white, faintly barred grey. Broad but pointed wings grey above barred blackish, black flight feathers. Under wing-coverts white, finely barred grey. Very short tail dark from above, grey from below, narrow white tip. Imm streaked brown, black and cinnamon. Long tail. Voice: a loud and long 'yekyekyekyekyek'. (See Plate C for bird in flight).

8 **SOLITARY EAGLE** *Harpyhaliaetus solitarius* Aguila solitaria (Arg, Bol). L ♂ 75–80, ♀ 80–85 cm. Beak black, iris brown, legs and cere yellow. All black with a white band across the tail halfway along. Long, broad wings and a short tail. Imm has a blackish-brown back, yellowish-brown breast and belly streaked black. Tail without any clear barring. (See Plate C for bird in flight). ▶

Plate 22

9 CROWNED EAGLE *Harpyhaliaetus coronatus* Aguila coronada (Arg, Bol), Aguia-cinzenta (Br).
L ♂ 75–79, ♀ 80–84 cm. Habitat: savannahs with trees, chaco woodlands. Black beak, brown iris and
yellow cere and legs. All grey with a prominent crest, (pale grey on the head, brownish-grey on the back
and wings, dark yellowish-grey on underparts). Enormous wings from below are grey on the coverts and
blackish on the flight feathers. Shortish tail grey at the base, a broad whitish band across halfway down, a
broad black subterminal band and narrow white tip. Imm: nape and sides of the neck ochreous, back
brownish, breast and belly creamy with streaking high on the sides of the breast. Wings: secondaries
brownish, primaries black. Tail light brown with faint subterminal band. (See Plate C for bird in flight).

Plate 23

KITES, HARRIERS, HAWKS AND EAGLES (FAMILY ACCIPITRIDAE)

1 ROADSIDE HAWK *Buteo magnirostris* Taguató común (Arg), Yndaje (Par), Gavilán común (Bol,
Uru), Gaviao-carijó (Br). L ♂ 35, ♀ 38 cm. Habitat: open woods, clearings, forest edges. Iris yellow. Hood
and back blackish-brown. Whitish breast and belly streaked (imm) or finely barred (adult). Wings with
cinnamon on the primaries, translucent from below. Brown tail with four darker bands. Imm back flecked
with brown and whitish-ochre. Some specimens greyer, others almost black. Perches very upright in the
open. Voice: soaring, a loud '*cheecheecheecheechee…*'; perched, a loud '*cheeuuuu-we*'. (See Plate D for bird
in flight).

2 WHITE-RUMPED HAWK *Buteo leucorrhous* Taguató negro (Arg), Gavilán rabadilla blanca (Bol).
L ♂, ♀ 38 cm. Habitat: upland humid forests up to 2000 m. Head, back and underparts black, thighs
reddish-brown. Rump and under tail-coverts white. Short, rounded black wings with white or cream
under wing-coverts. Long tail black with two narrow white bands. Imm blackish streaked with reddish-
brown. A pale form has a brownish-grey back and white underparts. (See Plate D for bird in flight).

3 SHORT-TAILED HAWK *Buteo brachyurus* Aguilucho cola corta (Arg, Bol). L ♂ 38, ♀ 42 cm. Habitat:
edge of forests and woods, over clearings, near rivers and marshes. Crown, nape, face, hind-neck and back
all black. Forehead and underparts white. Wings are black, white undersides with dark tip to the flight
feathers. Short tail banded black and grey; below whitish with five grey bands, subterminal band darker.
Imm yellowish-brown streaked dark brown, and white forehead. Dark form all black except for lighter
flight feathers, and grey tail banded blackish. (See Plate D for bird in flight).

4 WHITE-THROATED HAWK *Buteo albigula* Aguilucho andino (Arg), Aguilucho chico (Ch).
L ♂, ♀ 46 cm. Habitat: southern Andean forests. Head and back brownish, underparts white flecked
with brown; flanks and belly reddish. Long, broad, brownish wings with dark tips to flight feathers.
Underwing whitish with tips of flight feathers dark grey. Imm underparts buffy with heavier dark brown
streaking. (See Plate D for bird in flight).

5 SWAINSON'S HAWK *Buteo swainsoni* Aguilucho langostero (Arg, Bol), Gaviao-papa-gafanhoto
(Br), Gavilán de Swainson (Uru). L ♂ 50, ♀ 55 cm. Habitat: grasslands and agricultural land. Head
brownish with white forehead and throat. Back darker. Breast brown; belly whitish, lightly flecked pale
brownish. Wings dark brown; under wing-coverts white, flight feathers grey and dark-tipped (blackish
border). Shortish tail. Imm underparts streaked, whitish throat. The dark form has the white forehead and
throat, but otherwise all blackish-brown, lighter tail with fine barring and black subterminal band. (See
Plate D for bird in flight).

6 WHITE-TAILED HAWK *Buteo albicaudatus* Aguilucho alas largas (Arg), Gaviao-de-rabo-branco
(Br), Aguila de cola blanca (Uru, Bol). L ♂ 53, ♀ 58 cm. Habitat: semi-arid open country, grasslands with
sparse trees. Black head, grey or blackish back, white underparts barred on the belly. Black wings with
cinnamon upper-coverts. Underwing white with fine blackish barring. Flight feathers greyish barred dark.
Tip of the primaries white. Tail white with fine dark barring and a black subterminal band. Imm heavily
streaked brown but barely so on the breast. (See Plate D for bird in flight).

7 RED-BACKED HAWK *Buteo polyosoma* Aguilucho común (Arg, Bol), Aguila de lomo rojo (Uru),
Aguilucho (Ch). L ♂ 47, ♀ 53–55 cm. Habitat: scrubby terrain, mountains and valleys. ♂: head and back
grey, underparts from chin white. White tail with black subterminal band, sometimes more indefinite
bands. ♀ is the same but with a reddish back. Imm is dark brown, streaked paler on the back, whitish with
dark streaking on the undersides. There are also various phases – blackish, chestnut, plain grey and grey
barred, but the tail remains the same in all but the imm. Voice: a shrill '*yekyekyekyek*', high-pitched, and a
long, shrill, harsh whistle. (See Plate D for bird in flight).

8 PUNA HAWK *Buteo poecilochrous* Aguilucho puneño (Arg), Aguilucho de la puna (Ch), Aguilucho
puna (Bol). L ♂ 51, ♀ 55 cm. Habitat: rocky slopes between 3500 and 4000 m. Very like the Red-backed
Hawk but larger and lacks typical grey and white plumage. Grey bellied, white or white barred belly.
A dark phase is common in this species, a grey phase less so. There is also a red phase. Imm generally
ochreous streaked brownish and red. (See Plate D for bird in flight).

Note: Some consider this a high-Andean race of the Red-backed Hawk.

▶

Plate 23

9 ZONE-TAILED HAWK *Buteo albonotatus* Gaviao-de-rabo-barrado (Br), Gavilán negro (Bol). L 50 cm. Habitat: open country with scattered trees. In flight it looks like a Turkey Vulture, but feathered head and barred tail give it away. All dark slaty. Tail with three bands of grey. Imm is brownish-black, sparsely dotted on underparts. Tail narrowly barred.

10 RUFOUS-TAILED HAWK *Buteo ventralis* Aguilucho de cola rojiza (Arg, Ch). L ♂ 55, ♀ 60 cm. Habitat: cool, temperate forests of the southern Andes. Head and back blackish-brown, white throat. Breast ochreous streaked brown, belly whitish-ochre. Thighs reddish-brown. Long, broad wings brownish with darker brown bars and tip of the primaries black. Under wing-coverts ochre with dark barring, flight feathers barred grey and white. Primaries black-tipped. Tail reddish-cinnamon with eight fine dark brown bars. Imm: back as above, underparts white streaked brown. There is a black form, all black with reddish tail. (See Plate D for bird in flight).

Plate 24
KITES, HARRIERS, HAWKS AND EAGLES (FAMILY ACCIPITRIDAE)

1 CRESTED EAGLE *Morphnus guianensis* Aguila monera (Arg), Aguila morena (Bol), Uiraçu-falso (Br). L ♂ 82–85, ♀ 87–90 cm. Habitat: tropical and sub-tropical forests. Beak dark grey, brown iris, yellow cere and legs. Pale grey head with black crest. Black back, grey breast. Rest of underparts white, faintly barred grey. Long, broad wings. Under wing-coverts white with flight feathers concentrically barred with almost continuous black dots. Black tail with three uniform pale grey bands. Imm has a white head and crest, white back and upper wing-coverts, tail finely barred. Dark phase with sides of the head and breast black, and dark barring on the underbody. (See Plate D for bird in flight).

2 HARPY EAGLE *Harpia harpyja* Harpía (Arg), Aguila harpía (Bol), Gaviao-real or Uiraçu-verdadeiro (Br). L ♂ 90, ♀ 100 cm. Habitat: tropical and sub-tropical forests. Black beak, grey cere; brown iris and thick, powerful yellow legs and feet. Grey head with prominent double crest. Black back and shoulders. Upper breast black, rest of underparts whitish. Thighs white, barred black. Upperwings black, barred with grey on the flight feathers; underwings white with black concentric barring. Long tail greyish, barred black and tipped ashy, or white and black from below. Imm: head, neck and crest white, light brownish-grey back, finely barred tail. (See Plate D for bird in flight).

3 BLACK-AND-WHITE HAWK-EAGLE *Spizastur melanoleucus* Aguila viuda (Arg), Aguila blanquinegra (Bol), Gaviao-pato (Br). L ♂ 53–55, ♀ 56–58 cm. Habitat: forests, usually along river courses. Black beak, orange cere; yellow iris and feet, the legs feathered, white. Head, neck and underparts all white but for a small black patch on crown and crest. Black back and blackish-brown short wings, flight feathers barred grey. Under wing-coverts white, dark barring on primaries and secondaries. Long tail greyish-brown with five black bands. Imm similar but browner on the back. (See Plate D for bird in flight).

4 ORNATE HAWK-EAGLE *Spizaetus ornatus* Aguila crestuda real (Arg), Aguila de penacho (Bol), Gaviao-de-penacho (Br). L ♂ 58–67, ♀ 63–73 cm. Habitat: forest edges. Dark grey beak, yellow cere and iris; feathered legs, yellowish feet. Black crown and long crest. Cheeks, sides of back of the neck and sides of the breast reddish. Black malar streak borders white throat and centre of breast. Black back. Black and white barred underparts, thighs and legs. Short, rounded wings. Flight feathers barred dark brown and black, upper wing-coverts blackish-brown edged paler. Long tail banded black and grey. Imm: white crest, head, neck, breast, belly, and under tail-coverts. Upperparts dark brownish. (See Plate D for bird in flight).

5 BLACK HAWK-EAGLE *Spizaetus tyrannus* Aguila crestada negra (Arg), Aguila tirana (Bol), Gaviao-pega-macaco (Br). L ♂ 65–70, ♀ 70–75 cm. Dark grey bill, yellow iris. Orange cere, feathered legs and yellowish feet. Head, back and breast blackish. Black and white crest. Flanks, belly, thighs and tarsi barred black and white. Faint barring in flight feathers. Underwing all concentrically barred dark grey and white. Long tail banded brownish-grey and black. Imm has a whitish eyebrow, creamy breast streaked dark. (See Plate D for bird in flight).

6 BLACK-AND-CHESTNUT EAGLE *Spizaetus isidori* Aguila poma (Arg), Aguila de copete (Bol). L ♂ 80, ♀ 90 cm. Habitat: montane forests from 600 to 2500 m. Beak dark grey, iris and cere yellow; feathered legs, yellowish feet. Black head, crest and back. Underparts bright chestnut flecked black. Throat and thighs black, leggings chestnut. Huge wings black above. The under wing-coverts are chestnut, flight feathers grey with black tips making a dark border. Tail ash-grey with wide black subterminal band. Imm: pale head, crest darker. Light brownish back flecked lighter, whitish underparts faintly streaked beige. Tail with three dark bands. (See Plate D for bird in flight).

Plate 24

Imm

1

Dark
form

2

Imm

3

6

Imm

5

Imm

Imm

4

Plate 25

CARACARAS (FAMILY FALCONIDAE)

1 **MOUNTAIN CARACARA** *Phalcoboenus megalopterus* Matamico andino (Arg), Matamico cordillerano (Bol), Carancho cordillerano (Ch). L ♂ 50, ♀ 54 cm. Habitat: upland steppes between 2000 and 4000 m. Grey beak, brown iris, orange cere and legs. Head, back, throat and breast black, rump and underparts white. Black wings with the tips of the primaries and secondaries white. Under wing-coverts white. Black tail with white tip. Imm uniformly light brown with a bit of whitish flecking in the wing. (See Plate E for bird in flight).

2 **WHITE-THROATED CARACARA** *Phalcoboenus albogularis* Matamico blanco (Arg), Carancho cordillerano del sur (Ch). L ♂ 47–50, ♀ 52–54 cm. Habitat: forests, woodlands, grassy valleys and hillsides. Greyish beak, brown iris, yellow cere and legs. Head and back black, rump and underparts white. Long wings. Upperwing black with the tips of the flight feathers white. Under wing-coverts white. Long black tail with a white band at the tip. Imm overall darkish brown flecked and streaked. Yellowish on rump and reddish-brown tail. Voice: a sporadic '*we?or'oo*', sometimes a cackling '*kakakakakakaka*'. (See Plate E for bird in flight).

3 **STRIATED CARACARA** *Phalcoboenus australis* Matamico grande (Arg), Carancho negro (Ch). L ♂ 59, ♀ 62 cm. Habitat: seashore, marine mammal colonies, rookeries of penguins and other seabirds. Beak grey at the base, yellowish at the tip, brown iris; orange cere and legs. Black head, neck and back with fine streaking around the neck and down on to breast. Belly and thighs cinnamon. Long, black wings, secondaries edged whitish. Underwing brownish-grey with white on the primaries. Long, black tail with white tip. Imm more uniform dark brown. (See Plate E for bird in flight).

4 **CRESTED CARACARA** *Polyborus plancus* Carancho (Arg, Bol), Traro (Ch), Caracará (Br), Carancho común (Uru), Carcaña (Bol), Kara kara (Par). L ♂ 54–56, ♀ 58–60 cm. Habitat: sparsely wooded open country, steppes, agricultural land, hills and marshes. Beak bluish-grey, yellowish at the base. Brown iris, orange cere, yellow legs. Orange around the bare face. Crown black and slightly crested at nape. White throat. Back dark brown, breast ditto barred whitish (streaked in the imm). Rest of the bird darkish brown. Under tail-coverts whitish finely barred dark. Dark primaries have white at the base forming a white wing patch; secondaries barred. All wing-coverts dark. Long whitish tail finely barred black with a broad blackish terminal band. Voice: courtship call '*krakkrakkrak*', followed by '*arrrrrrarrrrarr*'. (See Plate E for bird in flight).

5 **YELLOW-HEADED CARACARA** *Milvago chimachima* Chimachima (Arg, Bol, Uru), Carrapateiro (Br), Kiri kiri (Par). ♂ 36, ♀ 39 cm. Habitat: open areas in woods or grasslands dotted with trees. Grey beak, brown iris, yellow cere and whitish legs. Head, breast and belly creamy, dark brown post-ocular streak. Back and wings dark brown, feathers edged ochre. Rump and tail ochreous, the tail finely barred brown, subterminal dark band. There is an ochre patch in the wing seen in flight. Under wing-coverts brownish-cinnamon. Imm all brown and streaked underparts. Voice: loud, high-pitched '*cheeeeee*', descending.(See Plate E for bird in flight).

6 **CHIMANGO CARACARA** *Milvago chimango* Chimango (Arg, Bol, Uru, Br), Tiuque (Ch). L ♂ 37–40, ♀ 40–44 cm. Habitat: grasslands, steppes, agricultural land, woodland edges. Grey beak, brown iris; cere and legs yellow. Head and back cinnamon-brown (some populations dark, some lighter, almost sandy). Pale rump. Lighter underparts to creamy belly. Wings brownish with white patch at the base of the primaries visible in flight. Lighter underwing. Tail ochre with brown markings, darker subterminal band and pale tip or tail whitish with fine brown barring and a broad subterminal band. Imm has streaking on the breast and underparts. (See Plate E for bird in flight).

Plate 25

Imm

4

2

3

6

1

5

Imm

Plate 26

FOREST-FALCONS, KESTRELS AND FALCONS (FAMILY FALCONIDAE)

1 **LAUGHING FALCON** *Herpetotheres cachinnans* Guaicurú (Arg, Bol), Acaua (Br), Halcón reidor (Ch), Macono (Bol), Macaguá (Par). L ♂ 43, ♀ 45 cm. Habitat: tropical, sub-tropical and chaco forests. Head whitish-ochre streaked with brown. Blackish face-mask extends onto nape. Dark brown back. Underparts whitish-ochre. Short, broad wings. Long, blackish tail with ochre bands. Voice: a long counterpoint duet '*whey whey whey whey whey*'. (See Plate E for bird in flight).

2 **BARRED FOREST-FALCON** *Micrastur ruficollis* Halcón montés chico (Arg), Halcón cuello rojizo (Bol), Gaviao-caburé (Br). L ♂ 35, ♀ 40 cm. ♂: head and back dark grey, lores and around the eye yellow. Reddish breast. Underparts finely barred light grey and dark brown. Short, rounded wings. Underwing barred like the underparts. Long brownish tail. ♀ is browner version of ♂. Imm lacks reddish breast and bars on underside broader. Voice: at dawn and dusk, calls '*Ka-oo... kaa-oo...*'. (See Plate E for bird in flight).

3 **COLLARED FOREST-FALCON** *Micrastur semitorquatus* Halcón montés grande (Arg), Gaviao-relogio (Br), Halcón de collar (Bol). L ♂ 50, ♀ 55 cm. Dark blackish head, white cheeks, dark 'sideburns'. White half-collar. Blackish-brown back, whitish underparts. Short rounded wings. Underwing white, flight feathers barred. Long, rounded tail blackish with three narrow white bands. Imm very varied but has facial pattern and half-collar; chestnut wash on breast. Incompletely barred underparts. Dark form: all black with fine grey tail bands, and yellowish-brown instead of white on cheeks and underparts. Voice: '*c-c-co-cow-cow cooooow cooooow cooooow*'. (See Plate E for bird in flight).

4 **SPOT-WINGED FALCONET** *Spiziapteryx circumcinctus* Halconcito gris (Arg). L ♂ 26, ♀ 28 cm. Habitat: open country with sparse trees, scrubland and open woodland. Grey head with prominent white eyebrow and malar stripe. Back brownish-grey streaked black. Large white rump-patch. Underparts light grey with brownish streaking. Short, rounded wings with white spotting. Flight flappy and un-falconlike, but fast when swooping on prey. (See Plate E for bird in flight).

5 **AMERICAN KESTREL** *Falco sparverius* Halconcito colorado (Arg, Bol), Halcón común (Bol), Cernícalo (Ch), Halconcito común (Uru), Quiriquiri (Br), Taguato'í (Par). L ♂ 27, ♀ 29 cm. Habitat: open country, grasslands, agricultural land, hills and edges of woods. ♂: dark grey head, white cheeks with two stripes downwards, one from the eye, the other on the ear-coverts. Back chestnut with dark barring. Creamier on breast and belly. Lower breast and flanks with black dots. Wing-coverts bluish-grey with black spots. Long tail cinnamon with black subterminal band and white tip. ♀: back, wing-coverts and tail chestnut, barred black. Underparts whitish streaked with cinnamon. Imm: ♀ like the adult, ♂ is streaky-breasted. Perches on wires and posts. Hovers. (See Plate E for bird in flight).

6 **APLOMADO FALCON** *Falco femoralis* Halcón plomizo (Arg), Falcao-de-coleira (Br), Halcón azulado (Uru), Halcón perdiguero (Ch), Kiri kiri guasu (Par). L ♂ 35, ♀ 39 cm. Habitat; areas dotted with trees, open grassland, steppes, agricultural land, open woods. Black head; forehead and long eyebrow ochreous. Black line down from the eye, and another from eye to nape. Slate-grey back. Throat white. Breast pale, dark streaks. Black 'waistcoat' from flanks. Long, pointed wings with dark grey coverts, barred dark grey and whitish below. Long tail dark with five or so white bands. Imm has black and brown back, dark streaking on the breast and a plain brown 'waistcoat'. (See Plate E for bird in flight).

7 **BAT FALCON** *Falco rufigularis* Halcón negro chico (Arg, Bol), Halcón golondrina (Bol), Cuaré (Br). L ♂ 23, ♀ 28 cm. Habitat: forests, chaco woods or savannahs. Head and back black. White throat extends backwards to form a half-collar. Upper breast with a cinnamon wash; lower breast and upper belly including flanks black, finely barred white. Lower belly and thighs rufous-chestnut. Long, pointed wings dark brown, coverts edged whitish. Under wing-coverts blackish with white markings. Tail black with five narrow bands and tip white. Imm has brown back and 'waistcoat'. (See Plate E for bird in flight).

8 **PEREGRINE FALCON** *Falco peregrinus* Halcón peregrino (Arg, Bol, Uru, Ch), Falcao-peregrino (Br). L ♂ 40–42, ♀ 45–48 cm. Habitat: open country, sea coasts, mountains and foothills, cities. Crown and nape dark brownish, prominent black line down from the eye on the face. Some races almost hooded, with this line very broad, but usually the side of the neck between shoulders and ear-coverts is pale. Back bluish-grey with some darker bars. Throat and upper breast whitish. Some streaking on buff lower breast, barring on the belly. Wings are long and pointed. Under wing-coverts grey, flight feathers grey, barred white. Tail like the back but faintly barred. There is a paler form with unmarked underparts but faint barring on the flanks. Imm is cinnamon on the underparts, heavily streaked dark brown. Voice: a pitiful, harsh '*he-aaaay he-aay*', or repetitive '*hick-chap, hick-cap hic hic hic chap*'. (See Plate E for bird in flight).

Note: One very light form was considered to be a separate species, the Pallid Falcon, *Falco kreyenborgii*.

9 **ORANGE-BREASTED FALCON** *Falco deiroleucus* Halcón negro grande (Arg), Falcao-de-peito-vermelho (Br), Halcón pechianaranjado (Bol). L ♂ 31, ♀ 33 cm. Habitat: open woods, savannahs, chaco forest edges. Head and neck black; white throat and orange-cinnamon upper breast which extends backwards to form an incomplete collar. Lower breast, upper belly and flanks black, barred orange-cinnamon. Lower belly and thighs chestnut. Under wing-coverts dark with white and yellowish-brown markings, flight feathers dark grey with whitish bars. Long tail black with four narrow whitish bands and whitish tip. Imm pale breast and belly, former streaked and latter barred dark. (See Plate E for bird in flight).

Plate 26

Imm 8

Pale form

Dark form

Imm

Imm

Imm

1

9

2

3

6

7

4

♂

♀

5

Plate 27

GUANS AND CHACHALACAS (FAMILY CRACIDAE)

1 CHACO CHACHALACA *Ortalis canicollis* Charata (Arg, Bol). L 50–55 cm. Habitat: chaco woodlands and riverine forests. Blackish bill, pink legs. Head and neck grey, back olive-brown. Underparts ochreous grey, belly and rump cinnamon. Greyish-brown wings; tail olive-grey with reddish outer tail feathers. Usually in pairs or small flocks, they move with agility among the branches. Voice: a loud and demented duet at dawn: '*karakaká-charatá-karakaká-charatá…*'.

2 SPECKLED CHACHALACA *Ortalis guttata* Aracua (Br), Guaraca manchada (Bol). L 50 cm. Habitat: forests and thickets. Small red wattle partly feathered. Head brown. Above dark olive-brown. Chestnut rump. Neck and breast with conspicuous white edge to dark brown feathers. Tail bronze-olive, outer feathers extensively reddish-tipped. The Bolivian race has a greyer head. Belly greyish. Primaries brown.

3 ANDEAN GUAN *Penelope montagnii* Pava de monte andina (Arg), Pava andina (Bol). L 56–60 cm. Habitat: montane forests between 2200 and 2500 m. Pinkish-brown bill, pink legs. Bare face grey, orange throat. Head and neck brownish-grey, brown back with reddish lower back and rump. Greenish-grey breast. Feathers on head, neck and breast edged whitish. Reddish-brown belly. Brown wings; tail greenish-brown with the outer feathers darker and shot blue.

4 RUSTY-MARGINED GUAN *Penelope superciliaris* Yacupoí (Arg, Bol), Yaku po'i (Par), Jacupemba (Br). L 60–65 cm. Habitat: rainforest canopy and lower in thicker-foliaged trees. Dark olive bill, reddish legs. Bare face bluish-grey, throat wattle red. Head and neck dark brown. White eyebrow. Back and rump chestnut, breast greyish-brown with a greenish tint, feathers edged buffy. Belly dark grey with feathers edged reddish. Wings olivaceous, feathers edged reddish; tail dark olive-brown.

5 RED-FACED GUAN *Penelope dabbenei* Pava de monte alisera (Arg), Pava cara roja (Bol). L 65–70 cm. Habitat: alder woods between 1700 and 2700 m. Bill and legs brown. Bare face and wattles red. Black forehead; crown and sides of the head brown with whitish flecking. Neck, back, breast and wings blackish-brown. Feathers of the lower neck, breast, upper back and scapulars edged whitish. Belly greyish-brown, rump with a reddish tone. Tail dark brown with greenish sheen.

6 DUSKY-LEGGED GUAN *Penelope obscura* Pava de monte común (Arg), Pava de monte (Uru), Jacuguaçu or Jacuaçu (Br), Pava pata negra (Bol). L 70–75 cm. Habitat: woods and gallery and transition forests. Blackish bill, dark grey legs. Bare face grey, wattles red. Crown and forehead black. Neck, breast and upperparts brown with greenish sheen and feathers edged white. Underparts brown, shot green. Dark brown tail. Voice: a loud '*kraah kraah krah*'; also a noisy wing-drumming '*tup tup tup*' ending in a long '*trrrrrrrr*'.

7 COMMON PIPING-GUAN *Aburria pipile* Pava campanilla or Yacutinga cariazul (Bol), Cujubi (Br). L 65 cm. Habitat: forests. Wattle and bare face blue. Red legs. Overall black; crest and nape feathers white at the base. Breast and wing-coverts flecked white. Large white wing patch.

8 BLACK-FRONTED PIPING-GUAN *Aburria jacutinga* Yacutinga (Arg), Jacutinga (Br). L 75 cm. Habitat: forests, near water-courses. Bill blue at the base, rest black; legs red. Wattle blue under the bill, and red under the throat. White eye-ring. Forehead, face and throat black. Crown and long nape-feathers white. Rest of the bird blackish-brown with purple sheen. Lower neck and breast feathers edged white. Wings dark with a white patch on the coverts. Brownish tail with outer feathers bluish. Voice: a very high-pitched piping whistle on a single note.

9 BARE-FACED CURASSOW *Crax fasciolata* Muitú (Arg), Muitú común or Pava pintada (Bol), Mutum-de-penacho (Br). L ♂ 77, ♀ 75 cm. Habitat: sub-tropical and chaco woods and forests. ♂ has a yellow bill with black tip and greyish legs. ♀ has brownish bill and pink legs. ♂ all black with white belly and undertail, white tip to tail. ♀ head and neck black, curly top-knot black and white. Back black with white barring, breast black with buff barring. Rest of underparts ochreous. Wings black with whitish bars, tail black with fine white bars and tip whitish.

Plate 27

Plate 28

QUAIL AND WOOD-QUAIL (FAMILY PHASIANIDAE)

1 **SPOT-WINGED WOOD-QUAIL** *Odontophorus capueira* Urú (Arg, Br), Capoeira (Br). L 26–30 cm. Habitat: sub-tropical forests. Thick but stubby beak black, grey legs. Bare face around the eye red. Reddish-brown crown, yellowish-chestnut eyebrow. Upperparts reddish-brown with black markings and white streaks along the shaft of the feathers. Sides of the head, throat and underparts grey. Wings blackish-brown with white spotting and lines. Tail reddish-brown with ochre bands. Voice: at dusk call loudly '*guroo-guroo-guroo-guroo-gurú-gurú-guroo…*' answered by other roosts within hearing.

2 **CALIFORNIA QUAIL** *Callipepla californica* Codorniz de California (Arg), Codorniz (Ch). L 25–26 cm. Habitat: foothills of the southern Andes. Black bill, blackish legs. ♂: forehead and fore-crown cinnamon-olive; fine white line from throat to eye and another from ear to ear over fore-crown. Black forward-leaning crest. Hind crown olive-brown. Chin and throat black, fore-neck and breast bluish-grey. Hind-neck grey, feathers edged black and a white spot on each feather. Upperparts olive-brown. Upper belly yellowish with black spots, lower reddish and black. Flanks brown with whitish streaking. Brown wings, secondaries edged ochre. Grey tail. ♀ has a brownish head and shorter crest, sides of the face and throat whitish finely streaked black. Fine black and cinnamon markings on the brown neck. Greyish-brown breast; belly white with black barring, rest of underparts white. Wings and tail like the ♂. Usually in flocks these birds run rapidly over the ground. Voice: when flushed, a characteristic '*quit*'.

CRAKE (FAMILY RALLIDAE)

3 **SPECKLED CRAKE** *Coturnicops notata* Burrito enano (Arg), Pinto-d'água-carijó (Br), Burrito pintado (Uru). L 12.5 cm. Habitat: dense vegetation of marshes and flooded grasslands. Tiny brown bill, olive legs. Crown and nape dark olive-brown, speckled with white. Dark lores. Whitish eyebrow. Hind-neck, sides of neck and upperparts olive-brown spotted with black and white, rump finely barred white. White throat. Fore-neck, breast and belly whitish, flecked with brown. Sides of the breast, flanks and under tail-coverts barred. Wings dark olive-brown with a white patch on the secondaries seen in flight. Coverts olive-brown with white speckling. Dark brown tail.

4 **OSCELLATED CRAKE** *Micropygia schomburgkii* Maxalalagá (Br), Burrito menor (Bol). L 14 cm. Habitat: marshy areas and bogs in savannahs. Greenish bill. Red-brown legs. Overall buffy-cinnamon. Dark hind-crown with white spotting. Back, sides of the breast and wing-coverts with white dots ringed black. Centre of belly whitish.

5 **RED-AND-WHITE CRAKE** *Laterallus leucopyrrhus* Burrito colorado (Arg), Burrito de patas rojas (Uru), Pinto-d'água-avermelhado (Br). L 16.5 cm. Habitat: marshes and swamps. Greenish-brown bill; reddish legs. Forehead, fore-crown, face and ear-patches reddish. Rest of the head olive-brown. Hind neck and shoulders reddish-brown; lower back, rump and tail dark olive-brown. Throat, fore-neck, breast and belly white. Sides of neck and breast reddish. Flanks barred black and white. Under tail-coverts white. Brown wings, coverts olive-brown and reddish.

6 **RUFOUS-SIDED CRAKE** *Laterallus melanophaius* Burrito común (Arg), Pinto-d'água-comum (Br), Burrito silbón (Bol), Burrito de patas verdes (Uru). L 17.5 cm. Habitat: marshes and other water bodies. Green bill, olive-green legs. Head olive-brown, lores grey. Ear-patches, sides of the neck and breast reddish. Hind neck and back olive-brown, rump and tail darker. Throat and underparts white, flanks heavily barred with black. Reddish undertail and brown wings. Voice: a duet, each bird singing alternate notes of a rapid descending trill.

7 **RUFOUS-FACED CRAKE** *Laterallus xenopterus* Not illustrated. L 14 cm. Known from a single specimen taken in Paraguay in 1933. Upper upperparts to mantle rufous, as are the sides of the head. Wing-coverts and scapulars black, prominently barred white. Back, rump and forward underparts yellowish-buff. White belly.

Plate 28

Plate 29

CRAKES AND RAILS (FAMILY RALLIDAE)

1 **GREY-BREASTED CRAKE** *Laterallus exilis* Not illustrated. L 14.5 cm. Accidental in southern South America. Top of the head dark grey. Upper back rufous, blackish tail. Sides of the head, neck and breast grey. Barred black and buff on flanks and lower belly.

2 **BLACK CRAKE** *Laterallus jamaicensis* Burrito cuyano (Arg), Pidencito (Ch). L 15 cm. Habitat: edge of marshes and rivers. Fore-neck and breast grey. Belly and flanks barred grey and white. Reddish nape. Shoulders and olive-brown, hindmost upperparts (including tail and wing-coverts) darker but barred white.

3 **DOT-WINGED CRAKE** *Laterallus spilopterus* Burrito negruzco (Arg), Burrito overo (Uru). L 17 cm. Habitat: grass and dense vegetation, usually near brackish or saline marshes. Legs and bill greenish-grey. Forehead black, crown and upperparts black streaked olive-brown. Face, throat and breast lead grey, whitish belly. Flanks and under tail-coverts barred black and white. Wings dark brown, coverts brown and black with white tips; tail olive-brown.

4 **AUSTRAL RAIL** *Rallus antarcticus* Gallineta chica (Arg), Pidén austral (Ch). L 22 cm. Habitat: damp grassland around marshes, lakes and bogs. Red bill, violet legs. Crown, hind-neck and back yellowish-brown with black streaks. Throat and sides of the face pale grey. Fore-neck, breast and belly slate-grey, flanks barred black and white. Wing-coverts reddish-brown, flight feathers black and tail brownish.

5 **GREY-NECKED WOOD-RAIL** *Aramides cajanea* Chiricote (Arg, Par, Bol, Uru), Três-potes (Br). L 40 cm. Habitat: grassy edges of marshes and swamps, ponds in woods. Green bill, yellowish at the base; red legs. Head brownish-grey, back olive-brown. Rump, upper tail-coverts and tail black. Throat white, neck grey, browner round the back. Chestnut breast; black belly, flanks and under tail-coverts. Wings olive-brown, chestnut primaries. Voice: loud and strident '*chiri cot.. chiri.. cot.. chiri cot*', usually at dusk.

6 **GIANT WOOD-RAIL** *Aramides ypecaha* Ipacaá (Arg), Gallineta grande (Uru), Ypaka'a (Par), Saracuraçu (Br). L 48 cm. Habitat: lakes, marshes, rivers and swamps, usually near woods. Greenish-yellow bill; red legs. Grey face, greyish-brown crown. Nape and back of the neck reddish. Back olive-brown. White throat; fore-neck and breast grey. Rest of underparts pinkish-buff. Under tail-coverts and tail black. Wing-coverts olive-brown, primaries reddish, secondaries olivaceous. Voice: a series of loud, screamed '*ha - ha -patter-ha*' singly, as a duet or in a cacophonous chorus.

7 **SLATY-BREASTED WOOD-RAIL** *Aramides saracura* Saracura (Arg), Saracura-do-mato (Br). L 38 cm. Habitat: forests, sometimes far from water. Green bill, red legs. Grey head. Hind-neck and shoulders brown, back olivaceous. Whitish throat; fore-neck, breast and rest of underparts grey. Brown wings with olivaceous coverts. Rump, undertail and tail black. Voice: a strident and ascending series of '*wheat*'.

8 **ASH-THROATED CRAKE** *Porzana albicollis* Burrito grande (Arg, Bol), Sana-carijó (Br), Ñahana'i (Par). L 27 cm. Habitat: grassy edges to open marshes. Green bill, pink legs. Crown and upperparts (including tail) dark brown with black markings. Lighter throat. Uniform grey undersides but flanks barred. Voice: a duet: one '*piri-piri-pir-pir-pir-piri*', the other '*row, rrrow, K-rrrrooow, k-rrrooow*' (rhymes with 'cow').

9 **YELLOW-BREASTED CRAKE** *Poliolimnas flaviventer* Burrito amarillo (Arg), Burrito de pecho amarillo (Uru). L 13 cm. Habitat: marshes with dense vegetation, flooded grasslands. Green bill; yellow legs. Crown dark brown, whitish eyebrow. Back dark brown and black streaked white. White throat, creamy yellow breast and whitish belly. Flanks and under tail-coverts barred dark brown and white. Tail brown. Wings: brown primaries, coverts yellowish-brown with black barring and white markings.

10 **PAINT-BILLED CRAKE** *Neocrex erythrops* Burrito pico rojo (Arg), Turuturu (Br). L 19 cm. Habitat: dense vegetation around lakes. Bill red at the base, rest yellowish-green; red legs. Head, hind-neck, back, wings and tail brown; whitish throat. Front of neck, breast and belly grey. Flanks, under tail-coverts and thighs barred brown and white.

11 **SPOTTED RAIL** *Pardirallus maculatus* Gallineta overa (Arg, Uru, Bol), Saracura-carijó (Br), Pidén moteado (Ch). L 30 cm. Habitat: edges of streams, lakes and marshes with dense vegetation. Long green bill with red base; reddish legs. Brownish head with darker crown, face with white spots. Back and upper wing-coverts brownish with black markings and white streaks. Whitish throat. Black neck flecked with white. Breast and belly barred black and white, under tail-coverts white. Tail and wings brownish.

12 **PLUMBEOUS RAIL** *Pardirallus sanguinolentus* Gallineta común (Arg, Bol), Pidén (Ch), Gallineta de pico rojo y azul (Uru), Sana (Br). L 32–40 cm. Habitat: taller vegetation of marshes, swampy areas and lake edges. Bill lime-green with a red spot at the base of the lower mandible, blue at the base of the upper. Pink legs. Head grey. Crown and nape brownish-grey, back olive-brown. Throat, fore-neck, breast and belly lead-grey. Under tail-coverts and flanks brownish-grey. Wings brownish with olive-brown coverts. Tail blackish-brown. Voice: a duet: while the ♀ says '*dumph..doomph*', the ♂ calls '*wee-wheat, weeuu-heet…*', ending in several unwinding '*whee-ooo*'s.

13 **BLACKISH RAIL** *Pardirallus nigricans* Gallineta negruzca (Arg), Saracura-sana (Br), Ñahana hû (Par). L 36 cm. Habitat: marshes and swamps. Green bill and red legs. Upperparts olive-brown. Whitish throat. Underparts lead-grey. Under tail-coverts and tail black. Brown wings. Voice: a duet of high-pitched whistled '*dweeet dweet doe-wheet…*'.

Plate 29

Imm

13

12

4

11

5

7

6

9

2

3

8

10

Plate 30

GALLINULES AND COOTS (FAMILY RALLIDAE)

1 PURPLE GALLINULE *Porphyrula martinica* Pollona azul (Arg), Polla de agua azul (Bol), Gallineta azul (Uru), Frango-d'água-azul (Br). L 33 cm. Habitat: marshes, swamps and flooded fields. Bill red with yellow tip, pale blue frontal shield; legs yellow. Head, neck, breast, belly and flanks blue-violet, a green sheen on the nape and sides of the neck and breast. Lower belly and thighs dark brown. Under tail-coverts white. Back greenish-blue turning greenish-brown on lower back and rump. Flight feathers: blue-green outer vane, brownish inner vane. Wing-coverts pale blue and olive, tail olive-brown. Imm: head and hind-neck brown, olive-brown on the back, redder on the rump. Throat, fore-neck and rest of the underparts olive-white. Greater-coverts pale blue. Brown tail.

2 AZURE GALLINULE *Porphyrula flavirostris* Pollona celeste (Arg), Polla de agua celeste (Bol), Frango-d'água-pequeno (Br). L 33 cm. Habitat: dense vegetation of marshes and swamps. Bill, shield and legs yellow. Head olive-brown; face, neck, shoulders, sides of the breast and flanks pale blue. Back and wing-coverts olive-brown with black markings. Throat and rest of underparts white; bluish wings, black tail.

3 SPOT-FLANKED GALLINULE *Gallinula melanops* Pollona pintada (Arg), Tagüita (Ch), Gallineta de pico verde (Uru), Ñahana (Par), Polla de agua chica (Bol), Frango-d'água-carijó (Br). L 28–30 cm. Habitat: around floating vegetation on lakes and marshes. Bill and frontal shield lime-green, legs yellowish-green. Head brownish-grey with lores, forehead and central crown black. Back olive-brown. Neck and underparts lead-grey, whitish belly. Flanks brown with round white spots. Under tail-coverts white. Wings dark brown with chestnut coverts. Tail olive-brown.

4 MOORHEN or COMMON GALLINULE *Gallinula chloropus* Pollona negra (Arg), Gallineta de agua (Bol), Frango-d'água-comum (Br), Ñahana (Par), Polla de agua (Ch), Tagüita del norte (Ch). L 35–40 cm. Habitat: lakes and marshes. Shield and base of bill bright red, tip yellow; legs green, lower tibia red. Head and neck blackish, upper back with bluish-grey tones. Lower back and rump dark olive-brown. Underparts dark bluish-grey. Flanks dark greyish-brown with white tips to feathers forming a white line along the side. Outer under tail-coverts white, central black. Wings and tail dark brownish.

5 ANDEAN COOT *Fulica ardesiaca* Gallareta andina (Arg), Tagua americana (Ch), Gallareta americana (Bol). L 55 cm. Habitat: between 3000 and 3500 m in *puna*, on lakes. Bill yellowish-white, dark red, knob-shaped shield. Green legs. Head and neck black; upperparts, wing-coverts and tail slate-grey. Brownish flight feathers. Outer under tail-coverts white, central black.

6 RED-GARTERED COOT *Fulica armillata* Gallareta ligas rojas (Arg), Tagua (Ch), Gallareta grande (Uru), Carqueja-de-bico-manchado (Br). L 50 cm. Habitat: open water of lakes and marshes with vegetation. Yellow bill and frontal shield with a wine-red band separating the two. Olivaceous legs with a red 'garter' at the lower end of the tibia. Head and neck black, rest of the bird slate-grey, paler on the underparts. Under tail-coverts white. Dark brown wings with white edge to the outer primaries. Voice: noisy, with several calls, the most often heard being rapid and repeated '*keop*'.

7 WHITE-WINGED COOT *Fulica leucoptera* Gallareta chica (Arg), Tagua chica (Ch), Gallareta de alas blancas (Uru, Bol), Carqueja-de-bico-amarelo (Br). L 42 cm. Habitat: clearings among reeds on lakes and marshes. Pale yellow bill, shield whitish, to orange in breeding condition; greenish-yellow legs. Head and neck black, slate-grey upperparts, lead-grey underparts. Under tail-coverts white. Slate-grey wings have white tips to the secondaries and outer vane of first primary (in spite of the name this is not usually a good field recognition mark).

8 RED-FRONTED COOT *Fulica rufifrons* Gallareta de escudete rojo (Arg, Uru), Carqueja-de-escudo-roxo (Br), Tagua de frente roja (Ch). L 46 cm. Habitat: lakes and marshes, near reedbeds. Bill yellow, narrowly red at the base, pointed shield deep wine-red. Legs green. Head and neck black, upperparts slate-grey, rump olive-brown. Underparts lead-grey; outer under tail-coverts white bracketing black, often made very visible as a flag to mark territory. Brownish wings. Shy. Voice: several calls, the most common a fast, guttural '*do-go-do-go-do-go-do-go…*'.

9 GIANT COOT *Fulica gigantea* Gallareta gigante (Arg, Bol), Tagua gigante (Ch). L 65 cm. Habitat: open lakes in high Andes, between 3500 and 4500 m. Bill whitish with black tip and pale point, orange at the base rising to a peculiar two-lobed frontal shield, orange to dark red, giving the bird a strange domed forehead. Legs red. Head and neck black, rest of the bird dark slate-grey. Vocalisations include a deep, growled '*arrr.. arrr.arr..arrr..togo..arr…..togo…*'.

10 HORNED COOT *Fulica cornuta* Gallareta cornuda (Arg, Bol), Tagua cornuda (Ch). L 60 cm. Habitat: open lakes in high Andes between 3500 and 4800 m. Bill yellowish-green, black carunculation from the shield (the 'horn') slopes down and forward along the bill, giving a 'roman nose' profile. Legs yellowish-green. Head and neck black, rest of the bird slate-grey, paler on the undersides. Whitish under tail-coverts.

Plate 30

Imm

1

2

3

4

5

6

7

8

9

10

Plate 31

FINFOOTS (FAMILY HELIORNITHIDAE)

1 SUNGREBE *Heliornis fulica* Ipequí (Arg, Bol), Ypeky (Par), Patito cuello listado (Bol), Picaparra (Br). L 28–30 cm. Habitat: quiet waters on streams, rivers and marshes in rainforests. Crown and hind-neck black. Black line from eye to the base of neck. Throat, foreneck and sides of head white. Back and wings olive-brown, underparts white; flanks with olive-brown wash. Very shy. Swims with body half submerged. Voice: at dawn, sonorous whistles, all on the same note: '*hoo, hoo, hoo, hoo*'.

LIMPKIN (FAMILY ARAMIDAE)

2 LIMPKIN *Aramus guarauna* Carau (Arg), Carao (Uru, Bol, Br), Caraú (Bol), Karâu (Par). L 66 cm. Habitat: marshes, lagoons. Overall dark blackish-brown with white flecking on head, neck and shoulders. Chin and throat whitish. Voice: a very loud '*krrrrow, ker-row, krow*'.

SERIEMAS (FAMILY CARIAMIDAE)

3 RED-LEGGED SERIEMA *Cariama cristata* Chuña de patas rojas (Arg, Uru), Seriema (Br), Chuña patiroja or Socori (Bol). L 95 cm. Legs red. Head grey. Large tufted crest from the forehead. Back greyish flecked with brown. Whitish belly. Voice: a series of very loud, descending and speeding-up '*keck.keck...keck..keck keck*', immediately answered by others nearby.

4 BLACK-LEGGED SERIEMA *Chunga burmeisteri* Chuña patas negras (Arg), Chuña patinegra or Socori patinegra (Bol). L 78 cm. Habitat: open woods. Bill and legs black. Plumage overall grey, finely barred whitish. Belly whitish-ochre. Wings dark grey with broad ochreous barring. Central tail feathers dark grey, outer tail feathers broadly barred brown and ochre. Shy. Voice: calls socially, usually at dawn, a chorus of very loud '*car-caw-who*'s, descending in pitch but not in volume.

STONE CURLEWS AND THICK-KNEES (FAMILY BURHINIDAE)

5 PERUVIAN THICK-KNEE *Burhinus superciliaris* Chorlo cabezón (Ch). L 40 cm. Habitat: sandy areas, stony steppes and arid land. Black bill with yellowish-green at the base. Yellowish-green legs. Above grey, streaked darker. Throat, lower breast and belly white. Broad white post-ocular streak almost around the crown, bordered by black above. Fore-neck and upper breast grey. Wings dark brown with white bands; coverts grey. Underwing white. Central tail feathers grey, outers with white sub-terminal patch and black tip.

PLOVERS AND LAPWINGS (FAMILY CHARADRIIDAE)

6 PIED LAPWING *Vanellus cayanus* Chorlo de espolón (Arg), Batuira-de-espolao (Br), Tero de espolón or Leque de espolón (Bol). L 26 cm. Bill black, legs red. Pink metacarpal spur at the bend of the wing. Face and sides of head black, extending down the sides of the neck. Crown and nape greyish-brown, extending down the back of the neck to shoulders. White lines from forehead to lower nape separate the two. Brownish back, black and white lines along the scapulars. Throat, upper breast and lower underparts white with broad black band across lower breast. Wings: coverts greyish-brown, secondaries white, primaries black. Tail white with broad black terminal band.

7 SOUTHERN LAPWING *Vanellus chilensis* Tero común (Arg, Uru, Bol), Leque (Bol), Tetéu (Par), Queltehue (Ch), Quero-quero (Br). L 36 cm. Habitat: meadows. Bill, wing-spurs and legs reddish. Forehead, throat and fore-neck black, all with a white margin. Breast black. Rest of the head and neck, and back grey. Long, slender crest black. Underparts white. Wings: flight feathers black, upper coverts bronze-green, greater-coverts white; under wing-coverts white. Tail white with broad sub-terminal black band. Voice: calls loudly '*tay, tay, tay-oh, tay-row*' as it dives on intruders. Southern form calls '*rare rare, ray-oh, ray-oh*'.

8 ANDEAN LAPWING *Vanellus resplendens* Tero serrano (Arg, Bol), Queltehue de la puna (Ch), Avefría serrana (Bol). L 32 cm. Habitat: steppe or damp pastures near water between 2000 and 3000 m. Bill black with yellow base, legs and wing-spurs pink. Head, neck and breast grey, whitish throat. Back brownish with green sheen. A white half-collar between the hind-neck and back. Undersides white. Wings dark brown with white at the base of the flight feathers. Lesser upper wing-coverts have a purple sheen, greaters are white. Under wing-coverts white. Tail white with blackish-brown broad sub-terminal band. Voice: a sharp, nasal, repeated '*keyer*'.

9 BLACK-BELLIED PLOVER *Pluvialis squatarola* Chorlo ártico (Arg, Ch), Chorlo blanco (Uru), Batuiruçu-de-aixa-preta (Br). L 27 cm. Habitat: mud flats in estuaries, or lake shores. Bill and legs black. N-br plumage: forehead and eyebrow whitish, as too the face, fore-neck, breast and flanks, but these faintly streaked brownish. Back greyish-brown, feathers edged whitish. Rump whitish. Tail white barred with brown, tip brown. Rest of the underparts whitish. Wing-coverts dark brownish-grey, feathers edged whitish. Flight feathers white at the base forming a wing-bar seen in flight. Axillaries black seen in flight. Br plumage: face, fore-neck, breast, belly, flanks and axillaries black; lower belly and under tail-coverts white. Rest of the head white with crown streaked brown. Back brown, black and whitish. Rump and wing-bar white.

▶

10 GOLDEN PLOVER *Pluvialis dominica* Chorlo pampa (Arg, Uru), Batuiruçu (Br), Chorlo dorado (Ch, Bol), Playero dorado (Bol). L 27 cm. Habitat: pampas grasslands, shorter grasses near water; also by sea and estuaries. Bill black, legs dark grey. N-br plumage: face, neck and breast whitish flecked with light brown. Forehead, eyebrow and rest of underparts whitish. Back darker brown, feathers edged whitish. Dark brown wings with coverts as on back. Axillaries light brownish-grey. Br plumage: crown and hind-neck black flecked with yellow, back dark brown with golden-yellow spots. Forehead, eyebrow, sides of the neck and of the breast white. Throat, face, fore-neck, breast and belly black.

Plate 32

PLOVERS AND LAPWINGS (FAMILY CHARADRIIDAE)

1 PACIFIC GOLDEN PLOVER *Pluvialis fulva* Not illustrated. No local names. L 25 cm. Habitat: open fields, seashore and river sides. Above light brown, spotted, feathers edged yellow. Brow yellowish-cream. Brownish breast spotted yellow. Rest of underparts buff-brown. White belly. Brown wings.

2 COLLARED PLOVER *Charadrius collaris* Chorlito de collar (Arg, Bol, Uru), Chorlo de collar (Ch), Batuíra-de-coleira (Br). L 16 cm. Habitat: shores and sandbanks of rivers, lakes and marshes. Forehead, throat and underparts white. Fore-crown, lore stripe and band across upper breast black. Face, nape and hind-neck reddish-cinnamon. Back brownish. Rump white, brownish down the centre. Brownish tail with outermost feathers whitish. Imm similar but collar and crown earthy brown. Voice: a short occasional 'peep'.

3 TWO-BANDED PLOVER *Charadrius falklandicus* Chorlito doble collar (Arg, Ch, Uru), Batuíra-de-coleira-dupla (Br). L 19 cm. Habitat: seashores, lake shores. Hind-crown and back of the neck reddish-cinnamon. Upperparts greyish-brown. Underparts white with two black bands (wide one across breast, narrow one, sometimes incomplete, across lower throat). Central tail brown, outers whitish. N-br plumage: reddish and black on head turn greyish-brown as do breastbands.

4 PUNA PLOVER *Charadrius alticola* Chorlito puneño (Arg), Chorlitejo serrano (Bol), Chorlo de la puna (Ch). L 18 cm. Habitat: lakes and watercourses in high Andes between 3000 and 4000 m. Underparts white (no collar); fore-crown, ear-patch and line down the sides of the neck black. Nape and hind-neck reddish. Back and wing-coverts brownish. Primaries brownish with white towards the base forming a band seen in flight; secondaries brownish with white tips. Tail brown centrally, white outers. Winter plumage lacks the colour on the head, the black and reddish turn brown.

5 SNOWY PLOVER *Charadrius alexandrinus* Chorlo nevado (Ch), Chorlito patinegro or Frailecito (Bol). L 17 cm. Habitat: seashores. Forehead, lores, brow, slight hind-collar and all underparts white. Above sandy-grey. Black band across mid-crown and black spot on sides of breast. Dark ear-coverts. Dark wings, feather shafts white. Tail blackish-grey with outer feathers white.

6 SEMIPALMATED PLOVER *Charadrius semipalmatus* Chorlito palmado (Arg), Chorlo semipalmado (Ch), Chorlito semipalmado (Bol), Batuíra-de-bando (Br). L 18 cm. Habitat: seashore, lake shores. N-br plumage: bill black with reddish at the base, legs yellow. Head and back earthy brown; forehead, eyebrow, post-ocular spot, throat and nuchal collar white. Underparts white with brownish band across breast. Dark brownish wing with whitish wing-bar in flight, coverts brownish; tail brownish with white tip. Br plumage: bill black with orange at the base, orange legs. Face, fore-crown and breastband black, otherwise like n-br plumage.

7 KILLDEER *Charadrius vociferus* Chorlo gritón (Ch). L 24 cm. Habitat: fields, cultivated areas, lake shores. Forehead, throat, post-ocular streak, ring around neck and underparts all white. Fore-crown, lores, line through ear-coverts right round nape, collar and breast band black. Above grey-brown. Cinnamon-buff rump. Blackish wings, secondaries and greater-coverts tipped white. Brown central tail feathers; the rest buff, all with broad, black sub-terminal band and white tip.

8 RUFOUS-CHESTED DOTTEREL *Charadrius modestus* Chorlo pecho canela (Arg), Chorlo chileno (Ch), Batuíra-de-peito-tijolo (Br). L 20 cm. Habitat: peat bogs, sandy, rocky and mud coasts of sea or lakes, short grass areas on islands, and on raised pebble beaches. Black bill, legs greenish-grey. Grey face; white ring almost around head through forehead, eyebrow and across nape. Crown, hind-neck, back and rump brownish. Fore-neck and breast reddish-cinnamon with a black band separating this from the white underparts. Brown wings. Tail: brown central feathers, white outers. In winter plumage breast turns brownish and head-band almost disappears.

9 DIADEMED SANDPIPER-PLOVER *Phegornis mitchellii* Chorlito de vincha (Arg), Chorlito cordillerano (Ch), Chorlito de ciénaga (Bol). L 19 cm. Habitat: rivers and bogs in the high Andes. Black bill, yellowish legs. Forehead and crown, sides of the face and neck, brown. Crown circled by white band. Nape and hind-neck chestnut. Upper breast white. Back brown. Underparts greyish-white with brownish barring. Wings greyish-brown, secondaries white-tipped. Brown tail with outer feathers barred white.

▶

Plate 32

10 TAWNY-THROATED DOTTEREL *Oreopholus ruficollis* Chorlo cabezón (Arg), Chorlo de campo (Ch), Chorlo canela (Uru), Chorlito cabezón (Bol), Batuíra-de-papo-ferrugíneo (Br). L 28 cm. Habitat: uplands, steppes. Black bill, salmon-orange legs. Crown, neck and upperparts (including upper wing-coverts) greyish-brown streaked with black and cinnamon, boldly on the back and wing-coverts. Forehead and eyebrow ochreous. Dark line through the eye. Brownish-grey rump. Throat and fore-neck cinnamon; breast greyish-brown; buff belly. A black mark, often shaped like a horseshoe, in the centre of the lower breast and upper belly. Primaries brown with shaft and adjacent area whitish; secondaries brown, white-tipped. Grey tail with black sub-terminal band. In flight emits a mournful but beautifully modulated whistle '*whee-roo wheeee-roooo, whee-roo*'.

11 MAGELLANIC PLOVER *Pluvianellus socialis* Chorlito ceniciento (Arg), Chorlo de Magallanes (Ch). L 20 cm. Habitat: downwind shores of ponds and lakes in southern Patagonia, and seashores in winter. Bill black, short legs pink, bright cerise eye. Dumpy and ground-dove-like. Forehead and throat whitish, lores blackish. Rest of the head, neck, breast and upperparts dove-grey. Belly, flanks and underwing white; flight feathers darkish with strong white band at their base. Tail centrally blackish, outer feathers white. Voice: a mournful '*wheeoo*', and a rapid trilling '*peereepeereepeereep…*' in courtship.

Plate 33

OYSTERCATCHERS (FAMILY HAEMATOPODIDAE)

1 AMERICAN OYSTERCATCHER *Haematopus palliatus* Ostrero común (Arg), Pilpilén (Ch). L 44 cm. Habitat: seashore, sandy or muddy beaches, sometimes shingle. Pinkish legs. Eye-ring red. Head, back and breast blackish-brown. Rump and undersides white invading up and around the front bend in the wing. There is a large white wing patch seen in flight on the secondaries. Tail dark brown with white at the base. Voice: a series of whistles: longish, sharp '*wheat*', other calls rapid '*piripiripiripirip*' usually ending in a duet '*pirrrrippirrrrhh….*'.

2 MAGELLANIC OYSTERCATCHER *Haematopus leucopodus* Ostrero austral (Arg), Pilpilén austral (Ch). L 44 cm. Habitat: sandy or shingle shores, short grass around ponds and sheep pens. Whitish legs. Eye-ring yellow. Head, neck, back, breast, primary flight feathers and distal third of the tail black. Secondaries, rump, base of the tail and belly white. No white before the bend of the wing (except when wings deliberately drooped in distraction display). Voice: a long, piercing and high-pitched '*wheeeeep*' and a series of rapid whistled '*diddlediddle*'s.

3 BLACKISH OYSTERCATCHER *Haematopus ater* Ostrero negro (Arg), Pilpilén negro (Ch). L 50 cm. Habitat: rocky shores. Whitish-pink legs. Head, neck, upper back, breast and undersides black. Rest of upperparts dark blackish-brown. Flight feathers blackish. Tail almost black. Voice: very similar to American Oystercatcher.

STILTS AND AVOCETS (FAMILY RECURVIROSTRIDAE)

4 SOUTH AMERICAN STILT *Himantopus mexicanus* Tero-real (Arg, Uru), Perrito (Ch), Cigüeñela or Viuda patilarga (Bol), Pernilongo (Br). L 42 cm. Habitat: edges of ponds, marshes and rivers, sometimes ploughed fields. Long, slender, straight bill black; bright pink legs. Nape, back of the neck, scapulars and wings black; forehead, crown, fore-neck, breast, belly, rump and tail white. When alarmed emits a repeated and penetrating '*hep*', like a little bark.

5 ANDEAN AVOCET *Recurvirostra andina* Avoceta andina (Arg, Bol), Caití (Ch). L 47 cm. Habitat: edges of lakes, streams and puddles, between 3000 and 4000 m. Long, slender, upturned bill black, legs and webbed feet bluish-grey. White, with black back, wings and tail. Voice: a bisyllabic '*do-it*', nasal and penetrating.

JACANAS (FAMILY JACANIDAE)

6 WATTLED JACANA *Jacana jacana* Jacana (Arg, Ch, Uru), Aguapeaso (Par), Gallito del agua (Uru, Bol), Gallareta (Bol), Jaçana or Piaçoca (Br). L 22–24 cm. Habitat: floating vegetation of marshes and swamps. Bill yellow with a red base and 'wattles', a red frontal shield; olivaceous legs. Head, neck, breast and belly black. Back, scapulars and wing-coverts chestnut. Flight feathers bright primrose-yellow tipped with black; outer primary's outer vane also blackish. Imm: crown reddish-brown, ochre eyebrow. Hind-neck dark brown, throat and fore-neck whitish, yellower on the breast. Underparts white. Back and tail brown, chestnut rump. Wings as in the adult but not so bright. Voice: a strident, sharp, raucous, penetrating series of '*weck. weck weck. weck… weck*'s.

PAINTED SNIPE (FAMILY ROSTRATULIDAE)

7 SOUTH AMERICAN PAINTED SNIPE *Nycticryphes semicollaris* Aguaterо (Arg), Narceja-de-bico-torto (Br), Becasina pintada (Uru), Becaciona pintada (Ch). L 22 cm. Habitat: marsh edges and flooded tall grasslands. Down-curved bill pale green and yellow at the base. Green legs. Black head with a white crown stripe as far as the nape. Narrow whitish eyebrow. Neck and breast dark brown. Two stripes starting at the sides of the breast carry over onto the back and scapulars. Rest of the underparts white. Back greyish-brown, rump with ochre and brown speckling. Wings dark grey with round white dots, black streaks and brown bars. Tail cinnamon and brown.

Plate 33

Plate 34

SANDPIPERS, SNIPE AND ALLIES (FAMILY SCOLOPACIDAE)

1 **GREATER YELLOWLEGS** *Tringa melanoleuca* Pitotoy grande (Arg, Ch), Patiamarillo mayor (Bol), Chorlo mayor de patas amarillas (Uru, Bol), Maçarico-grande-de-perna-amarela (Br). L 35 cm. Habitat: winters on marshes, lake- and seashores. Long, slender bill black. Legs yellow. N-br plumage: upperparts brownish-grey speckled white, rump white. Throat and eyebrow whitish. Sides of head and neck, fore-neck, breast and flanks whitish, lightly flecked with greyish-brown. Rest of underparts white. Tail white. Br plumage: more heavily speckled, darker upperparts. Often flocks with other species. Voice: a series of usually more than three '*tew-tew-tew*'s, strident and sharp.

2 **LESSER YELLOWLEGS** *Tringa flavipes* Pitotoy chico (Arg, Ch), Chorlo patas amarillas or Archibebe patiamarillo menor (Bol), Chorlo menor de patas amarillas (Uru), Maçarico-de-perna-amarela (Br). L 28 cm. Habitat: edge of the sea and lakes, and in marshes. Slender black bill, yellow legs. N-br plumage: upperparts greyish-brown flecked with white. Throat and rump white. Pale eye-ring. Breast and flanks flecked grey-brown. Rest of underside white. Tail white. Br plumage: similar, back more spotted, breast and flanks more heavily flecked. Voice: a short sharp '*key-ep*' alarm; also quick '*tewtew*'.

3 **SOLITARY SANDPIPER** *Tringa solitaria* Pitotoy solitario (Arg, Ch), Mbatuitui (Par), Chorlito solitario (Uru, Bol), Archibebe solitario (Bol), Maçarico solitario (Br). L 30 cm. Habitat: often on puddles in clearings in woods, also marshes, river banks, lake shores. N-br plumage: upperparts brownish-grey, slight grey and brown streaking. White eye-ring. Neck and breast whitish streaked with greyish-brown. Flanks whitish with brownish barring. Outer tail feathers white with brownish barring giving a chequered effect. Br plumage: similar, back has darker ground colour and is spotted with white. Generally solitary.

4 **WILLET** *Catoptrophorus semipalmatus* Not illustrated. Playero ala blanca (Arg), Playero grande (Ch), Maçarico-de-asa-branca (Br). L 40 cm. N-br plumage: upperparts grey, white rump. Underparts white with grey on the fore-neck. Wings: primaries black with white basal half, secondaries white. Remarkably sharp black and white wing-pattern in all plumages. Br plumage: brown streaking on neck, barring on breast, white scalloping on darker back. Migrates from N America, rarely as far as Tierra del Fuego.

5 **WANDERING TATTLER** *Heteroscelus incanus* Playero gris (Ch). L 25 cm. Habitat: seashores and rocky coasts. Above grey. Long white brow. Underparts white, slightly streaked grey on breast.

6 **SPOTTED SANDPIPER** *Actitis macularia* Playerito manchado (Arg), Playero manchado (Ch), Chorlito manchado (Bol, Uru), Maçarico-pintado (Br). L 19 cm. Habitat: riverbanks. N-br plumage: head and upperparts olive-brown, whitish eyebrow. Underparts white. Wing brownish with white wing-bar. Tail brownish-grey with outer feathers barred with white. Br plumage: darker back, underparts spotted black all over. Peculiar wobbly bat-like flight. Bobs its body.

7 **TEREK SANDPIPER** *Xenus cinereus* Not illustrated. No local names. Habitat: seashores. Like a short-legged Yellowlegs, with an upturned bill and shortish orange legs. A rare accidental wanderer.

8 **UPLAND SANDPIPER** *Bartramia longicauda* Batitú (Arg, Ch, Uru, Bol), Maçarico-do-campo (Br). L 28 cm. Shortish bill black, legs yellowish. Head, neck and breast cinnamon, streaked black; eyebrow whitish. Back brownish and black, feathers edged ochreous. Underparts white, flanks barred. Br plumage: same but brighter. Shy. Perches on fence posts. Voice: a melodious whistle.

9 **ESKIMO CURLEW** *Numenius borealis* Playero esquimal (Arg), Chorlo polar (Uru), Zarapito boreal (Ch), Maçarico-esquimó (Br). L 34 cm. Habitat: short-grass wintering grounds in Pampas. Downcurved bill. Crown brown streaked ochre. Ochreous eyebrow. Back brownish flecked ochre. Head, neck and breast ochreous flecked with brown; whitish belly. Flanks barred ochre and brown. Now virtually extinct (less than ten birds may survive).

10 **WHIMBREL** *Numenius phaeopus* Playero trinador (Arg), Maçaricao (Br), Zarapito (Ch). L 42 cm. Habitat: seashore, muddy estuaries, bogs. Long, downcurved bill, long legs. Whitish eyebrow, dark through the eye. Brownish back flecked with white. Breast whitish with brown flecking, rest of underparts white.

11 **HUDSONIAN GODWIT** *Limosa haemastica* Becasa de mar (Arg), Becacina de mar (Bol), Becasina de mar (Uru), Zarapito de pico recto (Ch), Maçaricao-de-bico-virado (Br). L 38 cm. Habitat: muddy estuaries, shores of lakes, rivers or the sea, marshes. Bill slightly up-turned. N-br plumage: brownish-grey upperparts, whitish rump and throat. Neck, breast and flanks grey, rest of the underparts whitish. Marked wing-bar in flight. Br plumage: white eyebrow. Back black, feathers edged reddish. White rump. Underparts reddish-chestnut flecked on neck, barred black and white on the rest. Black tail.

12 **MARBLED GODWIT** *Limosa fedoa* Zarapito moteado (Ch). L 43 cm. Habitat: rare migrant on seashore. Long bill slightly upturned. Tail finely barred black and reddish.

13 **RUDDY TURNSTONE** *Arenaria interpres* Vuelvepiedras (Arg), Playero vuelvepiedras (Ch), Vira-pedras (Br), Revuelvepiedras (Uru). L 23 cm. Habitat: seas and estuarine shores. N-br plumage: back brownish, feathers edged whitish. Lower back white. Rump brown top half, white lower half. Fore-neck and breast brownish, darker lower. Underparts white. Wings dark brown with white in a bold pattern. Br plumage: back and wing-coverts are russet with black on the scapulars, tail white with a black subterminal band. Face boldly black and white. Breast black.

►

Plate 34

14 SURFBIRD *Aphriza virgata* Not illustrated. Playero de las rompientes (Arg, Ch). L 25 cm. N-br plumage: upperparts brownish-grey, white rump. Eyebrow and throat contrastingly white; grey breast. Underparts white. Dark wings show a white band in flight. Tail white with black tip.

Plate 35

SANDPIPERS, SNIPE AND ALLIES (FAMILY SCOLOPACIDAE)

1 RED KNOT *Calidris canutus* Playero rojizo (Arg), Playero ártico (Ch), Chorlo rojizo (Uru), Maçarico-de-papo-vermelho (Br). L 26 cm. Habitat: winters on seashore. N-br plumage: white eyebrow. Upperparts pale greyish-brown with blackish streaks. Rump greyish-white streaked brown. Underparts white with slight streaking on the throat, neck, breast and flanks. Wings brownish, white bar in flight. Br plumage: cinnamon.

2 LEAST SANDPIPER *Calidris minutilla* Playero enano (Ch). L 15 cm. Habitat: seashores and inland waters. Above greyish-brown, feathers edged reddish. Dark along rump. Breast heavily flecked darker. White lower breast and belly. Dark flight feathers.

3 SANDERLING *Calidris alba* Playerito blanco (Arg), Playero blanco (Ch), Maçarico-branco (Br), Chorlito blanco (Uru). L 18 cm. Habitat: shores of lakes and sea. N-br plumage: upperparts pale grey; eyebrow and undersides all white. White tail with central feathers dark brown. Wings have dark brownish flight feathers and show a white wing-bar in flight.

4 WHITE-RUMPED SANDPIPER *Calidris fuscicollis* Playerito rabadilla blanca (Arg), Correlimos de rabadilla blanca (Bol), Chorlito de rabadilla blanca (Uru), Maçarico-de-sobre-branco (Br), Playerito de lomo blanco (Ch). L 18 cm. Habitat: seashores, lakes and marshes. N-br plumage: upperparts grey slightly flecked brown. Rump and upper tail-coverts white. Eyebrow and belly white; breast pale grey flecked darker, flecking extending onto the flanks. Voice: as takes flight, a rapid *'tzeep, tzeep'*.

5 SEMIPALMATED SANDPIPER *Calidris pusilla* Playerito enano (Arg), Playero semipalmado (Ch), Maçarico-rastreirinho (Br). L 15 cm. Habitat: seashore and by lakes. Feet partly webbed. N-br plumage: white eyebrow. Upperparts dark brownish, feathers edged paler; underparts white, sides of the breast greyish-brown. Wing-bar seen in flight. Tail brownish, outer feathers greyer.

6 WESTERN SANDPIPER *Calidris mauri* No local names. L 16 cm. In n-br plumage almost identical to Semipalmated Sandpiper, but bill longer and seems slightly drooped at the tip. Legs blacker. Accidental.

7 BAIRD'S SANDPIPER *Calidris bairdii* Playero unicolor (Arg), Chorlito unicolor (Uru), Chorlito de alas largas (Bol), Maçarico-de-bico-fino (Br). L 18 cm. Habitat: shores of lakes, rivers and the sea, and in short grass. N-br plumage: crown and upperparts dark brown, feathers edged lighter. Face and breast cinnamon-brown with brown flecking. Eyebrow, throat, flanks and the rest of the underparts white. Wings brownish with tips of the coverts whitish forming a slight wing-bar. Rump brownish. Br plumage similar but brighter in that the back feathers have black and are edged ochreous. Voice: on taking flight, a *'prreeeep'*. (Could be confused with the White-rumped Sandpiper but browner, no white rump, no flecking on the flanks, and the call set it apart.)

8 PECTORAL SANDPIPER *Calidris melanotos* Playerito pectoral (Arg), Playero pectoral (Ch), Maçarico de colete (Br), Chorlo de pecho gris (Uru). L 23 cm. Habitat: short grassland or edges of marshes and flooded areas. N-br plumage: upperparts dark brownish with the feathers edged lighter, rump dark brownish. Eyebrow and throat whitish. Neck and breast flecked and fairly heavily spotted brown. There is a sharpish cut-off between breast and white belly. Rest of the underside white. Wings dark with the coverts edged whitish. Brown tail, centrally darker. Br plumage: upperparts darker and with black streaks and spots. Voice: known as 'creekers' for their *'creeeeek'* call, similar to Baird's but louder and longer.

9 CURLEW SANDPIPER *Calidris ferruginea* Playerito errante (Arg). L 20 cm. Longish down-curved bill blackish-olive; legs olive-brown. N-br plumage: olive-brown upperparts, white rump. Whitish eyebrow. Breast white flecked with brownish. Wings: dark flight feathers, grey coverts and a wing-bar. Dark tail. Br plumage is generally chestnut, darker on the crown and with white under tail-coverts.

10 STILT SANDPIPER *Calidris himantopus* Playerito zancudo (Arg), Chorlito Zancudo (Bol), Chorlito semipalmado de pico largo (Uru), Playero de patas largas (Ch), Maçarico-pernilongo (Br). L 21 cm. Habitat: marshes and shores of lakes. Bill slightly down-curved at tip, black; long legs greenish. N-br plumage: brownish-grey upperparts slightly streaked white on neck. Back feathers edged whitish. Rump white. White eyebrow. Underparts white, faintly flecked with grey on neck, sides of breast, and flanks. Wings dark brown, coverts edged whitish. Light grey-brown tail. Br plumage: white eyebrow contrasts with dark crown and cinnamon face and ear-coverts. Back feathers darker and edges whitish. Underparts white, streaked brown on fore-neck, barred brown on breast, belly, flanks and under tail-coverts.

11 BUFF-BREASTED SANDPIPER *Tryngites subruficollis* Playerito canela (Arg), Chorlito canela (Bol), Maçarica-acanelado (Br), Chorlito acanelado (Uru). L 18 cm. Habitat: short-grass uplands. Bill black, legs yellowish. N-br plumage: dark streaked crown, rest of upperparts heavily blackish and cinnamon with creamy-edged feathers. Underparts buff. Undertail whitish. Dark wings with coverts like the back. Underwing white, dark bordered. Br plumage is similar but more contrasting back, brighter cinnamon underparts.

Plate 35

Plate 36

SANDPIPERS, SNIPE AND ALLIES (FAMILY SCOLOPACIDAE)

1 LONG-BILLED DOWITCHER *Limnodromus scolopaceus* Becasina boreal (Arg). L 30 cm. Habitat: shores of sea or lakes. Green legs. N-br plumage: greyish crown, whitish eyebrow. Head and neck greyish with flecking. Upperparts greyish, white rump. Underparts whitish. Tail white, barred black. Br plumage: reddish-brown upperparts with black markings, underparts reddish with black barring.

2 COMMON SNIPE *Gallinago g. paraguaiae* Becasina común (Arg, Uru), Becacina (Ch), Becacina paraguaya (Bol), Batuíra or Narceja (Br), Jakavere (Par). L 30 cm. Habitat: flooded grassland, edges of marshes, peat bogs. Very long bill. Head dark brown with crown stripe. Upperparts dark brown, scapulars blackish, outer vane yellowish forming noticeable 'skunk' stripes. Eyebrow and throat whitish; breast ochreous streaked with dark brown. Belly white, flanks whitish with brownish and cinnamon barring. Tail: central feathers black with white tip, outers barred whitish and grey.

3 GIANT SNIPE *Gallinago undulata* Becacina real (Bol), Narcejao or galinhola (Br). L 38 cm. Habitat: bogs. Throat whitish. Dark brown stripes on crown, brows and malar region. Below whitish. Flanks barred black. Upperparts dark brown, speckled. Tail barred brown and buff.

4 CORDILLERAN SNIPE *Gallinago stricklandii* Becasina grande (Arg, Ch, Bol). L 38 cm. Habitat: peat bogs, marshy places. Upperparts banded black, chestnut and ochre. Face whitish with dark brown freckling. Whitish throat. Breast ochreous with dark brown wavy barring, cinnamon on the neck. Ochreous belly and flanks, the latter barred with dark brown and cinnamon. Found in the damp sub-Antarctic of southern Tierra del Fuego.

Note: The following three species once composed a separate family. They are lobe-toed waders which swim with ease. Found on lakes, marshes and at sea.

5 RED PHALAROPE *Phalaropus fulicarius* Falaropo pico grueso (Arg), Pollito de mar rojizo (Ch). L 20–23 cm. N-br plumage: crown and line behind the eye dark. Upperparts grey. Forehead, eyebrow and underparts white; strong wing-bar.

6 RED-NECKED PHALAROPE *Phalaropus lobatus* Falaropo pico fino (Arg), Pollito de mar boreal (Ch). L 17–20 cm. N-br plumage: upperparts greyish with flecking on the back. Dark crown and eye-stripe. Forehead, eyebrow, sides of head and neck, and underparts white. Sides of the breast greyish.

7 WILSON'S PHALAROPE *Phalaropus tricolor* Falaropo común (Arg), Faláropo tricolor (Bol), Chorlo blanco nadador (Uru), Pollito de mar tricolor (Ch), Pisa-n'água (Br). L 22–25 cm. N-br plumage: pale grey upperparts. Eyebrow, rump and underparts white. Dark line through the eye. Greyish tail.

SEED-SNIPE (FAMILY THINOCORIDAE)

8 RUFOUS-BELLIED SEED-SNIPE *Attagis gayi* Agachona grande (Arg, Bol), Kulle-kulle (Bol), Perdicita cordillerana (Ch). L 30 cm. Habitat: stony steppes high in the Andes, and in boggy areas in the valleys. Dark back cryptic, with grey, cinnamon and ochre patterns. Whitish-grey throat. Fore-neck and breast pale cinnamon with fine wavy black barring. Belly and under tail-coverts ochre-cinnamon. When flushed flies fast.

9 WHITE-BELLIED SEED-SNIPE *Attagis malouinus* Agachona patagónica (Arg), Perdicita cordillerana austral (Ch). L 27 cm. Habitat: Breeds up by the snow-line on the scree, winters on the Patagonian steppes. Cryptic back dark brown with ochre, chestnut and whitish patterns. Whitish throat. Fore-neck and breast chestnut with dark brown and whitish speckling. Belly and under tail-coverts white. Hard to see, flies fast when flushed.

10 GREY-BREASTED SEED-SNIPE *Thinocorus orbignyianus* Agachona de collar (Arg, Bol), Puco-puco mayor (Bol), Perdicita cojón (Ch). L 22 cm. Habitat: rolling steppe and gentle slopes. ♂: head, neck and breast grey, with black streaks on crown and ear-patch. Rest of upperparts cryptic, brown with black and ochre markings. White throat bordered by a black line. A black band separates breast from white belly. ♀ has a speckled head, neck and breast, ochre and brownish, otherwise like the ♂. Voice: territorial flight-call a sonorous, deep, repetitive 'coop coop coop coop' from dawn.

11 LEAST SEED-SNIPE *Thinocorus rumicivorus* Agachona chica (Arg), Chorlo agachón (Uru), Perdicita (Ch), Agachona de corbata or Puco-puco menor (Bol). L 19 cm. Habitat: the flats, often near pebbly areas. ♂: upperparts cryptically light brown, ochre and blackish. Throat white bordered black, this joined with a vertical black line down the centre of the grey breast to the black bordering the lower breast, forming an 'anchor'. White belly. ♀ like ♂ but breast cryptically brown with speckling and only traces of the 'anchor'. Voice: calls on territory a sonorous 'toodle-doo toodle-doo...' ending with a guttural 'whorrrwhorrrwho'.

Plate 36

Plate 37

SHEATHBILL (FAMILY CHIONIDIDAE)

1 SNOWY SHEATHBILL *Chionis alba* Paloma-antártica (Arg, Ch), Paloma de mar (Uru), Pomba-antártica (Br). L 40 cm. Bill pinkish-yellow, dark tip. It emerges from a horn-coloured sheath around the base. Bare patch on the face. Pink caruncles. Legs greyish. Plumage impeccably white all over. Tame, struts and walks around between the colonial breeders like a pigeon in a park, which it resembles in form and flight.

SKUAS AND JAEGERS (FAMILY LARIDAE, SUBFAMILY STERCORARIINAE)

2 POMARINE JAEGER *Stercorarius pomarinus* Salteador grande (Arg), Salteador pomarino (Ch), Gaviota de rapiña pomarina (Uru), Gaivota-rapinheira-pomarina (Br). L 53–56 cm. Brownish bill with black tip; top of the head black, sides of same and half-collar on sides and hind-neck yellowish. Brownish back. Throat, fore-neck and belly white, breast marked with brown. Flanks and under tail-coverts barred or mottled brown. Wings brown with whitish at the base of the primaries. Tail long, brown, wedge-shaped, central feathers trailing, long, rounded and twisted about the shaft. The dark morph has undersides as dark as the back. Breeds in the Arctic. Migrates at sea with migrating Arctic Terns.

3 PARASITIC JAEGER *Stercorarius parasiticus* Salteador chico (Arg,Ch), Gaviota-rapinheira-comum (Br), Gaviota salteadora chica (Uru). L 46 cm. Bill brown, legs black. Top of the head, hind-neck, back and tail black. Sides of the head and neck yellowish. Underparts white with a brown band across the breast. Belly and under tail-coverts brownish. Wings brown with white at the base of the primaries. Wedge tail longish, with two central feathers protruding and pointed. Dark morph: neck and underparts lighter brown than the back. Imm: barred brownish on the underside and lacks the elongated central tail feathers. Sometimes, while moulting or having been broken off, the two central tail feathers are not seen in adults either. From the Arctic. Feeds by piracy.

4 LONG-TAILED JAEGER *Stercorarius longicaudus* Salteador coludo (Arg), Gaviota salteadora de cola larga (Uru), Salteador de cola larga (Ch), Rabo-de-junco-preto (Br). L 53–58 cm. Brown bill, black tip; legs grey. Top of the head black, back greyish-brown. Sides of the head and neck yellowish. Underparts white, darker flanks. Black primaries, brownish coverts. Brown tail with two central feathers extremely long and pointed (though these can break off or be moulted). Imm: greyish-brown on the back, white underside slightly flecked on the breast, and lacks the long tail. An Arctic breeder.

5 GREAT SKUA *Catharacta skua* Escúa común (Arg), Gaviota parda (Uru), Gaivota-rapinheira-grande (Br), Salteador (chileno) (Ch). L 57–59 cm. Bill and legs black. Brown upperparts with faint whitish streaking on the neck (hackles) and faint chestnut streaking lower on the back. Throat lighter. Breast and belly lighter brown. (The Brown Skua is all dark plain-chocolate coloured, the Chilean is paler with light cinnamon on body and underwing). In all forms there is a white patch near the end of the wing formed by the white bases of the primaries, seen in flight. The tail is slightly wedge-shaped. Though mostly a scavenger and predator, it sometimes practices piracy on terns, gulls and cormorants.

Note: This includes the Brown Skua (*Catharacta s.antarcticus*) from the Atlantic coast, and Chilean Skua (*C.s.chilensis*) of Tierra del Fuego and the Pacific.

6 SOUTH POLAR SKUA *Catharacta maccormicki* Escúa polar (Arg), Salteador polar (Ch). L 55 cm. Bill and legs black. Upperparts dark brown. Neck ochreous. Head and underparts sandy-brown. Wings dark with contrasting white patch near the tip. Brown, rounded tail. Nests in Antarctica, sharing snow-free areas with other colonial nesters which become skua food.

SKIMMERS (SUBFAMILY RYNCHOPINAE)

7 BLACK SKIMMER *Rynchops niger* Rayador (Arg, Uru, Ch, Bol), Cortamar (Uru), Pa'â guasu (Par), Corta-água (Br). L 50 cm. Habitat: rivers, lakes, estuaries. Characteristic bill red at the base, rest black. Forehead, face and underparts white, upperparts black. Long black wings with tips of secondaries white. Underwing greyish. Short, slightly notched tail dark brown centrally, rest white. In n-br plumage the upperparts are dark brown with a white collar round the back of the neck. Imm is mottled brown on the back. A dark form has a very narrow wing-bar on the secondaries, no white on the tail and brownish underwing. Flies just above the water with lower mandible of the open bill slicing through the water. Voice: when flocked the clamorous calling is characteristic.

Plate 37

Plate 38

GULLS (SUBFAMILY LARINAE)

1 **DOLPHIN GULL** *Leucophaeus scoresbii* Gaviota gris (Arg), Gaviota austral (Ch). L 44 cm. Habitat: around rubbish, docks and colonies of other sea-birds. Bill and legs red. Head, neck and underparts grey; back and wing-coverts black. Flight feathers with white tips. Underwing light grey, tail white. Imm: brownish hood and dirty grey neck and upper breast; rump, lower breast and belly white; bill brownish-pink with black tip. Brown legs. Solitary or in groups, noisy and boisterous. Voice: a raucous, screamed '*keeay, keeay, keeay*'. Moves up the coast in winter as far as southern Buenos Aires province.

2 **BAND-TAILED GULL** *Larus belcheri* Gaviota cangrejera (Arg), Gaviota peruana (Ch), Gaviota de cola negra (Uru). L 49 cm. Habitat: river mouths and estuaries. Yellow bill with red tip and black subterminal band right across. Yellow legs. Head, neck, underparts, rump and tail white, the tail with a broad black subterminal band. Back and wing-coverts black, primaries black, secondaries grey with white tip. In winter the head is brownish and the eyelids white. Imm: mottled grey and black with a hint of brown, has a pale yellow bill tipped black, and grey legs. Voice: calls are guttural.

Note: The South Atlantic population is considered by some to be a separate species, Olrog's Gull, *Larus atlanticus*.

3 **KELP GULL** *Larus dominicanus* Gaviota cocinera (Arg, Uru), Gaviotao (Br), Gaviota dominicana (Ch). L 60 cm. Yellow bill with a red spot near the tip of the lower mandible. Legs pale greenish-yellow. Head, neck, undersides, rump, tail and leading edge of the wing all white. Back and top of the wings black, flight feathers tipped white. Imm: mottled brownish, rump barred brownish and white; blackish bill. Alone or in groups, very rowdy. A scavenger and carrion-eater, thief of other birds' eggs and young. Often inland far from the sea or water. Voice: an onomatopoeic '*kelp, kelp*'.

4 **GREY-HOODED GULL** *Larus cirrocephalus* Gaviota capucho gris (Arg), Gaivota-de-cabeça-cinza (Br), Gaviota cabecigris (Bol). L 46 cm. Habitat: on lakes and marshes, sometimes on the seashore. Bill and legs red. White iris. Head and throat grey. Rump, tail and underparts white. Back and wing-coverts grey. Two outer primaries black with subterminal white at the base and onto the coverts. Rest of the flight feathers grey. In n-br plumage only a grey nuchal band. Imm: whitish mottled brown on head and back, with brown wings and white tail with brownish sub-terminal band. Noisy.

5 **ANDEAN GULL** *Larus serranus* Gaviota andina (Arg, Ch, Bol). L 46 cm. Habitat: high in the Andes between 3500 and 4000 metres, but in winter descends to 2000 metres or less. Bill and legs dark red. Black head with a white crescent behind the eye. Back and wing-coverts grey. Three outer primaries black with streak along the shaft and subterminal band white. Inner primaries greyish-white with broad black band at tip. Grey secondaries. Neck, underparts and tail white with faint pink wash on breast. In winter the head is flecked with grey, with a grey patch around the eye. Imm: head, neck and back whitish with brownish spotting, brownish secondaries, subterminal band on the tail and brown bill and legs. Voice: a raucous '*kaaaaay*'.

6 **FRANKLIN'S GULL** *Larus pipixcan* Gaviota chica (Arg), Gaviota de Franklin (Ch), Gaviota menor (Bol). L 36 cm. Habitat: inland on rivers, lakes or the sea coast. Migratory from North America. N-br plumage: bill and legs brownish. Forehead and fore-crown white, rest of the crown brownish flecked with white. Back and wing-coverts grey. Throat, fore-neck, lower hind-neck, rump, tail and underparts white. The five outer primaries black with white tip, the rest of the flight feathers grey with white tip. In br plumage, red bill and reddish legs; black head, otherwise like winter. Imm: white forehead; crown, sides of the head and upperparts greyish-brown. Tail grey with broad black subterminal band. Brown bill and legs.

7 **BROWN-HOODED GULL** *Larus maculipennis* Gaviota capucho café (Arg, Uru), Gaviota cabecicafé (Bol), Gaviota cahuil (Ch), Gaivota-maria-velha (Br). L 42 cm. Habitat: marshes, lakes, seashore, pastures and arable land. Bill and legs dark red. Brown iris. Head and throat dark brown, white crescent behind the eye. Back and wing-coverts grey. Neck, rump, tail and underparts white. Outer primaries black and white with white tip, middle primaries with white sub-terminal band, inner ones and secondaries grey. From below the wing is grey with black primaries and a white subterminal band. In winter the crown is white with dark spot before the eye and another on the ear-patch. Imm: spotted brown on the back and wing-coverts with a dark sub-terminal band on the tail. Gregarious; follows the plough. Voice: alarm and aggressive scream a high-pitched raucous '*kaaaaay*'.

8 **SABINE'S GULL** *Xema sabini* Gaviota de Sabine (Ch). L 33 cm. Black bill with yellow tip. Dark legs. Grey head. Upper back and wing-coverts grey. Neck, underparts, secondaries and forked tail white. Primaries black with white tips. Rare visiting migrant on seashores.

9 **SWALLOW-TAILED GULL** *Creagrus furcatus* Gaviota de las Galapagos (Ch). L 51 cm. Habitat: at sea. Dark bill pale-tipped. Greyish-white legs. Whitish head with dark ring around the eye. Upperparts grey. White below. Forked tail white. Br plumage has a dark grey head, pink legs. Primaries black and white. Secondaries and tail white.

Plate 38

Plate 39

TERNS (SUB-FAMILY STERNINAE)

1 **BLACK TERN** *Chlidonias niger* Gaviotín negro (Arg, Ch, Uru). L 22–24 cm. Habitat: sea coasts and lakes. N-br plumage: eye-stripe, hind-crown, nape and part of hind-neck black. Forehead, fore-crown, sides of head, throat and all underparts white. Back, wings and short, slightly forked tail lead-grey. Narrow white border along the leading edge of the wing. Br plumage: head, neck, breast and belly black; undertail white. Imm: like n-br but head and back have brownish spots.

2 **LARGE-BILLED TERN** *Phaetusa simplex* Atí (Arg, Uru), Gaviotín de pico grande (Bol), Pa'â (Par), Trinta-réis-grande (Br), Gaviotín de pico grueso (Uru). L 37–39 cm. Habitat: rivers, lakes, sand-banks. Large yellow bill. Top of the head black. Back and square tail grey. Throat, neck and underparts white. Black primaries, white secondaries, grey coverts making a very distinct wing-pattern. N-br plumage: crown is grey, post-ocular streak and nape darker. Imm: like n-br but with brownish spotting on the back. Voice: loud call.

3 **GULL-BILLED TERN** *Sterna nilotica* Gaviotín pico grueso (Arg), Gaviotín de pico negro (Uru), Trinta-réis-de-bico-preto (Br). L 38 cm. Habitat: lakes, rivers and sandy seashores. Heavy bill black. Crown, nape and sides of the head black. Back, slightly forked tail and wing-coverts grey. Underparts white. Grey primaries. N-br plumage: forehead and fore-crown white, rest of the crown and nape grey finely streaked black. Imm like n-br but speckled with brown on head and back.

4 **SOUTH AMERICAN TERN** *Sterna hirundinacea* Gaviotín sudamericano (Arg, Ch), Gaviotín común (Uru), Trinta-réis-de-bico-vermelho (Br). L 40–41 cm. Habitat: sea coast, on islands or beaches. Bill and legs red in br plumage, black in n-br plumage. Top half of the head black, back and wing-coverts grey. Rump and deeply-forked tail white. Tail extends beyond the folded wings. Throat and breast pale greyish, rest of the underparts white. Flight feathers grey, outer primaries with outer vane slate-grey. In n-br plumage the forehead and breast are white. Voice: a loud, nasal and high-pitched '*care, careware*'; when angry screams '*CAAARE*'.

5 **COMMON TERN** *Sterna hirundo* Gaviotín golondrina (Arg), Golondrina de mar (Uru), Gaviotín boreal (Ch), Trinta-réis-boreal (Br). L 33–40 cm. Habitat: coast, sometimes inland. Bill black with a bit of red at the base, the red brightening and extending in br plumage. N-br plumage: forehead and fore-crown white. Hind-crown and nape white with black flecking. Grey back, dark grey wing-coverts. Primaries have dark outer web, lighter inner web, and secondaries are grey and white. Border of the wing, rump and underparts white. Tail forked but does not extend beyond the folded wing. In br plumage the top half of the head is black, breast and belly grey. Imm like n-br but flecked brown on the back. On migration.

6 **ARCTIC TERN** *Sterna paradisaea* Gaviotín ártico (Arg, Uru, Ch), Trinta-réis ártico (Br). L 35 cm. Habitat: at sea. Bill and legs black. N-br plumage: crown and nape black, flecked with white. Back grey. Underparts and rump white. Grey wings with white on the secondaries. Tail slightly longer than the folded wing, deeply forked, light grey, darker on outer tail feathers. Br plumage: black top half of head, grey body. White separates the black from the grey running from the base of the bill to the back of the neck. Imm like n-br but upperparts ash-brown. Performs the longest migration known, a figure-of-eight from the Arctic, through the North and South Atlantic Oceans, to Antarctic and back.

7 **ANTARCTIC TERN** *Sterna vittata* Gaviotín antártico (Arg, Ch, Uru), Trinta-réis antártico (Br). L 37–40 cm. Habitat: Atlantic coast. Bill and legs red. Top half of the head black bordered below by a wide white band from the base of the bill to the neck. Back and wing-coverts blue-grey, rump and deeply forked tail white, outer vanes of tail feathers grey. Throat, breast and underparts grey, undertail-coverts white. Wings grey with the outer vanes of the outer primaries dark. 'Winter' plumage has a white fore-crown and forehead. Imm like this but also white underparts. Voice: alarm call a strident '*key-up, key-up*'.

8 **SNOWY-CROWNED TERN** *Sterna trudeaui* Gaviotín lagunero (Arg), Gaviotín piquerito (Ch), Gaviotín de antifaz negro (Uru), Trinta-réis-de-corona-branca (Br). L 34 cm. Habitat: fresh water, occasionally seashore. Bill yellow crossed by a black band before the tip (in n-br plumage black with yellow tip). Top of the head, throat and rump white. Striking black line through the eye. Rest of the head, upperparts and underparts grey. Underwing white, forked tail grey with outer feathers white. In n-br plumage the crown is grey. Imm is like winter plumage adult but with brown flecking on the back and wing-coverts. White forehead, blackish bill, yellowish legs.

Plate 39

Plate 40

TERNS (SUB-FAMILY STERNINAE)

1 SOOTY TERN *Sterna fuscata* Gaviotín apizarrado (Ch), Trinta-réis-das-rocas (Br). L 40 cm. Habitat: at sea. Forehead and underparts white. Above blackish-brown. Deeply forked tail black with outer feathers white.

2 SPECTACLED TERN *Sterna lunata* Gaviotín pascuense (Ch). L 36 cm. Habitat: inshore waters and at sea. Bill and feet black. Eye-line, crown and nape black. Forehead, eyebrow, around neck and underparts white. Dark grey upperparts. Deeply forked tail with outer feathers white.

3 YELLOW-BILLED TERN *Sterna superciliaris* Gaviotín chico común (Arg), Trinta-réis-anao (Br), Gaviotín de cejas blancas (Uru), Atî (Par), Gaviotín pico amarillo (Bol). L 23 cm. Habitat: fresh water, sometimes seen on the seashore. Bill and legs yellow. Crown, nape and back of the neck black, line from bill to eye black. Forehead extending back towards the eye white. Back and upperwing-coverts grey, underparts white. Four outer primaries black edged white on inner vane, rest of the flight feathers grey, secondaries white-tipped. Forked tail grey. In n-br only the nape and hind-neck are black and flecked with white. Imm has crown flecked blackish, back and wing-coverts brown-spotted.

4 PERUVIAN TERN *Sterna lorata* Gaviotín chico (Ch). L 23 cm. Habitat: coastal waters. Yellow bill with black tip. Forehead and throat white. Crown and nape black. Grey above, greyish underparts. Black outer primaries, rest grey with white shafts.

5 LEAST TERN *Sterna antillarum* Gaviotín chico boreal (Arg). L 22 cm. Habitat: coasts and at sea. Bill black in n-br plumage, yellow with black tip in br plumage. N-br plumage: white forehead and crown; nape and hind-neck black with white flecking. Back and upperwings grey, underparts and forked tail white. Wings with outer primaries black. In br plumage the crown, nape and hind-neck are black as is a line from eye to bill, otherwise like n-br. Imm has dark flecks on the nape, a dark post-ocular stripe, ochre dots on the grey back. On migration.

6 ROYAL TERN *Sterna maxima* Gaviotín real (Arg, Uru), Trinta-réis-real (Br). L 48 cm. Habitat: sea coast. Huge red bill. Crown and long nuchal feathers (crest) black. Forehead, rump, underparts, deeply forked tail and border of the wing white. Upperparts and wings grey, outermost primaries dark grey. In n-br and imm plumages crown and nape are flecked black and white, and imm has dark flecking on the back, yellow bill and legs. Voice: a strident call in flight – 'gerrep, gerrep'.

7 ELEGANT TERN *Sterna elegans* Gaviotín elegante (Ch). L 40 cm. Habitat: coastal waters and seashores. Orange bill, black legs. Forehead and fore-crown white. Hind-crown and nuchal crest black. Neck, underparts, rump and forked tail white. Back and wings grey. In br plumage top half of the head is all black. Migrant from the north.

8 SANDWICH TERN *Sterna sandvicensis* Gaviotín pico negro (Arg), Gaviotín de Sandwich (Ch). L 40 cm. Habitat: marine environments. Bill black with a yellow tip. N-br plumage: white forehead, fore-crown flecked black and white. Hind-crown black with nuchal tuft. Grey upperparts. Wings grey with white margins on the inner web of the primaries. Underparts, rump and forked tail white. In br plumage has black top half of the head and black nuchal feathers in a crest. Imm has black-and-white flecked forehead and crown and upperparts mottled black and white. Bill black. Migrant from North America.

9 CAYENNE TERN *Sterna eurygnatha* Gaviotín pico amarillo (Arg), Trinta-réis-de-bico-amarelo (Br), Gaviotín del Brasil (Uru). L 40 cm. Habitat: marine environments; breeds on islands and beaches. Bill yellow. Grey upperparts, white underparts. Black top half of the head with long black nuchal feathers in a crest as in Royal Tern.

10 INCA TERN *Larosterna inca* Gaviotín monja (Ch). L 40 cm. Habitat: islands and rocky shores; cliffs. Red bill and feet. Overall slate-grey. White line from gape to below eye, feathers long and droopy. Primaries and outer tail feathers black. Inner primaries edged white, secondaries tipped white. Forked tail.

11 BROWN NODDY *Anous stolidus* Gaviotín de San Félix (Ch), Andorinha-do-mar-preta (Br). L 39 cm. Habitat: coastal and at sea. Bill and feet black. Overall dark brown. Top half of head pale grey, forehead and brow white. Long, graduated tail not forked.

12 FAIRY TERN *Gygis alba* Gaviotín albo (Ch), Grazinha (Br). L 31 cm. Habitat: Coastal and at sea. All white but for black bill, feet and eye-ring.

Plate 40

Plate 41

PIGEONS AND DOVES (FAMILY COLUMBIDAE)

1 ROCK DOVE *Columba livia* Paloma doméstica (Arg, Uru), Paloma (Par, Ch), Pombo or Pombo-doméstico (Br). L 33 cm. Habitat: narrow canyons as in cities. Plumages vary greatly: original plumage blue-grey with green or violaceous sheen on the neck. Two black bars on the wing. Voice: 'cootooroocoo cootooroocoo' in courtship or 'boo-hoo-hoo boo-hoo' at the nest, or in courtship.

2 BAND-TAILED PIGEON *Columba fasciata* Paloma de nuca blanca (Arg, Bol). L 36 cm. Habitat: cloud forest between 1800 and 2500 m, descending to 1000 m in winter. Yellow bill and legs, red eye-ring. White collar round back of the neck. Bronzy-green shoulders. Grey tail with black band.

3 CHILEAN PIGEON *Columba araucana* Paloma araucana (Arg), Torcaza (Ch). L 35 cm. Habitat: cool temperate forests. Head, neck and breast vinaceous-chestnut; white nuchal collar. Grey tail with black subterminal band.

4 SCALED PIGEON *Columba speciosa* Paloma trocal (Arg, Bol), Pomba-trocal (Br), Paloma guacoa (Bol). L 30-32 cm. Habitat: subtropical rainforests. Red bill. Chestnut head. Feathers on neck and breast 'scaled'. Violaceous sheen on shoulders, purplish on wing-coverts.

5 PICAZURO PIGEON *Columba picazuro* Paloma picazuro (Arg), Asa-branca or Pombao (Br), Pykasûrô (Par), Picazuró or Paloma torcaza (Bol), Paloma grande de monte (Uru). L 36 cm. Vinaceous head, scaly on hind-neck. Brownish back grading to lead-grey on rump. Underparts vinaceous-grey. Greater-coverts with white tips forming a white line visible in flight. Voice: 'or whooo? who? who? or whooo?' repeated three or four times. Expanding into areas where not previously known.

6 SPOT-WINGED PIGEON *Columba maculosa* Paloma manchada (Arg, Bol), Paloma de alas manchadas (Uru), Pomba-do-orvalho (Br). L 33 cm. Habitat: woodland with clearings. Grey bill. Head, neck and underparts powder grey, darker on the back to lead-grey rump. Wing-coverts with white spots which give the bird its name. Voice: like Picazuro Pigeon, but hoarse.

7 PALE-VENTED PIGEON *Columba cayennensis* Paloma colorada (Arg, Bol), Pomba-galega (Br), Pykasû (Par). L 28-31 cm. Habitat: forests and woodland. Breast vinaceous. Back and wing-coverts purplish-chestnut; rump and tail, belly, flanks and undertail grey. Grey tail has sandy-grey terminal band. Voice: like Picazuro Pigeon, but higher-pitched and longer first 'haw whooo?'.

8 PLUMBEOUS PIGEON *Columba plumbea* Paloma plomiza (Bol), Pomba-amargosa (Br). L 33 cm. Habitat: forests. Brownish. Underwing-coverts brown.

9 EARED DOVE *Zenaida auriculata* Torcaza (Arg), Avoante or Pomba-de-bando (Br), Tórtola torcaza (Bol), Mbairari (Par), Torcaza común (Uru), Tórtola (Ch). L 26 cm. Habitat: woods, stubble fields, steppe, gardens. Auricular spot blue-black. Pinkish-grey breast. Wings with two to six largish black spots. Tail grey with white tips to outer feathers. Very abundant. Voice: gentle, deep toned descending 'whoo.. whoo.. whoo.. who-who' repeated sporadically. *(See Plate 42 for illustration of bird in flight).*

10 WHITE-WINGED DOVE *Zenaida asiatica* Paloma de alas blancas (Ch). L 31 cm. Habitat: arid areas, cultivated fields, riversides. Eye-ring cobalt blue. Black mark on each side of the neck with a golden spot below it. Wing-coverts brown with white tips forming a broad bar seen on folded wing.

11 PLAIN-BREASTED GROUND-DOVE *Columbina minuta* Palomita enana (Arg), Palomita sabanera or Chaicita enana (Bol), Rolinha-de-asa-canela (Br). L 14 cm. Habitat: open and semi-open areas. Tiny. Brownish-grey upperparts. Pinkish-grey breast. Wing-coverts dotted blue, underwing reddish.

12 RUDDY GROUND-DOVE *Columbina talpacoti* Palomita colorada (Arg), Rola or Rolinha (Br), Palomita colorada (Bol), Pycu'i pytâ (Par), Torcacita rojiza (Uru), Tortolita rojiza (Ch). L 17 cm. Habitat: savannahs, woods and forest edges. ♂: ruddy chestnut upperparts, whitish throat, pinkish-grey underparts. Wing-coverts with biggish black spots. Shortish tail with central feathers brown, outer feathers black with chestnut tips. ♀ like ♂ but olive-brown upperparts, ochre-brown underparts. Voice: a tri-syllabic 'oo-who who? .. oo-who who? .. oo-who who? ..' repeated 4 to 10 times; pause, then repeated.

13 PICUI GROUND-DOVE *Columbina picui* Torcacita (Arg), Tortolita cuyana (Ch), Torcacita común (Uru), Pycu'ipe (Par), Palomita común (Bol), Rolinha-branca (Br). L 18 cm. Habitat: woods, savannahs, fields and gardens. ♂: bluish on the crown; dove-grey; paler, almost white ventrally with a vinaceous wash on the breast and a touch of brown on the back. Upperwing-coverts black-tipped forming a continuous bar, greaters white, secondaries black – a striking wing pattern. Tail with outer tips white. ♀: as ♂ but browner upperparts, and no bluish crown. Voice: ♂'s a disyllabic 'coo-rue..coo-rue..coo-rue..coo-rue..' the 'rue' a minor third up, four to ten times, pause and then repeated.

14 GOLDEN-BILLED GROUND-DOVE *Columbina cruziana* Tortolita quiguagua (Ch). L 18 cm. Habitat: mountains between 2000 and 4000 m, in grassy fields and cultivated land. ♂: brownish-grey above. Vinaceous below. Whitish throat and central belly. Black flight feathers. Purplish-scarlet bar on wing. ♀ is grey below.

Plate 41

Plate 42

PIGEONS AND DOVES (FAMILY COLUMBIDAE)

1 SCALY DOVE *Columbina squammata* Torcacita escamada (Arg), Pyku'ípini (Par), Palomita escamosa (Bol), Fogo-apagou (Br). L 19 cm. Habitat: gardens, open areas with trees, farms. Whole bird has scaled appearance. Voice: dove-like and clear, four- or five-syllabled '*togo-at'a'go*'.

2 BLUE GROUND-DOVE *Claravis pretiosa* Palomita azulada (Arg), Pomba-de-espelho (Br), Palomita azul (Bol), Jeruti hovy (Par). L 20 cm. Habitat: woods and forests. ♂: blue-grey; coverts lead-grey with black spots. Tail centrally lead-grey, outer feathers black. ♀: back and breast brown, central tail feathers chestnut, outers black. Voice: '*oop…oop… oop…oop…*'.

3 PURPLE-WINGED GROUND-DOVE *Claravis godefrida* Palomita morada (Arg), Pararu (Br). L 20–22 cm. Habitat: subtropical rainforests. ♂: blue grey. Blue band on lesser wing-coverts, reddish-chestnut on greater. Central tail feathers blue-grey, the rest white. ♀: reddish-brown. Central tail feathers reddish-brown, outers grey, then black, ending in reddish tip.

4 BARE-FACED GROUND-DOVE *Metriopelia ceciliae* Palomita moteada (Arg, Bol), Tortolita boliviana (Ch). L 17 cm. Habitat: rocky areas with scrub between 2500 and 3500 m. Bare face yellowish-orange. Grey-brown upperparts, feathers edged ochreous. Flight feathers blackish-brown, secondaries tipped whitish. Central tail feathers chestnut hued, outers almost entirely black with whitish tip.

5 BARE-EYED GROUND-DOVE *Metriopelia morenoi* Palomita ojos desnudos (Arg). L 17 cm. Habitat: stony brushland steppe between 2000 and 3200 m. Bare skin around eye reddish-orange. Completely brown, wings dark, underwing blackish. Central tail feathers brown, outers black with white tip.

6 GOLDEN-SPOTTED GROUND-DOVE *Metriopelia aymara* Palomita de alas doradas (Arg), Palomita ala dorada or Palomita aymara (Bol), Tortola de la puna (Ch). L 17 cm. Habitat: steppes and deep valleys between 3000 and 4000 m. Entirely greyish-brown. Cinnamon patch on underwing. Wing-coverts with golden spots. Central tail feathers greyish, outers black.

7 BLACK-WINGED GROUND-DOVE *Metriopelia melanoptera* Palomita de alas negras (Arg), Tórtola cordillerana (Ch), Palomita ala negra (Bol). L 23 cm. Habitat: steppes and deep valleys up to 3000 m. Overall brownish-grey. Wings: blackish flight feathers, pale shoulders. Undertail black; tail centrally brown, outer feathers black.

8 WHITE-TIPPED DOVE *Leptotila verreauxi* Yerutí común (Arg), Juriti (Br), Jeruti (Par) Paloma montaraz común (Bol), Paloma de axilas rojas (Uru). L 30 cm. Habitat: woodlands. Grey crown. Nape, hind-neck and back with green and violet sheen. Brownish back, white throat. Rest of underparts vinaceous; belly and undertail whitish. Brownish wings with rich cinnamon underwing. Brown tail with white on outer feathers. Voice: a deep, resonant '*coo-cooooo*', rather like blowing across a bottle, repeated.

9 LARGE-TAILED DOVE *Leptotila megalura* Yerutí coluda (Arg, Bol). L 32 cm. Habitat: woodlands between 1500 and 2500 m. Grey forehead; crown, hind-neck and upper back shot violaceous. Lower back, wing-coverts and rump olive-brown, whitish throat. Underparts vinaceous-ochre, undertail white. Dark brownish flight feathers, underwing cinnamon. Long tail dark brown, white-tipped outer feathers. Voice: five-syllabled, sonorous '*who who who who whooooo*'.

10 GREY-FRONTED DOVE *Leptotila rufaxilla* Yerutí rojiza (Arg, Bol), Gemedeira (Br), Paloma de axilas rojas y frente gris (Uru). L 28 cm. Habitat: forests. Bare, red eye-ring. Grey forehead, crown blue-grey. Hind-neck and back with violaceous sheen. Lower back and wing-coverts dark olive-brown. Throat white, underparts red-ochre, paler on belly. White under tail-coverts. Brown wings with cinnamon underwing. Dark tail with white on tips of outer feathers. Voice: a quiet, low-pitched '*horwoooo*'.

11 RUDDY QUAIL-DOVE *Geotrygon montana* Paloma montera castaña (Arg, Bol), Parirí (Br). L 25 cm. Habitat: rainforests. Bare red skin around the eye. ♂: back, wings and short tail reddish-chestnut with purple sheen on nape and back. White line below the eye and on shoulders. Chestnut band on the sides of the head. White throat, vinaceous breast, ochre belly; underwing cinnamon. ♀: cinnamon, with green sheen on olive-brown back and central tail. Belly and undertail ochreous. Brown wings.

12 VIOLACEOUS QUAIL-DOVE *Geotrygon violacea* Paloma montera violacea (Arg), Paloma-perdiz rojiza or Ququisa (Bol), Juriti-vermelha (Br). L 24 cm. Habitat: forests. Red eye-ring. ♂: sides of the head grey. Forehead and throat white. Crown grey with violaceous sheen, hind-neck and upper back metallic violaceous; lower back, rump and tail-coverts olive with violaceous edging. Fore-neck and breast vinaceous, rest of underparts white. Wings and tail chestnut. ♀: forehead chestnut, olive back with darker tips to the feathers, brown breast, wings and tail.

13 WHITE-THROATED QUAIL-DOVE *Geotrygon frenata* Paloma montera grande (Arg), Paloma-perdiz parda or Ququisa (Bol). L 30 cm. Dark upperparts with violaceous sheen. Narrow black line through the eye, another (malar stripe) under the face to the nape. White throat. Brownish-grey underparts. Wings and tail brownish, secondaries edged chestnut. Voice: a deep sonorous '*boooooop*' repeated sporadically.

Plate 42

Plate 43

PARROTS AND PARAKEETS (FAMILY PSITTACIDAE)

1 HYACINTH MACAW *Anodorhynchus hyacinthinus* Guacamayo azul (Bol), Arara-azul-grande (Br). L 92 cm. Habitat: savannahs with trees, forests. Dark cobalt-blue plumage. Bare skin at base of lower mandible and around eye yellow.

2 GLAUCOUS MACAW *Anodorhynchus glaucus* Arara-azul-pequena (Br). L 70 cm. Habitat: nests in river banks. Above pale blue. Head, neck, flanks, wings, tail and belly greenish-blue. Once common, now probably extinct (perhaps through disease).

3 BLUE-AND-YELLOW MACAW *Ara ararauna* Arara-de-barriga-amarela or Canindé (Br), Paraba azul amarillo (Bol). L 80 cm. Habitat: palm groves and forests. Bare facial skin white with lines of tiny blackish-green feathers. Forehead and crown green. Black throat. Above, wings and tail pale blue. Yellow underparts.

4 MILITARY MACAW *Ara militaris* Guacamayo verde (Arg), Guacamayo de frente roja (Bol). L 70 cm. Habitat: forests. Bare face pink with black lines of tiny feathers. Green with scarlet forehead; pale blue lower back, rump and all tail-coverts. Central tail feathers red, outers pale blue. Flight feathers blue. Underwing and undertail bronzy-green.

5 RED-AND-GREEN MACAW *Ara chloroptera* Guacamayo rojo (Arg), Paraba roja (Bol), Arara-vermelha-grande (Br). L 78 cm. Habitat: forests. Upper beak whitish, lower mandible black. Dark grey feet. Bare face white with fine lines of tiny black feathers. Overall scarlet. Lower back, rump, all tail-coverts pale blue. Blue wings with lesser-coverts red, medial-coverts yellowish-green and greaters blue. Central tail feathers reddish-brown with blue-green tips, next pair blue with red, outermost entirely blue. Undertail and underwings red.

6 GOLDEN-COLLARED MACAW *Ara auricollis* Maracaná de cuello dorado (Arg, Bol), Maracana-de-colar (Br), Parabachi cuello amarillo (Bol). L 40–45 cm. Black beak with whitish tip, pink feet. Bare face yellowish-white. Overall green. Forehead, crown and cheeks black. Yellow collar round hind-neck. Blue flight feathers. Outer tail feathers blue with red inner webs. Central tail feathers red with distal third blue. Voice: in flocks calls loudly.

7 BLUE-WINGED MACAW *Ara maracana* Maracaná de dorso rojo (Arg), Maracana (Br). L 40 cm. Habitat: forests. Black beak, pinkish-brown feet. Bare face yellowish-pink. Overall green, a small red patch on the forehead. Bluish-green crown and ear-patch. Belly and rump red. Blue wings with green coverts. Tail pale blue with red basal half. Undertail olive-brown.

8 BLUE-CROWNED PARAKEET *Aratinga acuticaudata* Calancate (Arg, Bol), Periquitao-de-cabeça-azul (Br). L 34-36 cm. Creamy beak with black tip and mandible. Yellowish-pink feet. Bare patch on face yellowish-white. Generally green but metallic pale blue on forehead, crown, lores, cheek, ear-patch and part of the throat. Yellowish-green on breast and belly. Sharp-pointed green tail with red on inner web of outer feathers. Voice: strident and rough.

9 MITRED PARAKEET *Aratinga mitrata* Loro de cara roja (Arg), Loro cariroja (Bol). L 35-37 cm. Beak whitish, feet brownish. Bare face-patch pink. Green overall, with red splashed on forehead, cheeks and throat. Fore-neck, breast, scapulars, belly and back with scattered red feathers. Wings and tail green. Flocks. Voice: typical *Aratinga* voice strident and coarse.

10 WHITE-EYED PARAKEET *Aratinga leucophthalmus* Loro de ala roja (Arg), Maracaná (Uru), Loro ala roja (Bol), Marakana (Par), Periquitao-maracana (Br). L 36 cm. Habitat: savannahs, woods and forests. Yellow beak, dark grey feet. Bare ring around the eye whitish-pink. Overall green, neck breast and belly lighter. Some scattered red feathers on throat and nape. Edge of the wing and lesser under wing-coverts red, greaters yellow. Flight feathers and tail yellowish-green from below. Voice: raucous call in flight.

11 SUN CONURE *Aratinga solstitialis* Jandaia-de-testa-vermelha (Br). L 33 cm. Habitat: farmland, forest. Dark green. Forehead and face, belly and flanks red. Crown with yellow. Under tail-coverts olive. Blue flight feathers. Wing-coverts green and yellow. Under wing-coverts yellow and orange.

12 PEACH-FRONTED PARAKEET *Aratinga aurea* Cotorra de frente naranja (Arg), Periquito-rei or Periquito-estrela (Br), Cotorra frentidorada (Bol). L 25 cm. Habitat: savannahs. Beak and feet black. Generally green overall, forehead and area around the eye yellow. Blue on the cere, lores and crown. Yellowish-green breast and belly. Primaries green with dark tip, secondaries blue with internal vane olive. Coverts and scapulars green, yellowish underwing. Green tail.

13 BLACK-HOODED PARAKEET *Nandayus nenday* Ñenday (Arg) Periquito-de-cabeça-preta (Br), Cotorra cabecinegra or Nenday (Bol). L 32 cm. Habitat: palm savannahs. Black beak, brown feet. Overall green with black hood. Breast and belly yellowish-green with blue tips to the feathers. Yellow thighs, scarlet garters. Blue and green wing and tail. Pairs or in flocks. Voice: unpleasantly noisy.

▶

Plate 43

14 BURROWING PARROT *Cyanoliseus patagonus* Loro barranquero (Arg, Uru), Tricahue (Ch). L 46 cm. Habitat: brushland and steppe. Yellowish-white bare patch on face. Head, cheeks and scapulars olive-brown. Back, rump, tail-coverts and flanks pale yellow. Throat and breast greyish-brown, whitish spots on sides of breast. Red patch in the middle of yellow belly. Flight feathers blue, brown from below. Upper coverts green, yellowish underwing. Olive-green tail. A northern race has olive-brown belly, small red patch in the middle, olive lower back and rump. Noisy and gregarious.

Plate 44

PARROTS AND PARAKEETS (FAMILY PSITTACIDAE)

1 BLAZE-WINGED PARAKEET *Pyrrhura devillei* Periquito alianaranjado (Bol). L 25 cm. Habitat: forests. Green, scaly red on belly. Underwing scarlet on lesser-coverts, yellow on greaters.

2 REDDISH-BELLIED PARAKEET *Pyrrhura frontalis* Chiripepé de cabeza verde (Arg), Chiripepe (Uru), Chiri pepe (Par), Tiriba-de-testa-vermelha (Br). L 25 cm. Habitat: woods and forests. Green head. Red patch on belly. Green upperparts. Some blue in the wing. Tail reddish from below. In flocks. Voice: in flight a sharp '*shek…chek.*' and '*cheery..cheery.. chaychay*'.

3 GREEN-CHEEKED PARAKEET *Pyrrhura molinae* Chiripepé de cabeza gris (Arg, Bol). L 25 cm. Habitat: woods and forests up to 2000 m. Crown and cheeks green. Red belly. Tail mostly red. Voice: similar to Reddish-bellied Parakeet; fast '*cheery..cheery.. chaychay*'.

4 AUSTRAL PARAKEET *Enicognathus ferrugineus* Cachaña (Arg, Ch). L 34 cm. Habitat: cool temperate woods and forests, clearings. Olive-green with forehead, belly patch and tail reddish. Feathers on crown and neck have dark edges. Flight feathers green and brown.

5 SLENDER-BILLED PARAKEET *Enicognathus leptorhynchus* Choroy (Ch). L 40 cm. Habitat: stands of *Araucaria* woods and cool temperate forests. Long slender bill. Dark green. Forehead, lores and bare skin around eye reddish, orange-washed. Reddish tail.

6 MONK PARAKEET *Myiopsitta monachus* Cotorra (Arg), Cotorra común (Uru), Cata aliazul (Bol), Caturrita (Br). L 30 cm. Habitat: farmland, open woods. Upperparts bright green. Grey face and breast. Blue flight feathers. Huge stick and twig nests on pylons or high in trees.

7 GREY-HOODED PARAKEET *Bolborhynchus aymara* Catita serrana grande (Arg, Bol). L 19 cm. Habitat: steep bushy valleys between 1400 and 3400 m. Upperparts generally green. Brownish-grey hood. Voice: flight call a clicking '*tikitiklik tsi-tsi*'.

8 MOUNTAIN PARAKEET *Bolborhynchus aurifrons* Catita serrana chica (Arg), Catita frentidorada (Bol), Perico cordillerano (Ch). L 18 cm. Habitat: scrubby vegetation on mountains, valleys. Yellow beak. Bright green, yellow on forehead. Southern form has pink beak, bluish wash on breast.

9 BLUE-WINGED PARROTLET *Forpus xanthopterygius* Catita enana (Arg), Catita enana común (Bol), Membéi (Par), Tuim (Br). L 12 cm. Habitat: savannahs, woods and forests. Tiny. All green. ♂: blue on lower back, rump and wing. Short tail green. Voice: a short '*click, chick-click*'.

10 CANARY-WINGED PARAKEET *Brotogeris versicolurus* Catita de alas amarillas (Arg), Periquito-de-asa-branca (Br), Periquito aliamarillo (Bol). L 21-22 cm. Habitat: open woods and savannahs. All green. Greater wing-coverts yellow. Long, sharp tail green.

11 RED-CAPPED PARROT *Pionopsitta pileata* Catita de cabeza roja (Arg), Cuiú-cuiú (Br). L 22 cm. Habitat: woods and forests. Green. ♂: red head, crown and around the eye; green nape (♀ just green with blue on the forehead). Blue in the flight feathers; violet-blue on primary coverts and outer tail feathers. Mostly in pairs, and small flocks. Voice: in flight '*kerrrrry* [with rolled 'r']… *kerry.. kery*'.

12 SCALY-HEADED PARROT *Pionus maximiliani* Loro choclero (Arg, Bol), Maitaca (Br). L 28 cm. Habitat: savannahs, woods and forests up to 2000 m. Green, feathers of head and neck edged blue-grey and appearing like scales. Breast washed blue. Undertail red. Outer tail feathers blue. Voice: in flight '*chack, chuk, choclock..*' and variations, differing according to race across its range.

13 RED-SPECTACLED PARROT *Amazona pretrei* Charao (Arg, Br), Papagaio-da-serra (Br). L 32–33 cm. Habitat: forests, especially *Araucaria*. Green with brown edging to feathers, most obvious on back. Face and shoulders all red. Primary coverts red.

14 ALDER PARROT *Amazona tucumana* Loro alisero (Arg, Bol). L 32 cm. Habitat: woods and forests between 1800 and 2500 m. In winter descends to 500 m. Green with dark edging to feathers. Red forehead. Blue in flight feathers. Red patch on outer primary coverts. Voice: in flight a loud '*crow-ay-oh, creeayoh, crayoh…*'.

15 TURQUOISE-FRONTED PARROT *Amazona aestiva* Loro hablador (Arg, Bol), Ajuru (Par), Papagaio-verdadeiro (Br). L 38 cm. Habitat: savannahs, woods and forests. Green-bodied. Blue forehead; crown and face yellow. Feathers on hind-neck and back edged black, less so on underparts. Short, square tail. Voice: in flight a loud and hollow '*a-rrrow* (to rhyme with cow), *a-rrow* (with toe), *how-rrow* (cow)'.

▶

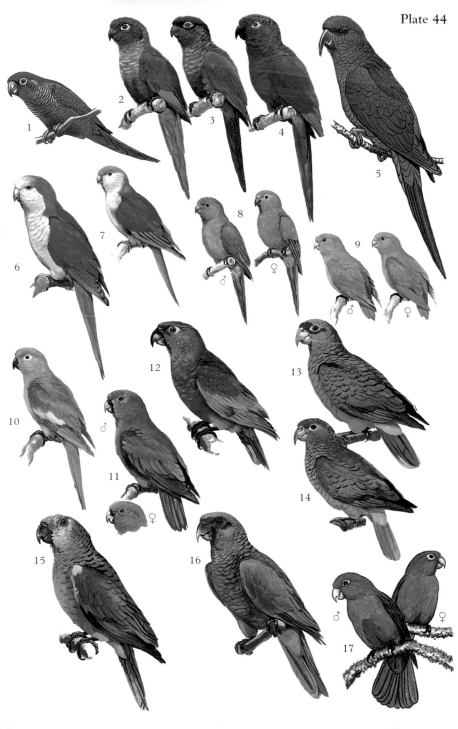

Plate 44

16 **VINACEOUS-BREASTED PARROT** *Amazona vinacea* Loro vináceo (Arg), Papagaio-de-peito-roxo (Br). L 34 cm. Habitat: mostly in *Araucaria* forests. Green with red forehead, lores and feathers on the throat. Throat and breast vinaceous with black tips to the feathers giving a scaled effect. Red patch on wing-coverts.

17 **BLUE-BELLIED PARROT** *Triclaria malachitacea* Loro de vientre azul (Arg), Sabiá-cica (Br). L 24 cm. Habitat: rainforests. Green with a large 'heavy' tail. ♂ with violet-blue on lower breast and belly. ♀ has no blue. Voice: strident '*vee-vee, jellied-jellied*' from the ♂ while the ♀ calls '*diot, diot, diot*'.

Plate 45

CUCKOOS (FAMILY CUCULIDAE)

1 **ASH-COLOURED CUCKOO** *Coccyzus cinereus* Cuclillo chico (Arg), Cuclillo gris (Bol), Cuclillo de ojo colorado (Uru), Papa-lagarta-cinzento (Br). L 23 cm. Habitat: savannahs and woodland. Black bill, red eye. Lead-grey head; back and underparts brownish-grey, paler on throat and breast. Undertail yellowish. Tail with white tip. Voice: a harsh '*che-rro, che-rro, che-rro*' repeated sporadically.

2 **BLACK-BILLED CUCKOO** *Coccyzus erythrophthalmus* Cuclillo de ojo colorado (Arg), Cuclillo pico negro (Bol). L 28 cm. Habitat: woods and forests. Bill all black; eye-ring red. Upperparts brownish, underparts greyish. Brown tail with dark subterminal band and white tips to the outer feathers.

3 **YELLOW-BILLED CUCKOO** *Coccyzus americanus* Cuclillo de alas rojizas (Arg), Tujacue (Par), Cuclillo de pico amarillo (Uru), Cuclillo picoamarillo (Bol), Papa-lagarta-norte-americana (Br). L 28 cm. Habitat: woods and savannahs. Bill: yellow lower mandible. Yellow eye-ring. Upperparts brownish-grey, underparts greyish-white. Flight feathers greyish-brown with cinnamon on the inner web. Brownish central tail feathers, blackish outers with white tips.

4 **PEARLY-BREASTED CUCKOO** *Coccyzus euleri* Cuclillo ceniciento (Arg), Papa-lagarta-de-euler (Br). L 24 cm. Habitat: forests and ecotones. Yellow mandible, black maxilla. Red eye-ring. Brownish-grey above, pale grey below.

5 **DARK-BILLED CUCKOO** *Coccyzus melacoryphus* Cuclillo canela (Arg, Bol), Papa-lagarta (Br), Cuclillo de pico negro (Uru, Ch). L 28 cm. Habitat: woods and savannahs. Black bill. Head lead-grey with black post-ocular streak. Underparts ochreous. Tail with white tip. Voice: a series of six to eight hollow, rapid '*coocoocoocoocoocoocoocoocoo*' descending slightly in pitch. Another is a harsh and rapid '*charr-charr-chao-chur-churr*' and '*cherrrrooouuuu*'.

6 **SQUIRREL CUCKOO** *Piaya cayana* Tingazú (Arg, Bol), Urraca canela (Uru), Tingasu (Par), Alma-de-gato (Br). L 45 cm. Thicker parts of foliage in woods and forests up to 2000 m. Upperparts chestnut. Fore-neck pinkish hue, underparts lead-grey. Immense chestnut tail with white spots, below black with large round white spots. Voice: three calls: a whistled series '*whit whit whit whit whit…*', an occasional loud '*whit..whey*', and a quiet rolled '*Chrrrrrrrr…*'

7 **STRIPED CUCKOO** *Tapera naevia* Crespín (Arg, Bol, Uru), Saci (Br), Chochi (Par), Nequí (Bol). L 28 cm. Habitat: savannahs, woods and groves. Crest. Whitish eyebrow. Back with heavy dark streaking. Underparts ochre-white. Long ladder tail brownish-grey with tips ochreous. Voice: day and night a two-syllabled short high whistle, the second note half a tone higher '*fee fee… fee fee…*'.

8 **PHEASANT CUCKOO** *Dromococcyx phasianellus* Yasíyateré grande (Arg), Cucú faisán (Bol), Peixe-frito-verdadeiro (Br). L 35 cm. Habitat: forests. Crown and crest chestnut. White post-ocular streak. Throat, neck and breast ochreous with dark brown spots. Dark tail with white tip and borders, from below with white spots. Voice: a whistled two note '*fee fee*' with a final trill, repeated.

9 **PAVONINE CUCKOO** *Dromococcyx pavoninus* Yasíyateré chico (Arg), Jasy jatere (Par), Peixe-frito-pavonino (Br). L 25 cm. Habitat: rainforests. Brown crown and crest, ochre post-ocular streak. Dark upperparts. Long tail dark, tipped white; from below grey with white spots. Voice: typical high '*fee fee*' whistle followed by '*feefeefee*'.

10 **GREATER ANI** *Crotophaga major* Anó grande (Arg, Bol), Ano guasu (Par), Anu-coroca (Br), Pirincho negro grande (Uru). L 45 cm. Habitat: in vegetation near water. White eye. All glossy black with blue sheen, large tail purplish with sheen. Voice: a chorus of '*toodle-doodle-doodle..*' low, hollow, while others of the group '*shhhrrrrrrr..*' endlessly.

11 **SMOOTH-BILLED ANI** *Crotophaga ani* Anó chico (Arg), Pirincho negro chico (Uru), Ano (Par), Anó común or Maúri común (Bol), Anu-preto (Br). L 33 cm. Habitat: bushes at the edge of woods and savannahs. Dark eye. All dull brownish-black, 'dirtier' around the head. Voice: high whistled '*coo-reeek keyoreek..*', emitted in flight. In flight, flap and glide alternately.

12 **GROOVE-BILLED ANI** *Crotophaga sulcirostris* Anó de pico surcado (Arg), Matacaballos (Ch). L 30 cm. Bill with less elevated culmen and grooved along the sides. Can be confused with the Smooth-billed Ani but bill smaller and tail shorter.

▶

Plate 45

13 GUIRA CUCKOO *Guira guira* Pirincho (Arg, Bol), Pirincho común (Uru), Piririgua (Par), Serere (Bol), Anu-branco (Br). L 40 cm. Habitat: open areas in savannahs, gardens, wood edges and fields. An untidy bird with the head reddish-ochre and feather shafts dark. Dark brown back with whitish shafts. Back and rump white. Underparts ochreous, throat and breast streaked dark. Long tail yellowish-ochre at the base, central feathers dark brown, rest black with broad white tip. Voice: series of descending '*kee-ey, kee-ey, kee-eh, kee-orr, keeorr, cure curecure*'; alarm a long high-pitched '*keerrrrrrrrrrr*'; flight call a quiet '*yew yew yew yew...*'

Plate 46

BARN OWLS (FAMILY TYTONIDAE)

1 BARN OWL *Tyto alba* Lechuza de campanario (Arg, Bol), Suindara (Br), Suinda (Par), Lechuzón de campanario (Uru), Lechuza (Ch). L 45 cm. Habitat: around villages in open areas. Long legs. Upperparts and wing-coverts ochre-grey with white spotting. White heart-shaped face, dark-margined. Underparts whitish with brown spotting (some birds are lavender-fronted). Underwings and undertail ochre with dark barring and speckling. Tail like the back with narrow dark bars. Alone or pairs. Voice: a loud hushing '*SSHHHHHT*' repeated sporadically. Also during the nesting season a long, high-pitched '*cliclicliclicliclicli...*'.

TYPICAL OWLS (FAMILY STRIGIDAE)

2 TROPICAL SCREECH-OWL *Otus choliba* Alicucu común (Arg), Kavure (Par), Tamborcito común (Uru), Corujinha-do-mato (Br), Chiñicito pampero or Autillo común (Bol). L ♂ 23, ♀ 24 cm. Habitat: forests, woods, gardens and savannahs. Upperparts brownish with white streaks and black and ochre spots. Grey face. Throat and upper breast grey with transverse dark bars. Rest of underparts whitish with heavy dark brown streaks crossed by finer bars. White lines bracket upper back. Wings and tail ochre with brown and white bands. There is a reddish form, similar but with chestnut as a base colour. Singly or in pairs. During daylight they keep motionless in trees, ears erect. Voice: a low-pitched rolled trill '*rrrrrr-koo*' or '*rrrrrr-cuckOO*'.

3 LONG-TUFTED SCREECH-OWL *Otus atricapillus* Alicucu grande (Arg), Corujinha-sapo (Br), Autillo vermiculado (Bol), Tamborcito grande (Uru). L 27 cm. Habitat: forests. Head and upperparts chestnut with black streaks on head, brown streaks on back. Breast chestnut with heavy black streaking, belly whitish with chestnut bars and streaks. Wings dark brown with chestnut bars, chestnut tail barred blackish. Voice: '*woo — rrrrrrrrrrrr..*', starting with a wobble up and down on the '*woo*'. Short ear-tufts.

Note: The western form of this species, the Vermiculated Screech-owl (*O. a. guatemalae*) has until recently been considered a separate species. The plumage is not chestnut but brown-based. The call omits the initial '*woo*' of the Long-tufted — just a very long, low pitched trill like a toad's call.

4 SPECTACLED OWL *Pulsatrix perspicillata* Lechuzón grande de collar (Arg, Bol), Murucututu (Br). L 45 cm. Habitat: woods and forests between 500 and 2000 m. Head and back brown. White brow, whitish collar. Upper breast brown, lower and belly ochreous. Wings and tail dark brown with faint paler barring. Voice: a series of five to seven '*pooooh*'s, accelerating and descending in pitch.

5 TAWNY-BROWED OWL *Pulsatrix koeniswaldiana* Lechuzón chico de collar (Arg), Murucututu-de-barriga-amarela (Br). L 38 cm. Habitat: forests and woods. Upperparts dark brown. Face brown and whitish with bright ochre brow. Dark brown throat. White half-collar. Breast brown with ochre tinge. Rest of underparts ochre. Brown wings with fine paler bands. Tail brown with narrow bands and white tip. Voice: a series of four to six '*who's*', also a loud '*whirrrrrr*'.

6 GREAT HORNED OWL *Bubo virginianus* Ñacurutú (Arg, Uru, Bol), Tucúquere (Ch), Buho americano (Bol), Corujao-orelhudo or Jacurutu (Br). L 51 cm. Habitat: woods, savannahs, palm groves, steppes and mountains. Long ear-tufts. Crown, hind-neck and upper back buff with dark brown markings. Rest of upperparts and wing-coverts brown and buff with whitish speckling. Face whitish-ochre framed by dark lines. Lower throat white. Rest of the underparts whitish with wavy dark barring. Wings and tail dark ochre with brown bands. Singly or in pairs. Immobile during daylight hours in trees or on the ground midst tussocks or bushes. Voice: a loud '*who who WHO-oo*'.

7 MOTTLED OWL *Ciccaba virgata* Lechuza estriada (Arg), Coruja-do-mato (Br), Lechuza colilarga (Bol). L 35 cm. Habitat: woods and forests. Ochre brow. Face and upperparts dark brown finely barred chestnut. Underparts ochre flecked with cinnamon. Thighs and feathered tarsi cinnamon. Wings barred cinnamon and dark brown. Dark brown tail with narrow cinnamon bars and ochre tip. Voice: a series of six or seven '*who?*' rising slightly in the middle, then dropping off again.

8 BLACK-BANDED OWL *Ciccaba huhula* Lechuza negra (Arg, Bol), Coruja-preta (Br). L 35–40 cm. Habitat: woods and forests. Head and underparts black with white barring; upperparts and wings dark brown barred white. Tail black with four narrow white bands and white tip. Voice: a low-pitched, loud '*HORwoo woo*' sporadically. Also a series: '*who who who who HOR who*', slightly rising in pitch.

Plate 46

Reddish
form

Plate 47

TYPICAL OWLS (FAMILY STRIGIDAE)

1 **RUSTY-BARRED OWL** *Strix hylophila* Lechuza listada (Arg), Coruja-listrada (Br). L 34 cm. Habitat: forests and woods. Head and upperparts chestnut, heavily barred dark brown. White collar. Ventrally chestnut and whitish barred dark brown. Voice: a raucous '*WHO?*'; also a guttural '*who who Who? WHO?... Who! who who who who*', rising and falling in volume.

2 **RUFOUS-LEGGED OWL** *Strix rufipes* Lechuza bataraz (Arg), Concón (Ch). L 37 cm. Habitat: woods, savannahs. Dark brown barred white with cinnamon tinge on belly. Thighs reddish-cinnamon. Voice: a loud and hoarse di-syllabic '*poorr, poorr*'.

Note: It is likely that this includes two species, *Strix chacoensis* in the north and the typical form in the Patagonian Andes. Measurements and calls are noticeably different, not plumage.

3 **LEAST PYGMY-OWL** *Glaucidium minutissimum* Caburé-miudinho (Br). L 14 cm. Habitat: woods. Brown head with white dots. White nuchal collar. Upperparts white, reddish-brown streaks on neck and sides of breast. Above reddish-brown. Voice: '*oo-oo*' or '*oo-oo-oo*' more like a screech-owl than a pygmy-owl.

4 **FERRUGINOUS PYGMY-OWL** *Glaucidium brasilianum* Caburé chico (Arg, Bol), Chuncho del norte (Ch), Kavure'i (Par), Caburé (Uru, Br). L ♂ 17, ♀ 18.5 cm. Habitat: savannahs, woods and forests. Head brown with ochre streaking. Upperparts dark brown. Simulated eyes on nape. Wings brown with ochre-white spots. Dark tail with five or six fine whitish bars. Moves tail jerkily from side to side. Voice: a series of monotone whistled '*too..too..too..too..*', three per second. Another, especially when angry: '*fweet fweet FWEET −cheerrr, cherrr, cherr, cherr*'.

5 **AUSTRAL PYGMY-OWL** *Glaucidium nanum* Caburé grande (Arg), Chuncho (Ch). L ♂ 19.5, ♀ 21 cm. Habitat: woods and forests. Brown head with longish ochre streaks. Fine white brow. Back brown with a touch of cinnamon; white spots on scapulars. Black and white design on the hind-neck simulating eyes. Face brown with buff spots. White throat. Brown collar. Breast cinnamon-brown with ochre and white streaking. Streaks run into each other to form three longitudinal lines. Brown wings with whitish dots. Tail brown with chestnut bands. There is also a reddish form. Voice: just like the Ferruginous Pygmy-owl.

Note: Now considered a race of *Glaucidium brasilianum* by some authors.

6 **ANDEAN PYGMY-OWL** *Glaucidium jardinii* Caburé andino (Arg), Mochuelo andino (Bol). L 16 cm. Habitat: forests. Generally reddish with round white spots on head, ochre dots on back. Two dark false eyes on the back of the head. Short white brow. Tail with four dark bands. Voice: two or three '*yurr, yurrr's*' followed by two short whistles per second '*too..too..too..too..too...*'.

7 **BURROWING OWL** *Athene cunicularia* Lechucita de las viscacheras (Arg, Bol), Chiñi (Bol), Buraqueira or Coruja-de-campo (Br), Urukure'a (Par), Pequén (Ch), Lechuza común (Uru). L 26 cm. Habitat: open country and grasslands. Light brown back with mostly white and some cinnamon spots. Face and throat white. Breast whitish with brownish splotches, white belly. Wings spotted with large whitish dots. Brown tail with whitish bars. Singly or in pairs on the ground, fence posts or telephone poles. Diurnal and nocturnal. Voice: alarm and annoyance scolding a loud '*CHEEEEay -cheecheecheechee...*' day and night. During the hours of darkness a reedy high '*woo who WHO, oo, oo*'.

8 **BUFF-FRONTED OWL** *Aegolius harrisii* Lechucita canela (Arg, Uru), Lechucita acanelada (Bol), Caburé-acanelado (Br). L 22 cm. Habitat: open forest and woods. Black around the eyes. Forehead and brow cinnamon. Dark brown head and cinnamon cheeks bracketed by black lines. Underparts intense cinnamon, paler on belly. Upperparts brown with cinnamon band across mantle; lower back chestnut. Brown wings with round white spots. Tail black with three transverse rows of white dots. Woods and forests. Voice: a quiet, long '*Hooorrrrrrrr*', changing in volume.

9 **STRIPED OWL** *Asio clamator* Lechuzón orejudo (Arg, Bol), Ñacurutu hû (Par), Lechuzón (Uru), Coruja-orelhuda (Br). L 34 cm. Habitat: savannahs, gallery forests, woods in open countryside. Long, black ear-tufts. Crown, hind-neck and upper back ochre broadly barred dark brown. Rest of upperparts similar but striped and speckled. Whitish throat, chestnut cheeks. Dark around the eyes. Face framed by a dark line, chestnut on throat. Breast ochre and white with large dark brown streaks. Wings and tail with dark brown bands. Voice: a loud, very high-pitched whistle, '*pheeeeeew*', descending.

10 **STYGIAN OWL** *Asio stygius* Lechuzón negruzco (Arg), Lechuzón negrusco (Bol) Mocho-diabo (Br). L 43 cm. Habitat: savannahs and woods. Upperparts dark brown with cinnamon markings on nape and back. Face dark brown. Auricular region spotted ochre. Black ear-tufts. Underparts cinnamon with brown markings. Cinnamon tarsi. Brown wings with some cinnamon markings, brown tail with cinnamon bands and ochre tip.

11 **SHORT-EARED OWL** *Asio flammeus* Lechuzón de campo (Arg), Lechuzón campestre (Bol), Mocho-do-banhados (Br), Nuco (Ch), Lechuzón de pajonal (Uru). L 38 cm. Habitat: grasslands, savannahs. Short 'ears'. Upperparts ochre and dark brown with some white markings, mostly on wing-coverts. Whitish face with dark around the eyes. Underparts whitish with an ochre tinge, flecked brown, finer on belly. Wings and tail ochre with pale cinnamon tint, and dark brown bands and speckling. On the ground and on fence posts. Flies low, quartering the ground; often diurnal. Voice: '*Key-ek, kyerk*' or '*cha-ek, cha-ey, chayy*'.

Plate 47

Plate 48

NIGHTJARS AND NIGHTHAWKS (FAMILY CAPRIMULGIDAE)

1 **CHESTNUT-BANDED NIGHTHAWK** *Lurocalis nattereri* Atajacaminos castaño (Arg, Bol), Tuju (Br). L 23 cm. Habitat: savannahs, woods and forest. Dark brown upperparts with chestnut markings on the head, the rest spotted with white and chestnut. White throat. Breast dark brown with chestnut and ochre, belly barred dark brown. Blackish wings with small chestnut rings and dots. Scapulars white, streaked and marked with dark brown. Short tail dark brown with grey and ochre barring. Folded wings longer than tail when perched (on branches), and show no white patch. Voice: calls on the wing flying over forests, '*whit whoowit...chew it*' sporadically.

2 **LESSER NIGHTHAWK** *Chordeiles acutipennis* Gallina ciega peruana (Ch), Bacurau-de-asa-fina (Br), Añapero chico or Cuyabito (Bol). L 21 cm. Habitat: savannahs and open country. Above and breast greyish with black spots. A large white triangle at the throat. Lower breast and belly barred buff and brown. Blackish wings with white (♂) or buff (♀) band across the four outermost primaries. Wing-coverts and inner flight feathers marked with buff. Blackish tail barred creamy; outer tail feathers with a white sub-terminal patch (♂), lacking in the ♀. Voice: '*krop – gaw gaw gaw gaw*'; also a toad-like purring while on the ground.

3 **COMMON NIGHTHAWK** *Chordeiles minor* Añapero (Arg, Uru), Añapero migratorio (Bol). L 23 cm. Habitat: savannahs and fields. Upperparts streaked dark brown with cinnamon and whitish dots and markings. White throat. Breast dark brown with cinnamon spots, rest of underparts whitish with dark barring. Wings dark, showing a white patch half way along the primaries. Tail brown with fine white bars. ♀ has ochreous throat and tail bars. In flocks. Voice: (contact call?) a hoarse '*been*' or '*bane*'. Migratory from North America.

4 **NACUNDA NIGHTHAWK** *Podager nacunda* Ñacundá (Arg), Corucao (Br), Añapero ñacundá (Bol), Dormilón de vientre blanco (Uru). L 30 cm. Habitat: open grasslands and savannahs. Upperparts brown, profusely speckled and vermiculated ochre and cinnamon, with black markings. White throat and half-collar. Breast brown with white markings. Rest of underparts white. Wings with large white diagonal wing-bar and under wing-coverts. Tail with dark bands on central feathers, outers subterminally black and broad white tip. Voice: a quiet guttural '*whoorr ho-oooor, who're*'. Also a quiet, deep, hollow, resonant '*brooopoop*'.

5 **PAURAQUE** *Nyctidromus albicollis* Atajacaminos de collar blanco (Arg), Lui ryevu (Par), Atajacaminos coliblanca (Bol), Curiango or Bacurau (Br). L 30 cm. Habitat: savannahs, clearings in forests, open woods. Crown grey with black markings. Face chestnut with dark brown. Upperparts grey with brown markings. Scapulars ochre-grey with dark brown markings edged cinnamon, some feathers chestnut. Upper breast with white half-collar, rest of underparts ochreous with dark brown vermiculations. Dark brown wings with white patch at the base of the primaries. Outer tail black, inner white, central grey with fine darker bars. ♀ has cinnamon-ochre wing patch and tail like back. Crepuscular and nocturnal. Voice: a four-note '*coo-wee-ah-oo*' the '*wee*' higher-pitched, the rest descending; repeated over and over again.

6 **OCELLATED POORWILL** *Nyctiphrynus ocellatus* Atajacaminos ocelado (Arg, Bol), Bacurao- ocelado (Br). L 20 cm. Habitat: forests. Generally reddish-brown, finely barred black. Head greyish with black markings. Throat white. Breast dark greyish. White dots on wing-coverts and belly, black dots on wing and scapulars. Tail with black bars, outers with white tips. Voice: a pitiful descending '*we err, we err, we err*', like the mewing of a cat.

7 **RUFOUS NIGHTJAR** *Caprimulgus rufus* Atajacaminos colorado (Arg, Bol), Joao-corta-pao (Br). L 31 cm. Habitat: woods and forests. General coloration reddish-brown. Head with fine chestnut and ochre speckling and black streaking. Upperparts dark brown, finely speckled cinnamon and ochreous. Throat dark brown with chestnut barring and narrow white collar. Rest of underparts speckled chestnut and ochreous. Black wings with chestnut speckling and spots, black and chestnut primaries. Tail like back but trailing half of outer feathers white. ♀ has no white on outer tail, and ochreous collar. Voice: a fastish, urgent 4-syllable '*chop...weep whip wheew*', melodious and rhythmical, the last three notes whistled, repeated.

8 **SILKY-TAILED NIGHTJAR** *Caprimulgus sericocaudatus* Atajacaminos ahumado (Arg). L 30 cm. Habitat: forests. Generally dark brown, speckled ochreous. Ochreous collar, nuchal band chestnut. Throat and breast with pale dots, rest of underparts barred. Primaries dark brown with reddish bands on outer vanes. No white wing patch. Round tail with narrow chestnut bands. Outer tail feathers with diagonal white band, white tip on ♂, reddish on the ♀. Voice: '*choo, Wheew, WHEEW*' rhythmical, rising in pitch.

Plate 48

Plate 49

NIGHTJARS AND NIGHTHAWKS (FAMILY CAPRIMULGIDAE)

1 BAND-WINGED NIGHTJAR *Caprimulgus longirostris* Atajacaminos común (Arg, Bol), Bacurau-da-telha (Br), Gallina ciega (Ch), Dormilón (Uru). L 25–27 cm. Habitat: steppes and woods. Upperparts blackish with grey and cinnamon markings. Nuchal half-collar cinnamon. Throat and breast dark, finely barred ochre-white. Narrow white band across upper breast. Belly ochreous, barred dark brown. Blackish wings with diagonal white patches. Coverts with cinnamon markings. Central tail feathers like back, rest black with white patches at base, and white tips; from below tail looks white with broad black band. ♀ has a narrow cinnamon wing-band, ochre collar, and tail with no white. Voice: a very high, repeated '*so weet*' or '*fee-owe-we*'.

2 WHITE-WINGED NIGHTJAR *Caprimulgus candicans* Bacurau-rabo-branco (Br). L 22 cm. Habitat: edge of gallery forests. Generally pale grey, head more reddish, all speckled. Belly, under wing-coverts and outer tail white. Central pair of tail feathers light grey. Primaries black with white at the base, seen in flight. ♀ has barred flight feathers and tail. Rare.

3 LITTLE NIGHTJAR *Caprimulgus parvulus* Atajacaminos chico (Arg, Bol), Bacurau-pequeno (Br), Kuchu'i guy guy (Par), Dormilón chico (Uru), Cuyabo común (Bol). L 20 cm. Habitat: savannahs, woods. Head dotted with grey, with black crown-stripe from forehead to nape. Cinnamon half-collar at nape with grey and black spotting. Rest of upperparts greyish-brown speckled with white. Wings brown with white spots and wing-patch (ochre in ♀). Scapulars white with ochre margins. Throat white. Breast greyish-brown with whitish markings. Belly ochre, barred chestnut-brown. Tail greyish-brown with cinnamon markings and white tip. Tail shows a white area at tip from below. Singly or in pairs, on the ground or low branches. Voice: a rolling, melodious, rhythmic '*choorree – froofroofroofroo*'.

4 LADDER-TAILED NIGHTJAR *Hydropsalis climacocerca* Dormilón coludo blanco (Bol), Acurana (Br). L ♂ 28, ♀ 23 cm. Habitat: riverside and sandbars. ♂: above grey with black vermiculations. Breast buff-grey. White belly. White band on primaries. Doubly forked tail – like a W – central and outer feathers elongated. Tail almost all white; central feathers with black bands, outers barred black and white. ♀ redder overall. Cinnamon wing-band. Tail shorter than ♂ and barred black and cinnamon. Voice: '*Crip crip*'.

5 SCISSOR-TAILED NIGHTJAR *Hydropsalis brasiliana* Atajacaminos coludo chico (Arg), Dormilón de cola larga (Uru), Yvyra'u jetapa (Par), Dormilón coludo (Bol), Bacurau-tesoura (Br). L ♂ 50, ♀ 30 cm. Habitat: woods, savannahs. Upperparts greyish-brown with white markings, black markings on head. Underparts whitish with cinnamon flecks on throat, dark brown barring, wider on belly. Wings brown with buff barring. Greyish tail with dark brown bands. Two outer tail feathers long, brown then white. ♀ is generally more ochreous, more barred on undersides and lacks long tail feathers. Voice: a high-pitched, quiet, short '*tsip, tsip, tsip...*', about one per second.

6 LYRE-TAILED NIGHTJAR *Uropsalis lyra* Atajacaminos lira (Arg, Bol). L ♂ 80, ♀ 25 cm. Habitat: Tall grass and open woods near the tree-line. Head grey with black markings; reddish collar. Upperparts reddish with black markings. Underparts ochre with black markings. Black wings with reddish bars. Tail reddish with black bands, outer feathers extremely long (66 cm), black, paling to white tip. ♀ has black crown with reddish dots; blackish tail with red bands, no long feathers on tail.

7 LONG-TAILED NIGHTJAR *Macropsalis creagra* Atajacaminos coludo grande (Arg), Bacurau-tesoura-gigante (Br). L ♂ 76, ♀ 34 cm. Habitat: forests and woods. Ochreous with black markings. Head dark brown. Reddish collar on neck. White throat. ♂'s outer tail feathers long (62 cm) and black with white on inner webs and tip. ♀ has short tail grey with outer feathers ochre marked with black.

8 SICKLE-WINGED NIGHTJAR *Eleothreptus anomalus* Atajacaminos de los pantanos (Arg), Curiango-do-banhado (Br). L 19 cm. Generally coloured grey with black markings. Reddish neck. Underparts ochre-brown. Wing-coverts and secondaries greyish-brown with black markings, primaries notably curved, black with white tips. Short tail ochre-brown barred blackish, whitish tip. ♀ similar but with reddish patches on the wing and without the white tips on the primaries. Voice: vocalisations are unknown, but there is a knocking noise produced by ♂'s wing.

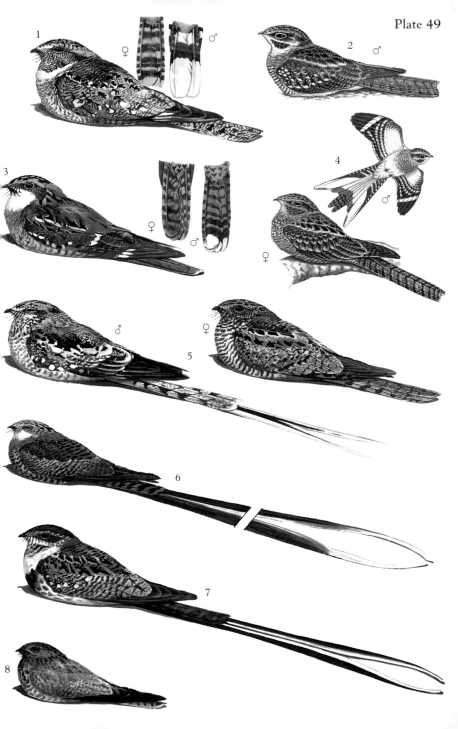

Plate 49

Plate 50

POTOOS (FAMILY NYCTIBIIDAE)

1 LONG-TAILED POTOO *Nyctibius aethereus* Urutaú de cola larga (Arg), Mae-da-lua-parda (Br). L 44 cm. Habitat: forests. Reddish-brown with wing and breast feathers edged black. Huge tail graduated, with pointed central tail feathers. Voice: a loud '*woreWHO?-oo*' repeated sporadically; more active on moonlight nights.

2 COMMON POTOO *Nyctibius griseus* Urutaú (Arg, Uru), Urutau (Br, Par), Urutaú común or Guajojó (Bol). L 38 cm. Habitat: savannahs, woods and forest edges, or clearings. Overall greyish-brown spotted and streaked with black, with cinnamon on breast and wing-coverts. Whitish throat. Greyish-brown wings with ochre spots on outer vane of primaries. Leading edge of wing black. Tail barred black and grey. Solitary. Voice: a series of five to eight sad and mournfully long whistles descending irregularly in pitch and volume, about one per second.

SWIFTS (FAMILY APODIDAE)

3 SOOTY SWIFT *Cypseloides fumigatus* Vencejo ahumado chico (Arg, Bol), Andorinhao-preto-da-cascata (Br). L 17 cm. Habitat: over forests. Overall uniform blackish-brown. Tail square.

4 GREAT DUSKY SWIFT *Cypseloides senex* Vencejo ahumado grande (Arg), Andorinhao-velho-da-cascata (Br), Mbyju'i ita (Par). L 20 cm. Habitat: flocks over rainforests, occasionally to ground level in clearings. Uniform sooty brown, head paler. Square tail shortish. Voice: a loud and raucous '*Cheeeerrrrr, cheeeerrrr*'. Roosts and nests at waterfalls.

5 DARK BROWN SWIFT *Cypseloides rothschildi* Vencejo pardusco (Arg). L 19 cm. Habitat: savannahs, woods up to 2000 m. All brown. Generally like the Great Dusky Swift but different distribution.

6 WHITE-COLLARED SWIFT *Streptoprocne zonaris* Vencejo de collar blanco (Arg), Andorinhao-de-coleira (Br), Vencejo cuelliblanco (Bol), Vencejo de collar (Uru). L 22 cm. Habitat: grasslands and mountains up to 3000 m. A large blackish swift with a complete white collar, broader on the breast. Tail slightly forked. Imm has incipient or no collar. Voice: flight call a penetrating and loud '*chirreee chirreee chirreee*'.

7 BISCUTATE SWIFT *Streptoprocne biscutata* Vencejo de nuca blanca (Arg), Andorinhao-de-coleira-falha (Br). L 20.5 cm. Habitat: forests in mountains. A large, blackish swift with an incomplete collar, interrupted on the sides of the neck.

8 CHIMNEY SWIFT *Chaetura pelagica* Andorinhao-migrante (Br), Vencejo de chimenea (Ch). L 13 cm. Habitat: open country, woods and over forests. Above and wings uniformly dark brown. Whitish throat. Rest of underparts light brown. Short, square tail.

9 ASHY-TAILED SWIFT *Chaetura andrei* Vencejo de garganta blanca (Arg), Andorinhao-do-temporal (Br), Vencejo gargantiblanco (Bol). L 12 cm. Habitat: savannahs and woods. Upperparts deep grey-brown, paler underparts. Pale throat, rump and upper tail-coverts. Tail short, grey; barbs black and project beyond the tip of the vaning. Voice: flight call a '*teep teep teebleep tseep teep*'.

10 GREY-RUMPED SWIFT *Chaetura cinereiventris* Vencejo de vientre gris (Arg), Mbyju'i (Par), Vencejo de vientre gris (Bol), Andorinao-de-sobre-cinzento (Br). L 11 cm. Habitat: forests. Crown, mantle and wings shiny black. Lower back, rump and upper tail-coverts grey. Lores, undertail and tail black. Barbs project beyond tail. Throat whitish, breast and belly grey. Roosts and nests in tall hollow trees.

11 WHITE-TIPPED SWIFT *Aeronautes montivagus* Vencejo montañés (Bol), Andorinhao-serrano (Br). L 12 cm. Habitat: mountains. Dark brown. Throat, breast and mid-belly dingy white. Flanks and under tail-coverts ashy-brown. Tips of tail feathers white.

12 ANDEAN SWIFT *Aeronautes andecolus* Vencejo blanco (Arg, Bol), Vencejo chico (Ch). L 13.5 cm. Habitat: mountains up to 3000 m. A slender swift with brown upperparts. Rump, sides of the neck and underparts white. Wings and longish forked tail brown. Very fast in flight. Voice: flight call a high-pitched '*tseerrr tseerrr...*'

Plate 50

Plate 51

HUMMINGBIRDS (FAMILY TROCHILIDAE)

1 SCALE-THROATED HERMIT *Phaethornis eurynome* Picaflor ermitaño grande (Arg), Rabo-branco-de-garganta-rajada (Br), Mainumby ruguaitî (Par). L 16 cm. Habitat: woods and forests. Long, curved bill. Brow cinnamon-yellow. Black eye-stripe. Throat black with white-edged feathers giving a scaly effect. Tail with white tip. Long central feathers. Voice: a high-pitched, four-beat, whistled *'teree tilteetew... teree tilteetew...'*, persistently repeated.

2 PLANALTO HERMIT *Phaethornis pretrei* Picaflor ermitaño chico (Arg, Bol), Mainumby ruguaitî (Par), Rabo-branco-de-sobre-amarelo (Br). L 15 cm. Habitat: woods and forests. Long, curved bill. Dark eye-stripe with yellowish-white lines above and below. Plain buff throat. Rest of underparts reddish-ochre. Tail with long central feathers two-thirds bronze-green, the rest white. Voice: a three-syllable, high-pitched, whistled *'tseesyepsyep... tseesyepsyep...'*, persistently repeated.

3 SWALLOW-TAILED HUMMINGBIRD *Eupetomena macroura* Picaflor golondrina (Bol), Tesourao (Br). L 18 cm. Habitat: savannahs and thickets, scrub. Mostly blue-green. Head, neck and breast violet blue. Long forked tail dull dark blue. Voice: a loud *'tzuk'*.

4 BLACK JACOBIN *Melanotrochilus fuscus* Picaflor negro (Arg, Uru), Beija-flor-preto-e-branco (Br). L 11 cm. Habitat: bushes in clearings, thickets. ♂: black but for the back, upper tail-coverts and wing-coverts all of which are bronze-green. Wings greenish-brown. Black central tail feathers, rest white with black tips. ♀: black with wide chestnut band either side of the throat. Tail purple, white outer vane of outer feathers. Whitish flanks in both sexes.

5 GREEN VIOLETEAR *Colibri thalassinus* Picaflor de cara azul (Arg), Picaflor penacho azul (Bol). L 11 cm. Habitat: woods and forests up to 3000 m. Brilliant green; throat and breast with black on each feather giving a scaly appearance. Violet ear-patch. Brown wings. Central tail green, bluish sheen on outers. Black subterminal band.

6 SPARKLING VIOLETEAR *Colibri coruscans* Picaflor de cara azul (Arg, Bol). L 14 cm. Habitat: bushy terrain on hills between 1500 and 2000 m. Brilliant green; chin-spot, throat, centre of belly and ear-patch purplish-blue. Fore-neck and breast feathers with dark marking producing a scaly effect. Brown wings. Central tail feathers bluish-green, rest green. Subterminal purplish-blue band.

7 WHITE-VENTED VIOLETEAR *Colibri serrirostris* Picaflor de penacho purpúreo (Arg, Bol), Beija-flor-de-orelha-violeta (Br). L 13 cm. Habitat: bushy terrain and savannahs. Green; purplish-blue ear-patch. Violet below cheeks. White spot behind the eye. Under tail-coverts white. Brown wings. Bluish-green tail with dark subterminal band.

8 BLACK-THROATED MANGO *Anthracothorax nigricollis* Picaflor de garganta negra (Arg, Bol), Beija-flor-preto (Br), Mainumby (Par). L 12 cm. Habitat: forests. Slightly curved bill. ♂: green. Throat, centre of breast and belly black bordered blue. Brown wings. Central tail feathers green, outers purple. ♀: upperparts green with bluish hue. Underparts white with broad black stripe from throat to belly. Central tail green, outers reddish at the base, subterminal band black, white tips.

9 BLACK-BREASTED PLOVERCREST *Stephanoxis lalandi* Picaflor copetón (Arg), Mainumby apiratî (Par), Beija-flor-de-topete (Br). L 9 cm. Habitat: forests. ♂: forehead and crown violet-blue with long, black, pointed crest. White spot behind the eye. Upperparts brilliant green. Grey from behind the eye, down the sides of both neck and breast, to flanks and belly. Fore-neck and centre of breast bluish-black. Wings violet-brown. Central tail feathers brilliant green, outers green at the base, then black, with white tips. ♀: upperparts and central tail feathers brilliant green. Outer tail feathers almost completely black with white tips. Underparts whitish-grey; white mark behind the eye. No crest.

10 FESTIVE COQUETTE *Lophornis chalybea* Picaflor abanico (Arg), Tufinho-verde (Br), Picaflor coqueta abanico puntiblanco (Bol). L 8 cm. Habitat: damp shrubby areas in savannahs. ♂: dark head, green forehead; chin-spot and line to below the eye dark green. From the cheek project long green feathers, white tipped. Upperparts green, white across the rump. Green throat. Breast and belly violet-grey. Green flanks. Greenish-brown wings. Purplish-green tail. ♀: upperparts green. Whitish band across the rump. Throat and cheeks whitish, rest of underparts dark grey. Tips to outer tail feathers grey. No long cheek feathers.

11 GLITTERING-BELLIED EMERALD *Chlorostilbon aureoventris* Picaflor verde común (Arg, Bol), Picaflor común (Uru), Mainumby (Par), Besourinho-de-bico-vermelho (Br). L 9 cm. Habitat: woods, shrubby areas, savannahs and gardens. Red bill, black tip. ♂: green. Throat and fore-neck brilliant greenish-blue. Forehead golden-green. Whitish lower belly. Sometimes a white spot behind the eye. Brown wings. Bluish tail. ♀: green. Pale grey underparts. White mark behind the eye. Bluish tail with white tips to outer feathers. Voice: a high-pitched *'turtle...turtlee..turtlee..'*, repeated sporadically.

12 FORK-TAILED WOODNYMPH *Thalurania furcata* Picaflor záfiro (Br), Beija-flor-tesoura-verde (Br). L ♂ 11, ♀ 10 cm. Habitat: Damp shrubby areas and forests. ♂: green with mantle, lower breast and belly violet. Throat and upper breast brilliant emerald-green. Under tail-coverts white. Bluish-brown wings. Bluish-black forked tail. ♀: upperparts green, bluish on rump. Underparts grey. Undertail white. Brown wings. Green central tail feathers, outers green at the base, then bluish, with grey tips.

Plate 51

Plate 52

HUMMINGBIRDS (FAMILY TROCHILIDAE)

1 **VIOLET-CAPPED WOODNYMPH** *Thalurania glaucopis* Picaflor verde de frente azul (Arg), Tesoura-de-fronte-violeta (Br). L 12 cm. Habitat: forests. ♂: green, forehead and crown bluish-violet. Whitish belly. Bluish-brown wings. Dark blue forked tail. ♀: upperparts golden-green with feathers edged dark giving a scaled effect. Underparts grey. Tail slightly forked. Central feathers green, outers with green at the base, then blue, white tips.

2 **RUFOUS-THROATED SAPPHIRE** *Hylocharis sapphirina* Picaflor de barba castaña (Arg, Bol), Beija-flor-safira (Br). L 9.5 cm. Habitat: bushy terrain in savannahs. Red bill with black tip. ♂: upperparts, lower breast and belly brilliant green. Throat and malar stripe chestnut. Fore-neck and upper breast violet. White vent, under tail-coverts chestnut. Brown wings. Central tail feathers bronze-green with a purplish sheen, outers chestnut edged black. ♀: upperparts bronze-green. Throat and under tail-coverts reddish. Underparts whitish-grey, feathers in fore-neck and upper breast tipped greenish-blue. Tail like ♂'s but tips of outer feathers white.

3 **WHITE-CHINNED SAPPHIRE** *Hylocharis cyanus* Picaflor lazulita (Arg, Bol), Beija-flor-roxo (Br). L 9 cm. Habitat: bushes, woods, forests. Red bill, black tip. ♂: green; head, throat and neck violet-blue. Tiny white chin-spot. Undertail and tail blue-black. Greenish-brown wings. ♀: upperparts green. Whitish-grey underparts with green spots on throat and breast. Under tail-coverts grey with black dots. Blue-black tail with grey tips to outer feathers. Voice: '*tsee tsee tsee...*'.

4 **GILDED HUMMINGBIRD** *Hylocharis chrysura* Picaflor bronceado (Arg, Bol, Uru), Kuarahy áva (Par), Beija-flor-dourado (Br). L 9 cm. Habitat: savannahs, thickets, forests, woods. Sexes alike. Red bill, black tip. Uniformly golden-green, pale reddish on chin. Brown wings. Bronze-green tail. Voice: a high-pitched '*tseerrtseerrtseerr*', repeated at intervals.

5 **WHITE-THROATED HUMMINGBIRD** *Leucochloris albicollis* Picaflor garganta blanca (Arg, Uru), Papo-branco (Br). L 10.5 cm. Habitat: thickets, woods, groves. Sexes alike. Head and upperparts green. Chin green, feathers edged white. Throat, belly and undertail white. Breast brilliant green. Greenish-brown wings. Tail blue with broad white tip. Voice: '*tseentseentseentseen...*', repeated sporadically.

6 **WHITE-TAILED GOLDENTHROAT** *Polytmus guaynumbi* Picaflor dorado (Arg, Bol), Beija-flor-dourado-de-bico-curvo (Br). L 11 cm. Edge of forests, savannahs, thickets near rivers. Slightly curved bill reddish. ♂: underparts bronze-green. Two whitish lines on the face, one behind the eye, one below. Dark auricular streak. Underparts golden-green, middle of belly white. Under tail-coverts whitish. Brown wings. Green tail, white outer vane of outer feathers, and tips white. ♀: upperparts like ♂, underparts whitish-ochre with green dots on throat and upper breast. Tail as in the ♂.

7 **WHITE-BELLIED HUMMINGBIRD** *Amazilia chionogaster* Picaflor de vientre blanco (Arg, Bol). L 11 cm. Habitat: thickets and woods. Sexes alike. Upperparts golden-green, underparts white with green spots on throat and fore-neck. Brown wings. Bronze-green tail with white tip. Voice: sings a persistent, high-pitched clear '*tsing...tsing...tsing...*' from an exposed perch.

8 **VERSICOLOURED EMERALD** *Amazilia versicolor* Picaflor esmeralda (Arg, Bol). L 8 cm. Habitat: edges of and clearings in forests, gallery forests. Forehead and crown greyish-brown. Upperparts green, underparts golden-green. Vent and undertail grey. Brownish wings. Tail olive-green with dark subterminal band and paler tip. ♀ white on throat and fore-neck.

9 **GLITTERING-THROATED EMERALD** *Amazilia fimbriata* Picaflor diamante cabeza parda (Bol), Beija-flor-de-garganta-verde (Br). L 8 cm. Habitat: forests, scrub, grasslands and cerrado. Brilliant green. White mid-line from breast to belly. Central tail feathers bronze, outers black.

10 **SPECKLED HUMMINGBIRD** *Adelomyia melanogenys* Picaflor de garganta púrpura (Arg, Bol). L 9 cm. Habitat: thickets and forests between 500 and 3000 m. Short bill. Upperparts brilliant bronze-green. Sides of head dark. Post-ocular streak white. Underparts ochreous with green dots on throat. Greenish flanks. Greenish-brown wings. Central tail feathers olive-green, the rest grey at the base, dark violet toward the tip which is buff-white.

11 **ANDEAN HILLSTAR** *Oreotrochilus estella* Picaflor serrano grande (Arg, Bol), Picaflor de la puna (Ch). L 13 cm. Habitat: bushy areas in rocky places between 3200 and 4000 m. Descends in winter. Black bill slightly curved. ♂: greenish-brown upperparts. Throat and fore-neck green with lower border black. Underparts white with red medial line through breast and belly. Brown wings. Central tail feathers green, rest white. ♀: upperparts greenish-brown. Underparts greyish. Throat whitish with greyish-green freckles. Brown wings. Central tail feathers green, next pair with white tips, outers all white.

12 **WHITE-SIDED HILLSTAR** *Oreotrochilus leucopleurus* Picaflor serrano chico (Arg, Bol), Picaflor cordillerano (Ch). L 13 cm. Habitat: arid bush and rocky areas between 1000 and 4000 m. Descends in winter. Slightly curved bill. ♂: upperparts brown. Throat and fore-neck green, bordered below by a black line. Breast and belly white with black medial stripe. Greenish-brown wings. Central tail feathers greenish-brown, outers white. ♀: underparts greyish. Throat white with green spots. Tail green with white tips to outers.

Plate 52

Plate 53

HUMMINGBIRDS (FAMILY TROCHILIDAE)

1 **WEDGE-TAILED HILLSTAR** *Oreotrochilus adela* Picaflor andino castaño (Bol). L 12 cm. Habitat: rocky mountain steppe. ♂: above brown. A fan of green feathers on side of the neck. Chestnut flanks; black mid-breast and belly. ♀: olive-brown. Below cinnamon; throat white, dotted brown.

2 **GIANT HUMMINGBIRD** *Patagona gigas* Picaflor gigante (Arg, Ch, Bol). L 22 cm. Habitat: arid bush, preferably with cacti, between 1000 and 4000 m. Huge. Sexes alike. Upperparts greenish-brown. Whitish rump. Under tail-coverts white. Brown wings. Greenish-brown tail.

3 **GREEN-BACKED FIRECROWN** *Sephanoides sephanoides* Picaflor rubí (Arg), Picaflor (Ch). L 11 cm. Habitat: open woods and damp thickets, gardens. Straight black bill. ♂: forehead and crown red. Upperparts bronze-green. White spot behind the eye. Underparts greyish with bronze-green speckling on throat and breast. ♀ lacks red on the head, and underparts less speckled.

4 **JUAN FERNANDEZ FIRECROWN** *Sephanoides fernandensis* Picaflor de Juan Fernández (Ch). L 13 cm. Habitat: thickets and gardens. ♂ generally cinnamon with crown brilliant red. ♀: crown metallic blue-green, upperparts brilliant green. Below white, with green dots on throat and flanks.

5 **BLUE-CAPPED PUFFLEG** *Eriocnemis glaucopoides* Picaflor de frente violácea (Arg), Picaflor pantalón grande (Bol). L 11 cm. Habitat: thickets and forests between 1000 and 2000 m. ♂: green. Forehead, fore-crown, belly and under tail-coverts blue. White thighs. Brown wings. Forked tail blue-black. ♀ like ♂ but blue only on under tail-coverts. Cinnamon underparts.

6 **RED-TAILED COMET** *Sappho sparganura* Picaflor cometa (Arg, Bol). L ♂ 22, ♀ 15 cm. Habitat: thickets, woods and mountains up to 3000 m. ♂: brown head. Reddish to purple upperparts. Brilliant golden-green throat. Underparts green. White under tail-coverts. Brown wings. Long tail deeply forked, banded black and orange-red, black tip. ♀: upperparts bronze-green. Underparts pale greyish with green freckles. Shorter tail, banded green (or bronze according to light) and black, outers buff. Voice: a high-pitched and harsh 'chaychaychaychait cheechaychay...', repeated.

7 **LONG-BILLED STARTHROAT** *Heliomaster longirostris* Picaflor estrella (Arg), Picaflor estrella pico largo (Bol), Bico-reto-cinzento (Br). L 12 cm. Habitat: thickets, edges of woods and forests. Long bill black. Crown greenish-blue; white spot behind eye. White line on cheek. Black chin. Throat brilliant violet-red. Upperparts bronze-grey. Under tail-coverts with white spots. Brown wings. Central tail feathers bluish-green, outers tipped white. ♀ like ♂ but green crown and throat feathers edged white.

8 **BLUE-TUFTED STARTHROAT** *Heliomaster furcifer* Picaflor de barbijo (Arg, Bol), Bico-reto-azul (Br), Picaflor de garganta rojiza (Uru). L 12.5 cm. Habitat: savannahs, thickets and woods. Long black bill. ♂: crown brilliant green. Upperparts bronze-green. Throat brilliant violet-red. Long metallic blue feathers on sides of neck. Underparts violet-blue. Brown wings. Longish forked tail bluish-green. ♀: white spot below eye. Brownish head. Upperparts bronze-green. Underparts pale grey. Tail blackish and green, shorter than ♂'s. Voice: flight call a clear, sharp 'tsee....tsee....tsee...'.

9 **OASIS HUMMINGBIRD** *Rhodopis vesper* Picaflor del norte (Ch). L 12–13.5 cm. Habitat: thickets in damper valleys. ♂: bronze-green above, whitish below. Shiny pinkish-violet throat. Rump reddish. Central tail feathers short and green, outers long and dark brown. ♀ lacks violet throat. Below pale coffee-brown. Normal tail with black sub-terminal band on outer three pairs of feathers.

10 **PERUVIAN SHEARTAIL** *Thaumastura cora* Picaflor de Cora (Ch). L ♂ 13, ♀ 8 cm. Habitat: thickets in arid areas. ♂: above bronze-green. Throat brilliant pinkish-violet. Below white, greyish on belly. Long central pair of tail feathers. ♀ lacks brilliant throat. Short tail tipped white.

11 **SLENDER-TAILED WOODSTAR** *Microstilbon burmeisteri* Picaflor enano (Arg, Bol). L 7–8 cm. Habitat: woods between 1000 and 3000 m. Tiny. Short bill. ♂: upperparts brilliant dark green. Throat with long brilliant reddish-violet feathers at sides. Underparts grey with green spots on the sides of the breast and flanks. Under tail-coverts and thighs whitish. Brown wings. Tail green, outermost pair long and dark brownish. ♀: upperparts green. Pale patches on sides of back. Underparts pale cinnamon. White spot behind the eye. Buff brow. Brown wings. Short tail pale cinnamon with black subterminal band. Loud buzzing flight in display – like a large beetle's noise. Voice: flight call a high 'teeayoh... teeayoh...', fast.

12 **AMETHYST WOODSTAR** *Calliphlox amethystina* Picaflor amatista (Arg, Bol), Estrelinha or Tesourinha (Br). L 9 (♂), 7.5 (♀) cm. Habitat: thickets, forests. ♂: upperparts brilliant bronze-green. White spot behind the eye. Throat and sides of neck violet-red. White breast. Rest of underparts greenish-grey. Brown wings. Tail forked. Central tail feathers green, the rest purple. ♀: bronze-green upperparts. Long post-ocular streak. Ochre throat with green dots. Whitish band across breast. Rest of underparts cinnamon. Short, square tail with central feathers green, outers black with cinnamon tips.

13 **CHILEAN WOODSTAR** *Eulidia yarrellii* Picaflor de Arica (Ch). L 8 cm. Habitat: gardens and thickets in arid regions. ♂: above olive-green. Purplish-red throat. Rest of underparts very pale cinnamon. Central tail feathers short and green, outers long, slender and dark brown. ♀: bronze above. Below pale cinnamon. Short tail centrally green, outer feathers tipped white.

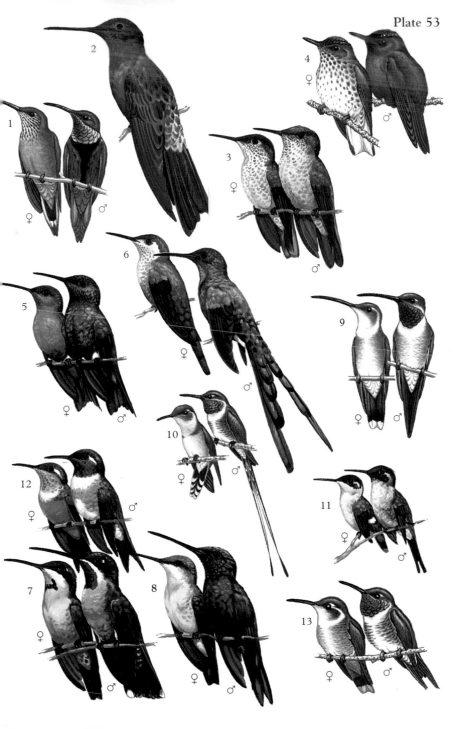

Plate 53

Plate 54

TROGONS (FAMILY TROGONIDAE)

1 **BLACK-THROATED TROGON** *Trogon rufus* Surucuá amarillo (Arg, Bol), Surucuá-de-barriga-amarela (Br). L 24 cm. Habitat: forests. ♂: throat black. Upperparts bronze-green. Belly, flanks yellow. Tail from below barred black and white. ♀: upperparts olive-chestnut. Tail barred black and white. Voice: a series of five or more slow, whistled, melodious '*wheeew… wheeew… wheeew….*'.

2 **SURUCUA TROGON** *Trogon surucura* Surucuá común (Arg), Suruku'a (Par), Surucuá-de-peito-azul (Br). L 25 cm. Habitat: rainforests. ♂: face black. Breast metallic blue, upperparts shiny green. Belly red. Tail white from below. ♀: dark grey, pinkish belly. Voice: a series of monotone whistled '*took took took chook chook chook…*' 8 to 14 or more times. Angry call a sporadic rattled '*pirrrrr*'.

3 **BLUE-CROWNED TROGON** *Trogon curucui* Surucuá de pecho verde (Arg), Surucuá purpúreo (Bol). L 23 cm. Habitat: forests and woods. ♂: face and throat black. Breast and upperparts metallic green. Belly and under tail-coverts red. Tail finely barred black and white. ♀: grey upperparts, belly reddish. Voice: a longish series of '*tootootootootootootoo…*' at about three per second.

MOTMOTS (FAMILY MOMOTIDAE)

4 **BLUE-CROWNED MOTMOT** *Momotus momota* Burgo (Arg), Udu-de-coroa-azul (Br), Burgo verde (Bol). L 43 cm. Blue forehead, black face. Green upperparts. Green throat. Breast and belly green. Black mark on breast. Two central tail feathers project with bare barbs and racket-shaped tips. Voice: a deep, hollow '*wurup….wurup…*', sporadically.

5 **RUFOUS MOTMOT** *Baryphthengus ruficapillus* Yeruvá (Arg, Bol), Burgo rojizo (Bol), Juruva (Br). L 45 cm. Habitat: lower storeys of forest. Crown chestnut. Upperparts green. Face black. Breast with big black spot. Voice: at dusk a repeated '*whodledoo…..woodledoodledoo*', low-pitched and hollow-sounding.

KINGFISHERS (FAMILY ALCEDINIDAE)

6 **RINGED KINGFISHER** *Ceryle torquata* Martín pescador grande (Arg, Uru, Bol), Martín pescador (Ch), Javatî guasu (Par), Martim-pescador-grande (Br). L 45 cm. Habitat: streams, rivers and lakesides. Upperparts blue-grey. Neck white. Breast and belly chestnut in ♂; ♀ has blue-grey breast. Voice: a rattled '*trek…trek..trek…*', or spaced '*trek's*.

7 **AMAZON KINGFISHER** *Chloroceryle amazona* Martín pescador mediano (Arg, Bol, Uru), Martim-pescador-verde or Ariramba-verde (Br), Javatî (Par). L 35 cm. Habitat: rivers, streams and the edges of marshes and lakes. Upperparts metallic green. Throat and belly white. ♂ has a chestnut breast, ♀ white breast with green on the sides. Voice: a sharp '*kyekyekyekyekyek…*', descending in volume and pitch.

8 **GREEN KINGFISHER** *Chloroceryle americana* Martín pescador chico (Arg, Ch, Uru, Bol), Javatî mirî (Par), Martim-pescador-pequeno (Br). L 22 cm. Habitat: ponds, lakes, rivers, marshes and ditches. Head and upperparts blackish bronze-green. Throat, collar and underparts white, but ♂ has a chestnut breast, while the ♀ has two dark green bands across breast. Voice: a rapid '*kikikikikikikik…*', clicking and descending.

9 **GREEN-AND-RUFOUS KINGFISHER** *Chloroceryle inda* Martín pescador rojizo (Bol), Martim-pescadoir-do-mata (Br). L 22 cm. Habitat: watercourses in deep forest. Above petroleum-green dotted white on rump. Underparts chestnut. ♀: breast band barred green and white.

10 **PYGMY KINGFISHER** *Chloroceryle aenea* Martín pescador enano (Arg), Martín pescador pigmeo (Bol), Arirambinha (Br). L 12 cm. Habitat: forest pools. Tiny. Upperparts bronze-green. Underparts red; centre of belly white. ♀: has green across breast.

PUFFBIRDS (FAMILY BUCCONIDAE)

11 **WHITE-NECKED PUFFBIRD** *Notharchus macrorhynchus* Chacurú grande (Arg, Bol), Makuru (Par), Capitao-do-mato (Br). L 25 cm. Habitat: forests. Strong, heavy bill black. Head, back and breast-band black. Throat, a complete collar, upper breast white. Cinnamon belly and vent.

12 **WHITE-EARED PUFFBIRD** *Nystalus chacuru* Chacurú listado (Arg), Chacurú cariblanco (Bol), Chakuru (Par), Joao-bobo or Dormiao (Br). L 22 cm. Habitat: clearings in forests or woods. Head and back dark brown except for white lores and ear-coverts, these last almost surrounded by black. Underparts and complete collar white but with ochre wash on breast. Voice: ♂ and ♀ duet '*feefeefee, feyfeyfey, feefeefee, feyfeyfey…*'.

13 **SPOT-BACKED PUFFBIRD** *Nystalus maculatus* Durmilí (Arg), Chacurú dormido (Bol), Rapazinho-dos-velhos (Br). L 20 cm. Habitat: dry woods. Dark crown and upperparts spotted and barred ochre. Cinnamon hind-collar and breast. Belly white with heavy dark streaking as also on breast. Voice: a rhythmic '*to you, to you, to you, to you…*', descending in tone and volume, repeated sporadically.

14 **RUSTY-BREASTED NUNLET** *Nonnula rubecula* Chacurú chico (Arg, Bol), Macuru (Br). L 14 cm. Habitat: edge of clearings in forests. White eye-ring. Head and upperparts brown. Neck, breast and flanks cinnamon. Whitish belly.

▶

JACAMARS (FAMILY GALBULIDAE)

15 **RUFOUS-TAILED JACAMAR** *Galbula ruficauda* Yacamará (Arg), Yacamará común (Bol), Bico-de-agulha-de-rabo-vermelho (Br). L 25 cm. Long, sharp bill slightly down-curved. Upperparts, breast and topside of tail bronze-green. Throat and upper breast white. Belly and underside of tail chestnut.

Plate 55

TOUCANS (FAMILY RHAMPHASTIDAE)

1 **CHESTNUT-EARED ARAÇARI** *Pteroglossus castanotis* Tucán de cara castaña (Arg, Bol), Arasari (Par), Araçari-castanho (Br). L 40 cm. Habitat: forests. Serrated bill black with yellow on the sides of the upper mandible. Black crown with chestnut centre stripe. Back and long graded tail greenish-brown. Throat, sides of the neck and collar chestnut. Rump and a band across the belly red. Forehead, fore-neck and upper breast black; lower breast and belly yellow. Thighs and wings brown. Voice: a high-pitched screechy '*tseeetcheeek*' with the quality of scraping glass.

2 **SPOT-BILLED TOUCANET** *Selenidera maculirostris* Tucán pico manchado (Arg), Araçari-poca (Br). L 37 cm. Habitat: dense middle layers and canopy of rainforests. Both sexes have pale greenish bill with black spots and bars, bare green faces. ♂: black head, neck, breast and belly; olive-green back. Yellow lower flanks and red under tail-coverts. Tip of tail chestnut. Slight yellow collar on hind-neck. ♀ is brown where ♂ is black, otherwise similar. Voice: a toad-like '*gwok, chwawk, gwork, walk...*' in a series of five to seven, sporadic, quiet and low-pitched.

3 **SAFFRON TOUCANET** *Baillonius bailloni* Tucán amarillo (Arg), Arasari pakova (Par), Araçari-banana (Br). L 37 cm. Green bill red at the base. Bare face red. Forehead, face and underparts yellow. Upperparts greyish-olive. Red rump. Long tail. Voice: a quiet, sneezy '*tissip, sip*'.

4 **RED-BREASTED TOUCAN** *Ramphastos dicolorus* Tucán de pico verde (Arg), Tuca sa'yju (Par) Tucano-de-bico-verde (Br). L 45 cm. Habitat: forests and woods. Yellowish-green bill. Bare face red. Upperparts, wings and tail black. Rump, lower breast and belly red. Throat and breast yellow. Voice: raucous and coarse '*yehhhk, eehhhp...*', several calling together.

5 **TOCO TOUCAN** *Ramphastos toco* Tucán grande (Arg, Bol), Tucanuçu (Br). L 55 cm. Habitat: forest edge, woods and clearings, gardens. Orange-yellow bill, red in parts during breeding, and a black oval patch near the tip. Bare orange face and blue eye-ring. All black but for a large white bib on throat and breast, white rump and red vent. In pairs and loose flocks, family groups. Often in the open and above the forests. Usually silent in flap-glide flight. Voice: loud, raucous '*aaaacks*' and '*aaarks*', several calling at the same time, answering each other.

Plate 55

Plate 56

WOODPECKERS (FAMILY PICIDAE)

1   **ARROWHEAD PICULET** *Picumnus minutissimus* Carpintero ventriocre (Bol), Pica-pau-anao-escamado (Br), Ypeku ne'i (Par). L 9 cm. Habitat: savannahs and mangroves. Above brown with white dots. Below whitish, feathers edged black giving scaly effect. Forehead and crown of ♂ red, ♀'s dotted white.

2   **MOTTLED PICULET** *Picumnus nebulosus* Carpinterito pardo (Arg), Carpintero enano (Uru), Pica-pau-anao-carijo (Br). L 11 cm. Habitat: savannahs and woods. Red forehead. Crown black with white dots (brown with white dots in ♀). Overall ochre-brown, throat lightly barred black and white. Black central tail feathers, next white then black again, outer ones black and white.

3   **OCHRE-COLLARED PICULET** *Picumnus temminckii* Carpinterito de cara canela (Arg), Ypeku ne'i (Par), Pica-pau-anao-de-coleira (Br). L 9 cm. Habitat: thickets and forests. Top of the head black with red tips to the feathers of the forehead, white tips to the rest. Face and broad hind collar cinnamon-ochre. Rest of upperparts and wing-coverts brown. Underparts barred black and white. Tail as Mottled Piculet – black and white longitudinally. ♀ lacks the red dots on forehead.

4   **WHITE-BARRED PICULET** *Picumnus cirratus* Carpinterito común (Arg), Carpintero variado (Bol), Pica-pau-anao-barrado (Br). L 9 cm. Habitat: savannahs, woods, thickets and forests. Black head dotted white, through red dots on forehead and crown of ♂ (absent in ♀). Underparts barred greyish-white and black. Upperparts greyish-brown (greenish-brown in ♀). Tail as in most of the genus, black and white lengthways.

Note: This includes the north-western form which is considered by some to be a separate species, the Ocellated Piculet, *Picumnus dorbignyanus*, which is untidily barred on the underparts.

5   **WHITE WOODPECKER** *Melanerpes candidus* Carpintero blanco (Arg, Uru, Bol), Birro (Br), Ypeku la novia (Par), Viudita (Bol). L 27 cm. Habitat: savannahs, woods and palm groves. Head, underparts and rump white. Yellow on ♂'s nape absent in ♀. Black line under the eye joins the black back, wings and tail. In small flocks or family groups, sometimes singly. Voice: a loud and noisy 'wheeerrr… wheeerrr…'

6   **YELLOW-FRONTED WOODPECKER** *Melanerpes flavifrons* Carpintero de frente amarillo (Arg), Carpintero frentiamarillo (Bol), Benedito-de-testa-amarela (Br). L 19 cm. Habitat: forests and woods. Yellow forehead. Red crown and nape (black in ♀). Black face and down the neck. Back and wing-coverts black with blue sheen. Some white feathers on hind-neck and central back. White rump and upper tail-coverts. Throat, malar region and fore-neck yellow. Breast greyish-green, lower breast and belly red. Flanks, under tail-coverts and thighs barred black and yellowish-white. Black tail. Voice: a fast, reedy, whistled 'peereepeep' answered by 'pireepeepee'. When angry or territorial the pair duets 'yek, yeck, yek, yeck…'.

7   **WHITE-FRONTED WOODPECKER** *Melanerpes cactorum* Carpintero de los cardones (Arg, Bol), Pica-pau-de-testa-branca (Br). L 18 cm. Habitat: savannahs and woods. White forehead. Face and rest of the head black with a red patch on the crown of ♂, missing on ♀. Nape and hind-neck grey, black line down side of the neck. Black back with some white feathers. Rump and upper tail-coverts with white barring. Yellow throat. Ochre-grey breast. Flanks and under tail-coverts barred black and white. Wings dark with round white spots. Tail barred black and white. Drills bark to obtain sap, as well as feeding on insects and their larvae.

8   **CHEQUERED WOODPECKER** *Picoides mixtus* Carpintero bataraz chico (Arg), Pica-pau-chorao (Br), Carpintero chorreado (Bol, Uru). L 15 cm. Habitat: savannahs and woods. Forehead and crown dark brown streaked with white (plain in ♀). Red nape (absent in ♀). White superciliary extending down the neck, and another white line below the eye. Pale chestnut ear-patch. Upperparts, wings and tail black, dotted and barred white. Underparts white dotted black. Flanks and undertail barred black and white. Voice: a high-pitched, fast, laughing 'cheercheer- cheercheercheer'.

9   **STRIPED WOODPECKER** *Picoides lignarius* Carpintero bataraz grande (Arg), Carpinterito (Ch). L 18 cm. Habitat: woods. Forehead and crown dark brown with fine white streaking. Red nape (not in ♀). White brow and line beneath eye both extend onto neck. Grey ear-patch. Upperparts, wings and tail dark brown with white bands. Flight feathers and coverts barred and dotted. Underparts white streaked dark. Belly, flanks, thighs and undertail barred black and white.

10 **SMOKY-BROWN WOODPECKER** *Veniliornis fumigatus* Carpintero olivaceo ahumado (Arg), Carpintero pardo oliva (Bol). L 17 cm. Habitat: woods and forests between 1700 and 2500 m. Overall olive-brown. Red crown (absent in ♀). Brown wings with white markings on the inner vanes seen from the underside. Dark tail.

11 **LITTLE WOODPECKER** *Veniliornis passerinus* Carpintero olivaceo común (Arg), Ypeku para (Par), Carpintero olivaceo (Bol), Pica-pauzinho-anao (Br). L 15 cm. Habitat: woods and forests. Forehead, crown and sides of head brown, forehead with whitish flecking. Red nape (but not so in ♀). Olive upperparts with some spotting on the wing-coverts. Outer vane of the primaries bright olive-green, inner vanes brown with whitish markings. Underparts pale brown with fine ochre barring. Tail brown, olive at the base.

Plate 56

Plate 57

WOODPECKERS (FAMILY PICIDAE)

1 DOT-FRONTED WOODPECKER *Veniliornis frontalis* Carpintero oliváceo listado (Arg), Carpintero frentinegro (Bol). L 16 cm. Habitat: woods and forests between 500 and 2000 m. Dark brown forehead, crown and nape with white dots (♀), ♂ has crown and nape red. Two white lines, one above and one below the eye. Brown ear-patch. Upperparts olive with ochre spotting. Pale-barred primaries. Coverts olive with pale spots. Underparts pale brown with fine white barring. Throat whitish with blackish streaks. Dark brown tail with faint ochre barring.

2 WHITE-SPOTTED WOODPECKER *Veniliornis spilogaster* Carpintero oliváceo manchado (Arg), Carpintero manchado (Uru), Pica-pauzinho-verde-carijó (Br). L 17 cm. Habitat: woods and forests. Forehead and crown dark brown with red streaks (♂) or fine white streaks (♀). A white line above the eye, another below. Upperparts olive with heavy yellowish bands. Brown wings with large ochre spots. Throat and neck streaked black and white. Breast and belly marked with whitish. Flanks, thighs and under tail-coverts banded brown and white. Dark brown tail with ochre barring. Voice: a rapid, laughing 'churchurrchurrchurrchurrchurr..'.

3 GOLDEN-GREEN WOODPECKER *Piculus chrysochloros* Carpintero dorado amarillo (Arg, Bol), Pica-pau-dourado-escuro (Br). L 20 cm. Habitat: woods and savannahs. Head olive, but in ♂ forehead, crown, nape and malar stripe are all red. Yellow line from bill below eye. Green ear-patch. Orange on sides of the neck. Upperparts and wing-coverts olive-green. Underwing spotted with chestnut. Throat orange. Rest of the underparts barred yellow and olive. Tail brown, greenish at the base and dark at the tip.

4 WHITE-BROWED WOODPECKER *Piculus aurulentus* Carpintero dorado verde (Arg), Pica-pau-dourado (Br). L 22 cm. Habitat: rainforests. ♂ forehead, crown, nape and malar stripe red (♀ red only on nape and malar stripe). Face olive with yellow lines above eye and below face. Upperparts golden-green. Yellow throat. Neck and the rest of the underparts barred dark grey and whitish. Black tail.

5 GOLDEN-OLIVE WOODPECKER *Piculus rubiginosus* Carpintero dorado gris (Arg, Bol). L 22 cm. Habitat: woods and forests between 1000 and 3000 m. Forehead and crown grey. Red line from bill over the eye to nape and red malar stripe (♂). ♀ just has a red nape. Pale face. Olive-green back. Throat streaked dark brown and whitish. Underparts barred dark grey and yellowish-white. Tail dark, greenish at the base. Voice: a loud 'tee-or', sporadically.

6 GREEN-BARRED WOODPECKER *Colaptes melanochloros* Carpintero real (Arg), Ypeku (Par), Carpintero pecho dorado (Bol), Carpintero de nuca roja (Uru), Pica-pau-verde-barrado (Br). L 26 cm. Habitat: woods, forest edges, savannahs, palm groves. Forehead and crown black. Lores, face and ear-coverts whitish. Red nape. ♂ has red malar stripe. Upperparts barred blackish-brown and yellowish-white. Rump whitish or yellowish with dark triangular markings. Throat white flecked with black. Underparts yellowish-green on breast with large black dots. Under tail-coverts barred black and whitish. Dark wings barred yellowish-white with yellow shafts. Black tail, outer feathers barred yellow. Voice: calls often duetted: 'wick,wick,wick,wick,wick', somewhat raucous. Drumming call is rhythmic 'brrrrr...brrrrr...brrrbrrr' rhythmically.

Note: Two species were lumped together and became one; the southern and western form (Golden-breasted Woodpecker, *Colaptes melanolaimus*) is still considered separate by some.

7 CHILEAN FLICKER *Colaptes pitius* Pitío (Arg, Ch). L 33 cm. Habitat: woodland edges and clearings in the Patagonian Andean woods. Forehead, crown and nape dark grey. Face, chin and throat buff. Upperparts dark brown barred buff. White lower back and rump. Barred upper tail-coverts; black tail. Underparts barred and spotted dark brown and white. Centre of belly yellowish-white. Yellow shafts to flight feathers which are spotted yellow on inner vanes. Voice: calls are a rapid 'gligligligligli' and the onomatopoeic 'pit.. piteeoo... piteeoo... pit-you..' which gives it its local name.

8 ANDEAN FLICKER *Colaptes rupicola* Carpintero de las piedras (Arg, Bol), Pitío del norte (Ch). L 33 cm. Habitat: rocky slopes between 2000 and 3500 m. Top parts of head dark grey. Sides of head and neck greyish. Malar stripe black (red at the dorsal end in ♂). Upperparts brown barred whitish. Rump yellowish-buff, upper tail-coverts same barred black. Underparts greyish with black spots on breast. Dark wings barred buff and whitish; yellow shafts to flight feathers. Black tail, outer feathers barred buff. On the ground.

9 FIELD FLICKER *Colaptes campestris* Carpintero campestre (Arg, Bol), Carpintero de campo (Uru), Ypeku ñu (Par), Pica-pau-do-campo (Br). L 33 cm. Habitat: savannahs, steppe and meadows. Top parts of the head black. Lores, around the eyes and throat whitish. Upperparts barred dark brown and whitish. Malar stripe red in ♂, black and white in ♀. Rump and lower back white. Breast yellow. Underparts whitish, barred brown. Yellow-shafted flight feathers spotted. Black tail. Voice: a fast, high-pitched 'whitwhitwhitwhitwhit' and 'k'yeh k'yeh, kyekyeh'.

10 PALE-CRESTED WOODPECKER *Celeus lugubris* Carpintero de cabeza pajiza (Arg), Carpintero cabeciblanco (Bol). L 23 cm. Habitat: savannahs, woods and palm groves. Dark face. Red malar stripe in ♂ only. Head with long, shaggy, pale yellow crest. Upperparts dark brown with yellow barring. Yellow rump. Throat yellowish-ochre. Dark brown underparts with chestnut barring on belly. All tail-coverts chestnut. Flight feathers dark, barred chestnut. Yellowish under wing-coverts. Black tail.

Plate 57

Plate 58

WOODPECKERS (FAMILY PICIDAE)

1 BLOND-CRESTED WOODPECKER *Celeus flavescens* Carpintero de cabeza amarilla (Arg), Carpintero cabeciamarillo (Bol), Ypeku akâ sa'yju (Par), Pica-pau-de-cabeça-amarela (Br). L 23 cm. Habitat: woods and forests. Yellow head with long crest. Red malar stripe (absent in ♀). Upperparts black barred yellow. Yellow rump. Ochre-yellow throat. Underparts black. Wings dark with yellow barring on flight feathers. Black tail. Voice: loud, high-pitched '*week, weeek, week, week, wek*', dropping off at the end, almost like a break in the voice.

2 HELMETED WOODPECKER *Dryocopus galeatus* Carpintero listado de cara canela (Arg), Pica-pau-de-cara-amarela (Br). L 33 cm. Habitat: rainforests. Head, throat, malar stripe and nape red with cinnamon face in ♂; cinnamon throat, face and malar stripe in ♀. Creamy white line down the sides of the neck. Upper back and tail black, lower back and rump ochre-white. Black wings with cinnamon at the base of the primaries. Fore-neck black. Rest of underparts barred black and ochre. Rare.

3 BLACK-BODIED WOODPECKER *Dryocopus schulzi* Carpintero negro de garganta blanca (Arg). L 32 cm. Habitat: woods and savannahs. Head red; grey ear-coverts, white throat, (♀ has black forehead). White line under the eye to nape and thence down the sides of the neck. Rest black. White at the base of the primaries seen in flight. Voice: loud contact call '*tsee-ah….tsee- ah…*'.

4 LINEATED WOODPECKER *Dryocopus lineatus* Carpintero negro de garganta blanca (Arg), Carpintero negro listado (Bol), Ypeku akâ pytâ (Par), Pica-pau-de-banda-branca (Br). L 35 cm. Habitat: woods and forests. Forehead, crown, nape and malar stripe red, (malar stripe only in ♂). Upperparts black. White line from bill, under the eye, down the neck and along scapulars (absent in some races). Black fore-neck; barred underparts. Black tail. ♀ has a white throat (speckled in ♂), black forehead and face. White under wing-coverts and base of the flight feathers.

5 ROBUST WOODPECKER *Campephilus robustus* Carpintero listado de garganta roja (Arg), Pica-pau-rei (Br). L 37 cm. Habitat: rainforests. Red head, throat and neck. White malar stripe in ♀. Black and white ear-spot. White upperparts with cinnamon wash on rump and tail-coverts. Underparts barred black and white. Black wings with cinnamon spots on flight feathers. White under wing-coverts. Black tail.

6 CRIMSON-CRESTED WOODPECKER *Campephilus melanoleucus* Carpintero listado de garganta negra (Arg), Carpintero negro picoamarillo (Bol), Pica-pau-de-topete-vermelho (Br). L 35 cm. Habitat: forests. Red head (♀ with black forehead and along centre of forecrest, white from bill to nape). ♂ has black and white ear-spot. Black throat, neck, upperparts and tail. White line down the side of the neck and onto the back forming a 'V'. Breast and belly barred. White at the base of the primaries.

7 CREAM-BACKED WOODPECKER *Campephilus leucopogon* Carpintero negro de dorso blanco (Arg), Pica-pau-de-barriga-preta (Br), Carpintero lomo crema (Bol). L 35 cm. Habitat: savannahs, woods and forests up to 2500 m. Red head and upper neck. Black and white ear-spot in ♂. ♀ has black forehead and forecrest, white malar stripe and black line under eye. Cream back. The rest of upperparts, tail and all underparts black. Chestnut patch at the base of the primaries seen in flight from below.

8 MAGELLANIC WOODPECKER *Campephilus magellanicus* Carpintero negro gigante (Arg), Carpintero (Ch). L 44 cm. Habitat: Patagonian Andes forests and woods. Head: red with slight crest in ♂, black with long, floppy, forward-curling crest in ♀. Rest of the bird all black but for white patch on secondaries, spots on primaries, and under wing-coverts. Voice: double rapped '*budoom*' typical of the genus, and screechy '*piss-ah, …p'saaaah*'.

Plate 58

Plate 59

WOODCREEPERS (FAMILY DENDROCOLAPTIDAE)

1 **PLAIN-BROWN WOODCREEPER** *Dendrocincla fuliginosa* Trepador pardo (Arg, Bol), Arapaçu-liso (Br). L 21 cm. Habitat: rainforests. All brown with ochre streaks on crown, paler throat. Wings with chestnut hue. Tail chestnut.

Note: Some consider this southern form a separate species, the Plain-winged Woodcreeper, *Dendrocincla turdina*, the specific name referring to its thrush-like appearance.

2 **OLIVACEOUS WOODCREEPER** *Sittasomus griseicapillus* Tarefero (Arg, Bol), Arapaçu-verde (Br), Guiri (Par). L 15 cm. Habitat: woods and forests. Small. Short bill. Head dark brown with olive tones. Upperparts brownish with chestnut tinge. Cinnamon throat. Breast and belly cinnamon with olive tinge. Wings brown and chestnut with cinnamon wing band on flight feathers. Chestnut tail. Works up tree trunks to the top, then glides to the bottom of another. Voice: a series or 6 to 18 high-pitched whistles descending '*fweeep, fweeep, fweeep, fweeep...*'.

3 **SCIMITAR-BILLED WOODCREEPER** *Drymornis bridgesii* Chinchero grande (Arg), Arañero grande (Uru), Arapaçu-platino (Br), Trepador chinchero (Bol). L 33 cm. Habitat: open woods, savannahs and gardens. Long curved bill. Head dark chestnut. Face and nape pale chestnut. Two whitish lines across face, one above and one below the eye. Breast and belly whitish, feathers edged dark giving a streaky effect. Primaries dark brown, secondaries chestnut. Tail chestnut. Quite terrestrial. Voice: a sharp '*cheedle*' contact call, and long '*tweedle-tweedle-tweed-twee-twee...*', accelerating and losing volume.

4 **WHITE-THROATED WOODCREEPER** *Xiphocolaptes albicollis* Trepador grande de pico negro (Arg), Arapaçu-de-garganta-branca (Br). L 31 cm. Habitat: forests and woods. Heavy, slightly down-curved bill black. Dark brown head with ochre streaking. Face paler. White throat. Olive-brown upperparts and breast with long ochre streaks. Belly and thighs olive-brown barred dark brown. Chestnut wings and tail. Voice: calls at dusk and dawn a series of very loud and well-spaced whistles descending in volume and pitch '*tee-ay, heechee, hechee, hichee, hitchy...*'.

5 **GREAT RUFOUS WOODCREEPER** *Xiphocolaptes major* Trepador gigante (Arg), Arapaçu-do-campo (Br), Trepador grande colorado (Bol). L 34 cm. Habitat: woods. Heavy, slightly decurved bill pale. Overall rufous, more cinnamon on head, paler on throat. Chestnut on upperparts. Faint streaking on breast, slight barring on flanks. Pale chestnut on belly.

6 **BLACK-BANDED WOODCREEPER** *Dendrocolaptes picumnus* Trepador grande rojizo (Arg, Bol). L 25 cm. Habitat: woods and forests. Head brown streaked buff. Upperparts reddish-brown. Rump, tail and wings chestnut. White throat with dark streaking. Forehead and breast chestnut streaked buff. Belly pale reddish-brown faintly barred dark brown.

7 **PLANALTO WOODCREEPER** *Dendrocolaptes platyrostris* Trepador chico de pico negro (Arg), Arapaçu-grande (Br). L 25 cm. Habitat: woods and forests. Black bill. Dark head streaked ochre. Upperparts brown with long ochre streaks. Rump chestnut. Whitish throat. Breast olive-brown with ochre streaking. Belly light chestnut barred dark brown. Chestnut wings and tail. Voice: at dusk and dawn calls a series of descending whistles '*hee, hee, he, he, hey, hay, huh*'.

8 **NARROW-BILLED WOODCREEPER** *Lepidocolaptes angustirostris* Chinchero chico (Arg), Arañero chico (Uru). Arapasu'i (Par), Arapaçu-do-cerrado (Br), Trepador chico común (Bol). L 20 cm. Habitat: open woods. Long decurved bill pinkish. Dark head streaked buff. Whitish brow. Back of the neck dark brown streaked whitish. Upperparts brown with chestnut tinge. White throat. Breast and belly whitish with dark streaking. Wings and tail chestnut. Voice: a series of loud, clear, accelerating '*freeew, freew, freee, free freefreefreefree...*' descending in volume.

9 **SCALED WOODCREEPER** *Lepidocolaptes squamatus* Trepador escamado (Arg), Arapaçu-escamado (Br). L 18 cm. Habitat: rainforests. Longish decurved bill. Overall has a 'scaly' look. Head and hind-neck cinnamon, feathers edged dark brownish. Whitish throat. Upperparts cinnamon-brown faintly streaked buff. Breast and belly whitish, feathers edged dark brown. Chestnut tail.

10 **LESSER WOODCREEPER** *Lepidocolaptes fuscus* Trepador enano (Arg), Arapaçu-rajado (Br). L 16 cm. Habitat: rainforests. Decurved bill. Upperparts brown, streaked buff on head and mantle. Post-ocular streak ochreous. Rump and tail chestnut. Underparts buff, streaked pale chestnut.

11 **RED-BILLED SCYTHEBILL** *Campylorhamphus trochilirostris* Picapalo de pico rojizo (Arg, Bol). L 29 cm. Habitat: woods, savannahs and gallery forests. Very long, strongly decurved bill red. All upperparts chestnut, whitish streaking on head. Whitish throat streaked chestnut. Breast and belly light chestnut, heavily streaked pale on breast, less or not at all on the belly.

12 **BLACK-BILLED SCYTHEBILL** *Campylorhamphus falcularius* Picapalo de pico negro (Arg), Arapaçu-de-bico-torto (Br). L 26 cm. Habitat: rainforests at lower levels. Very long, decurved bill black. Brown upperparts, darker and streaked brown on head and neck. Chestnut wings and tail. Whitish throat. Underparts olive with narrow pale streaking on breast. Voice: '*bzhi, bzhiu, bzhiuy...*', up to ten times, accelerating; also a fast, high-pitched '*chiddle chiddle...chiddlechiddle*'.

Plate 59

Plate 60

OVENBIRDS AND ALLIES (FAMILY FURNARIIDAE)

1 **GREYISH MINER** *Geositta maritima* Minero chico (Ch). L 14 cm. Habitat: arid lower slopes of mountains. Buff flanks. Dark greyish tail, with outer web of outer feathers whitish. Dark wings.

2 **CREAMY-RUMPED MINER** *Geositta isabellina* Caminera de alas largas (Arg), Minero grande (Ch). L 17 cm. Habitat: high montane steppe and rocky valleys between 2000 and 3500 m. Upperparts brown. Underparts pale brownish-white with no streaking. Central tail feathers and the tips of the outers dark; base of the outers and upper tail-coverts cream, contrasting markedly.

3 **RUFOUS-BANDED MINER** *Geositta rufipennis* Caminera rojiza (Arg, Bol), Minero cordillerano (Ch). L 17 cm. Habitat: high mountain steppe and rocky landscape between 600 and 4000 m. Upperparts brown. Slight pale eyebrow. Underparts sandy. Flight feathers rufous with dark trailing border seen in flight. Tail cinnamon with dark subterminal band. Voice: a loud, coarse, high-pitched '*schewip, schewip, schewip, schewip…*'. Also a quiet contact '*tirup… trup*'.

4 **PUNA MINER** *Geositta punensis* Caminera chica (Arg, Bol), Minero de la puna (Ch). L 15 cm. Habitat: between 3000 and 5000 m in arid *puna*. Upperparts sandy brown. Underparts whitish, no streaks on breast. Pale cream and sandy-grey pattern in tail. Cinnamon flight feathers.

5 **COMMON MINER** *Geositta cunicularia* Caminera común (Arg, Bol), Minero (Ch), Pampero común (Bol), Corre-caminos (Uru), Curriqueiro (Br). L 16 cm. Habitat: arid and semi-arid areas. Pale brown upperparts. Pale eyebrow. Buff underparts with faint streaking on breast. Flight feathers rufous. Upper tail-coverts and central tail feathers creamy white contrasting sharply with dark tail. Terrestrial. Voice: a '*chirrrirrrriirrrr…*' often in flight.

6 **SHORT-BILLED MINER** *Geositta antarctica* Caminera patagónica (Arg), Minero austral (Ch). L 16 cm. Habitat: open short-grass. Upperparts greyish-brown. No rufous in the wing. Underparts sandy whitish. Dusky mottling on breast. Voice: '*wetook, wetook, wetook, wetook, wetook…*'.

7 **SLENDER-BILLED MINER** *Geositta tenuirostris* Caminera de pico largo (Arg), Pampero pico largo (Bol). L 18 cm. Habitat: stony steppes at 3000 to 4000 m. Large. Bill long and decurved. Upperparts brown. Underparts sandy with streaking on breast. Flight feathers rufous. Tail rufous, but central feathers dark brown.

8 **SCALE-THROATED EARTHCREEPER** *Upucerthia dumetaria* Bandurrita común (Arg, Bol), Bandurrilla (Ch). L 22 cm. Habitat: scrubby steppe and mountainous terrain. Long, decurved bill. Upperparts earthy brown. Whitish eyebrow. White throat and buff breast, with feathers edged dark looking scaly. Voice: a long '*clicklicklicklicklicklickli…*', high-pitched and piercing, ascending.

9 **WHITE-THROATED EARTHCREEPER** *Upucerthia albigula* Bandurrilla de Arica (Ch). L 21 cm. Habitat: arid hillsides and valleys. Long, pale cinnamon brow. Wings with rufous patch on primaries seen in flight. Tail: dark brown central feathers, outers cinnamon-rufous.

10 **BUFF-BREASTED EARTHCREEPER** *Upucerthia validirostris* Bandurrita ocrácea (Arg), Bandurrilla de la puna (Ch). L 21 cm. Habitat: high mountains between 2000 and 4000 m. Very long decurved bill. Upperparts brown. Eyebrow and underparts ochreous. Central tail feathers brown, outers chestnut.

11 **PLAIN-BREASTED EARTHCREEPER** *Upucerthia jelskii* No local common name. L 19 cm. Habitat: high elevation hillsides and arid valleys. Upperparts light brown. Long buff brow. Below buff with faint scaling on breast. Small rufous patch at base of inner primaries seen in flight. Tail as upperparts but ruddier. Voice: sings '*clicky clicky clicky clicky..*' from the top of a bush

12 **ROCK EARTHCREEPER** *Upucerthia andaecola* Bandurrita de cola castaña (Arg), Bandurrilla de las piedras (Ch). L 19 cm. Habitat: high Andean rocky hillsides up to 4000 m. Cinnamon-brown upperparts. Ochre eyebrow. Underparts evenly buff with darker streaks. Wing shows brown and chestnut in flight. Tail chestnut.

13 **STRAIGHT-BILLED EARTHCREEPER** *Upucerthia ruficauda* Bandurrita de pico recto (Arg), Bandurrilla de pico recto (Ch). L 19 cm. Habitat: upland Patagonia and high Andean steppe to 4000 m. Bill longish and almost straight. Upperparts brown. Buff eyebrow. Throat and breast whitish. This, and the rest of the underparts streaked. Chestnut wings, bright chestnut tail.

14 **CHACO EARTHCREEPER** *Upucerthia certhioides* Bandurrita enana (Arg). L 17 cm. Habitat: arid woods. Upperparts brown. Notable white throat. Underparts paler greyish-brown, more cinnamon on flanks. Rufous band in the brown wing visible in flight. Tail chestnut-brown. Found low in bushes and trees. Voice: a series of up to ten piercing '*chip*' whistles.

15 **BAND-TAILED EARTHCREEPER** *Eremobius phoenicurus* Bandurrita cola negra (Arg). L 17.5 cm. Habitat: taller scrub in steppes. Upperparts earthy brown. Long, whitish eyebrow. Underparts buff with faint dark brown streaking. Tail basally chestnut with terminal third black. Runs across open spaces, tail held high like a banner. Voice: a sharp, high-pitched '*chrrrrrrrr…*' trill followed by one or several '*tee..tee…tee..tee's*'.

▶

Plate 60

16 CRAG CHILIA *Chilia melanura* Chiricoca (Ch). L 18 cm. Habitat: rocky slopes and cliffs with some bushes. Above brown. White brow. Rufous lower back, rump and under tail-coverts. Tail black, reddish at the base. White throat and breast. Belly dusky brown. Dark flight feathers with rufous at the base, forming a wing-bar visible in flight.

Plate 61

OVENBIRDS AND ALLIES (FAMILY FURNARIIDAE)

1 BLACKISH CINCLODES *Cinclodes antarcticus* Remolinera negra (Arg), Churrete austral (Ch). L 17.5 cm. Habitat: rocky and gravel seashores. Overall blackish-brown with slightly paler throat. Unafraid of people.

2 DARK-BELLIED CINCLODES *Cinclodes patagonicus* Remolinera estriada (Arg), Churrete (Ch). L 20 cm. Habitat: lakes, streams, rivers or the seashore. Sooty brown. White eyebrow. Throat whitish with flecking. Underparts greyish, breast with bold whitish streaking. Belly grey. Wing with buff wing-band. Outer corners of tail buff. Always near water. Voice: a piercing '*weep weep weep tirrrrRRRrrr*', often duetted, emitted while dancing with wings raised.

3 GREY-FLANKED CINCLODES *Cinclodes oustaleti* Remolinera chica (Arg), Churrete chico (Ch). L 17.5 cm. Habitat: seashores, mountain streams and rivers to 4000 m. Sooty brown. Narrow white eyebrow. Throat freckled. Underparts greyish, breast with pale streaking. White belly. Wing shows buff wing-band in flight. Dot of white at bend of the folded wing. Underwing white. Tail sooty brown, with the tips of outer feathers dark buff.

4 BAR-WINGED CINCLODES *Cinclodes fuscus* Remolinera común (Arg), Churrete acanelado (Ch), Meneacola (Uru, Bol), Churrete cordillerano (Bol). L 17 cm. Habitat: rivers, streams and lake-shores. Upperparts greyish-brown. Buff eyebrow. Breast pale greyish, belly whitish. Wing-band noticeable in flight. Whitish tips to outer tail feathers. There are variations in the various races.

5 CHESTNUT-WINGED CINCLODES *Cinclodes f. comechingonus* Remolinera serrana (Arg). Habitat: near mountain streams, on rocky mountain slopes. Rufous wing-bar and tail corners. Voice: high-pitched '*weet weet churrr*'. Endemic to mountains of Córdoba (C Argentina).

Note: Until recently considered a separate species.

6 LONG-TAILED CINCLODES *Cinclodes pabsti* Pedreiro (Br). L 22 cm. Habitat: farmland above 800 m. As large as and not unlike a mockingbird. Not restricted to water like most others of the genus.

7 WHITE-WINGED CINCLODES *Cinclodes atacamensis* Remolinera castaña (Arg), Churrete de alas blancas (Ch), Churrete castaño (Bol). L 20 cm. Habitat: shores of high Andean and mountain streams and rivers to 4000 m. Darkish brown with chestnut tinge. Contrasting white eyebrow and throat. Greyish breast with whitish flecking. Large white wing-bar.

8 SEASIDE CINCLODES *Cinclodes nigrofumosus* Churrete costero (Ch). L 25 cm. Habitat: rocky coasts and surf. Large. Dark brown above. White throat. Underparts dusky brown, heavily streaked white on breast. Buff on flanks. Cinnamon wing-bar.

9 CANEBRAKE GROUNDCREEPER *Clibanornis dendrocolaptoides* Espinero del monte (Arg). L 20 cm. Habitat: cane thickets and dense gallery understorey. Upperparts chestnut, paler back. Buff eyebrow. Throat whitish, sides spotted dark brown. Greyish underparts.

10 RUFOUS HORNERO *Furnarius rufus* Hornero común (Arg, Bol), Hornero (Uru), Joao-de-barro (Br), Tiluchi (Bol), Ogaraity (Par). L 19 cm. Habitat: open areas with scattered trees; parks and gardens. Upperparts lightish bright brown. Pale underparts. Tail bright rufous. Struts on the ground. Voice: loud and un-musical duet: one bird an accelerating clatter, the other regular high-pitched '*peep*'s.

11 CRESTED HORNERO *Furnarius cristatus* Hornero copetón (Arg), Hornero crestón (Bol). L 15.5 cm. Habitat: open dry woodland. Crested. Upperparts lightish bright brown, paler underparts. Belly white, rufous tail. Voice: shriller imitation of Rufous Hornero '*pfwee - tittle tittle*', followed by rattle. Also '*chichichichi chee chee chee chee chee*', descending.

12 CURVE-BILLED REEDHAUNTER *Limnornis curvirostris* Pajera de pico curvo (Arg, Uru), Junqueiro-bico-curvo (Br). L 18 cm. Habitat: usually bulrushes, sometimes reeds. Quite long, curved bill. Upperparts chestnut. Whitish brow and throat. Underparts whitish with buff tinge. Rounded chestnut tail. Voice: '*frrriiiick tic tic tic ti titirrrrr*' ascending and descending in pitch, sometimes duetted.

13 STRAIGHT-BILLED REEDHAUNTER *Limnoctites rectirostris* Pajera de pico recto (Arg, Uru) Junqueiro-bico-reto (Br). L 16.5 cm. Habitat: damp grasslands. Long, straight bill. Olive-brown upperparts. Eyebrow and underparts white. Graduated and pointed tail chestnut.

14 DES MUR'S WIRETAIL *Sylviorthorhynchus desmursii* Colilarga (Arg, Ch). L 23.5 cm. Habitat: cane thickets in the understorey of cool and temperate woods. Very long tail (15 cm) of two wiry central feathers. Cinnamon all over, lighter below. Buff eye-line. Voice: a fast and high-pitched '*cooteeroocooteeroocooteeroocooteeroo…*'.

▶

Plate 61

Plate 61 (continued)

15 **THORN-TAILED RAYADITO** *Aphrastura spinicauda* Rayadito (Arg, Ch). L 14 cm. Habitat: woods and forests. Large cinnamon eyebrow. Tail mostly chestnut. Wings dark with two prominent cinnamon bands. Underparts whitish. Tit-like as it searches leaves and twigs for its insect food. Voice: '*tirrr, tirrr, tirrr…*' and '*tsip, tsip, tsiprrrirrrirrrirrrirrri…*' fast and very high-pitched.

16 **MASAFUERA RAYADITO** *Aphrastura masafuera* Not illustrated. Rayadito de Mas Afuera (Ch). L 15 cm. Habitat: dense low vegetation. Dusky head, buff-grey brow.

17 **WREN-LIKE RUSHBIRD** *Phleocryptes melanops* Junquero (Arg, Uru), Totorero (Bol), Trabajador (Ch, Bol), Bate-bico (Br). L 13 cm. Habitat: reed-beds. Upperparts brown streaked black and whitish. Whitish eyebrow. Underparts whitish with cinnamon wash. Voice: an even, rapid clicking interspersed with occasional '*bzzht*', buzzy and questioning.

18 **STREAKED TIT-SPINETAIL** *Leptasthenura striata* Tijeral listado (Ch, Bol). L 16 cm. Habitat: mountain scrub with cactus or dwarf trees. Crown with stripes. Nape and back streaked. Throat and breast lightly streaked.

19 **STRIOLATED TIT-SPINETAIL** *Leptasthenura striolata* Grimpeirinho (Br). L 13.5 cm. Habitat: *Podocarp* and *Araucaria* pine stands at high elevations. Crest. Crown streaked black and light brown. Back streaked. Buff brow. Central tail feathers dark, outers reddish.

Plate 62 (continued)

16 OLIVE SPINETAIL *Cranioleuca obsoleta* Curutié oliváceo (Arg), Arredio-meridional (Br), L 12.5 cm. Habitat: canopy and the edges of forests and woods. Upperparts olive-brown. White eyebrow. Underparts ochreous. Wing-coverts and tail chestnut. Searches twigs and branches for insects. Voice: a series of high-pitched '*tseep*'s accelerating and ending in a trill.

17 STRIPE-CROWNED SPINETAIL *Cranioleuca pyrrhophia* Curutié de cabeza estriada (Arg). Trepadorcito (Uru). L 13 cm. Habitat: drier woods and savannahs. Brown crown with darker streaking. White eyebrow. Black post-ocular streak. Brown back. Face and underparts white. Voice: an accelerating '*tee teetee tititititi...*', ending in a trill.

Plate 62

OVENBIRDS AND ALLIES (FAMILY FURNARIIDAE)

1 **PLAIN-MANTLED TIT-SPINETAIL** *Leptasthenura aegithaloides* Coludito común (Arg, Bol), Tijeral (Ch). L 15 cm. Habitat: Patagonian and Andean steppes and valleys. No crest. Black crown streaked cinnamon. Buff underparts. Black tail with buff on outer vanes and buff outer feathers. Voice: a buzzy '*bzzz bzbzbzbzbz*'.

2 **TUFTED TIT-SPINETAIL** *Leptasthenura platensis* Coludito copetón (Arg, Uru). L 15 cm. Habitat: woods with clearings. Upperparts greyish earthy brown. Prominent crest streaked. Whitish throat streaked grey. Greyish underparts. Brown wings with chestnut band. Long brown tail, outer feathers cinnamon. Voice: '*tswee tswee tswee tittle-tit*' ending in a rattle.

3 **BROWN-CAPPED TIT-SPINETAIL** *Leptasthenura fulginiceps* Coludito de cabeza rojiza (Arg, Bol). L 15.5 cm. Habitat: bushy steppes and steep valleys. Upperparts cinnamon-brown. Slight crest. Underparts lighter. Rufous wings.

4 **ARAUCARIA TIT-SPINETAIL** *Leptasthenura setaria* Coludito de los pinos (Arg), Grimpeiro (Br). L 17.5 cm. Habitat: *Araucaria* forests. Crested. Crown black streaked whitish. Back bright chestnut. Whitish throat streaked grey-brown. Underparts cinnamon. Tail centrally brown, outer feathers chestnut.

5 **CHOTOY SPINETAIL** *Schoeniophylax phryganophila* Chotoy (Arg, Uru). L 22 cm. Habitat: open woods, savannahs and clumps of low bushy trees. Chin spot yellow above a black throat. Cinnamon breast, rest of underparts whitish. Voice: a rapid '*rrrrtooo chicheetitichichicheecheychachochoochew*' low-pitched and hollow-sounding, duetted.

6 **RUFOUS-CAPPED SPINETAIL** *Synallaxis ruficapilla* Pijuí de cabeza rojiza (Arg), Pijuí de vientre sepia (Bol), Pichororé (Br). L 15 cm. Habitat: forest edges and overgrown clearings. Forehead and crown bright chestnut. Buff eyebrow. Face grey. Upperparts chestnut. Underparts grey. Wing brilliant chestnut. Tail chestnut. Voice: a quiet, insistent '*drrrrrt wee*'.

7 **BUFF-BROWED SPINETAIL** *Synallaxis superciliosa* Pijuí de ceja canela (Arg). L 16.5 cm. Habitat: understorey of forests, edges of bushy clearings. Crown, wings and tail bright rufous. Narrow buff eyebrow. Back brown. Throat speckled with black. Underparts pale grey. Voice: a fairly quiet '*tipooee*'..

Note: Some consider this species a race of Azara's Spinetail, *Synallaxis azarae*.

8 **SOOTY-FRONTED SPINETAIL** *Synallaxis frontalis* Pijuí común de cola rojiza (Arg, Bol), Petrim (Br), Coludito de frente parda (Uru). L 16 cm. Habitat: thickets and trees in open country, woods and savannahs. Forehead grey. Chestnut crown. Underparts grey. Most of wing chestnut. Tail chestnut. Voice: a slow, deliberate '*teeoopooee*'.

9 **CHICLI SPINETAIL** *Synallaxis spixi* Chiclí (Arg), Joao-teneném (Br), Coludito de boina roja (Uru). L 16 cm. Habitat: savannahs, woods and thickets. Forehead and crown chestnut. Underparts grey. Wing-coverts chestnut. Wings and tail brown. Voice: '*wee'tiddledidee......wee'tiddledidee*', repeated.

10 **PALE-BREASTED SPINETAIL** *Synallaxis albescens* Pijuí común de cola parda (Arg), Pijuí cola parda (Bol), Ui-pí (Br). L 15 cm. Habitat: savannahs, woods and thickets. Grey forehead, chestnut crown. Underparts whitish-grey. Wings and tail brown. Voice: '*wee bidget ..wee bidget…*', repeated.

11 **PLAIN-CROWNED SPINETAIL** *Synallaxis gujanensis* Güitio espinoso (Bol), Joao-teneném-becuá (Br). L 16 cm. Habitat: lower vegetation in forests and woodland. Upperparts all olive-brown. Buff brow. Underparts whitish, breast washed dingy. Tail and wings rufous.

12 **GREY-BELLIED SPINETAIL** *Synallaxis cinerascens* Pijuí ceniciento (Arg), Coludito plomizo (Uru), Joao-teneném-da-mata (Br). L 13.5 cm. Habitat: undergrowth and cane thickets in rainforests. Forehead, crown, hind-neck, back and rump brown. Face and underparts dark grey. Wing-coverts and tail chestnut, flight feathers mostly so. Voice: loud '*sweet teewee*' with variations ('*see-weet tibee*').

13 **YELLOW-CHINNED SPINETAIL** *Certhiaxis cinnamomea* Curutié rojizo (Arg, Bol), Kurutie (Par), Coludito rojizo (Uru), Curutié (Br). L 14 cm. Habitat: grassy marshes and wet areas. Upperparts cinnamon-brown. Dark eye-stripe contrasting with paler eyebrow. Underparts white. Rufous wings and tail. Voice: a duetted '*too too tootrrrrrrrrrr…*'.

14 **OCHRE-CHEEKED SPINETAIL** *Poecilurus scuttatus* Pijuí ocráceo (Arg), Estredlinha-preta (Br). L 14 cm. Habitat: undergrowth in woods and forests. Brown upperparts. Buff-white eyebrow. White throat with black spot. Breast cinnamon. Belly white. Voice: variations on '*seet tseewee*', fairly quiet.

15 **SULPHUR-BEARDED SPINETAIL** *Cranioleuca sulphurifera* Curutié ocráceo (Arg), Coludito de garganta amarilla (Uru). L 15 cm. Habitat: reedbeds in marshes. Upperparts to central tail feathers brown. Buff eyebrow. Yellow throat. Face and breast white with fine grey streaking. Outer tail rufous. Voice: a rapid '*trrrrr tirictirictirictiric trrr*'.

◀

Plate 62

Plate 63

OVENBIRDS AND ALLIES (FAMILY FURNARIIDAE)

1 **LESSER CANASTERO** *Asthenes pyrrholeuca* Canastero coludo (Arg, Bol), Canastero chico (Uru), Canastero de cola larga (Ch). L 15 cm. Habitat: Patagonian shrubby steppe. Slender pointed bill. Upperparts greyish-brown. Slight buff eyebrow. Cinnamon chin patch. Underparts pale greyish-brown. Brown wings with cinnamon wing-bar. Tail is centrally darkish brown; outer feathers chestnut. Voice: a '*tweet tweet tiddly frriiiip frriiiip frriiiip*', these last trilled and ascending.

2 **CREAMY-BREASTED CANASTERO** *Asthenes dorbignyi* Canastero rojizo (Arg, Bol), Canastero del norte (Ch). L 16 cm. Habitat: high mountain valleys with scrubby steppe vegetation. Upperparts brown. Grey eyebrow. Chestnut chin spot. Rump chestnut, contrasting with blackish tail. Underparts creamy-white with cinnamon flanks and vent.

3 **CHESTNUT CANASTERO** *Asthenes steinbachi* Canastero castaño (Arg). L 16 cm. Habitat: steep valleys with scrubby vegetation. Brown upperparts. Grey eyebrow. No chin spot, which distinguishes this species from Creamy-Breasted Canastero. Rump chestnut as also two outer pairs of tail feathers. Vent pale cinnamon. Chestnut patch on secondary flight feathers.

4 **SHORT-BILLED CANASTERO** *Asthenes baeri* Canastero chaqueño (Arg), Lenheiro (Br), Canastero de garganta castaña (Uru). L 15 cm. Habitat: woods. Short, quite stout bill. Upperparts earthy grey-brown. Underparts buff-grey. Eyebrow grey. Cinnamon chin spot. Wings brown with cinnamon band. Central tail feathers blackish, outers chestnut. Voice: a high-pitched, fast '*seep seep seepseepseep…*', speeding up to and ending in a trill.

5 **PATAGONIAN CANASTERO** *Asthenes patagonica* Canastero de garganta negra (Arg). L 15 cm. Habitat: scrubby and bushy steppes. Upperparts grey-brown. Throat white with black speckling. Underparts grey. Under tail-coverts pale cinnamon. Dark brown tail with chestnut on outer feathers. Voice: a long descending trill; also up to 20 or more rapid '*chip chip chip chip…*', slowing.

6 **DUSKY-TAILED CANASTERO** *Asthenes humicola* Canastero de pecho rayado (Arg), Canastero (Ch). L 16 cm. Habitat: arid, bushy steppes. Upperparts brown. Whitish eyebrow. Throat white speckled dark. Breast and belly whitish-grey streaked with brown. Flanks and under tail-coverts cinnamon. Lesser wing-coverts rufous. Dark brown tail.

7 **CORDILLERAN CANASTERO** *Asthenes modesta* Canastero pálido (Arg, Bol), Canastero chico (Ch). L 15 cm. Habitat: grasslands and low scrub in Patagonia and mountains. Brownish upperparts. Buff eyebrow. Orange chin spot. Throat and upper breast faintly streaked whitish. Underparts buff-grey. Brown wings with cinnamon bar. Chestnut outer vanes of tail feathers. Carries tail erect; runs on the ground. Voice: a trill which starts slowly and gains speed and pitch.

8 **AUSTRAL CANASTERO** *Asthenes anthoides* Canastero manchado chico (Arg), Canastero del sur (Ch), Canastero dorso manchado (Bol). L 16 cm. Habitat: bushy steppes. Upperparts light brown, heavily streaked black. Whitish eyebrow. Yellow chin spot. Underparts buff with slight dark freckling on breast. Wings brown with cinnamon bar. Tail dark brown with buff outer tips.

9 **CORDOBA CANASTERO** *Asthenes sclateri* Canastero manchado serrano (Arg). L 16 cm. Habitat: high montane grasslands. Upperparts pale brown streaked dark brown. Whitish brow. Orange chin spot. Underparts buff-grey. Brown wings with cinnamon bar; wing-coverts cinnamon. Tail brown with cinnamon on outer feathers.

10 **HUDSON'S CANASTERO** *Asthenes hudsoni* Canastero manchado pajizo (Arg), Canastero listado (Uru). L 18 cm. Habitat: tall grass and sedges. Cinnamon-brown upperparts heavily streaked with dark brown, feathers edged paler. Whitish brow. Orange chin spot. Cinnamon-ochre underparts. Wings with cinnamon band. Long brown tail, outer feathers cinnamon. Voice: a short, ascending trill.

11 **SCRIBBLE-TAILED CANASTERO** *Asthenes maculicauda* Canastero estriado (Arg, Bol). L 17.5 cm. Habitat: usually on the ground in high steppes at 3000 to 4500 m. Upperparts dark brown streaked buff. Chestnut forehead. White throat. Underparts whitish with slight streaking on breast. Brown wings have chestnut bar. Tail brightish brown finely streaked and dotted black. Voice: '*tree tree tree tree…*' accelerating and ending in a trill.

12 **BAY-CAPPED WREN-SPINETAIL** *Spartanoica maluroides* Canastero enano (Arg, Uru). L 13 cm. Habitat: sedges and tall grass. Tiny. White iris. Forehead and crown rufous. Slight whitish eyebrow. Olive-brown back with heavy black streaking at nape and upper back. Underparts whitish, cinnamon wash on breast. Wings with cinnamon at the base of the primaries. Brown tail long, with central feathers having a black streak. Voice: a grasshopper-like buzz, long and tuneless, rising and falling away.

Plate 63

Plate 64

OVENBIRDS AND ALLIES (FAMILY FURNARIIDAE)

1 **LITTLE THORNBIRD** *Phacellodomus sibilatrix* Espinero chico (Arg, Uru). L 15 cm. Habitat: woods, savannahs and fields with scattered trees. Chestnut forehead. Upperparts greyish-brown. Underparts whitish. Brown wings with chestnut wing-coverts. Dark brown tail with chestnut outer feathers. Voice: a duetted series of sharp, piercing, loud and straight '*tee tee tee*'s, where one bird goes faster than the other (three notes for two) so the effect is a '*tee teeter tee teeter teeter tee tee teeter...*'.

2 **RUFOUS-FRONTED THORNBIRD** *Phacellodomus rufifrons* Espinero de frente rojiza (Arg, Bol), Joao-de-pau (Br). L 16.5 cm. Habitat: woods and savannahs. Forehead and fore-crown rufous. Whitish brow. Brown upperparts, wings and tail. Underparts whitish-buff. Voice: has an introductory invitation '*ti ti ti...*', then a duetted long and loud '*titititi tee tee tee tee tee...*'

3 **STREAK-FRONTED THORNBIRD** *Phacellodomus striaticeps* Espinero de frente estriada (Arg, Bol). L 16 cm. Habitat: high, steep valleys and bushy steppe between 1500 and 3000 m. Brown upperparts, more rufous and slightly streaked buff on the forehead and fore-crown. Pale brow. Central tail feathers darker, outers rufous. Brown wings with rufous bar and coverts. Underparts buff-grey. Voice: '*wip wip weep weeep WEEEP weeep weep weep wip wip*' rising and falling in volume and pitch, piercing, loud and almost hysterical.

4 **RED-EYED THORNBIRD** *Phacellodomus erythrophthalmus* Joao-botina (Br). L 17.5 cm. Habitat: edge of the forests. Hills to the coast. Red eye. Reddish-brown upperparts. Forehead, throat and upper breast brighter rufous. Rest of underparts paler than back. Tail chestnut. Voice: duets.

5 **GREATER THORNBIRD** *Phacellodomus ruber* Espinero grande (Arg, Bol), Graveteiro (Br), Tiluchi espino (Bol). L 20 cm. Habitat: woods and gallery forests, always by the water. Yellow eye. Upperparts brown, more chestnut on crown and outer tail feathers. Underparts whitish. Voice: '*poo tew tew tew too too tootootoochoochew*' whistled, descending in pitch but accelerating in tempo.

6 **FRECKLE-BREASTED THORNBIRD** *Phacellodomus striaticollis* Espinero de pecho manchado (Arg, Bol), Tío-tío (Uru), Tio-tio (Br). L 17 cm. Habitat: woods, thickets, savannahs. Reddish-brown forehead and crown. Eyebrow and throat whitish. Back and wings chestnut. Underparts whitish with cinnamon-ochre freckles on breast. Central tail brown, outer feathers chestnut. Voice: four to six loud, clear, deliberate '*peep*'s, shrill and penetrating; also '*whit teeep peepeepeepeepee*' duetted, descending in pitch and volume.

Note: Included in this is a north-western form, the Spot-breasted Thornbird, *Phacellodomus maculipectus*, which some consider a separate species.

7 **LARK-LIKE BRUSHRUNNER** *Coryphistera alaudina* Espinero crestudo (Arg), Crestudo (Bol), Copetón (Uru), Corredor-crestudo (Br). L 15 cm. Habitat: chaco and open woods, savannahs and pastures with scattered shrubs and trees. Erect crest dark. White around eye. Streaked upperparts blackish, feathers edged ochre and whitish. Underparts whitish streaked chestnut. Tail blackish with contrasting rufous base of the outer feathers. Groups of four to six, usually on the ground. Voice: calling is a social thing and consists of a mixed chorus of quiet '*freeeps*', '*chucks*', trills, rolled rrrrr's, '*peep*'s etc.

8 **FIREWOOD-GATHERER** *Anumbius annumbi* Leñatero o Añumbí (Arg), Espinero común (Uru), Cochicho (Br). L 20 cm. Habitat: open woods and scattered trees in open country. Upperparts brown, streaked darker. Forehead chestnut. Whitish brow. Throat white bordered with a line of blackish dots. Underparts buff. Wings brown with cinnamon wash. Central graded tail feathers brown, outers with white terminal spots. Voice: (often duetted) '*tip tip tip tiptiptititrrrrr*', accelerating, repeated.

9 **PEARLED TREERUNNER** *Margarornis squamiger* No local names known. L 15 cm. Habitat: montane forests, woods, in upper vegetation. Rufous upperparts. Long, yellowish brow. Yellowish throat. Below grey-brown with yellowish 'droplets' edged darker; streakier on under tail-coverts.

10 **RUFOUS CACHOLOTE** *Pseudoseisura cristata* Casaca-de-cuoro (Br). L 23 cm. Habitat: woods and open areas with scattered trees. Golden eye. Large, erect crest. Overall bright cinnamon-rufous. Wing tips darker. Voice: duets.

11 **BROWN CACHOLOTE** *Pseudoseisura lophotes* Cacholote castaño (Arg), Caserote (Uru), Coperete (Br). L 26 cm. Habitat: woods, savannahs, open areas with trees. All brownish with a chestnut tinge. Large crest darker. Face and throat more chestnut. Underparts greyer chestnut. Under tail-coverts, rump and tail brighter. Brown wings. Often on the ground, strutting. Voice: a duet of rowdy, screeched, raucous screams, very loud and piercing, ending faster and quieter.

12 **WHITE-THROATED CACHOLOTE** *Pseudoseisura gutturalis* Cacholote pardo (Arg). L 25 cm. Habitat: shrubby steppe in arid areas. Slight crest, often not raised. Greyish-brown above. Small white throat patch with black spotted edge. Greyer underparts. Wings and tail browner. Voice: a series of duetted, clear, far-carrying whistled notes '*teeew teeew teeew ...*', accelerating.

Plate 64

Plate 65

OVENBIRDS AND ALLIES (FAMILY FURNARIIDAE)

1 BUFF-BROWED FOLIAGE-GLEANER *Syndactyla rufosuperciliata* Ticotico común (Arg), Trepador chorreado (Uru), Tirirí (Bol), Trepador-quiete (Br). L 17 cm. Habitat: woods and forests. Upperparts olive-brown. Ochreous eyebrow. White throat. Underparts olive, streaked buff. Wings brownish-rufous. Tail bright chestnut. Voice: a quite slow, rattled '*rikitikitikitikiteekeeteekeetikitikiti*', rising and falling in pitch, slowing in the middle.

2 WHITE-BROWED FOLIAGE-GLEANER *Anabacerthia amaurotis* Ticotico de ceja blanca (Arg), Limpia-folha-miúda (Br). L 16.5 cm. Habitat: lower storey of rainforests. Upperparts rufous-brown with black tips to feathers on nape. Pale streaks on crown. Light buff eyebrow. Underparts olive-brown with paler buff streaking on breast. Bright rufous tail.

3 BLACK-CAPPED FOLIAGE-GLEANER *Philydor atricapillus* Ticotico de cabeza negra (Arg), Limpia-folha-coroada (Br). L 16 cm. Habitat: rainforests. Black forehead, crown and post-ocular streak, the last between two buff lines. Upperparts rufous. Bright rufous neck and underparts. Wings brown. Bright cinnamon-rufous tail.

4 PLANALTO FOLIAGE-GLEANER *Philydor dimidiatus* Limpia-folia-do-brejo (Br). L 17 cm. Habitat: rainforests, gallery forests, woods. Bright rufous overall, paler below. Brow cinnamon, framed by a darkish post-ocular stripe below it, and sides of crown brownish-grey above it. Rare.

5 OCHRE-BREASTED FOLIAGE-GLEANER *Philydor lichtensteini* Ticotico ocráceo chico (Arg), Limpia-folha-ocrácea (Br). L 16 cm. Habitat: the middle storey of rainforests. Grey head with cinnamon-buff eyebrow. Upperparts olive-brown, underparts cinnamon. Chestnut wing-coverts. Central tail feathers olive-brown, outers chestnut.

6 BUFF-FRONTED FOLIAGE-GLEANER *Philydor rufus* Ticotico ocráceo grande (Arg), Ticotico común (Bol), Limpia-folha-testa-baia (Br). L 18.5 cm. Habitat: rainforest canopy. Ochre-buff forehead, eyebrow and underparts. Grey crown, nape and line through the eye. Back olive-brown. Tail and wings rufous. Voice: a series of 12 or so '*chiddle*'s, rising and descending.

7 WHITE-EYED FOLIAGE-GLEANER *Automolus leucophthalmus* Tacuarero ojo blanco (Arg), Barranqueiro-olho-branco (Br). L 18 cm. Habitat: rainforest undergrowth and cane thickets. White eye. Upperparts chestnut. Slight eyebrow cinnamon. White throat. Buff underparts. Flight feathers chestnut with dark inner vanes. Tail rufous-chestnut. Voice: '*chick..chick chickooee, chickooee...*' and a loud and fast '*kireekireekireekireekiree...*', long or short.

8 HENNA-CAPPED FOLIAGE-GLEANER *Hylocryptus rectirostris* Fura-barreira (Br). L 20 cm. Habitat: low at forest edges and gallery forests. Crown and hind-neck bright rufous. Light brown back. Wings and tail rufous. Underparts ochre, paler on throat, darker on flanks. Voice: said to be loud and like a clucky hen, '*ka ka ka*' and '*có-có-có-ray-eh*'.

9 SHARP-BILLED TREEHUNTER *Heliobletus contaminatus* Ticotico de dorso estriado (Arg), Trepadorzinho (Br). L 12 cm. Habitat: lower storey of rainforests. Crown and back brown, former streaked black, latter streaked buff. Long, buff eyebrow. Yellowish throat. Rest of underparts streaked brown and ochreous. Dark brown wings. Chestnut tail.

10 STREAKED XENOPS *Xenops rutilans* Picolezna grande (Arg, Bol), Bico-virado-carijó (Br). L 12.5 cm. Habitat: lower storeys of forests. 'Upturned' bill. Olive-brown crown streaked buff. Buff eyebrow. White malar streak. Back reddish-brown with scattered buff streaks. Underparts olive-brown with pale buff streaks. Rump and tail rufous. Wings cinnamon and black in a bold pattern. Voice: three to six sharp, descending '*peeep*'s.

11 PLAIN XENOPS *Xenops minutus* Picolezna chico (Arg), Picolezna oscuro (Bol), Bico-virado-miudinho (Br). L 11 cm. Habitat: lower storey of rainforests. 'Upturned' bill. Upperparts olive-brown. Buff eyebrow. White malar streak. Rump rufous. Throat whitish. Rest of underparts greyish-brown. Black wing with chestnut band. Tail chestnut and blackish. Voice: a single sharp '*peeeep*' or a accelerating trill descending in pitch.

12 WHITE-THROATED TREERUNNER *Pygarrhichas albogularis* Comesebo (Arg), Comesebo grande (Ch). L 15 cm. Habitat: forests of the Patagonian Andes. Bill appears to turn upwards slightly and has pale lower mandible. Dark brown upperparts. Chestnut rump and tail. Wings boldly patterned dark brown and chestnut. Striking white throat and most of breast. Rest of underparts dark brown with white splotches and dots. Nuthatch-like, it climbs on, over, under and up branches and trunks. Voice: a sharp '*tirick*' and variations on '*tsee tsee tseree*'.

13 RUFOUS-BREASTED LEAFTOSSER *Sclerurus scansor* Ogarití (Arg), Vira-folhas (Br). L 19 cm. Habitat: rainforests. Blackish head and back, the latter with chestnut tone. Chestnut rump. Whitish throat speckled with dark brown. Underparts chestnut with slight buff streaking on chest. Dark wings. Black tail. On or near the ground.

▶

Plate 65

14 SHARP-TAILED STREAMCREEPER *Lochmias nematura* Macuquiño (Arg, Bol), Joao-porca (Br). L 15 cm. Habitat: waterside, by running streams. Overall blackish-brown but whitish brow, and underparts with white 'scaling'. Tail black. Wings blackish. Voice: an accelerating trill, high-pitched and penetrating.

Plate 66

ANTBIRDS (FAMILY FORMICARIIDAE)

1 SPOT-BACKED ANTSHRIKE *Hypoedaleus guttatus* Batará goteado (Arg), Chocao-carijó (Br). L 21 cm. Habitat: dense canopy of rainforests. ♂: upperparts black spotted white. Throat white. Breast black with large white spots. Belly white, grading to buff-cinnamon. Wings brown with white dots. Tail barred black and white. ♀: patterned like ♂ but spotting and barring is buff. Voice: a longish, trilled '*drrrrrrrrew*' rising and falling in pitch and volume. Also a piercing, explosive '*peeeeeeeeooo*'.

2 GIANT ANTSHRIKE *Batara cinerea* Batará gigante (Arg), Coludo copetón (Bol), Matracao (Br). L 35 cm. Habitat: forests and woods. Impressively massive. ♂: topknot black. Upperparts, wings and tail black, barred right across white. Neck and underparts grey. ♀: fore-topknot chestnut, hind part black. Same pattern as ♂ but topside dark brown barred buff-cinnamon, and buff neck and underparts. In spite of the size, remarkably hard to see in thick undergrowth and bushes. Voice: not unmusical: '*rrrrrrrtewtewtewtewtewtewtewtewtewtewtewtip*'. Alarm '*drrrrrrrrchick*'.

3 LARGE-TAILED ANTSHRIKE *Mackenziaena leachi* Batará silbón grande (Arg), Borralhara-assobiadora (Br). L 26 cm. Habitat: middle and lower storey of rainforests where the vegetation is most dense. ♂: black. Upperparts and wings barred and dotted with white. ♀: blackish. Similarly patterned but spotting is rufous on crown and neck, buff on rest of upperparts and even paler on underparts. Both sexes have rufed tail. Voice: a series of 16 or so high-pitched, clear whistles '*feefeefeefeefeefeefeefeefeefee...*', rising then falling back in volume and pitch, followed by a coda of four accelerating and descending notes.

4 TUFTED ANTSHRIKE *Mackenziaena severa* Batará silbón chico (Arg), Borralhara (Br). L 23 cm. Habitat: dense lower vegetation in rainforests. Reddish eye. ♂ entirely sooty black, darker on prominently crested crown. ♀: crested crown rufous. Above and below blackish-brown, heavily banded buff. Tail dark grey, more lightly barred. Voice: a quite slow or deliberate whistled '*feeew feeew feeew feeew feeew feee fee*' loud, penetrating and rising in pitch.

5 GREAT ANTSHRIKE *Taraba major* Batará mayor (Arg), Batará grande (Bol), Choró-boi (Br), Mbatara guasu (Par). L 20 cm. Habitat: woods and forests, savannahs, scrubby woodland, even fairly arid areas. Both sexes have startling red eyes and white underparts. ♂: Black above, white bars on wings and under tail. ♀ is brown where ♂ is black, and lacks barring. Voice: a musical '*tew dididi*', alarm an ugly '*kwehk*'.

6 WHITE-BEARDED ANTSHRIKE *Biatas nigropectus* Batará de pecho negro (Arg), Papo-branco (Br). L 17 cm. Habitat: lower and middle vegetation of rainforests. ♂: head and breast black. White chin extends back under the eye to form a yellowish collar. Underparts olive-brown. Chestnut wing-coverts and tail. Belly cinnamon-grey. ♀: forehead and crown chestnut. Whitish brow. White chin and throat extend to a buff nuchal collar. Breast and belly olive-buff.

7 BARRED ANTSHRIKE *Thamnophilus doliatus* Batará listado (Arg, Bol), Choca-barrada (Br), Che oro para (Par). L 16 cm. Habitat: woods and savannahs. Yellowish eye. ♂: black cap. Upperparts, wings and tail black barred white. Below white barred black. ♀: cap, back, wings and tail chestnut. Face and neck streaked black and white. Underparts buff.

8 BLACK-CAPPED ANTSHRIKE *Thamnophilus schistaceus* Batará apizarrado (Bol). L 15 cm. Habitat: thickets under forests. The form whose range is covered by this work, in spite of the name, has no black cap. ♂: uniform grey, lighter below. ♀: crown chestnut. Olive-brown back. Face and underparts bright buff.

9 VARIABLE ANTSHRIKE *Thamnophilus caerulescens* Batará o choca común (Arg), Choca-da-mata (Br), Batará plomiza (Bol), Curruca azulada (Uru). L 14.5 cm. Habitat: occupies varied habitats from forests and woods to fairly arid scrubland with scattered trees. ♂: cap black. Wings and tail black with white spots on tips of feathers. Dark grey face, and rump, paler breast. Buff lower belly, though this varies, increasing to include breast and even back in western forms. ♀: chestnut cap. Back grey or olive-brown. Breast grey. Cinnamon belly. Wing-coverts dark with white spots. Tail same but spots on tips. Voice: a nasal '*there there there there there...*' up to 12 times; also a single scolding note, raucous and repeated.

10 RUFOUS-CAPPED ANTSHRIKE *Thamnophilus ruficapillus* Batará pardo (Arg, Bol), Curruca bataraz (Uru), Choca-de-chapéu-vermelho (Br). L 17 cm. Habitat: lower vegetation in copses, edge of woods and clearings, and even fairly open scrub country. Both sexes have rufous caps and brown backs. ♂: black-and-white barred breast. Dark tail with white tips to outer feathers. ♀: buff-grey underparts and chestnut tail. Voice: rather musical '*weepweepweepweepweepweepeepeepeep*', fairly fast, rising then falling in volume and pitch.

Plate 66

Plate 67

ANTBIRDS (FAMILY FORMICARIIDAE)

1 SPOT-BREASTED ANTVIREO *Dysithamnus stictothorax* Batará amarillo grande (Arg), Choquinha-de-peito-pintado (Br). L 12 cm. Habitat: lower vegetation in rainforests. Red eye. Crown grey (♂) or chestnut (♀). Back, wings and tail olive-grey. Arc of white dots from behind the eye down around ear-coverts. Wing-coverts black with white spots. White throat. Yellowish underparts freckled with grey on the breast.

2 PLAIN ANTVIREO *Dysithamnus mentalis* Batará amarillo chico (Arg), Burujara pequeña (Bol), Choquinha-lisa (Br). L 11 cm. Habitat: lower storeys of forests. Grey upperparts, more olive on back. An arc of white dots from eye round ear-coverts. Underparts plain yellowish. Wings and tail brown, coverts of the former white-tipped. ♀ differs in chestnut cap and buff spotting on wing-coverts. Voice: a rather nasal, accelerating '*tewp tewp tewp tewp tewp tew tewtew*' rising in pitch, followed by a rapid descending rattled '*tiddledoodledoo*' coda.

3 UNICOLOURED ANTWREN *Myrmotherula unicolor* No local names. L 9.5 cm. Habitat: forests. ♂: plain grey all over but for black throat scaled grey by lighter feather-borders. Plain wing-coverts. ♀: light brown above, olive wash on crown. Below light greenish-buff, paler on throat.

4 STRIPE-BACKED ANTBIRD *Myrmorchilus strigilatus* Batará estriado (Arg), Piu-piu (Br), Hormiguero moteado (Bol). L 16 cm. Habitat: terrestrial under the chaco woods. Upperparts heavily streaked black and chestnut. Pale eyebrow. Wings black and rufous with white streaks. Tail centrally chestnut, then dark, finally white edged on the outer vanes. Underparts creamy. Pale cinnamon flanks. ♂ has a black throat and breast, creamy and slightly streaked in the ♀.

5 BLACK-CAPPED ANTWREN *Herpsilochmus pileatus* Batará plomizo chico (Arg, Bol), Chororozinho-de-chapéu-preto (Br). L 12 cm. Habitat: woods and forests at all levels. ♂: black crown, white eyebrow. Grey back. Black wings with white spots on coverts. Black tail with broad white tip. Greyish underparts, paler on throat. ♀: brown forehead and streaks in the crown. Buff underparts. Voice: a rapid, ascending '*piripiripiripiripipip*', often echoed by ♀.

6 RUFOUS-WINGED ANTWREN *Herpsilochmus rufomarginatus* Batará de alas canelas (Arg, Bol), Chororozinho-de-asa-vermelha (Br). L 11 cm. Habitat: dense canopy of rainforests. Both sexes: broad white eyebrow. Upperparts grey with olive tint. White throat. Yellowish underparts. Wing-coverts with a white wing-bar. Outer parts of flight feathers chestnut, very noticeable in folded wing. Tail black, white-tipped. ♂ has a black cap, ♀ chestnut cap. Voice: '*pew pew pew...*' three to five times, sometimes with a rapid trill in the middle '*pew pew pirrrrr pew pew*'.

7 BLACK-BELLIED ANTWREN *Formicivora melanogaster* No local names. L 14 cm. Habitat: gallery forests and forest edges. Above dark slate-brown. Long white brow. Black below (♂) or buff-white (♀).

8 RUSTY-BACKED ANTWREN *Formicivora rufa* Papa-formigas-vermelho (Br), Choro ñanandy (Par). L 13 cm. Habitat: open gallery forests and woods. ♂: brown above, black below, divided by a white line from bill, over eye, down neck, sides of breast and along flanks, to cinnamon lower flank. Wing-coverts white-tipped. Tail dark brown with narrow white tip. ♀ has white undersides streaked black, otherwise like ♂.

9 BERTONI'S ANTBIRD *Drymophila rubricollis* Batará coludo canela (Arg), Trovoada (Br). L 13 cm. Habitat: rainforests, lower vegetation. ♂: forehead, crown and post-ocular black. Brow, lores and face white. Middle of the back, wing-coverts and tail black, feathers tipped white. Wings and shoulders brown. Underparts rich chestnut. ♀: a toned-down version of ♂, with a white chin. Voice: '*cheep cheep cheep chip chip chewy chewy*', descending in pitch.

10 DUSKY-TAILED ANTBIRD *Drymophila malura* Batará coludo estriado (Arg), Choquinha-carijó (Br). L 13 cm. Habitat: low in rainforests. ♂: upperparts grey, streaked white on head. Throat and breast dark brown streaked white. Buff-grey belly. Wing-coverts black dotted white. Wings and tail dark brown. ♀: a toned-down version of ♂. Buff streaks on head and breast, wings and tail light brown, though wing-coverts as in ♂. Voice: '*tseew tseew tsee tsee ti titititititirrrrr*', ending in a rattle.

11 STREAK-CAPPED ANTWREN *Terenura maculata* Batará enano (Arg), Zídede (Br). L 10 cm. Habitat: rainforest canopy. Streaky black and white head and upper back. Streaky grey and black throat and breast. Chestnut back. Dark brown tail. Yellowish belly. Black wing-coverts are white-tipped forming two wing-bars. ♀ is a wishy-washy version of the ♂ – more buff.

Plate 67

Plate 68

ANTBIRDS (FAMILY FORMICARIIDAE)

1 **MATO GROSSO ANTBIRD** *Cercomacra melanaria* No local names. L 17 cm. Habitat: lower vegetation of forests and woods. ♂: black with white across the back and shoulders, white-tipped wing-coverts. Tail graded. ♀ is grey, paler below, whitish throat and belly. Wings and tail like those of the ♂.

2 **WHITE-BACKED FIRE-EYE** *Pyriglena leuconota* Papa-taoca (Br). L 17.5 cm. Habitat: lower vegetation of rainforests. Bright red eye. ♂ all black with white patch on upper back. ♀ is brown above, buff below. White brow. White spot on back. Dark brown tail. Voice: a series of more than eight quite fast, whistled, '*fee fee fee fee...*'.

3 **WHITE-SHOULDERED FIRE-EYE** *Pyriglena leucoptera* Batará negro (Arg), Borralhara (Br). L 17 cm. Habitat: understorey of rainforests. Red eye. ♂ all black, but with white at the bend of the wing, on upper back and tipping wing-coverts. ♀: upperparts and wings chestnut-brown. Underparts buff-grey. Blackish tail. Voice: a clear, strident, whistled '*feew feew feew feew feew feew feew*', slightly descending in pitch.

4 **SQUAMATE ANTBIRD** *Myrmeciza squamosa* Papa-formigas-de-grota (Br). L 14.5 cm. Habitat: forest. Crown brown. Long white brow. Black face (and throat, ♂). Back, flight feathers and tail rufous (♂ with black spotting on upper back). Wing-coverts dark, tipped pale buff. Below buff-grey. ♂ has black spots in a band across mid-breast, whiter below.

5 **SHORT-TAILED ANTTHRUSH** *Chamaeza campanisona* Tovaca (Arg, Bol), Tovaca-campainha (Br), Tovakusu (Par). L 21 cm. Habitat: on the ground under rainforests where underbrush affords some protection from being seen but allows free running space. Forehead and crown cinnamon-brown. Upperparts olive-grey. White post-ocular streak. White throat with brown spotting. Underparts buff with brown flecking. Brown wings. Tail olive-brown with black subterminal band and white tip. Voice: starts quietly – a long series of '*who too too too too too...*' rising slowly in volume and pitch, and ending almost suddenly in a rapid, laughing, four-note descending coda '*woopwopwupwoo*'. It seems ventriloqual.

6 **RUFOUS-TAILED ANTTHRUSH** *Chamaeza ruficauda* Tovaca-de-rabo-vermelho (Br). L 20 cm. Like the previous species but lacks black on the tail; flanks heavily spotted with black that forms a noticeable band along the sides.

7 **RUFOUS-CAPPED ANTTHRUSH** *Formicarius colma* Galinha-do-mato (Br), Pollito hormiguero (Bol). L 17 cm. Habitat: forests. Crown and nape bright rufous. Above olive. Underparts black, paler on belly. Cinnamon on lesser wing-coverts and at the base of the flight feathers.

8 **VARIEGATED ANTPITTA** *Grallaria varia* Chululú pintado (Arg), Tovacuçu (Br). L 19 cm. Habitat: rainforest floor. Forehead brown streaked white. Crown and nape feathers grey edged black and with narrow white shaft streaking. Upperparts olive with buff streaks on feather shafts. Ear-coverts brown. White moustache. Dark brown throat streaked buff. Underparts scaled buff and cinnamon. Wings and tail rufous. Voice: though terrestrial, calls from elevated perch at dawn and dusk, a series of low-pitched (bottle-blowing) whistles '*whoop whoop hoop Hoop HOOP hoop hoop hoo hoo hoo hoo*', rising in pitch and volume in the middle of the phrase.

9 **WHITE-THROATED ANTPITTA** *Grallaria albigula* Chululú de garganta blanca (Arg), Chululú mediano (Bol). L 20 cm. Habitat: on the ground and low in montane forests. Head bright rufous. White eye-ring. Upperparts olive-brown. White throat stands out. Light grey underparts. Wings and tail cinnamon. Crepuscular (and later). Voice: a two-syllabled, evenly-pitched '*hooop hooop*', slow and deliberate.

10 **SPECKLE-BREASTED ANTPITTA** *Hylopezus ochroleucus* Chululú chico (Arg), Pinto-do-mato (Br). L 14 cm. Habitat: rainforest floor. Eye-ring. Upperparts olive-brown. Whitish throat bordered by dark lines. Buff underparts with black spots, thickest on breast and flanks. Brown wings and tail. Voice: a series of clear whistles '*foo foo few few few fay fay fee*', rising three full notes in pitch.

11 **RUFOUS GNATEATER** *Conopophaga lineata* Chupadientes (Arg), Tokotoko (Par), Chupa-dente (Br). L 12 cm. Habitat: forest undergrowth and bushes. A grey eyebrow (both) ends in a silvery-white tuft (♂). Upperparts brown. Face, throat and breast cinnamon. Whitish belly. Olive flanks. Brown wings and tail. Voice: a fairly quiet, accelerating '*too too to to ta ta te te ti ti titititititititee*', rising in tempo and pitch.

Note: Gnateaters were, and possibly still are, a separate family (Conopophagidae).

Plate 68

Plate 69

TAPACULOS (FAMILY RHINOCRYPTIDAE)

1 **CHESTNUT-THROATED HUET-HUET** *Pteroptochos castaneus* Hued-hued castaño (Ch). L 25 cm. Habitat: damp forests. Forehead, brow, throat, fore-neck and upper breast chestnut. Crown and back black. Upper tail-coverts bright reddish. Belly and flanks barred black and yellowish-white. Voice: a series of low-pitched, hollow-sounding '*too too too too…*'; a contact '*wet-huet*' is quiet and whistled.

2 **BLACK-THROATED HUET-HUET** *Pteroptochos tarnii* Huet-huet or Tapacola (Arg), Hued hued del sur (Ch). L 25cm. Habitat: cool temperate forests in the Patagonian Andes, scrubby ecotonal hillsides. Forehead and crown dark chestnut. Black throat and upperparts. Dark chestnut breast. Black wings and tail. Voice: a deep '*hooopooopooopooopooopooop…*' increasing slightly in pitch, volume and tempo; and an alarm '*wet-wet wet*'.

3 **MOUSTACHED TURCA** *Pteroptochos megapodius* Turca (Ch). L 24 cm. Habitat: scrubby slopes. Above grey-brown except for redder rump, tail and wings. Brow, chin and broad moustachial streak white. Dark face. Light brown breast; belly white, barred brown.

4 **WHITE-THROATED TAPACULO** *Scelorchilus albicollis* Tapaculo (Ch). L 19 cm. Habitat: dense scrub in semi-arid areas. Above brown; lores, brow and throat pure white. Breast and belly barred brown and buff. Voice: onomatopoeic '*tápa, tápa, tápaku, tápakculo, tápaculo*', amongst others.

5 **CHUCAO TAPACULO** *Scelorchilus rubecula* Chucao (Arg, Ch). L 17.5 cm. Habitat: Patagonia's subantarctic beech forests. Eyebrow, fore-neck and upper back chestnut. Underparts barred grey and black. Voice: from very dense vegetation calls a loud '*crrew diddlediddlecoo*', rapid and varied.

6 **CRESTED GALLITO** *Rhinocrypta lanceolata* Gallito copetón (Arg, Bol). L 22 cm. Habitat: scrubland and open woods. Crest and head brown with whitish streaks. Upperparts brown. Whitish underparts. Chestnut flanks. Brown wings. Runs rapidly across tracks and clearings with tail cocked. Voice: '*tirok*' or '*chowok*' occasionally; also a raucous scold '*jeep jeep-jeep*'.

7 **SANDY GALLITO** *Teledromas fuscus* Gallito de las arenas (Arg). L 16 cm. Habitat: arid scrub in sandy areas. Slight pale line through eye. Light cinnamon upperparts, sandy-grey below. Very shy and hard to see.

8 **COLLARED CRESCENT-CHEST** *Melanopareia torquata* Tapaculo-de-colarinho (Br). L 12 cm. Habitat: grassy areas with scattered bushes. Crown, back, wings and tail brown, redder on the last two. Bright cinnamon hind-collar. Long, narrow brow white. Black face, ear-coverts and down the neck. Underparts buff with narrow black collar edged white above it, across upper breast.

9 **OLIVE-CROWNED CRESCENT-CHEST** *Melanopareia maximiliani* Gallito de collar (Arg, Bol). L 15 cm. Habitat: tallish grass or patches of denser scrub. Upperparts olive-grey. Black face and ear coverts. Long buff brow. Cinnamon throat; black band across upper breast. Rest of underparts chestnut. Tail never held aloft. Hard to see though not shy. Voice: a monotone fairly slow trill which drops away slightly at the end; alarm is a rapid disyllabic '*chikchuck*'.

Note: This and the previous species are atypical Tapaculos; their status is very uncertain.

10 **SPOTTED BAMBOOWREN** *Psilorhamphus guttatus* Gallito overo (Arg), Tapaculo-pintado (Br). L 13 cm. Habitat: canebrakes at rainforest edge. Head, back, throat and upper breast grey with well-spaced white dots. Lower breast grades to buff, then cinnamon, and dots here are brown. Chestnut flanks barred dark brown. Wings chestnut with neatly white-tipped coverts forming lines of pearls. Tail brown with little white circles evenly spaced along it. ♀ unspotted. Voice: whistled, low pitch and volume '*roop doop doop hoop hoop…*' for up to five seconds, hollow and remarkably ventriloqual.

Note: Perhaps not a Tapaculo at all, but placed here until its true position is elucidated.

11 **OCHRE-FLANKED TAPACULO** *Eugralla paradoxa* Churrín grande (Arg), Churrín de la Mocha (Ch). L 15 cm. Habitat: dense cane thickets in subantarctic beech forests of the southern Andes. Upperparts, wings and tail dark grey. Cinnamon rump, flanks and vent. Underparts lighter grey. Very secretive. Voice: composed of phrases with an increasing number of explosive '*chek*'s.

12 **MOUSE-COLOURED TAPACULO** *Scytalopus speluncae* Churrín plomizo (Arg), Tapaculo preto (Br). L 11 cm. Habitat: cane thickets at the rainforest edge. Upperparts dark grey, underparts lighter grey. Faint barring. Hard to see. Voice: starts with rapid '*tiptiptiptip*' then a series of measured '*chip*'s or '*tewp*'s and a fast rattling trilled coda.

13 **MAGELLANIC TAPACULO** *Scytalopus magellanicus* Churrín andino-patagónico (Arg), Churrín (Ch), Churrín común (Bol). L 12 cm. Habitat: forests. All blackish-grey with cinnamon wash on under tail-coverts. Shiny white patch on crown and forehead very variable. Voice: a long series of loud, staccato, disyllabic '*k'trip k'trip k'trip k'trip k'trip…*', heard wherever there is a jumble of fallen tree-trunks or dense underbrush in forests where it creeps or scoots around mouse-like.

►

Plate 69

Plate 69 (continued)

14 **WHITE-BROWED TAPACULO** *Scytalopus superciliaris* Churrín de ceja blanca (Arg), Churrín gargantiblanco (Bol). L 12 cm. Habitat: at higher elevations where alders meet grasslands, usually near streams. Brownish upperparts and tail. Grey face, long white eyebrow and large white throat-patch. Grey breast. Voice: a slow, raucous '*tit-tew … tit-tew …*'.

Plate 70 (continued)

16 **SMALL-BILLED ELAENIA** *Elaenia parvirostris* Fiofío pico corto (Arg), Viudita de pico corto (Uru), Bobito copetón pico corto (Bol), Guaracava-de-bico-pequeno (Br), L 15 cm. Habitat: woods, forest edge and taller shrubs. Olive upperparts. Partly hidden white crown-patch. Pale eye-ring. Throat and breast grey. Whitish belly. Two wing-bars. Voice: '*t'p.. t'p.. t'p... we wheeew —we wheeew whirrwe*'.

17 **OLIVACEOUS ELAENIA** *Elaenia mesoleuca* Fiofío oliváceo (Arg), Tuque (Br). L 15 cm. Habitat: forests. Above olivaceous. Below grey; olive flanks. Two buff wing-bars. Brownish tail. Voice: a sharp '*whick —whickeer*'.

18 **SLATY ELAENIA** *Elaenia strepera* Fiofío plomizo (Arg, Bol), Bobito escandaloso (Bol). L 15.5 cm. Habitat: woods on slopes and forest edge. ♂: slate-grey. Two paler wing-bars. Grey breast. White on belly. ♀: more olive back and wing-bars buff. Yellowish-white belly. Voice: '*tip tip t'p trrrriiiiip*'.

19 **LESSER ELAENIA** *Elaenia chiriquensis* Fiofío belicoso (Arg), Bobito copetón moño blanco (Bol). L 13 cm. Habitat: bushes and trees in grassy areas. Very like others of the genus. Slight crest; underparts grey, with yellow wash on belly. Two whitish wing-bars. Voice: '*djíbou*'.

20 **HIGHLAND ELAENIA** *Elaenia obscura* Fiofío oscuro (Arg, Bol), Tucao (Br). L 19 cm. Habitat: forest edge. No crest or crown-patch. Slight eye-ring. Vent yellow. Two creamy wing-bars. Voice: contact '*pyrh*', also '*surely-sheroot*'.

Plate 70

TYRANTS – THE NEW WORLD FLYCATCHERS (FAMILY TYRANNIDAE)

1 **PLANALTO TYRANNULET** *Phyllomyias fasciatus* Mosqueta olivácea (Arg), Piolhinho (Br). L 11 cm. Habitat: forest canopy. Bill black. Upperparts olive, greyer on crown. Brow and eye-ring whitish. Olive-yellow breast. Two olive-yellow wing-bars. Voice: a soft, clear *'pee-poo-pwit'*.

2 **ROUGH-LEGGED TYRANNULET** *Phyllomyias burmeisteri* Mosqueta pico curvo (Arg), Tachurí pico curvo (Bol). L 11cm. Habitat: forest canopy. Quite heavy bill with pale lower mandible. Upperparts olive, crown duller. Throat and breast yellowish-grey, yellowish belly. Two buff wing-bars. Voice: series of high-pitched *'see-see-see-see-see-see...'*.

3 **GREENISH TYRANNULET** *Phyllomyias virescens* Mosqueta corona oliva (Arg). L 12.5 cm. Habitat: forest canopy. Olivaceous upperparts. Face speckled. Whitish brow and throat. Below yellow with olive-grey wash. Two yellow wing-bars.

4 **REISER'S TYRANNULET** *Phyllomyias reiseri* No local names. L 11.5 cm. Habitat: probably gallery forests. Like Greenish Tyrannulet but bright yellow-olive upperparts, greyish crown. Plain yellowish face. Two whitish-yellow wing-bars.

5 **SCLATER'S TYRANNULET** *Phyllomyias sclateri* Mosqueta corona gris (Arg), Tachurí verde grande (Bol). L 12.5 cm. Habitat: canopy of montane forests. Grey crown. Olive back and tail. White brow and throat. Grey breast, white belly. Two broad yellowish wing-bars. Voice: series of harsh notes.

6 **TAWNY-RUMPED TYRANNULET** *Phyllomyias uropygialis* Atrapamoscas rabadilla leonada (Bol). L 11.5 cm. Habitat: edge of woods and montane forests. Crown dark. Short white brow. Olive-brown back grading to tawny brown on rump. Two buff wing-bars. Throat pale grey, breast darker. Yellowish-white belly.

7 **SOUTHERN BEARDLESS TYRANNULET** *Camptostoma obsoletum* Piojito silbón (Arg), Risadinha (Br), Tachurí silbador (Bol), Piojito (Uru). L 10.5 cm. Habitat: open or thin woodland, gardens and forest borders. Upperparts greyish-olive. Crown with untidily raised feathers. Whitish throat. Greyish breast. Yellowish-white belly. Two buff wing-bars. Voice: fast giggling laugh *'teep leeteep leepleepleepleeplee'*, with *'wee-heys'* interspersed.

8 **MOUSE-COLOURED TYRANNULET** *Phaeomyias murina* Piojito pardo (Arg), Tachurí pálido (Bol), Bagageiro (Br). L 12.5 cm. Habitat: woods, gardens and open scrub. Brownish-olive. Whitish brow. Pale throat and greyish breast. Two whitish wing-bars. Voice: a dry, gravely *'jejejejejejeJOO'*.

9 **SCRUB FLYCATCHER** *Sublegatus modestus* Suirirí pico corto (Arg), Tachurí pico ancho (Bol), Viudita gris (Uru). L 14 cm. Habitat: dryish scrub and open woods. Short black bill. White eye-ring. Grey throat and breast contrasting with yellow belly. Voice: a high-pitched *'seepee…peepeepee…seee'*.

10 **SUIRIRI FLYCATCHER** *Suiriri suiriri* Suirirí común (Arg), Suirirí (Uru, Bol), Suiriri-cinzento (Br). L 15 cm. Habitat: woodland, scrub and open areas with scattered trees. Grey head and back, olive wash on latter. Pale rump. Pale eye-line and eye-ring. Ash-grey breast, white belly. Two cream wing-bars. Voice: a buzzing *'bzzeéeeoo'*.

11 **GREY ELAENIA** *Myiopagis caniceps* Fiofío ceniciento (Arg), Bobito gris (Bol). L 12 cm. Habitat: canopy and forest edge. ♂: grey. Narrow eye-ring whitish. Breast grey, white belly. Three white wing-bars. ♀: pale yellow wing-bars. Olive back, yellowish wash on belly.

12 **GREENISH ELAENIA** *Myiopagis viridicata* Fiofío corona dorada (Arg), Guaracava-de-olheiras (Br), Bobito verdoso (Bol). L 13cm. Habitat: forest edge, woods or scattered trees, bushes in open ground. Olive above. White eye-ring. No wing-bars. Throat pale, olive-grey breast, pale yellow belly. Voice: a rough and loud *'cherweep'*.

13 **YELLOW-BELLIED ELAENIA** *Elaenia flavogaster* Fiofío copetón (Arg), Bobito copetón vientre amarillo (Bol), Guyra káva (Par), Guaracava-de-barriga-amarela (Br). L 16 cm. Habitat: open woods and tall, scrubby bushes. Bushy crest; white crown-patch. Slight eye-ring. Upperparts brownish-olive. Yellowish-grey breast; yellowish belly. Two yellowish-white wing-bars. Voice: duet a fast, buzzing *'schzweeew….chiwip-eeew, chiwip-eeew…'*.

14 **LARGE ELAENIA** *Elaenia spectabilis* Fiofío grande (Arg), Guaracava-grande (Br), Fiofío grande corona blanca (Bol). L 18 cm. Habitat: forest borders, woods and shrubby clearings. Slight crest. Upperparts olive-brown. Breast grey. Yellowish belly. Three whitish wing-bars. Voice: *'wheeew…wheeew.. wheeew…p'teeew, p'teew'*.

15 **WHITE-CRESTED ELAENIA** *Elaenia albiceps* Fiofío silbón (Arg), Fío-fío (Ch), Fiofío común (Bol), Viudita chilena (Uru). L 15 cm. Habitat: beech forests in Andean Patagonia and woodlands further north. Crest divided to reveal white crown. Whitish eye-ring. Olive-grey head and upperparts. Breast grey with olive wash. Whitish belly, yellowish flanks. Two yellowish wing-bars. Voice: whistled *'feeew'*, *'fee-wheeew'* and buzzing *'bzeeew'*.

◀

Plate 70

Plate 71

TYRANTS – THE NEW WORLD FLYCATCHERS (FAMILY TYRANNIDAE)

1 **WHITE-THROATED TYRANNULET** *Mecocerculus leucophrys* Piojito gargantilla (Arg), Tachurí de anteojos (Bol). L 13 cm. Habitat: montane forests and woods in the lower vegetation. Above olive-brown. Narrow white brow. Large, puffed-out white throat very noticeable. Greyish breast. Pale yellowish belly. Two buff-cinnamon wing-bars and edges to flight feathers. Voice: a descending '*weedip...pew pew pew*'.

2 **BUFF-BANDED TYRANNULET** *Mecocerculus hellmayri* Piojito de los pinos (Arg), Tachurí enano (Bol). L 11 cm. Habitat: forest canopy and edges. Often in Podocarp woods between 1500 and 2300 m. Above greyish-olive. Lead-grey crown. Brow and throat whitish. Dark brownish wings with pale buff wing-bars. Voice: a series of four clear whistled notes, each inflected upwards.

3 **SOOTY TYRANNULET** *Serpophaga nigricans* Piojito gris (Arg, Bol), Joao-pobre (Br), Yrembe'y (Par), Tiqui-tiqui oscuro (Uru). L 12 cm. Habitat: reeds, banks, floating vegetation. Never away from water. Above brownish-grey. Below pale grey. Black tail which it fans on alighting. Voice: a thin, questioning '*tsewee?*'.

4 **WHITE-CRESTED TYRANNULET** *Serpophaga subcristata* Piojito común (Arg), Tiqui-tiqui (Uru), Piojito vientre blanco (Bol), Turi turi (Par), Alegrinho (Br). L 11 cm. Habitat: forest edge, woods and patches. Upperparts olive-grey, greyer on head. Hidden white crest. Yellow wash on belly. Two whitish wing-bars. Voice: song is '*chip chereep chip*'.

Note: The White-bellied Tyrannulet (*Serpophaga s. munda*) (**5**) is a race of the above with lead-grey upperparts, and no yellow wash on belly. Voice is the same.

6 **GREY-CROWNED TYRANNULET** *Serpophaga griseiceps* Not illustrated. Piojito trinador. L 10.5 cm. Habitat: *Larrea* (creosote bush) and open woods. Until recently thought to be the species above in its typical form. Very slightly smaller – otherwise the same. Voice very different; '*tweet-teeeerrrrrrrr*'.

7 **PLAIN TYRANNULET** *Inezia inornata* Piojito picudo (Arg), Amarelinho (Br), Piojito chico (Bol). L 10 cm. Habitat: chaco woods, forest edge and savannahs. Thickish bill, pale on lower mandible. Plain grey crown and nape. Back grey with olive tinge. White around lores and eye. Greyish breast. Yellowish belly. Two pale buff wing-bars. Voice: '*psee, tee-ee-ee-ee-ee-ee.*'.

8 **GREATER WAGTAIL-TYRANT** *Stigmatura budytoides* Calandrita (Arg), Rabicano (Bol), Papa-moscas-do-sertao (Br). L 14 cm. Habitat: woods, savannahs and scrubby steppes. Shaped like a small mocking-bird. Olive-grey upperparts. Brow and underparts pale yellowish. Tail longish, rounded and broadly tipped white. Voice: a vigorous syncopated duet: '*tit tiddledoo tit tiddledoo tititiddledoo tititiddledoo...*'.

9 **PIED-CRESTED TIT-TYRANT** *Anairetes reguloides* Cachudito de cresta blanca (Ch), Torito gargante (Bol). L 11 cm. Face, fore-crown, throat and ear-coverts black. Double crest white at the base with contrasting black. Above black with streaks from white feather edges. Two white wing-bars. Breast heavily streaked black and white. Flanks finely streaked grey and white.

10 **JUAN FERNANDEZ TIT-TYRANT** *Anairetes fernandezianus* Not illustrated. Cachudito de Juan Fernández (Ch). L 12.5 cm. Conspicuous long, curly crest black, also forehead. Wings with one broad white wing-bar from white greater wing-coverts. Below heavily streaked black on whitish. Endemic to Isla Robinson Crusoe, Juan Fernández Archipelago.

11 **YELLOW-BILLED TIT-TYRANT** *Anairetes flavirostris* Cachudito pico amarillo (Arg), Cachudito del norte (Ch), Torito pico amarillo (Bol). L 11.5 cm. Habitat: arid scrub. Bill with yellowish on lower mandible. Conspicuous black curly crest. Dark iris. Breast heavily streaked with broad black stripes, sharply cut-off at yellowish belly. Voice: a '*prrrrr...prrrrr...*' trill.

12 **TUFTED TIT-TYRANT** *Anairetes parulus* Cachudito pico negro (Arg), Cachudito (Ch), Cachudito de pico negro (Bol). L 10 cm. Habitat: scrubby bush. Bill black. Conspicuous black curly crest. Whitish iris. Breast whitish streaked blackish. Yellowish belly. Voice: a quiet, fast '*ootiddletip*' and a toneless, evenly rolled trill.

13 **MANY-COLOURED RUSH-TYRANT** *Tachuris rubigastra* Tachurí sietecolores (Arg), Siete-colores (Ch), Siete colores (Bol), Siete colores de laguna (Uru), Papa-piri (Br). L 11 cm. Habitat: reedbeds around marshes and lakes. Head black with blue sheen on sides. Partly-hidden red crown-patch. Long yellow brow. Bright olive back. White throat. Yellow breast and belly. Bright pinkish-red under tail-coverts. Curiously trusting for such a beautiful bird. Voice: '*teechew...weh...tichew-t'chew*', followed by a rolling trill.

Plate 71

Plate 72

TYRANTS – THE NEW WORLD FLYCATCHERS (FAMILY TYRANNIDAE)

1 **SHARP-TAILED GRASS-TYRANT** *Culicivora caudacuta* Tachurí coludo (Arg), Papa-moscas-do-campo (Br), Piojito coludo (Bol). L 11 cm. Habitat: tall grasses. Blackish crown. White eyebrow. Dark line through eye. Upperparts dark brown, heavily streaked buff. Long, slender, brown tail feathers pointed. Underparts white, cinnamon flanks. Voice: a thin questioning '*ree?....ree?....reee?..*', varying in number.

2 **BEARDED TACHURI** *Polystictus pectoralis* Tachurí canela (Arg), Tachurí canela enano (Bol), Tachurí (Uru), Papa-moscas-canela (Br). L 10 cm. Habitat: tall grasses and shrubs. ♂: blackish head streaked white. Whitish brow. Nape and back cinnamon-brown. Buff-white underparts. Wings dusky with two buff wing-bars. ♀ lacks dark head. Voice: '*swee... teesweeeerr*' and '*teetititisweeerrrr*', the end dropping to a deeper pitch.

3 **CRESTED DORADITO** *Pseudocolopteryx sclateri* Doradito copetón (Arg), Tricolino (Br). L 10 cm. Habitat: marshes and reeds. Olive-brown upperparts mottled darker. Dark face. Crest feathers longish, raised and parted to expose yellow stripe. Dark wings with two whitish wing-bars and whitish trim to flight feathers. Underparts bright yellow. Voice: a soft '*sick*' and '*tsik-tsik-tseelee*'.

4 **DINELLI'S DORADITO** *Pseudocolopteryx dinellianus* Doradito pardo (Arg), Doradito pico chico (Bol). L 11 cm. Habitat: reeds and sedges or bushes near water. Upperparts olive-brown, browner on crown and face. Below strong yellow. Wings (with slight buff wing-bars) and tail brown. Voice: a soft '*redek...redek...redidek*'.

5 **SUBTROPICAL DORADITO** *Pseudocolopteryx acutipennis* Doradito oliváceo (Arg, Bol). L 11.5 cm. Habitat: marshes, reeds and sedges, or bushes near water. Slight crest. Above olivaceous. Below bright yellow. Wings browner with two greyish wing-bars.

6 **WARBLING DORADITO** *Pseudocolopteryx flaviventris* Doradito común (Arg, Bol), Doradito de las pajas (Uru), Pájaro amarillo (Ch). L 12 cm. Habitat: in reeds at edges of marshes. Upperparts brown. Darker through face and on forehead. Underparts yellow. Brown wings with coverts edged buff. Tail brown. Voice: a quiet: '*tup..tup..tip.teroo*' or simply '*tup...tip*'.

7 **TAWNY-CROWNED PYGMY-TYRANT** *Euscarthmus meloryphus* Barullero (Arg), Barulhento (Br), Mosqueta de copete (Uru), Atrapamoscas copete castaño (Bol). L 11 cm. Habitat: bushy areas, scrub and edge of woods. Upperparts dull brown, darker on wings and tail. Hidden crown-patch orangy. Throat and breast greyish-white. Yellow wash on belly. Voice: calls singly a fast '*kwitrr*' or duets '*kwittikweer kwittikweer...*'.

8 **RUFOUS-SIDED PYGMY-TYRANT** *Euscarthmus rufomarginatus* No local names. L 12 cm. Habitat: savannahs with scattered bushes. Above brownish. Central crown with reddish-edged feathers. White throat; rest of underparts pale yellow. Buff flanks and under tail-coverts. Wings with two buff wing-bars. Long tail dusky brown.

9 **GREY-HOODED FLYCATCHER** *Mionectes rufiventris* Ladrillito (Arg). L 14 cm. Habitat: rainforests. Grey hood. Upperparts olive-brown. Underparts rufous, olive-washed on breast. Voice: like a reedy, accelerating mewing.

10 **SEPIA-CAPPED FLYCATCHER** *Leptopogon amaurocephalus* Mosqueta corona parda (Arg), Cabeçudo (Br), Tachurí cabeza parda (Bol). L 13 cm. Habitat: lower vegetation in woodland and forests. Brown crown. Dark ear-patch. Olive back, tail browner. Pale yellowish-grey throat, olive-yellow breast, pale yellowish belly. Two bold yellow-buff wing-bars and edging to flight feathers. Voice: '*twee-errrrrkk*' or '*dret-deedeedeedeedeedee deww*'.

11 **SOUTHERN BRISTLE-TYRANT** *Phylloscartes eximius* Mosqueta media luna (Arg), Barbudinho (Br). L 11 cm. Habitat: lower vegetation of forest edge. Bold head pattern: long, whitish, speckled eyebrow down around behind a 'half-moon' of black-tipped ear-coverts. Grey crown. Rest of upperparts olive. Wings and tail 'dirtier'. Throat white. Breast dirty yellow. Bright yellow belly. Perches very upright.

12 **YELLOW TYRANNULET** *Phylloscartes flaveolus* Mosqueta ceja amarilla (Arg), Atrapamosca amarillo (Bol), Marianinha-amarela (Br). L 11 cm. Habitat: thickets and cane on the edge of woods and the lower vegetation of forests. Brow and underparts yellow. Upperparts yellowish brownish-olive. Dark wings with two yellow wing-bars and flight feathers edged yellow. Voice: calls in duet: '*brrrr trípirew trípirew trípirew trípirew...*' seven to as many times again.

13 **MOTTLE-CHEEKED TYRANNULET** *Phylloscartes ventralis* Mosqueta común (Arg), Mosqueta chica olivácea (Bol), Borboletinha-do-mato (Br). L 12 cm. Habitat: forest canopy and edge. Upperparts olive. Yellowish brow and eye-ring. Slightly mottled cheeks. Whitish throat, greyish-yellow breast and yellow belly. Two bold wing-bars and borders of flight feathers yellow. Voice: a buzzing '*bzheeew...bzh..b*'

14 **SERRA DO MAR TYRANNULET** *Phylloscartes difficilis* Estalinho (Br). L 11 cm. Habitat: thickets at the edge of montane forests. Above uniform bright olive-brown, contrasting with ash-grey below. White eye-ring, white line before the eye and white throat. Pale yellow under tail-coverts. Dark-tipped ear-coverts.

▶

Plate 72

15 SAO PAOLO TYRANNULET *Phylloscartes paulistus* Mosqueta de oreja negra (Arg). L 11 cm. Habitat: lower storeys and borders of forests. Upperparts and breast olive. Long yellow brow from forehead and down behind black ear-coverts. Belly yellow. Wings and tail brownish. Two vague yellowish wing-bars and yellow trim to flight feathers. Voice: a whistled '*fwee-eet*'.

16 BAY-RINGED TYRANNULET *Phylloscartes sylviolus* Mosqueta cara canela (Arg). L 11 cm. Habitat: canopy and forest edge. Pale eye. Upperparts olivaceous. Eye-ring and foreface bright cinnamon. Below whitish. Throat yellowish. Longish, slender, half-cocked, dusky tail.

Plate 73

TYRANTS – THE NEW WORLD FLYCATCHERS (FAMILY TYRANNIDAE)

1 SOUTHERN ANTPIPIT *Corythopis delalandi* Mosquitero (Arg), Estalador (Br), Mosquitero verdoso (Bol). L 13 cm. Habitat: forests. Olive upperparts. Throat and belly white. Black band across breast. Voice: a shrilly high-pitched whistled '*pewrrréepirrréepipee*'.

2 EARED PYGMY-TYRANT *Myiornis auricularis* Mosqueta enana (Arg, Bol), Miudinho (Br). L 9 cm. Habitat: understorey of forest borders. Black on ear-coverts and under eye. Upperparts olive with grey band across hind-neck. Whitish throat streaked blackish. Underparts yellow. Dark wings and tail, all with outer vanes yellow. Two faint yellow wing-bars. Voice: '*prreeeep*' and '*tip tip tip treeep*'.

3 DRAB-BREASTED PYGMY-TYRANT *Hemitriccus diops* Mosqueta de anteojos (Arg), Olho-falso (Br). L 11 cm. Habitat: cane thickets on forest edge. Upperparts olive. White eye-ring and spot on lores. Underparts grey tinged mauve. Indistinct white spot on upper breast. Dark wings with flight feathers edged paler. Voice: a dry, double, mechanical trill '*trrrr trrrr*'.

4 EYE-RINGED TODY-TYRANT *Hemitriccus orbitatus* Tiririzinho-do-mato (Br). L 11.5 cm. Habitat: lower and middle storey of rainforests. Plain olive above. White eye-ring. Yellowish below, streaked olive on throat, olive wash on breast and yellow belly. Voice: '*teerreet*' and '*teereerreet*'.

5 BROWN-BREASTED BAMBOO-TYRANT *Hemitriccus obsoletus* No local name. L 11 cm. Habitat: cane thickets and undergrowth of montane forests. Above brownish-olive. Buff eye-ring, throat and breast. Belly whitish, yellower under tail-coverts. Voice: a series of '*tick*'s.

6 PEARLY-VENTED TODY-TYRANT *Hemitriccus margaritaceiventer* Mosqueta ojo dorado (Arg), Ñakyra'i (Par), Sebinho-de-olho-de-ouro (Br), Pico chato vientre perla (Bol). L 10 cm. Habitat: thickets on the edge of forests and woods. Longish bill. Wicked pale golden eye. Upperparts dirty olive. Grey head. Throat and breast whitish with grey streaking. Brownish wings with outer vanes of flight feathers yellowish-green. Two buff wing-bars. Often in pairs. Voice: '*tip…tip…tiptrrtrrrrr*'.

7 OCHRE-FACED TODY-FLYCATCHER *Todirostrum plumbeiceps* Mosqueta cara canela (Arg, Bol), Ferreirinho-de-cara-canela (Br). L 9 cm. Habitat: dense forest edge and thick cane. Crown grey. Face and throat cinnamon. Olive upperparts. Below whitish. Two buff-cinnamon wing-bars on darkish coverts. Voice: '*tip…tiptrurew……rrreew – prrrweprue*'.

8 RUSTY-FRONTED TODY-FLYCATCHER *Todirostrum latirostre* No local names. L 10 cm. Habitat: dense thickets at rainforest edge and in clearings. Above greyish-olive. Brown crown. Buff lores and around eye. White throat streaked grey. Breast and flanks olivaceous. White belly. Dark wings with two buff wing-bars. Flight feathers edged yellowish. Grey tail, feathers edged olive.

9 COMMON TODY-FLYCATCHER *Todirostrum cinereum* Titirijí lomicenizo (Bol), Relógio or Ferreirinho (Br). L 9 cm. Habitat: open woods, gardens, hedges and forest edge. Pale eye in a dark face. Pale grey nape; olive wash on back and rump. Wings dark, feathers noticeably edged yellow. Black tail, outers tipped white. Yellow underparts. Voice: includes repeated trills, and clicking.

10 LARGE-HEADED FLATBILL *Rhamphotrigon megacephala* Picochato cabezón (Arg, Bol). L 13 cm. Habitat: understorey of forests, especially with canes. Darkish head with yellowish brow and eye-ring. Olive above. Yellow below with olive-yellow breast. Two buff-cinnamon wing-bars. Voice: a two-note call with a long pause between notes '*wheeew …………… whoo*'.

11 YELLOW-OLIVE FLYCATCHER *Tolmomyias sulphurescens* Picochato sulfuroso (Arg, Bol), Bico-chato-de-orelha-preta (Br). L 15 cm. Habitat: forests, forest edge, woods. Olive-grey head with whitish around face and throat. Olive upperparts. Yellow below, greyer on breast. Two yellow wing-bars. Tail brownish with outer edge buff. Voice: a sharply ascending, questioning '*schzweeee?*' or '*jewee?*' repeated five or so times.

12 WHITE-THROATED SPADEBILL *Platyrinchus mystaceus* Picochato chico (Arg), Patinho (Br), Pico chato gargantiblanco (Bol), Jurupe'i (Par). L 10 cm. Habitat: forest undergrowth. Wide bill with pale lower mandible. Buff eye-line and eye-ring. Post-ocular and malar stripes blackish. Buff below the eye – all this makes a bold face pattern. Hidden crown yellow. Cinnamon-grey upperparts. Whitish throat. Cinnamon below. Short, dusky brown tail. Voice: a fast '*twee-dee-deetteeteet teeteet tweeteet teetwteet*'.

13 RUSSET-WINGED SPADEBILL *Platyrinchus leucoryphus* Picochato grande (Arg), Patinho gigante (Br). L 12.5 cm. Habitat: undergrowth of rainforests. Very wide, flat bill mostly yellowish. Eye-line whitish. Post-ocular stripe curling to meet malar stripe, both darkish brown. Upperparts olive-brown. Wing-coverts broadly edged rufous.

Plate 73

Plate 74

TYRANTS – THE NEW WORLD FLYCATCHERS (FAMILY TYRANNIDAE)

1 BRAN-COLOURED FLYCATCHER *Myiophobus fasciatus* Mosqueta chorreada (Arg), Filipe (Br), Atrapamosca pechirayado (Bol). L 12.5 cm. Habitat: dense vegetation in woods, scrubland and the edge of forests. Brown head and back. Underparts whitish with brown streaking on breast. Two buff wing-bars. Voice: a slowish *'pewee teeroo....peedledee tewoo...'* and fast, rolling *'pwee tittletittletittletittletit'*.

2 EULER'S FLYCATCHER *Lathrotriccus euleri* Mosqueta parda (Arg), Enferrujado (Br), Frailecito alirufo (Bol). L 13 cm. Habitat: lower storeys and edges of forests. Whitish lower mandible. Narrow eye-ring. Upperparts olive-brown. Throat whitish. Breast yellowish-olive. Yellowish belly. Two buff wing-bars. Voice: *'dzheeew.. dzheeew...'* or fast, buzzing, scolding *'bzhewbzhewbzhewbzhew...'*.

3 CINNAMON FLYCATCHER *Pyrrhomyias cinnamomea* Birro chico (Arg), Atrapamoscas acanelado (Bol). L 12.5 cm. Habitat: brush on edge of forests and woods. Chestnut head. Back olive-chestnut. Underparts chestnut. Two bright chestnut wing-bars, chestnut patch on inner flight feathers. Voice: rattled *'drrrrrr'*.

4 GREATER PEWEE *Contopus fumigatus* Burlisto gris grande (Arg), Atrapamoscas ahumado (Bol). L 17 cm. Habitat: edges of montane forests and woods. Slight crest. Overall grey, browner upperparts, paler throat and belly. Two faint wing-bars. Voice: calls at dawn *'per-wheeer'*; also repeated *'pip-pip-pip'*.

5 EASTERN WOOD-PEWEE *Contopus virens* Not illustrated. No local names. L 16 cm. Habitat: woods and forests. Pinkish-yellow lower mandible. Above dark greyish-olive. White throat and belly, olive-grey across breast. Tail blackish. Two wing-bars whitish. Migrant from North America.

6 TROPICAL PEWEE *Contopus cinereus* Burlisto gris chico (Arg, Bol), Papa-moscas-cinzento (Br). L 13.5 cm. Habitat: forest edge. Crown and back brownish-grey. Breast grey. Throat and belly whitish. Two whitish wing-bars. Voice: *'whip-whip-whip-whip'* or *'tips'* or *'dips'*. Shivers tail.

7 ALDER FLYCATCHER *Empidonax alnorum* Mosqueta boreal (Arg), Atrapamoscas pálido (Bol). L 14 cm. Habitat: clearings with bushes in light woodland. Greyish-olive upperparts. White throat. Greyish breast. Yellowish belly. Two whitish wing-bars. Voice: *'whit'* and *'tip'*; song *'free-bréw'*.

8 FUSCOUS FLYCATCHER *Cnemotriccus fuscatus* Mosqueta de ceja blanca (Arg), Guaracavuçu (Br), Atrapamoscas fusco (Bol). L 14 cm. Habitat: woods and forest undergrowth. All black bill. Yellowish-buff eyebrow. Upperparts brown. Throat white. Brownish-grey breast. Two pale cinnamon wing-bars. Pale yellowish belly. Voice: a high-pitched *'fee.... feee....'*.

9 BLACK PHOEBE *Sayornis nigricans* Pitajo negruzco (Arg). L 18 cm. Habitat: always by mountain streams on rocks and low bushes. All sooty black, white on lower belly, wing-coverts and flight feathers. Voice: *'feee...... feebee...feebee......feeep...fee..'*

10 VERMILION FLYCATCHER *Pyrocephalus rubinus* Churrinche (Arg, Uru), Saca-tu-real (Ch), Hijo del sol or Atrapamoscas sangre de toro (Bol), Guyra tata (Par), Verao or Príncipe (Br). L 14 cm. Habitat: open areas with scattered trees, woodland edge. ♂: blackish upperparts. Head and underparts bright red. Blackish wings and tail. ♀: upperparts greyish. Below whitish streaked brown. Voice: a musical *'pi pi pi pi prrreeee'* rising in pitch and volume, often at night.

11 D'ORBIGNY'S CHAT-TYRANT *Ochthoeca oenanthoides* Pitajo canela (Arg, Bol), Pitajo rojizo (Ch). L 15 cm. Habitat: bushy areas and copses of small trees at elevations of 2000 m and more. Eyebrow white. Grey-brown upperparts. Greyish throat. Underparts cinnamon-rufous. Tail brownish, outer vane white. Voice: fairly musical *'reeka - teeekera....reeka - teekera....'*.

12 PATAGONIAN TYRANT *Ochthoeca parvirostris* Peutrén (Arg), Viudita (Ch). L 13 cm. Habitat: from the canopy to thick undergrowth and edges of Southern-beech woods in the Patagonian Andes. Short bill. Head grey. Back brownish-grey. Grey breast, whitish belly. Two chestnut wing-bars. Voice: high-pitched whistled *'feee.... fefeeew feee - fefeeew'*.

13 WHITE-BROWED CHAT-TYRANT *Ochthoeca leucophrys* Pitajo gris (Arg, Ch). L 14.5 cm. Habitat: arid regions from 2000 m upwards. Long eyebrow white. Grey crown, browner back. Underparts pale grey, whiter on belly. Wings with two fine cinnamon wing-bars. Dark tail, outermost pair of tail feathers with white outer vane. Voice: a sharp *'keeew'*.

14 STREAK-THROATED BUSH-TYRANT *Myiotheretes striaticollis* Birro canela (Arg), Atrapamosca (Bol). L 22 cm. Habitat: bushy scrub valleys. Brown above. Whitish brow. Face white, heavily striped dark. Wings with cinnamon-rufous band and cinnamon under wing. Breast and rest of underparts bright cinnamon. Tail: central pair of feathers blackish, rest basally cinnamon.

15 RUFOUS-WEBBED TYRANT *Myiotheretes rufipennis* Birro gris (Arg). L 21 cm. Habitat: low scrub and rocky slopes at 3000 to 4000 m. Above ashy grey with paler brow and underparts, to white on belly. Under wing cinnamon. Flight feathers rufous. Rare.

Plate 74

Plate 75

TYRANTS – THE NEW WORLD FLYCATCHERS (FAMILY TYRANNIDAE)

1 **FIRE-EYED DIUCON** *Xolmis pyrope* Diucón (Arg, Ch). L 19 cm. Habitat: edge of Antarctic beech forests and transition to steppes where there are larger bushes. Fiery red eye. Grey: darker on crown, back and wings; paler breast and flanks; very pale grey belly. White throat and under tail-coverts. Tail very pale grey. Voice: a quiet '*peet*'.

2 **GREY MONJITA** *Xolmis cinerea* Monjita cenicienta (Arg), Monjita gris (Bol), Escarchero or Viuda Mora (Uru), Maria-branca, Primavera (Br). L 22 cm. Habitat: savannahs, open areas with scattered trees, woodland edge. Upperparts grey. Narrow white forehead and line under the eye. Dark moustache. White chin and throat. Pale grey breast grading to white belly. Wings: coverts finely tipped white. White patch at the base of black primaries. Black tail narrowly white-tipped. Perches exposed on look-outs.

3 **BLACK-CROWNED MONJITA** *Xolmis coronata* Monjita coronada (Arg), Monjita de corona negra (Bol), Viudita de boina negra (Uru). L 20 cm. Habitat: open woods or bushy steppe. Blackish crown; white supercilliary from forehead to nape forming a ring around crown. Throat and underparts white. Post-ocular black. Grey back. Wings black with white on tips of coverts and a patch in the primaries. Black tail. Perches high (often on telephone wires).

4 **WHITE-RUMPED MONJITA** *Xolmis velata* Noivinha-branca (Br). L 20 cm. Habitat: open areas around dwellings and farms. Head white, pale grey on hind-neck. Dirty grey back, white rump and base of tail. Terminal half of tail black. Underparts white. Wing with white stripe along base of the flight feathers. Pairs, perch up.

5 **BLACK-AND-WHITE MONJITA** *Xolmis dominicana* Monjita dominicana (Arg), Noivinha-rabo-preto (Br), Viudita blanca de cola negra (Uru). L 20 cm. Habitat: low-lying grasslands near water. ♂ white with black tail and wing, white patch on primaries. ♀: grey crown, nape and upper back. Rest of head, rump, underparts and scapulars white. Wings and tail as in ♂. Perches up on look-outs.

6 **WHITE MONJITA** *Xolmis irupero* Monjita blanca (Arg, Bol), Noivinha (Br), Viudita blanca común (Uru). L 17 cm. Habitat: open areas. Strikingly white with black bill, eye, tips of tail and primaries. Voice: calls softly at dawn and dusk. Perches very visibly on look-outs (bushes and small trees).

7 **RUSTY-BACKED MONJITA** *Neoxolmis rubetra* Monjita castaña (Arg). L 19 cm. Habitat: arid, bushy steppe. Chestnut crown, upperparts and flanks. Long white eyebrow. Face, throat and breast white with blackish streaking. Rest of underparts white. Black and chestnut wings, coverts and inner flight feathers pale-edged. Tail blackish with white outer vane of outer feathers.

Note: Some consider the Salinas Monjita (*N. r. salinarum*) a valid species. Habitat: edge of salt-flats, semi-open scrubland. It is smaller and has almost no streaking on face and breast, much whiter wing, no rufous on flanks and grey (paler) tail broadly black-tipped. Perches on look-outs and chases prey on the ground.

8 **CHOCOLATE-VENTED TYRANT** *Neoxolmis rufiventris* Chocolate (Arg), Cazamoscas chocolate (Ch), Gaúcho-chocolate (Br). L 23 cm. Habitat: in summer on open steppe with some grass or shrubs. Flocks and migrates to agricultural land in winter. Front half of the bird grey, browner on crown and back. Black face. Rufous belly and flanks. Wings: dark primaries, reddish secondaries white-tipped, pale coverts – quite a flashy show and falcon-like in flight. Black tail with outer border white. Voice: '*weepweepweepweepweepweep...*'. Perches on any available look-out (bush, fence) and pounces on prey on the ground.

9 **BLACK-BILLED SHRIKE-TYRANT** *Agriornis montana* Gaucho serrano (Arg), Mero gaucho (Ch), Arriero andino (Bol). L 22 cm. Habitat: rocky high mountain steppe. Black bill. Grey-brown upperparts and wings. Throat whitish with brown stripes. Light brownish-grey below, paler on belly. Tail: central pair grey-brown, rest white. Voice: an occasional quiet '*whee-wheeeee*' or simply '*wheeeee*', rising.

10 **WHITE-TAILED SHRIKE-TYRANT** *Agriornis andicola* Gaucho andino (Arg, Bol), Mero de la puna (Ch). L 26 cm. Habitat: high mountain steppe. Yellow lower mandible. Above and wings greyish-brown. Throat whitish striped dark brown. Greyish-brown breast. Greyish-white belly. All outer tail feathers white, central pair brown.

11 **GREAT SHRIKE-TYRANT** *Agriornis livida* Gaucho grande (Arg), Mero (Ch). L 27.5 cm. Habitat: arid sub-Andean scrub and valleys. Large, hook-tipped bill with lower base yellow. Upperparts dull greyish-brown with slight darker streaking. Whitish throat striped dark. Grey breast. Cinnamon belly. Dark wings. Tail blackish with white outer vane of outer feathers, and pale tip. Terrestrial, though it perches on available look-outs like fences and bushes.

12 **GREY-BELLIED SHRIKE-TYRANT** *Agriornis microptera* Gaucho común (Arg, Bol), Mero de Tarapacá (Ch). L 24 cm. Habitat: upland bushy steppe, comes down to fields to winter. Large bill. Whitish brow. White throat striped greyish-brown. Grey underparts, paler on belly. Brown wings, secondaries edged whitish. Dark tail with white outer vane of outer feathers.

▶

Plate 75

13 LESSER SHRIKE-TYRANT *Agriornis murina* Gaucho chico (Arg), Monjita parda (Bol). L 18 cm. Habitat: bushy terrain. Small. Bill less heavy (even proportionally) than other shrike-tyrants. Brownish-grey above. Eyebrow buff. Throat striped dark on whitish. Sandy-grey breast, creamy belly. Wing-coverts edged paler and secondaries edged whitish. Outer edge of dark, dusky tail finely white. Voice: an occasional '*phooeeay*' descending.

Plate 76

TYRANTS – THE NEW WORLD FLYCATCHERS (FAMILY TYRANNIDAE)

1 SPOT-BILLED GROUND-TYRANT *Muscisaxicola maculirostris* Dormilona chica (Arg, Bol), Dormilona chica (Ch). L 14 cm. Habitat: open, bare, scrubby areas in high mountain terrain and valleys. Pale spot at base of lower mandible. Short, pale brow from eye to bill. Sandy-brown upperparts; wing-coverts darker, edged cinnamon. Underparts whitish-buff, paler on throat. Tail blackish, edged white on outer vanes of outer feathers.

2 LITTLE GROUND-TYRANT *Muscisaxicola fluviatilis* Dormilona enana (Arg, Bol). L 14 cm. Habitat: mostly lowlands on river bars and short grass by water. Like the Spot-billed Ground-Tyrant, has a pale spot at the base of the bill. Plain head – no brow. Sandy-grey upperparts, darker wings. A touch of rufous in the wing. White belly. Short tail.

3 DARK-FACED GROUND-TYRANT *Muscisaxicola macloviana* Dormilona cara negra (Arg), Dormilona común (Bol), Dormilona tontita (Ch). L 16 cm. Habitat: valleys by water or near the sea. Blackish forehead and face. Brownish-grey upperparts. Pale grey underparts. Lighter throat. Tail black narrowly edged white on outer vane of outer feathers. Rapidly fans tail.

4 CINNAMON-BELLIED GROUND-TYRANT *Muscisaxicola capistrata* Dormilona de corona castaña (Arg, Bol), Dormilona rufa (Ch). L 17 cm. Habitat: breeds at rock-falls at foot of cliffs, heaps of tumbled boulders; winters on Andean meadows and steppes. Forehead and lores black. Crown chestnut. Upperparts brown. Pale throat. Greyish breast. Cinnamon flanks and belly. Dark wings. Tail as in all, blackish, white on outermost vanes. Voice: a long, clicking '*cooreecooreecooree...*' call in display flight.

5 RUFOUS-NAPED GROUND-TYRANT *Muscisaxicola rufivertex* Dormilona gris (Arg), Dormilona cenicienta (Bol), Dormilona de nuca rojiza (Ch). L 17 cm. Habitat: high-mountain meadows and rocky terrain. Upperparts grey but for chestnut patch on hind-crown (very pale in some races). Slight brow. Underparts very pale whitish-grey. Tail blackish, outer vanes of outer feathers white. Voice: '*see-hee, he-hee*' and variations. When it lands or stops running it fans tail very rapidly two or three times.

6 PUNA GROUND-TYRANT *Muscisaxicola juninensis* Dormilona de la puna (Arg, Ch, Bol). L 16 cm. Habitat: at high elevations in arid montane steppe. Smallish. Slight pale eyebrow. Crown chestnut. Upperparts sandy-grey. Pale grey underparts. Black tail with outermost web white, fanned rapidly two or three times when bird comes to a halt.

7 WHITE-BROWED GROUND-TYRANT *Muscisaxicola albilora* Dormilona de ceja blanca (Arg, Bol, Ch). L 17 cm. Habitat: montane steppes. Narrow white eyebrow. Brownish-grey fore-crown grades into chestnut hind-crown. Upperparts brownish-grey, pale grey below. Black tail with white outermost vanes. Fans tail rapidly when it stops.

8 CINEREOUS GROUND-TYRANT *Muscisaxicola cinerea* Dormilona cenicienta (Arg, Ch), Dormilona gris (Bol). L 16.5 cm. Habitat: at high elevations on *puna*. Black bill. Narrow white brow from eye forward. Crown grey. Overall grey, darker and with brownish wash on upperparts, paler below. Whitish throat. Black tail with white on outer vane of outer feathers.

9 WHITE-FRONTED GROUND-TYRANT *Muscisaxicola albifrons* Dormilona gigante (Ch, Bol). L 21.5 cm. Habitat: high Andean grasslands near cliffs. White forehead and slight brow. Central crown reddish-brown, rest just tinted. Upperparts darkish grey-brown, getting blacker on lower back and rump. Pale grey below, whiter on belly. Darkish wings with inner flight feathers edged white, coverts ditto. Black tail, outer edge white.

10 OCHRE-NAPED GROUND-TYRANT *Muscisaxicola flavinucha* Dormilona de nuca amarilla (Arg, Bol), Dormilona fraile (Ch). Habitat: high mountain meadows. L 20 cm. Large. Lores and forehead white, grey crown. Yellow nuchal patch. Grey above, whitish-grey below. Blackish tail with white outermost vanes fanned frequently.

11 BLACK-FRONTED GROUND-TYRANT *Muscisaxicola frontalis* Dormilona frente negra (Arg, Ch), Dormilona corona negra (Bol). L 19 cm. Habitat: high mountain terrain, descends after snow-storms. Bill longish and slightly decurved. Forehead and mid-crown black. White lores. Above grey, blackish on rump. Underparts dirty white, cleaner on throat. Tail as in all the genus, dark with narrow white outer edge.

12 ANDEAN NEGRITO *Lessonia oreas* Not illustrated. Sobrepuesto andino (Arg), Negrito (Bol), Colegial del norte (Ch). L 13 cm. Habitat: barren flats near water, between 3000 and 4000 m. ♂ black with a pale cinnamon-rufous back like a small mantle. Otherwise like Austral Negrito (**13**) but white at the base of the flight feathers visible in flight. ♀ is darker below than Austral Negrito.

▶

Plate 76

13 AUSTRAL NEGRITO *Lessonia rufa* Sobrepuesto (Arg), Negrito (Bol, Uru, Br), Colegial (Ch, Br).
L 12 cm. Habitat: lake shores or beaches. ♂ black with chestnut-rufous back in the shape of a small cape.
♀: head and wing-coverts brownish-grey, slight eyebrow. Brown back. Dark tail and flight feathers.
Whitish-buff underparts slightly streaked. Usually silent, but ♂ sings '*sipsipsipsip - sereen*' in display flight.
Terrestrial. Pursues its insect prey by running over open ground; when it comes to a halt it flicks the wings
fast two or three times.

Plate 77

TYRANTS – THE NEW WORLD FLYCATCHERS (FAMILY TYRANNIDAE)

1 CINEREOUS TYRANT *Knipolegus striaticeps* Viudita cenicienta (Arg). L 13 cm. Habitat: chaco
woods and clearings. ♂: bright red eye. All darkish grey, darker on crown and face. Two grey wing-bars.
♀: grey back, chestnut forehead, crown, nape and rump. Throat and breast buff with fine grey streaks on
breast. Rest of underparts whitish. Two cinnamon wing-bars. Dark tail with chestnut on outer feathers.
Voice: in ♂s display, they rise high then drop to a low perch, emitting '*tikitip*'.

2 HUDSON'S BLACK-TYRANT *Knipolegus hudsoni* Viudita negra chica (Arg). L 15 cm. Habitat:
scrubby open woodland. ♂: jet black, white in flight feathers and lower flanks. ♀: upperparts brownish,
rufous rump and base of tail which is black-banded. Underparts ochre streaked greyish-brown on breast.

3 ANDEAN TYRANT *Knipolegus signatus* Viudita plomiza (Arg, Bol). L 16 cm. Habitat: alder woods and
montane forests. ♂: bluish bill, red eye. Overall lead-grey. Hidden white on flight feathers. ♀ brown.
Bright rufous on rump. Two buff wing-bars. Ochre underparts very heavily streaked olive-grey, especially
on breast. ♂s perform a very high arc display flight, with whirring wings and a bill-snap on landing.

4 BLUE-BILLED BLACK-TYRANT *Knipolegus cyanirostris* Viudita negra de pico azul (Arg), Viudita
negra de monte (Uru), Maria-preta-de-bico-azulado (Br). L 15 cm. Habitat: scrub and woodland edge.
♂: pale blue bill and red eye. Black with hidden white on inner flight feathers. ♀: rufous brown above,
brighter on crown and rump. Underparts whitish, heavily streaked dark on breast. Two buff wing-bars.
♂s perform a flight display jumping up a metre or so, show white in the wing, and loop to same perch.

5 WHITE-WINGED BLACK-TYRANT *Knipolegus aterrimus* Viudita negra común (Arg), Maria-preta-
do-nordeste (Br). L 17 cm. ♂: jet black, white on primaries shown only in flight. ♀: brown above; rump and
base of tail bright rufous. Underparts buff. Wings dark with two broad buff wing-bars. Tail terminally
black. Voice: in aerial display, calls '*sip…sip…*' and produces mechanical clicks and thrums.

6 CRESTED BLACK-TYRANT *Knipolegus lophotes* Maria-preta-de-penacho (Br), Viudita negra de
copete (Uru). L 20 cm. Habitat: open grassy areas with bushes. Prominent crest. Overall glossy
blue-black. White base of flight feathers form a line seen in flight.

7 SPECTACLED TYRANT *Hymenops perspicillata* Pico de plata (Arg, Bol), Viuvinha-de-oculos (Br),
Viudita negra de bañado (Uru), Pico blanco (Par), Run-run (Ch). L 14 cm. Habitat: wetter tall grass areas
near marshes. ♂ black with white primaries, creamy bill and bare yellowish eye-ring. ♀: darker yellowish
eye-ring, slight pale eyebrow. Upperparts streaked; underparts buff with greyish streaking on breast.
Rufous primaries.

8 PIED WATER-TYRANT *Fluvicola pica* Viudita blanca (Arg), Viudita acuática (Bol), Lavadeira-de-
cara-branca (Br), Viudita blanca y negra (Uru). L 13 cm. Habitat: around marshes and along sluggish
rivers. Forehead, face and underparts white. Crown, nape, back, wings and tail black. Voice:
'*djjeeeoo…djjeeeoo*'. Fans tail.

Note: Some consider this southern form different from the typical species and call it the Black-backed
Water-tyrant, *Fluvicola albiventer*.

9 MASKED WATER-TYRANT *Fluvicola nengeta* Lavadeira-mascarada (Br). L 15 cm. Habitat: marshes
and adjacent bushes; riversides. Mostly white but black bill, line through face and eye, wings and tail.
Grey back.

10 WHITE-HEADED MARSH-TYRANT *Fluvicola leucocephala* Lavandera (Arg, Bol), Atrapamoscas
duende (Bol), Lavadeira-de-cabeça-branca or Freirinha (Br). L 12 cm. Habitat: reedbeds and marshes.
♂ all black with a white hood. ♀: upperparts grey-brown. Forehead, face, breast and belly whitish.
Blackish tail.

11 LONG-TAILED TYRANT *Colonia colonus* Yetapá negro (Arg, Bol), Jiovere hû (Par), Viuvinha (Br).
L ♂ 21, ♀ 14 cm. Habitat: high forest edge. All black with white rump; crown and nape silvery. ♂ has two
stiff tail feathers 9 cm long (sometimes broken off). Voice: a thin, high-pitched '*feee – ay*' dropping in
pitch.

12 COCK-TAILED TYRANT *Alectrurus tricolor* Yetapá chico (Arg), Galito (Br). L 19 cm. Habitat: tall
grasslands. Pale bill. ♂: black above and sides of breast. Face, slight brow and underparts white. White on
wing-coverts. Tail black, central feathers very broad and twisting to the vertical. ♀: brown upperparts and
sides of breast. Buff band across breast. Whitish belly. Normal tail.

▶

Plate 77

13 STRANGE-TAILED TYRANT *Alectrurus risora* Yetapá de collar (Arg), Tijereta de las pajas (Uru). L ♂ 32, ♀ 21 cm. Habitat: tall grass areas prone to flooding. Pale orange bill. ♂: black above. Wing feathers edged buff-white. Bare throat orange in breeding season, white when feathered. Black breast. White underparts. Tail black, two outer feathers very long, with a broad inner vane, twisted to the vertical. ♀: upperparts lightish brown, paler brow. Brown band across buff breast. Outer tail feathers long and racket-tipped.

14 STREAMER-TAILED TYRANT *Gubernetes yetapa* Yetapá grande (Arg, Bol), Jipiru (Par), Tesoura-do-brejo (Br). L 42 cm. Habitat: savannahs, tall grasslands on the edges of marshes and swamps. Crown and back grey, lightly streaked brownish. White throat. Brown band from ear-coverts bordering throat. Underparts grey. Blackish wings with bright cinnamon patch. Very long, deeply forked tail blackish. Voice: 'weeps', 'wierds' and 'who leaps' with variations.

Plate 78

TYRANTS – THE NEW WORLD FLYCATCHERS (FAMILY TYRANNIDAE)

1 YELLOW-BROWED TYRANT *Satrapa icterophrys* Suirirí amarillo (Arg), Suiriri-pequeno (Br), Vinchero (Uru), Atrapamoscas ceja amarilla (Bol). L 16 cm. Habitat: woodland and savannahs. Crown and upperparts dark olive; blackish on face, wings and tail. Broad bright yellow supercilliary and underparts. Wing-coverts and inner flight feathers edged pale buff.

2 SHORT-TAILED FIELD-TYRANT *Muscigralla brevicauda* Cazamoscas de cola corta (Ch). L 11 cm. Habitat: open, barren areas and bare agricultural fields. Small. Long legs pale. Short tail. Above dusky grey. Crown with a yellow patch. Lower back and rump yellow. Upper tail-coverts and base of tail bright chestnut. Very short tail black narrowly tipped white (♂ only). Wing-coverts tipped white forming two wing-bars. Below very pale grey, dirtier across the breast, to whitish lower belly.

3 CLIFF FLYCATCHER *Hirundinea ferruginea* Birro castaño (Arg), Viudita colorada (Uru), Atrapamoscas de precipicios (Bol), Gibao-de-couro (Br). L 18 cm. Habitat: around cliffs, rock-faces and cliff-like buildings in towns. Brownish-chestnut upperparts. Bright cinnamon-rufous rump. Chestnut below. Dark brown wings with large chestnut patch. Cinnamon-rufous tail with broad blackish band across tip. Voice: a high-pitched whistled 'wheep..wheedeedeedeedee… wheedeep'.

4 CATTLE TYRANT *Machetornis rixosus* Picabuey (Arg), Margarita (Uru), Atrapamoscas jinete (Bol), Guyra kavaju (Par). L 19 cm. Habitat: short grass areas; in town squares and on garden lawns (in winter). Grey head. Hidden orange flare on crown. Brownish back, wings and tail. White throat. Rest of underparts yellow. Usually in pairs. Terrestrial and around, or on, livestock. Voice: 'tsee tiwit' and a sharp 'tirik' – unmelodious.

5 SHEAR-TAILED GREY-TYRANT *Muscipipra vetula* Viudita coluda (Arg), Tesoura-cinzenta (Br). L 22 cm. Habitat: forest edge. Grey. Darker face and white throat. Blackish wings and tail, the latter long, heavy and markedly forked.

6 RUFOUS-TAILED ATTILA *Attila phoenicurus* Burlisto cabeza gris (Arg), Capitao-castanho (Br). L 18 cm. Habitat: in and under forest canopy. Grey head to hind-neck. Rest rufous, more orange on underparts, blacker on primaries. Voice: said to be a loud 'whee, whee, whee-bit'.

7 RUFOUS CASIORNIS *Casiornis rufa* Burlisto castaño (Arg), Caneleiro (Br), Cotinga rojiza (Bol). L 17 cm. Habitat: chaco woods, palm groves and gallery forest. Bill pale at the base. Rufous above. Paler throat cinnamon as also breast, paling to buff belly. Darker primaries. Voice: a high-pitched 'seep…seep seep tiptip'.

8 SIRYSTES *Sirystes sibilator* Silbador (Arg), Gritador (Br), Anambe ayvu (Par), Suirirí copetón (Bol). L 18 cm. Habitat: middle storey of forests, sometimes lower. Head with top-knotty crest, wings and tail blackish. Rest grey, slightly streaked on the back, lighter on rump and underparts. Wing-coverts and inner flight feathers edged whitish. Voice: a loud, penetrating, insistent, whistled 'fweeee, feee, feee, fee, fee', slightly descending in pitch.

9 DUSKY-CAPPED FLYCATCHER *Myiarchus tuberculifer* Burlisto cabeza negra (Arg, Bol), Maria-cavaleira-pequena (Br). L 17 cm. Habitat: canopy and edge of forests. Bill blackish. Blackish forehead and crown. Back olive-grey. Grey throat and breast. Yellowish belly. Wings dark brownish with indistinct buff wing-bars. Tail all dusky. Voice: 'wheeerr', dropping away.

10 SWAINSON'S FLYCATCHER *Myiarchus swainsoni* Burlisto pico canela (Arg), Irre (Br), Burlisto común ala larga (Bol), Mosqueta parda (Uru). L 18 cm. Habitat: woods and edges, trees in savannahs. Bill blackish upper, lower mandible pale skin colour. Above dingy brown. Throat and breast grey. Yellowish belly. Wing-coverts edged whitish forming wing-bars. Tail dark with pale outer webs. Voice: a disyllabic 'po -tty', a whistled 'whooOOoo' and a hoarse 'wherrr wherrrr'.

11 SHORT-CRESTED FLYCATCHER *Myiarchus ferox* Burlisto pico negro (Arg), Choperu (Par), Burlisto común ala corta (Bol), Maria-cavaleira (Br). L 19 cm. Habitat: edge of forests and gallery forests. Bill black. Above sooty-brown, darker on crown (which it can raise). Throat and breast grey. Yellowish belly. Wing-coverts edged greyish forming two paler wing-bars. Tail dusky. Voice: a quiet 'prrrt'.

▶

Plate 78

12 BROWN-CRESTED FLYCATCHER *Myiarchus tyrannulus* Burlisto cola castaña (Arg), Maria-cavaleira-de-rabo-enferrujado (Br), Burlisto cola castaña (Bol). L 19 cm. Habitat: savannahs and dry woodland. Dark bill. Above brownish, greyer on back. Throat and breast grey. Yellowish belly. Wing-coverts edged buff. Outer webs of flight feathers rufous. Tail brown and chestnut. Voice: loud '*wheep, whip…whip*'.

13 LESSER KISKADEE *Pitangus lictor* Benteveo pico fino (Arg), Pecho amarillo orillero (Bol), Bem-te-vizinho-do-brejo (Br). L 18 cm. Habitat: gallery forests. A smaller version of the Great Kiskadee, with a slender bill, and a more slender shape overall. Voice: a loud, nasal '*dzáy dzwee-dzwee-zwee*', accented on first syllable.

14 GREAT KISKADEE *Pitangus sulphuratus* Benteveo (Arg, Bol, Ch), Pitogüe (Par), Bem-te-vi or Bem-te-vi-de-coroa (Br), Frío or Cristofué (Bol), Benteveo común (Uru). L 22 cm. Habitat: extremely common almost everywhere – clearings, woods, gallery forests, near marshes, towns etc. Black cap with hidden yellow crown-patch and a white band right around from forehead, over eye to nape. Upperparts brownish. Black through the face. White throat. Yellow breast and belly. Wing feathers with cinnamon edging. Voice: loud and varied '*weh….weh…. teeweh……titi weh*' with variations, often duetted.

Plate 79

TYRANTS – THE NEW WORLD FLYCATCHERS (FAMILY TYRANNIDAE)

1 BOAT-BILLED FLYCATCHER *Megarhynchus pitangua* Pitanguá (Arg, Bol), Pitogüe guasu (Par), Nei-nei or Bem-te-vi-de-bico-chato (Br). L 22 cm. Habitat: tree-tops in semi-open forests. Large bill. Black head with hidden yellow crown-patch. Broad white eyebrows meet at nape. Olive-brown upperparts. Throat white. Rest of underparts yellow. Brown wings and tail. Voice: coarse; contact call a raucous '*kwee*' or '*kwek*'. Duetted '*chiriwee..chiriwee…..chiddlediwee..chiddlediwee…*'.

2 SOCIAL FLYCATCHER *Myiozetetes similis* Benteveo mediano (Arg), Pitogüe'i (Par), Bem-te-vizinho-penacho-vermelho (Br), Pitirre copete rojo (Bol). L 17 cm. Habitat: marshes and shrubby clearings. Top of the head and face black. Hidden crown-patch flame red. White brows which drop towards back, and do not meet at nape. Olive back and tail. White throat. Rest of underparts yellow. Wings blackish, feathers faintly edged cinnamon. Very often near water. Voice: a high-pitched '*tswee…tsweeedeedee*'.

3 THREE-STRIPED FLYCATCHER *Conopias trivirgata* Benteveo chico (Arg), Bem-te-vi-pequeno (Br), Atrapamoscas tri-listado (Bol). L 15 cm. Habitat: rainforests. Crown and eye-stripe black. White brow. Olive-grey back. Yellow underparts from throat and below eye-stripe downwards. Wings and tail dark brownish. Perch out on crowns and forest canopy. Voice: (sometimes duetted) '*djeeew…djeew*', rather harsh and excited.

4 GOLDEN-CROWNED FLYCATCHER *Myiodynastes chrysocephalus* Atrapamoscas corona dorada (Bol). L 21 cm. Habitat: montane forest edge and clearings. Darkish brown head, darker through the eye, with a white band ringing it above the eye and a yellow crown streak. Back olive-grey. Wings and edges of tail feathers rufous. From below the eye to under tail-coverts yellow, dirtier on the throat, faintly mottled pale olive across breast. Olive-grey malar stripe. Noisy.

5 STREAKED FLYCATCHER *Myiodynastes maculatus* Benteveo rayado (Arg, Bol, Uru), Vichivichi para (Par), Bem-te-vi-rajado (Br), Benteveo chico (Ch). L 21 cm. Habitat: woods and open areas with trees. A hidden yellow patch on crown. Dark face through the eye bordered pale below. All upperparts brown streaked paler. Underparts whitish streaked dark brown. Outer tail and rump rufous. Wings brownish with coverts and inner flight feathers edged whitish. Voice: loud, raucous and often duetted.

6 PIRATIC FLYCATCHER *Legatus leucophaius* Tuquito chico (Arg), Atrapamoscas ladrón (Bol), Bem-te-vi-pirata (Br). L 14 cm. Habitat: forests and woods. Crown (with hidden yellow flare) and face blackish. Eyebrow, malar stripe and throat whitish-grey. Grey-brown upperparts. Underparts greyish-yellow, streaked dark on breast. Whitish belly. Dark tail. Voice: vocal when nesting – a high-pitched '*peereepee - fee'ee*'.

7 VARIEGATED FLYCATCHER *Empidonomus varius* Tuquito chorreado (Arg), Peitica (Br), Atrapamoscas veteado (Bol), Suiriritî (Par), Suirirí rayado (Uru). L 18 cm. Habitat: gallery forests, woods, forest edge, savannahs with trees. Crown (with hidden yellow patch) and sides of head black. Eyebrow and malar stripe whitish. Brownish back. Rump and tail feathers edged chestnut. Underparts white, streaked brownish except on throat. Wings dark brown, coverts and flight feathers edged white. Almost totally silent – just a quiet '*seerr….seerrr…seepseerrree*' at dawn.

8 CROWNED SLATY-FLYCATCHER *Empidonomus aurantioatrocristatus* Tuquito gris (Arg), Suirirí de cabeza negra (Uru), Peitica-de-chapeu-preto (Br), Atrapamoscas copete negro-amarillo (Bol). L 17 cm. Habitat: tall dry woods, trees in savannahs and forest edge. Crown black with hidden yellow patch. Grey brow. Brownish-grey upperparts, dark grey underparts. Imm: pale brow and underparts, wing-coverts and flight feathers edged whitish. Voice: a series of '*seek… seek… seeseeseesee*' rising in pitch.

▶

Plate 79

9 **TROPICAL KINGBIRD** *Tyrannus melancholicus* Suirirí grande (Arg, Bol), Suiriri (Br), Suiriri guasu (Par), Benteveo real (Uru). L 22 cm. Habitat: savannahs, edge of clearings in woods or forests, open areas with scattered trees, gallery forests. Grey head with hidden orange crown-patch. Dark face. Back grey with olive tinge. Grey throat and breast, the latter grading to yellow on belly. Wings darkish, feathers narrowly edged pale. Blackish tail slightly notched. Perches on vantage-points. Voice: '*tseerrreee*', unmusical and sharp.

10 **FORK-TAILED FLYCATCHER** *Tyrannus savana* Tijereta (Arg, Bol, Uru), Tesoura (Br), Tuguái jetapa (Par), Cazamoscas tijereta (Ch). L 40 cm. Habitat: open country with trees. Black cap (with hidden yellow crown-patch), wings and very long forked tail. Grey back and white underparts. Voice: a single short '*tip*' contact, and variations with '*tip*' and trills, rolled, rattled and complicated.

11 **EASTERN KINGBIRD** *Tyrannus tyrannus* Suirirí de cabeza negra (Arg, Bol), Benteveo blanco y negro (Ch). L 20 cm. Habitat: edges or canopy of forests and woods, clearings with trees, pastures. Black cap (with hidden red crown-patch). Upperparts dark grey. Dark wings with flight feathers and coverts edged white. Tail black with white tip. Underparts white, greyish on breast.

Plate 80

TYRANTS – THE NEW WORLD FLYCATCHERS (FAMILY TYRANNIDAE)

1 **WHITE-NAPED XENOPSARIS** *Xenopsaris albinucha* Tijerilla (Arg), Tijerila (Br). L 12 cm. Habitat: scrubby woods by water. Spot on forehead, lores, neck and underparts white. Black crown (♂). Back brownish-grey. Dark wings with two white wing-bars and white borders to flight feathers. ♀ has a dusky crown.

2 **GREEN-BACKED BECARD** *Pachyramphus viridis* Anambé verdoso (Arg, Bol), Caneleirinho-verde (Br), Añambé verde (Uru). L 15 cm. Habitat: gallery forests, open woods and forest edge. ♂: black cap. Face and throat whitish. Grey collar round the nape. Back and tail olive. Yellow breast-band. Rest of underparts buff. ♀: crown and upperparts olivaceous but with the grey hind-collar. Broad yellow band across upper breast. Rest of underparts creamy. Chestnut wing-coverts; greenish flight feathers. Underwing yellow. Voice: a series of rising '*piripi pee pee PEE PEE*' and '*teeoolee...teeoolee...*'.

3 **CHESTNUT-CROWNED BECARD** *Pachyramphus castaneus* Anambé castaño (Arg, Bol), Caneleirinho (Br), Anambe hovy (Par). L 15 cm. Habitat: forest edge, clearings with scattered trees. Head, back and tail chestnut. Nuchal collar grey. Below paler chestnut, whiter on throat and lower mid-belly. Brown wings edged chestnut. Voice: a soft, melodious, high-pitched '*teeew teeew teeew...*'.

4 **WHITE-WINGED BECARD** *Pachyramphus polychropterus* Anambé común (Arg, Uru), Cabezón aliblanco (Bol), Canaleiro-preto (Br). L 15 cm. Habitat: woods (often open), forest edge, gallery forests. ♂: pale grey bill. Sooty black on crown grading to grey belly. Two broad white wing-bars and white tips to outer tail feathers. ♀: upperparts greyish-brown. Underparts grey, whitish belly. Cinnamon wing-bar. Tail brown with cinnamon tips to outer feathers. Voice: a melodious, quiet, accelerating '*too too too tootootoototo*'.

5 **BLACK-CAPPED BECARD** *Pachyramphus marginatus* Caneleiro (Br). L 14 cm. Habitat: rainforest canopy. ♂: crown and nape bluish-black. Back streaked grey and black. Grey rump. Black tail with white tip. Lesser coverts form two wing-bars; greaters are edged white as are the inner flight feathers. Face, ear-coverts, neck, breast, belly and flanks grey. White throat and under tail-coverts. ♀: rufous-brown cap, grey hind-neck. Olive back. Wings dark with wing-bar and edge of feathers cinnamon. Whitish throat. Below yellow, grey-washed on breast. Central tail feathers grey-brown with black sub-terminal band, outers black, all with cinnamon-buff tips.

6 **CRESTED BECARD** *Pachyramphus validus* Anambé grande (Arg), Anambé (Par), Caneleiro-de-chapéu-negro (Br). L 18 cm. Habitat: woods and trees in clearings. ♂: untidy crown and rest of upperparts black. White on scapulars. Dingy grey below. ♀: dark grey crown, rest of upperparts rufous. Cinnamon-buff underparts. Primaries blackish, rest of wing chestnut. Voice: twitters and a very high-pitched and thin '*tseeeeee*'.

7 **BLACK-TAILED TITYRA** *Tityra cayana* Tueré grande (Arg, Bol), Anambé-branco-de-rabo-preto (Br). L 21 cm. Habitat: canopy and exposed bare branches high in forests and edges of clearings. Red at basal half of bill and bare skin around eye. Bill tipped black. ♂: white with black head, wings and tail. Back ash-grey. ♀: similarly patterned, but dingy white with streaking on head, back and breast. Voice: a deep, guttural '*wert*', repeated, sometimes duetted.

8 **BLACK-CROWNED TITYRA** *Tityra inquisitor* Tueré chico (Arg), Anambe-branco-de-bochecha-parda (Br). L 18 cm. Habitat: canopy and edges of forests and woods. Bill all black. ♂: black cap from nape to bill and upwards. Black wings and tail. Rest white, ashy on back. ♀: similar but more orange face and ear-coverts. Dingier back streaked and speckled darker. Voice: a duetted, dry, mechanical, almost comical '*werek - terek - werek - terek...*'.

Plate 80

Plate 81

MANAKINS (FAMILY PIPRIDAE)

1 **GREENISH MANAKIN** *Schiffornis virescens* Bailarín oliváceo (Arg), Saltarín mayor (Bol), Flautim (Br). L 15 cm. Habitat: lower and middle storeys of rainforests and regrowth. Overall darkish olive-green with reddish-brown wings and tail. Voice: a whistled loud to piercing '*tee-oo hoo-eet*', repeated often.

2 **WING-BARRED MANAKIN** *Piprites chloris* Bailarín verde (Arg), Saltarín verde (Bol), Papinho-amarelo (Br). L 13 cm. Habitat: canopy and edge of forests. Yellow forehead, lores and eye-ring. Crown and back olive. Grey nape and face. Underparts yellow with greyish wash. Wings with two yellowish wing-bars. Voice: a loud, rhythmic '*whip whip pip piddipip pip pip whip whip*', faster in the middle and stressing the last syllables.

3 **BLACK-CAPPED MANAKIN** *Piprites pileatus* Bailarín castaño (Arg), Caneleirinho-de-chapéu-preto (Br). L 12.5 cm. Habitat: forests at higher elevations. Black cap. Reddish-brown back. Buff-chestnut below. White band at base of primaries. Tail rufous, central blackish. ♀ more olive on the back.

4 **HELMETED MANAKIN** *Antilophia galeata* Soldadinho (Br). L 14 cm. Habitat: impenetrable lower and middle levels of woods and gallery forests. ♂ black with red upper back, nape, crown and forehead, latter with a long tuft pointed forwards along top of bill. ♀ olive, paler below. Tuft only half the length of bill.

5 **WHITE-BEARDED MANAKIN** *Manacus manacus* Bailarín blanco (Arg), Rendeira (Br). L 10 cm. Habitat: forest edge. ♂: above mostly black. Puffed-out throat, breast and complete collar white. Belly and rump grey. ♀: olive, paler below and grey throat. Voice: '*cheepoo*'.

6 **BLUE MANAKIN** *Chiroxiphia caudata* Bailarín azul (Arg), Tangará or Dançador (Br). L 15 cm. Habitat: low and middle storey of forests, canopy of lower regrowth. ♂: red cap. Throat, face, hind-neck and wings black. Rest lovely blue. Tail black with central tail feathers elongated and blue. Imm ♂ olive with red cap. ♀ olive, paler below. Voice: a sharp, loud '*cheekoo chirroo*' and '*chiwee chiwee*', sometimes an angry, raucous '*choooo*'.

7 **BAND-TAILED MANAKIN** *Pipra fasciicauda* Bailarín naranja (Arg), Uirapuru-laranja (Br), Saltarín amarillo (Bol). L 10.5 cm. Habitat: rainforests. White eye. ♂: red head, more orange on forehead, cheeks and throat. Back and wings black, these last with white band. Breast red with yellow streaks. Belly yellow. Tail yellow at base, black tip. ♀ olive; yellowish underparts, yellow on belly.

COTINGAS (FAMILY COTINGIDAE)

8 **SWALLOW-TAILED COTINGA** *Phibalura flavirostris* Tesorito (Arg), Tesourinha (Br). L 22 cm. Habitat: open forest. Tail long and forked. Yellow bill. Black head, red nape. Back to upper tail-coverts broadly barred black and yellow. Yellow throat. Breast barred black and white. ♀ is a toned-down version of the above. Perches on exposed branches.

9 **HOODED BERRY-EATER** *Carpornis cucullatus* Corocochó (Br). L 23 cm. Habitat: middle storey of montane forests. ♂: black hood, throat and breast. Yellow collar across upper back and all lower underparts. Rich brown back. Olive-brown lower back, rump and tail. Wing-coverts edged yellow forming scalloped wing-bars. ♀ has greyish-olive where ♂ is black. Voice: a loud '*weeork......weeko*' at intervals.

10 **BARE-NECKED FRUITCROW** *Gymnoderus foetidus* Anambe-pombo (Br), Pavita pescuecipelada (Bol). L 36 cm. Habitat: gallery forests. ♂: black with bare neck wattled and warty, pale sky-blue. Silver-grey wings. ♀: overall greyish. Neck as in ♂.

11 **RED-RUFFED FRUITCROW** *Pyroderus scutatus* Yacutoro (Arg), Pavao-do-mato (Br). L 42 cm. Habitat: rainforest. Black, with gleaming red lower throat onto upper breast. Some reddish spots on rest of black, on lower underparts. Voice: calls at lek are a deep-toned whistle '*too-tooo*' – like blowing over the mouth of a large bottle – once or repeated.

12 **BARE-THROATED BELLBIRD** *Procnias nudicollis* Pájaro campana (Arg), Guyrapú (Par), Araponga (Br). L 27 cm. Habitat: rainforest canopy. ♂: white, green skin around face. ♀: blackish head. Upperparts olive. Below yellowish streaked olive. Voice: a startlingly loud metallic '*wehnk*' or '*weyink*'.

SHARPBILL (FAMILY OXYRUNCIDAE)

13 **SHARPBILL** *Oxyruncus cristatus* Picoagudo (Arg), Araponga-do-horto (Br). L 17 cm. Habitat: rainforest canopy. Sharp bill. Red eye. Crown black. Rest of head and throat speckled blackish-olive and white. Olive back and tail. Slight yellowish wing-bars. Breast and belly pale yellow spotted black. Voice: 'uncannily like ... a falling bomb, without the boom at the end!' (R. S. Ridgely).

PLANTCUTTERS (FAMILY PHYTOTOMIDAE)

14 **RUFOUS-TAILED PLANTCUTTER** *Phytotoma rara* Rara (Arg, Ch). L 19.5 cm. Habitat: open bushy areas, gardens, woodland edge. Red eye. ♂: cap and upperparts brick red, the latter streaked blackish and buff. White wing-coverts. Tail brick-red with a broad black terminal band. ♀: heavily streaked brown and buff. Tail rufous and black. Voice: a raucous, rapid '*kaykaykaykaykaykayKAY*', rising in volume and slightly in pitch.

▶

Plate 81 (continued)

15 WHITE-TIPPED PLANTCUTTER *Phytotoma rutila* Cortarramas (Arg, Bol), Corta-ramos (Br), Cortahojas (Bol), Corta-ramas (Uru). L 19 cm. Habitat: low trees and bushes in scrub and open woods. Amber eye. ♂: fore-crown and underparts brick red. Upperparts grey, slightly streaked. Two whitish wing-bars. Dingy tail with white tips to outer feathers. ♀: heavily streaked buff on brownish, grey on buff underparts. Buff wing-bars. Voice: like a creaking door on unoiled, rusty hinges.

CROWS AND JAYS (FAMILY CORVIDAE)

16 AZURE JAY *Cyanocorax caeruleus* Urraca azul (Arg), Gralha-azul (Br). L 37 cm. Habitat: upland forests with *Araucaria* pines. Blue, with head, fore-neck and upper breast black. Wings blue and black. Tail blue above, black below. Noisy and gregarious. Voice: raucous and rapid 'char char char char...'. Now rare.

17 PURPLISH JAY *Cyanocorax cyanomelas* Urraca morada (Arg, Uru, Bol), Cacaré (Bol), Akae hû (Par), Gralha-do-pantanal (Br). L 32 cm. Habitat: woods and gallery forests. All dingy brownish-purple but forehead, face and breast sooty black. Wings brownish. Tail purplish-blue. Usually in small loose flocks. Voice: contact call is a strange, metallic, buzzing 'beh'.

18 CURL-CRESTED JAY *Cyanocorax cristatellus* Gralha-do-campo (Br). L 32 cm. Habitat: edge of forests, woods and gallery forests. Black-hooded to upper breast and upper back. Frontal crest curls backwards. Rest of upperparts through purple-black to violet-blue on wings and basal half of tail. Lower breast, belly, flanks and distal half of tail white. Voice: loud 'jaar' call, repeated.

19 PLUSH-CRESTED JAY *Cyanocorax chrysops* Urraca común (Arg, Bol), Urraca azul (Uru), Suso (Bol), Akae para (Par), Gralha-picaça (Br). L 35 cm. Habitat: woods and forests, gallery forests, clearings and gardens. Head, neck and breast black. Cap with beret-like pom-pom at nape. Electric-blue brow above pale yellow eye; likewise on hind-neck and face. Dark violet on back extends to basal half of tail. Distal half of tail whitish. Below creamy. Forages in flocks of up to 15. Voice: rapid 'chucker-chuck', 'k'yaaaw', 'check - check' amongst other varied sounds.

Plate 82 (continued)

5 CLIFF SWALLOW *Hirundo pyrrhonota* Golondrina rabadilla canela (Arg), Andorinha-de-dorso-acanelado (Br), Golondrina de rabadilla parda (Uru), Golondrina rabadilla castaña (Bol). L 13 cm. Habitat: savannahs, fields and marshes. Forehead yellowish-buff. Crown shiny blue-black. Chestnut nape. Back blue-black. Cinnamon rump. Sides of neck chestnut. Breast and belly pale buff-grey. Migratory from N America.

Plate 82

SWALLOWS (FAMILY HIRUNDINIDAE)

1 **WHITE-WINGED SWALLOW** *Tachycineta albiventer* Golondrina ala blanca (Arg), Mbyju'i (Par), Golondrina verdosa (Bol), Andorinha-do-rio (Br). L 13.5 cm. Habitat: rivers and bodies of water in forests. Above black with a green sheen. Rump and underparts white. Wings with broad white patch.

2 **WHITE-RUMPED SWALLOW** *Tacycineta leucorrhoa* Golondrina ceja blanca (Arg), Mbyju'i (Par), Andorinha-de-sobre-branca (Br), Golondrina de rabadilla y cejas blancas (Uru), Golondrina azul de ceja blanca (Bol). L 13 cm. Habitat: woodland edge, fields, savannahs and waterside. Above (except rump) black with blue sheen. Rump and underparts white. Variable white line from forehead to brow. Migratory. Voice: complex, throaty, warbling and melodious song.

3 **CHILEAN SWALLOW** *Tachycineta leucopyga* Golondrina patagónica (Arg, Bol), Golondrina chilena (Ch), Mbyju'i (Par). L 12.5 cm. Habitat: clearings in southern-beech woods, forest edge, steppes, open spaces with scattered trees. Upperparts (except rump) black with purple-blue sheen. Rump and below all white. No brow. Under wing grey. Highly migratory. Voice: complex, melodious song.

4 **BROWN-CHESTED MARTIN** *Phaeoprogne tapera* Golondrina parda (Arg, Uru), Andorinha-do-campo (Br), Golondrina de río (Bol). L 17 cm. Habitat: woodland edge, savannahs, clearings with trees and marshes. Upperparts, breastband and line down central belly brown. Throat, sides of belly and flanks whitish. Voice: a musical descending arpeggio '*teeerrrrroop*', and in flight a '*deyeeet*'.

5 **PURPLE MARTIN** *Progne subis* Golondrina purpúrea (Arg), Golondrina de iglesias (Bol). L 17.5 cm. Habitat: clearings, often near water. Brilliant bluish-purple with black wings and tail. ♀ is duller with dingy grey on underside and whitish belly. Migratory from N America.

6 **GREY-BREASTED MARTIN** *Progne chalybea* Golondrina doméstica (Arg), Golondrina azul (Uru), Andorinha-doméstica-grande (Br), Mbyju'i (Par), Golondrina azul grande (Bol). L 18 cm. Habitat: savannahs, open areas, towns, sea cliffs and hills. Above bluish-black. Throat and breast grey with whitish wash. Rest of underparts whitish. ♀ has dingier upperparts. Voice: complex and not unmusical '*choorroolooleep*' or '*tooroolee*'.

7 **SOUTHERN MARTIN** *Progne elegans* Golondrina negra (Arg, Bol, Ch, Uru). L 19 cm. Habitat: near cliffs, buildings, open areas, hills, sea-coasts. Shiny blue-black. ♀ is dull black above, dingy sooty brown beneath. Voice: '*tooroolee...choorooleeep*' and variations, musical and richly throaty.

8 **BLUE-AND-WHITE SWALLOW** *Notiochelidon cyanoleuca* Golondrina barranquera (Arg), Andorinha-pequena-de-casa (Br), Golondrina ribereña (Uru), Golondrina de dorso negro (Ch), Golondrina azul chica (Bol). L 12 cm. Habitat: grasslands and open areas. Shiny blue-black hood and upperparts. Lower breast and belly white. Under tail-coverts, wings and tail black. Usually flies low. Voice: '*seep .. teeerrr ..... seep*'.

9 **BLACK-COLLARED SWALLOW** *Atticora melanoleuca* Golondrina de collar (Arg), Andorinha-de-coleira (Br). L 14.5 cm. Habitat: on rivers in rainforests. Upperparts jet black. Neat black band across upper breast. Underparts white. Wings and longish forked tail dull black.

10 **TAWNY-HEADED SWALLOW** *Alopochelidon fucata* Golondrina cabeza rojiza (Arg), Andorinha-morena (Br), Golondrina de cabeza castaña (Uru, Bol). L 12 cm. Habitat: savannahs, fields and aquatic habitats. Hind-crown dark brown. Rest of head and throat cinnamon. Underparts white. Back, wings and tail dark brown. Voice: a melodious '*seep..seep.....googlileep choorlip*'.

11 **ROUGH-WINGED SWALLOW** *Stelgidopteryx ruficollis* Golondrina ribereña (Arg), Golondrina canela (Bol), Golondrina de cuello rojizo (Uru), Andorinha-serrador (Br). L 13 cm. Habitat: Usually near rivers, also marshes and lakes. Upperparts brownish, paler on rump. Pale cinnamon throat. Greyish breast. Belly yellowish-buff. Under tail-coverts whitish. Voice: '*viveeek... eeveeek...eeooeeek*'.

12 **BANK SWALLOW** *Riparia riparia* Golondrina zapadora (Arg, Bol), Andorinha-do-barranco (Br), Golondrina barranquera (Ch). L 12cm. Habitat: savannahs, fields, rivers and wetlands. Above brown, below white with broad brown band on breast. Migratory from N America.

13 **BARN SWALLOW** *Hirundo rustica* Golondrina tijerita (Arg), Golondrina tijereta (Bol, Uru), Golondrina bermeja (Ch), Andorinha-de-bando (Br). L 16.5 cm. Habitat: savannahs, fields, wet areas. Upperparts dark shiny blue. Forehead and upper breast russet. Underparts cinnamon. Blackish tail, with elongated outer feathers with white spots. All this toned down in winter plumage. Imm has cinnamon forehead and throat, buff underparts. There is a small breeding population near Miramar in Buenos Aires province. Otherwise migratory from N America.

14 **ANDEAN SWALLOW** *Hirundo andecola* Golondrina de los riscos (Ch). L 15 cm. Habitat: arid *puna* and high Andean valleys. Above bluish-black with green sheen. Upper breast grey, paling to whitish on belly.

◀

Plate 82

Plate 83

WRENS (FAMILY TROGLODYTIDAE)

1 **DONACOBIUS** *Donacobius atricapillus* Angú (Arg), Japacanim or Batuquira (Br), Calandria de agua or Parulata de agua (Bol), Calandria estero (Par). L 21 cm. Habitat: reedbeds and waterside vegetation. Black face, cap and hind-neck. Very yellow eye. Brown back, chestnut rump. Black tail tipped white. Underparts yellowish-buff, whiter on throat. Bare orange on side of throat seen in displays. Dark wings with a large round white spot. Bird shaped more like a mockingbird. Voice: loud song includes '*cooee cooee cooee cooee*', and raucous '*teeyah, teeyah*'.

2 **THRUSH-LIKE WREN** *Campylorhynchus turdinus* Ratona (Bol), Catatau or Garrinchao (Br). L 21 cm. Habitat: canopy and edges of rainforest, secondary growth. Above grey. Long white brow. Flight feathers and tail faintly barred browner. Underparts white, slightly spotted brownish on flanks and under tail-coverts. Gregarious.

3 **GRASS WREN** *Cistothorus platensis* Ratona aperdizada (Arg), Corruíra-do-campo (Br), Chercán de las vegas (Ch), Cucarachero sabanero (Bol). L 10 cm. Habitat: sedges and grasses two or more feet tall. Dark brown upperparts heavily streaked whitish-buff. Cinnamon rump. Whitish throat. Rest of underparts buff. Tail barred buff and dark brown. Voice: song varies throughout the disjunct range but is loud, musical and complex.

4 **FAWN-BREASTED WREN** *Thryothorus guarayanus* No local names. L 14 cm. Habitat: thickets and forest edge. Crown, post-ocular streak and upperparts greyish-brown. Long white brow. Cheeks streaked. Throat pale buff. Rest of underparts cinnamon, ruddier on flanks. Wings and tail finely barred with dark brown.

5 **LONG-BILLED WREN** *Thryothorus longirostris* Garrinchao-de-bico-grande (Br). L 15 cm. Habitat: undergrowth, forest edge, clearings with bushes. Long bill. Above brown, reddish on back, wings and tail – these last finely barred dark brown. Long brow, throat and face white, ear-coverts slightly streaked. Below fawn, ruddier on flanks.

6 **HOUSE WREN** *Troglodytes aedon* Ratona común (Arg, Bol), Chercán (Ch), Masakaragua'i (Par), Corruíra or Cambaxirra (Br), Ratonera (Uru). L 11 cm. Habitat: ubiquitous in gardens and dense vegetation with clearings. Brown, lighter below. Barring in wings. Blackish barring in chestnut tail. Voice: scolds '*djjjiiiiit*'. Song is complex and warbling with trills and gurgles familiar to almost everyone.

7 **MOUNTAIN WREN** *Troglodytes solstitialis* Ratona ceja blanca (Arg, Bol). L 11 cm. Habitat: lower to middle storey of montane forests. Above chestnut-brown, darker on the head. Long white eyebrow. Underparts buff-grey. Under tail-coverts barred dark brown. Barring in the wings and on tail. Voice: song is very high-pitched and 'thin', almost inaudible and insect-like but for its complexity: '*sibleysibley diddlydisssy*'.

DIPPERS (FAMILY CINCLIDAE)

8 **RUFOUS-THROATED DIPPER** *Cinclus schultzi* Mirlo de agua (Arg). L 15 cm. Habitat: beside tumbling streams and on emergent rocks. Lead-grey with orange-chestnut throat and upper breast. Hidden white patch in the wing which is flashed from time to time. The short tail is usually slightly cocked. Unafraid.

GNATCATCHERS (FAMILY MUSCICAPIDAE, SUBFAMILY SYLVINAE)

9 **CREAMY-BELLIED GNATCATCHER** *Polioptila lactea* Tacuarita blanca (Arg), Balança-rabo-leitoso (Br). L 11 cm. Habitat: canopy and edge of rainforests. ♂: crown black. Otherwise ♂ and ♀ the same: blue-grey mantle; central tail feathers black, outers white; creamy underparts. Voice: a high-pitched '*feetfeetfeetfeetfeet*', up to five times.

10 **MASKED GNATCATCHER** *Polioptila dumicola* Tacuarita azul (Arg, Bol), Azulito (Uru), Balança-rabo-de-máscara (Br). L 12 cm. Habitat: open woods. ♂: blue-grey. Black forehead and mask. ♀ paler, lacks mask. Both have blackish wings with white on coverts and secondaries. Central tail feathers black, outers white. Pairs or more occur together. Voice: a loud '*dweet*', insistent scolding, and a melodious song '*tiddly tiddly peely peedlee siblyblit*'. Insistent alarm: '*weet weet weet weet...*'.

Plate 83

Plate 84

THRUSHES (FAMILY MUSCICAPIDAE, SUBFAMILY TURDINAE)

1 **SPOTTED NIGHTINGALE-THRUSH** *Catharus dryas* Zorzalito overo (Arg, Bol). L 16 cm. Habitat: undergrowth of montane forests. Black head. Orange bill, eye-ring and legs. Upperparts olive. Below yellow with large blackish spots. Voice: sings *'piree - pirilee - tirilolee…'*.

2 **VEERY** *Catharus fuscescens* Parulata cachetona (Bol), Sabiá-norte-americano (Br), Zorzal tropical (Ch). L 18 cm. Habitat: lower vegetation in forests and woods, forest edge. Reddish-brown upperparts, wings and tail. Darkish yellow throat and breast; sides flecked brown. Rest of underparts white.

3 **SWAINSON'S THRUSH** *Catharus ustulatus* Zorzal boreal (Arg), Zorzal chico (Bol). L 18 cm. Upperparts olive-brown. Breast spotted dark brown. Underparts whitish with dusky spots on flanks. Voice: *'quit'* on wintering grounds.

4 **YELLOW-LEGGED THRUSH** *Platycichla flavipes* Zorzal azulado (Arg), Sabiaúna (Br). L 21 cm. Habitat: rainforest canopy. Yellowish eye-ring and yellow legs. ♂: yellow bill. Head, breast, wings and tail black. Rest grey. ♀: all brownish, lighter below. Streaked throat.

5 **CHIGUANCO THRUSH** *Turdus chiguanco* Zorzal chiguanco (Arg), Chiguanco (Bol), Zorzal negro (Ch). L 27 cm. Habitat: on ground in clearings with scattered trees and shrubs; gardens. Bill and legs yellowish-orange. ♂ all sooty black, ♀ dark smoky-brown. Voice: simple song, lacking much in musical quality.

6 **GLOSSY-BLACK THRUSH** *Turdus serranus* Zorzal negro (Arg, Bol). L 25 cm. Habitat: montane forest. Orange-yellow bill and legs. ♂: orange eye-ring. All glossy black. ♀: brown, lighter below, streaked throat. Shy. Voice: shrill song.

7 **SLATY THRUSH** *Turdus nigriceps* Zorzal plomizo (Arg), Sabiá-ferreiro (Br), Zorzal cabeza negra or Chulupia cabeza negra (Bol). L 22 cm. Habitat: canopy of woods and forests. ♂: yellow bill, orange legs. Lead grey. White throat with black streaks. Underparts paler grey. ♀: upperparts, wings and tail brown. Throat buff, streaked dark. Brownish breast, whitish belly. Voice: high-pitched 'scraping' song.

Note: This may be two species: Andean Slaty Thrush *Turdus nigriceps* and Eastern Slaty Thrush *T. subalaris*. ♀s differ most – the Eastern almost nondescript, the Andean patterned like ♂ but in brown.

8 **RUFOUS-BELLIED THRUSH** *Turdus rufiventris* Zorzal colorado (Arg), Zorzal (Uru), Zorzal rojizo or Chulupia melodiosa (Bol), Sabiá-laranjeira (Br), Havía pytâ (Par). L 25 cm. Habitat: gardens and open woods, from the ground to mid-vegetation. Belly and under tail-coverts rufous. Voice: rich and melodious song, continuous and rollingly repeated phrases.

9 **AUSTRAL THRUSH** *Turdus falcklandii* Zorzal patagónico (Arg), Zorzal (Ch). L 25 cm. Habitat: woodland edge, gardens, lawns. Dark blackish head. White throat streaked. Below buff-brown. ♀ duller. Voice: song is not very inspiring though unmistakably a thrush.

10 **PALE-BREASTED THRUSH** *Turdus leucomelas* Zorzal sabiá (Arg), Parulata montañera (Bol), Capoeirao or Sabiá-barranco (Br), Havía morotî (Par). L 23 cm. Habitat: forest edges and clearings. Greyish head. Upperparts brown, more cinnamon on wings and tail. Throat streaked dark. Buff breast and flanks. Voice: melodious song with repeated phrases.

11 **CREAMY-BELLIED THRUSH** *Turdus amaurochalinus* Zorzal chalchalero (Arg), Korochire (Par), Chalchalero or Jichi tarumá (Bol), Zorzal argentino (Ch), Sabiapoca (Br), Sabiá (Uru). L 23 cm. Habitat: woods, denser gardens with clearings under trees. Head, back, wings and tail greyish-brown. Breast brownish-grey. Belly whitish. Voice: lovely thrush song with pauses.

12 **WHITE-NECKED THRUSH** *Turdus albicollis* Zorzal collar blanco (Arg), Zorzal paraguayo (Uru), Sabiá-coleira or Carachué-coleira (Br), Haviá (Par), Zorzal flancos canela (Bol). L 23 cm. Habitat: middle to lower storey of rainforests. Upperparts dark brown. Throat black and white streaked. White band below, on neck. Breast and flanks grey with cinnamon wash. Voice: slow, short-phrased song, rhythmically delivered.

MOCKINGBIRDS (FAMILY MIMIDAE)

13 **CHILEAN MOCKINGBIRD** *Mimus thenca* Tenca (Ch). L 28 cm. Habitat: gardens and open areas with trees and bushes. Above greyish. Broad whitish brow. Dark face. Whitish throat. Buff breast; pale belly.

14 **CHALK-BROWED MOCKINGBIRD** *Mimus saturninus* Calandria común (Arg, Bol, Uru), Saí (Bol), Guyra ñe'engatu (Par), Sabiá-do-campo (Br). L 25 cm. Habitat: open areas with short grass and bushes, open woods, gardens, and field edges. Above grey. Darker line through the eye. Broad whitish brow. Wing-coverts edged white. Tail with narrow white tip, broader on outer feathers. Below creamy grey, buff wash on undertail. Voice: alarm call *'dissht'*. Wonderful and varied songster and immitator.

15 **PATAGONIAN MOCKINGBIRD** *Mimus patagonicus* Calandria mora (Arg), Tenca patagónica (Ch). L 23 cm. Habitat: scrubby open areas with bushes. Above greyish. Slight brow. Wing-coverts blackish tipped white. Buff underparts. Tail dark, tipped white. Voice: song is thinner than Chalk-browed Mockingbird's but just as varied.

▶

Plate 84

16 WHITE-BANDED MOCKINGBIRD *Mimus triurus* Calandria real (Arg, Bol), Tenca de las alas blancas (Ch), Calandra-de-tres-rabos (Br), Calandria de tres colas (Uru). L 22 cm. Habitat: bushy steppes and open areas. Upperparts brownish-grey. Cinnamon rump. Brow and throat whitish. Underparts pale buff. Wings boldly black and white. Tail white but for black central pair of feathers. Voice: a great songster with varied and musical song also containing imitations.

17 BROWN-BACKED MOCKINGBIRD *Mimus dorsalis* Calandria castaña (Arg, Bol). L 25 cm. Habitat: arid mountain valleys, on the tops of bushes and on the ground. Back chestnut-brown, rump cinnamon. White brow. Buff underparts. Wings black and white. Tail white, centrally black. Voice: fairly quiet song.

Plate 85

PIPITS (FAMILY MOTACILLIDAE)

1 SHORT-BILLED PIPIT *Anthus furcatus* Cachirla uña corta (Arg, Bol), Cachila de uña corta (Uru), Caminheiro-de-unha-curta (Br). L 15 cm. Habitat: short grass in the lowlands, taller *puna* grasses in the Andes. Pink legs. A short hind claw. Washy brown above, streaked darker. Breast buff with broad dark streaking, the buff extending onto flanks, but not the streaking. Whitish belly. Outer tail feathers buff-white, rest of tail brownish. Voice: flight song a buzzing 'teee - clicliclicli ....teee - clicliclicli...', performed very high, with short glides.

2 HELLMAYR'S PIPIT *Anthus hellmayri* Cachirla pálida (Arg, Bol), Cachila pálida (Uru), Bailarín chico argentino (Ch), Caminheira-de-barriga-acanelada (Br). L 14 cm. Habitat: rocky, grassy hillsides in Andes and mountains in central Argentina, tall wet grass in its eastern distribution. Dark upperparts streaked light brown. Below buff streaked with fine dark brown on breast. Voice: flight song 'tsilly tsilly tsilly tsilly...', in descent. Also sings perched.

3 YELLOWISH PIPIT *Anthus lutescens* Cachirla chica (Arg, Bol), Caminero (Bol), Bailarín chico peruano (Ch), Caminheiro-zumbidor (Br), Guyra tape (Par), Cachila chica (Uru). L 13 cm. Habitat: short grass, often around lakes and dams. Above dark brown streaked buff. Below yellowish with speckled brown streaking on upper breast (new feathers), to plain whitish (old feathers). Brownish tail with white outer feathers. Voice: flight song is 'sips' while the bird is rising, then long butterfly-like gliding descent singing a characteristic buzzing 'dzzeeeeeeeeeeooooooow', descending in pitch.

4 CHACO PIPIT *Anthus chacoensis* Cachirla trinadora (Arg). L 13 cm. Habitat: short grass. Indistinguishable in the field from Yellowish Pipit, though streaks on back seem whiter than buff. Voice: flight song is remarkably different from Yellowish Pipit's. The bird rises very high and sings in a gliding descent a long series (50 or more syllables long) 'clicliclicliclidlidlidlidlidlewdlewdlewdlew dleedleedleedleedleecleecleeclicliclicli....', only to rise again and repeat.

5 CORRENDERA PIPIT *Anthus correndera* Cachirla común (Arg, Bol), Bailarín chico (Ch), Cachila de uña larga (Uru), Caminheiro-de-espora (Br). L 15 cm. Above heavily streaked dark and buff with two whitish 'skunk stripes' along scapulars. Breast buff with dark spotty streaks, these extending down flank. White on outer tail feathers. Voice: the flight song consists of a series of 'cloocleeclewclips' in ascent. Descent is in spiral, singing 'toodleedoocheeew.. toodleedoocheeew.... toodleedoocheeew' continually, right down to the ground, then up again to repeat.

6 OCHRE-BREASTED PIPIT *Anthus nattereri* Cachirla pálida (Arg), Caminheiro-grande (Br). L 15 cm. Habitat: rolling, dry, tall grasslands. Golden-buff upperparts streaked blackish. Golden breast with blackish streaks. Whitish belly. Pipit tail. Voice: short flight song and rapid descent.

7 PARAMO PIPIT *Anthus bogotensis* Cachirla andina (Arg, Bol), Miracielito (Bol). L 15 cm. Habitat: high upland *puna* grasslands. Overall buff with dark streaks above and slight speckling on upper breast. Dark tail with buff outers. Voice: sings on the ground or in low display flight 'deedle deedle dee'.

8 SOUTH GEORGIA PIPIT *Anthus antarcticus* Cachirla grande (Arg). L 16 cm. Habitat: on shorelines and grassy areas. The darkest pipit, almost olive-buff, and only on South Georgia Island in the South Atlantic. Heavily streaked back and 'skunk lines' on scapulars as in Correndera Pipit.

STARLINGS (FAMILY STURNIDAE)

9 EUROPEAN STARLING *Sturnus vulgaris* Estornino común L 22 cm. New plumage is dark, all body feathers tipped white. Brown wings and tail. White tips wear off to reveal br plumage – glossy iridescent black shot green and purple, with yellow bill. Imm greyish-brown upperparts, paler underparts. There is an established population in Buenos Aires which is expected to spread.

10 CRESTED MYNA *Acridotheres cristatellus* No local names. L 25 cm. Habitat: parks and gardens. Feeds out in surrounding fields. Chunky black bird with greener tint on underside; yellow bill and legs, pale orange eye. A white circular spot at the base of the primaries, striking in flight. Fine bluish tip to tail. Seen perched on fences. Established north of Mar del Plata, Argentina, (some 400 km south-east of Buenos Aires).

Plate 85

Plate 86

VIREOS (FAMILY VIREONIDAE)

1 **RED-EYED VIREO** *Vireo olivaceus* Chiví común (Arg), Juruviara (Br, Par), Chiví ojirrojo (Bol), Chivi-chivi (Uru), Verderón de ojos rojos (Ch). L 14 cm. Habitat: woods, forests and gardens. Brown eye. Grey crown, long, pale brow. Upperparts olive. Below whitish, washed grey-green on flanks. Voice: sings '*chivee - chividee - cheewee…*'.

2 **RUFOUS-CROWNED GREENLET** *Hylophilus poecilotis* Chiví coronado (Arg, Bol), Verdinho-coroado (Br). L 12.5 cm. Habitat: forests, usually middle storey. Crown chestnut. Ear-coverts speckled. Upperparts yellowish-olive. Below: whitish throat, rest yellowish. Voice: song a high-pitched '*Seeseeseeseesee*'.

3 **RUFOUS-BROWED PEPPERSHRIKE** *Cychlaris gujanensis* Juan chiviro (Arg, Uru, Bol), Sirirí (Bol), Pitiguari (Br), Chiviro (Par). L 16 cm. Habitat: woods and forests. Amber eye. Above olive. Grey head with long rufous brow. Whitish below with yellow band across upper breast. Voice: song a melodious '*toodletiddletoodletiddle*', repeated often. In winter a loud, descending '*tweeootweeootweeootweeoo*'.

WOOD WARBLERS (FAMILY EMBERIZIDAE, SUBFAMILY PARULINAE)

4 **TROPICAL PARULA** *Parula pitiayumi* Pitiayumí (Arg, Bol, Uru), Pyti'ajumi (Par), Reinita montañera (Bol), Mariquita (Br). L 10 cm. Habitat: middle storey in woods and gardens. Upperparts blue-grey but back olive. Breast orange. Yellowish belly. White wing-bars. Voice: a thin '*tsipsipsiprrreetsipi* – (trill) – *tsee*' and variations.

5 **BLACKPOLL WARBLER** *Dendroica striata* Arañero estriado (Arg, Bol), Mosquitero norteamericano (Uru), Monjita americana (Ch). L 13 cm. Habitat: forest edge. N-br plumage: yellowish head with dark streaks on crown. Streaked breast dark on yellow. Flanks streaked. Two white wing-bars.

6 **NORTHERN WATERTHRUSH** *Seiurus noveboracensis* No local names. L 14 cm. Habitat: near water. Above olive-brown. Buff-yellow brow. Yellowish-white below, streaked dark brown on breast. Plain belly. Voice: contact call '*stink*', loud and frequent.

7 **MASKED YELLOWTHROAT** *Geothlypis aequinoctialis* Arañero cara negra (Arg, Bol). L 14 cm. Pia-cobra (Br), Mosquitero amarillo (Uru). L 14 cm. Habitat: edges of marshes in trees and shrubs. ♂: black mask. Bright yellow below. ♀ lacks ♂'s black on face. Voice: loud, fast and clear song starting '*turee turee turee*' then '*tiddle*'s and '*dee*'s; warbles and trills follow – varied.

8 **SLATE-THROATED REDSTART** *Myioborus miniatus* Candelita gargantipizarra (Bol). L 14 cm. Habitat: montane forests and woods. Dark slate-grey hood and upperparts. Central crown rufous. Breast and belly bright yellow. Outer tail feathers white.

9 **BROWN-CAPPED REDSTART** *Myioborus brunniceps* Arañero corona rojiza (Arg), Candelita gorgojeadora or Arañero cabeza castaña (Bol). L 13 cm. Habitat: woods, forest edge, clearings with small trees, gardens. Chestnut cap. White eye-ring. Grey upperparts, olive wash on back. Below yellow. Voice: song a high-pitched '*seeseeseeseeseeseeseeseeseep*'.

10 **TWO-BANDED WARBLER** *Basileuterus bivittatus* Arañero coronado (Arg), Arañero coronado grande (Bol). L 14 cm. Habitat: lower storey of forests. Crown-stripe orange bordered black. Above olive, below yellow. Voice: song is a fast, seemingly endless '*chee chee choo choo chiddle chiddle chum chum tiddle chee chee choo choo chew chiddle chup chup tiddle….*'.

11 **FLAVESCENT WARBLER** *Basileuterus flaveolus* Canário-do-mato (Br). L 14 cm. Habitat: woods and gallery forests, shrubby clearings. Olive upperparts. Yellow brow. Below all yellow, tinged greenish on breast. Voice: song is a rhythmical '*didi deedee teetee dichoodichoo choochoo*'.

12 **PALE-LEGGED WARBLER** *Basileuterus signatus* Arañero ceja amarilla (Arg), Chiuí amarillento (Bol). L 13 cm. Lower storey in montane forests. Upperparts olive. Yellow brow. Dark lores. Yellow underparts, olive flanks. Voice: sings '*tsi tsi tsi tsi*', accelerating and ending with a trill.

13 **GOLDEN-CROWNED WARBLER** *Basileuterus culicivorus* Arañero común (Arg), Arañero coronado chico (Bol), Pula-pula (Br), Mosquitero chico (Uru). L 12 cm. Habitat: undergrowth of rainforests, woods. Orange-red crown stripe bordered black. Upperparts olive-grey. Below yellow. Voice: sings '*witty witty wee ti teeoo*'; or a sharp, buzzing '*bzheew*'.

14 **WHITE-BELLIED WARBLER** *Basileuterus hypoleucus* Pichito (Br). L 12.5 cm. Habitat: undergrowth of drier woods and gallery forest. Long brow white. Dark eye-stripe. Above olive-brown, below white. Voice: sings '*chee-titty-chee-chee-chee-chee-chée-choo*'.

15 **WHITE-BROWED WARBLER** *Basileuterus leucoblepharus* Arañero silbón (Arg), Mosquitero oliváceo (Uru), Pula-pula-assoviador (Br). L 14 cm. Habitat: undergrowth of forests and gallery woods. Grey head with two blackish crown stripes, pale brow, white eye-ring and throat. Upperparts olive. Grey breast, white belly, olive wash on flanks. Voice: song starts with isolated sharp '*tsip-tseep*' and continues with a rhythmically erratic '*ti tsi tsi dididi see didi day doe doo doo doo*' – stumbling and descending in pitch.

▶

Plate 86

16 RIVER WARBLER *Phaeothlypis rivularis* Arañero ribereño (Arg), Arañero ocráceo (Bol), Pula-pula-ribeirinho (Br). L 13 cm. Habitat: always near streams in forests. Upperparts olive, crown greyish with two faint darker stripes. Whitish-buff below. Voice: song may have an introductory *'tew wheet'* then *'titititititew teew teeew teew tew ...'* slowing down, 8 to 10 times – loud and clear.

BANANAQUIT (SUBFAMILY COEREBINAE)

17 BANANAQUIT *Coereba flaveola* Mielero (Arg), Cambacica or Mariquita (Br), Reinita común or Saí amarillo (Bol). L 11 cm. Habitat: semi-open woods and forests, gardens. Upperparts grey, darker on crown and tail. Long white eyebrow. Grey throat. Yellow breast and belly. Voice: song is a thin, high-pitched *'tsitsiweetsiwee'*.

Plate 87

TANAGERS (SUBFAMILY THRAUPINAE)

1 CHESTNUT-VENTED CONEBILL *Conirostrum speciosum* Saí común (Arg, Bol), Mielerito azul (Bol), Figuinha-de-rabo-castanho (Br). L 11 cm. Habitat: fairly high in open woods and gallery forest. ♂: upperparts, wings and tail blue-grey. Pale grey underparts. Under tail-coverts chestnut. White speculum in wings. ♀: blue grey head. White brow. Upperparts olive. Underparts whitish, buff on breast. Voice: a fast, rattled *'tiddly'* song.

2 CINEREOUS CONEBILL *Conirostrum cinereum* Comesebo chico (Ch), Mielerito gris (Bol). L 11 cm. Habitat: shrubbery and open areas with scattered trees; gardens. Upperparts olive-grey, crown darker. Long white brow. Dark wings with white patch at base of primaries. Below buff-grey.

3 TAMARUGO CONEBILL *Conirostrum tamarugense* Comesebo de los tamarugales (Ch). L 12 cm. Habitat: low scrubby woods. Grey above, rufous brow. Throat, upper breast and under tail-coverts rufous. Rest of underparts whitish-grey. Grey-brown wings with white patch on primaries.

4 FAWN-BREASTED TANAGER *Pipraeidea melanonota* Viuva (Arg, Uru), Tangará de antifaz (Bol), Sai guasu (Par), Viúva (Br). L 14 cm. Habitat: woods, forest edge and clearings. Black forehead, around eye and to ear-coverts. Crown and rump pale blue. Back rich purple-blue (♂) or grey-blue (♀). Below buff-fawn. Voice: a very high-pitched and thin *'sisisisisi...'* song of four to ten syllables.

5 GREEN-HEADED TANAGER *Tangara arcoiris* Tangará aroiris (Arg), Sete-cores (Br). L 14 cm. Habitat: high in the rainforest and edges. ♂: head shiny blue-green. Upper back golden-green. Mid-back black. Lower back orange. Bright blue breast, shiny green flanks. Wing-coverts purple-blue. Tail and flight feathers black, bordered green. ♀: a toned-down version of ♂. Voice: sings *'tchewee-chewee chewee'*.

6 RED-NECKED TANAGER *Tangara cyanocephala* Tangará cuello castaño (Arg), Saíra-militar or Saíra-lenço (Br). L 13 cm. Habitat: higher elevation rainforests and edges. Throat, forehead and crown blue. Black on back (streaked green in ♀). Face, ear-coverts and nape bright rufous. Breast, flanks and belly bright green.

7 CHESTNUT-BACKED TANAGER *Tangara preciosa* Tangará castaño (Arg), Saíra-sapucaia (Br), Tangará preciosa (Uru). L 15 cm. Habitat: forests and edges, clearings at all levels. ♂: coppery chestnut. Back and wing-coverts silvery buff. Underparts silvery buff. ♀: head and nape chestnut. Back, wings and tail green. Pale green below.

8 BURNISHED-BUFF TANAGER *Tangara cayana* Tangará pecho negro (Arg), Saíra-amarelo (Br), Sai (Par), Tanagrá pecho negro (Bol). L 15 cm. Habitat: at all levels in savannahs with scattered trees, scrub. ♂: black face, chin, throat and breast, the rest rich buff. Wings and tail blue-green. ♀: greener. No black.

9 BLUE DACNIS *Dacnis cayana* Saí azul (Arg, Br, Bol), Saíra (Br), Mielero turquesa (Bol). L 13 cm. Habitat: forest edge, regrowth, clearings with trees, gallery woods. ♂: throat and back black. Head, breast, belly and flanks turquoise. ♀: green, blue face and crown.

10 BLUE-NAPED CHLOROPHONIA *Chlorophonia cyanea* Tangará bonito (Arg), Bonito-do-campo (Br). L 11 cm. Habitat: rainforest canopy and edge. Bright green hood. Eye-ring bright blue (♂ also has bright blue on centre of back and rump). Breast, belly and flanks lemon-yellow (olive-washed in ♀).

11 GOLDEN-RUMPED EUPHONIA *Euphonia aureata* Tangará cabeza celeste (Arg, Bol), Gaturamo-rei (Br). L 11 cm. Habitat: high at forest edges, gardens, woods. ♂: back dark metallic blue. Crown and nape electric blue. Rump, breast and belly yellow. ♀: olive above except for blue crown and nape. Orange forehead. Yellow below. Voice: song starts with a sedate *'fwheeew... tooree... fooreeew... tooree'* then goes mad and rattles off ten or more seconds of very fast, incomprehensible *'fiddletoddleteeteetiddle...'*, repeated.

12 PURPLE-THROATED EUPHONIA *Euphonia chlorotica* Tangará garganta violácea (Arg, Bol), Fi-fi verdadeiro or Vivi (Br), Teteî (Par). L 10 cm. Habitat: high in forest edges, gallery woods, clearings, chaco woods. ♂: hood purple, including throat. Yellow fore-crown. Upperparts bluish-black. Underparts bright yellow. ♀: olive above. Narrow yellow forehead. Greenish-yellow on throat. White breast and belly. Voice: a high, whistled, piercing though plaintive *'fee-wee'*, over and over again.

13 VIOLACEOUS EUPHONIA *Euphonia violacea* Tangará amarillo (Arg), Gaturamo-verdadeiro (Br), Tiete'i (Par). L 12 cm. Habitat: rainforest edge, clearings, gardens, gallery forest. Above steel-blue. Fore-crown from above eye and all underparts yellow. Voice: fast, rattling, very varied *'clickety-tiddle'* song.

▶

Plate 87

14 CHESTNUT-BELLIED EUPHONIA *Euphonia pectoralis* Tangará alcalde (Arg), Ferro-velho (Br), Tiete (Par). L 12 cm. Habitat: high in forest canopy and edges. ♂: breast, head and all upperparts dark steel blue. Yellow spot at each side of breast. Belly, flanks and under tail-coverts dark chestnut. ♀: olive above. Greyish underparts. Under tail-coverts chestnut. Voice: song a very strange series of five or six raucous and buzzing '*bzh*'s, rapid – and rather ugly.

15 GREEN-CHINNED EUPHONIA *Euphonia chalybea* Tangará picudo (Arg), Cais-cais (Br). L 12 cm. Habitat: rainforest edge and large trees. ♂: above dark purplish with greenish sheen, extending onto chin. Forehead and all remaining underparts yellow. ♀: olive above and on throat. Underparts grey.

16 DIADEMED TANAGER *Stephanophorus diadematus* Frutero azul (Arg), Cardenal azul (Uru), Sanhaço-frade (Br). L 19 cm. Habitat: open country with patches of trees, gardens. Shiny purple-blue. Face, forehead and chin black. Fore-crown puffy, red. Hind-crown white. Wings and tail black, feathers edged blue. Voice: song is a fully melodious and clear '*wee tiwee tewee tier weedle doo*', varied and lovely.

17 BLUE-AND-YELLOW TANAGER *Thraupis bonariensis* Naranjero (Arg, Bol, Uru, Ch), Sanhaço-papa-laranjas (Br). L 17 cm. Habitat: arid woodland, gardens. ♂: blue hood and black face to around eye. Mantle black. Rump and underparts bright orange-yellow, paler on belly. Wings and tail black, feathers edged blue. Wing-coverts pale blue. ♀ dull: greyish above with slight olive wash. Drab buff below. Wings and tail darkish, faintly edged bluish-green. Rump with yellowish wash. Voice: sings a thin '*see-up…pichee see-up pidderee…*'.

Plate 88

TANAGERS (SUBFAMILY THRAUPINAE)

1 SAYACA TANAGER *Thraupis sayaca* Celestino (Arg, Bol), Sayubú oscuro (Bol), Frutero celeste (Uru), Sanhaço-cinzento (Br), Sai hovy (Par). L 16 cm. Habitat: forest edge, woods, gardens and savannahs. Above dull bluish-grey, below grey with a touch of blue. Wings and tail with greenish-blue edging. Voice: song is a high-pitched, thin '*sip - sisi say swee*' or '*see we say swee…. see we say swee*' with variations.

2 AZURE-SHOULDERED TANAGER *Thraupis cyanoptera* Sanhaço-de-encontro-azul (Br). L 18 cm. Habitat: montane coastal rainforests. Heavy bill. Dull bluish-grey above with hint of greenish wash on back. Wing and tail feathers edged blue. Below paler blue-grey. Lesser wing-coverts bright blue.

3 PALM TANAGER *Thraupis palmarum* Sanhaço-do-coqueiro (Br), Azulejo de palmares (Bol). L 18 cm. Habitat: forest edge, agricultural areas, always where there are palms. Overall olive-brownish-grey; paler on face and wing-coverts. Slightly darker back. Dark flight feathers, forming a markedly two-tone wing. Dark tail.

4 BRAZILIAN TANAGER *Ramphocelus bresilius* Fueguero escarlata (Arg), Tié-sangue (Br). L 18.5 cm. Habitat: forest edge and clearings with regrowth. Pale silvery bill. ♂ scarlet, black wings and tail. ♀ has brown upperparts but redder on back. Chestnut rump and underparts. Wings and tail dark brown.

5 SILVER-BEAKED TANAGER *Ramphocelus carbo* Pipira-vermelha (Br), Sangre de toro (Bol), Jurundi (Par). L 18 cm. Habitat: near water at forest edge, gardens. Lower mandible silvery white, (ash-grey in ♀). Overall black with reddish wash which comes through on forehead and breast. Flanks browner. ♀: dark brown head and upperparts, red shows through on breast, becomes dominant on rump; under tail-coverts quite pinkish-brown. Tail blackish. Noisy flocks in the lower vegetation.

6 HEPATIC TANAGER *Piranga flava* Fueguero común (Arg, Bol), Frutero rojo (Uru), Sanhaço-de-fogo (Br). L 17 cm. Habitat: open woods, gallery forests, savannahs with trees. ♂: red, browner on upperparts. ♀: yellow, greener on upperparts. Flicks tail up and down. Voice: contact call an audible '*chup*'.

7 SUMMER TANAGER *Piranga rubra* Piranga (Ch). L 16.5 cm. Habitat: woods near the water. ♂ entirely rosy-red with black in wings. ♀ yellow below, dingy green on upperparts. Once seen in Chile.

8 RED-CROWNED ANT-TANAGER *Habia rubica* Fueguero morado (Arg), Tié-do-mato-grosso (Br), Tangará copetón (Bol). L 18 cm. Habitat: low in rainforests. Crown crest bright scarlet. ♂: above brownish-red, rosier below. ♀: dull red crest. Brown, more buff on underparts. Noisy in small groups. Voice: musical, thrush-like song, loud, often follows series of scolding harsh '*chwits*' or '*chitchitchit*'.

9 WHITE-LINED TANAGER *Tachyphonus rufus* Frutero negro (Arg), Pipira-preta (Br). L 18 cm. Habitat: clearings, open woods, near water. ♂ like Ruby-crowned but lacks hidden red on crown. ♀ uniform chestnut, though slightly paler below. Voice: song a repeated '*cheep-chooi… cheep-chooi…*'.

10 RUBY-CROWNED TANAGER *Tachyphonus coronatus* Frutero coronado (Arg), Tié-preto (Br). L 17 cm. Habitat: forest edge. ♂: all shiny black. Hidden red crown-patch. White under wing-coverts. ♀: basically chestnut. Greyer on head, paler on belly. Faint streaking on breast. Bright tail. Voice: song a strong, whistled, staccato, rhythmically spaced '*cheeroo… churu….. whit… chew… chera… chira… whit… chut…*', on and on.

11 GREY-HEADED TANAGER *Eucometis penicillata* Frutero amarillento (Arg), Pipira-de-taoca (Br), Bachaquero (Bol). L 18 cm. Habitat: gallery forests, woods. Grey hood with paler erectile crown, even paler throat. Above brownish-olive. Underparts strong yellow.

Plate 89

TANAGERS (SUBFAMILY THRAUPINAE)

1 BLACK-GOGGLED TANAGER *Trichothraupis melanops* Frutero corona amarilla (Arg), Tangará corona amarilla (Bol), Tié-de-topete (Br). L 16 cm. Habitat: lower and middle storey in forests. ♂: black forehead and face (around eye). Yellow crown stripe. Above grey-brown, below buff. Black wings with white band at base of primaries seen in flight. Black tail. ♀ lacks black goggles and yellow crest. Voice: a melodious song 'swee tititwee... tweedle...tweedle twee... teeoee' and a contact 'tsip'.

2 WHITE-RUMPED TANAGER *Cypsnagra hirundinacea* Bandoleta (Br). L 15.5 cm. Habitat: open areas with bushes and low trees. Top of head, neck, upper back, upper tail-coverts, tail, all black. Wings black with a white patch at base of primaries, and white-edged secondaries. White line of upper-coverts. Lower back and rump white. Pinkish throat and cheeks, paling to pale buff on breast. Whitish belly. Voice: sings a wonderful duet from treetops in the early morning.

3 CHESTNUT-HEADED TANAGER *Pyrrhocoma ruficeps* Frutero cabeza castaña (Arg), Cabecinha castanha (Br). L 13 cm. Habitat: low in undergrowth of rainforests, in shadow. ♂: black forehead and face. Rest of hood chestnut. All the rest grey, paler below. ♀: cinnamon hood, lighter on throat. Olivaceous upperparts. Dingy buff underparts, paler on belly. Voice: a high-pitched song 'feeoofeeoofeeoo - fooeet fooeet'.

4 HOODED TANAGER *Nemosia pileata* Frutero cabeza negra (Arg), Saíra-de-chapéu-preto (Br), Tangará cabeza negra (Bol). L 13 cm. Habitat: forest clearings with low vegetation, gallery forests. Yellow eye and legs. ♂: black cap and sides of neck. White lores and underparts. Upperparts blue-grey. ♀: lacks black. With buff on sides of neck and breast.

5 GUIRA TANAGER *Hemithraupis guira* Saíra dorada (Arg), Tangará pecho rojizo (Bol), Saíra-de-papo-preto (Br). L 13 cm. Habitat: rainforest edge, woods, gallery forest. ♂: black throat and face framed by a yellow line. Upperparts yellowish-green. Breast and rump cinnamon. Grey flanks; pale, yellowish belly and under tail-coverts. Wings and tail dark, feathers edged greenish. ♀ nondescript: olive above, yellowish below. Grey flanks. Yellowish brow and rump. Voice: thin, high-pitched song 'tee...tee...tikitikitikitikitik'.

6 ORANGE-HEADED TANAGER *Thlypopsis sordida* Frutero cabeza naranja (Arg), Canário-sapé (Br), Tangará cabeza naranja (Bol). L 14 cm. Habitat: gallery woods and thin forest regrowth in the lowlands. Orange hood, more yellow on throat and face. Grey, washed olive above; buff-white below, slightly more buff on under tail-coverts. Greyer flanks. Voice: a high-pitched, thin song 'tsit-tsitseewitseew'.

7 RUST-AND-YELLOW TANAGER *Thlypopsis ruficeps* Frutero alisero (Arg). L 13 cm. Habitat: high montane woods near alders. Orange-chestnut hood, yellow on throat. Rest of upperparts olive. Below bright yellow. Olive wash on flanks. Imm has greenish-yellow head.

8 COMMON BUSH-TANAGER *Chlorospingus ophthalmicus* Fruterito yungueño (Arg), Tangará ojo blanco (Bol). L 14 cm. Habitat: at all levels in montane forests and woods. Head and upperparts greenish-brown. White post-ocular spot. Throat and belly white. Greenish-yellow across breast, down flanks and under tail-coverts. Wings and tail olivaceous. Voice: song is a long, irregular series of 'tsips'.

9 WHITE-BANDED TANAGER *Neothraupis fasciata* Cigarra-do-campo (Br). L 15.5 cm. Habitat: branches of trees, but also comes to the ground. Above grey. Below white, tinted grey on breast. Black face to ear-coverts. Narrow white brow. Blackish wing-coverts with medians tipped white forming one wing-bar.

10 MAGPIE TANAGER *Cissopis leveriana* Frutero overo (Arg), Morichero blanco (Bol), Aka'emi kavaru (Par). L 28 cm. Habitat: gardens, forest edges. Yellow eye. Head, upper back and breast black. Rest of upperparts and lower underparts white. Wings black with white tips to coverts and edges of inner flight feathers. Graded tail long, black, white-tipped. Voice: a high-pitched song 'sissopipee, sissopipee... siddly pireen, siddly pireen...', often duetted.

11 BLACK-FACED TANAGER *Schistochlamys melanopis* Chovy estero (Par), Sanhaço-de-coleira (Br). L 18 cm. Habitat: grasslands with scattered trees and bushes, edge of forest patches. Quite short, thick bill blue-grey with black tip. Mostly grey, paler below. Black forehead, face and throat. Imm olive, paler below. Yellow eye-ring. Also transition plumages.

12 SWALLOW TANAGER *Tersina viridis* Tersina (Arg), Saí-andorinha (Br). Tangará golondrina (Bol). L 14.5 cm. Habitat: forests and woods. Broad bill. ♂: black face and throat. Rest mostly shiny turquoise (or blue-green depending on angle of light) with barring on flanks. Black flight feathers and on tail, feathers edged blue. Belly and under tail-coverts white. ♀ green. Lower underparts pale yellow with green barring on flanks. Grey throat speckled. Perches conspicuously on emergent branches. Voice: high pitched, clear and 'tiddly' song with lots of 'tseees' thrown in.

Note: Until recently this species was considered to form a family all by itself. It certainly seems a very aberrant Thraupin.

Plate 89

Plate 90

CARDINALS, GROSBEAKS AND ALLIES (SUBFAMILY CARDENALINAE)

1 **BUFF-THROATED SALTATOR** *Saltator maximus* Picurero (Bol), Tempera-viola (Br). L 20 cm. Habitat: at all levels in humid forest edge, thickets, woods and clearings with scattered trees. Above bright olive. Short brow and chin white. Throat cinnamon-buff. Black malar stripe. Below greyish-buff.

2 **GREYISH SALTATOR** *Saltator coerulescens* Pepitero gris (Arg, Bol), Rey del bosque plomizo (Uru), Sabiá-gongá (Br). L 21 cm. Habitat: woods and gallery forests, pastures with scattered trees. Blackish bill. Above grey. Short buff brow. Below pale greyish becoming cinnamon on belly and under tail-coverts. Voice: song 'tup-tup-cheew… chup chup chweeee', sometimes duetted. Ugly-sounding contact call.

3 **GREEN-WINGED SALTATOR** *Saltator similis* Pepitero verdoso (Arg, Bol), Trinca-ferro-verdadeiro (Br), Rey del bosque verdoso (Uru). L 21 cm. Habitat: woods, forest edge, gallery forests, clearings. Olive-grey above. Long white brow. White throat bracketed by black malar stripes. Buff underparts. Edge of flight feathers olive-green. Voice: a slow, melodious song 'whee-teew-teewteew-whit …tew-tew-whee-tew-wheechew' with variations.

4 **THICK-BILLED SALTATOR** *Saltator maxillosus* Pepitero pico grueso (Arg), Bico-grosso (Br). L 20 cm. Habitat: canopy and forest edge. Fairly thick bill black with orange at base. Above grey. Long white brow. Black malar stripe. Below buff, greyer on breast. ♀ similar but with olive-brown upperparts.

5 **GOLDEN-BILLED SALTATOR** *Saltator aurantiirostris* Pepitero de collar (Arg), Patetao (Br), Rey del bosque común (Uru), Pepitero (Ch). L 21 cm. Habitat: scrub, woods and gardens. ♂: bright orange bill. Black face, ear-coverts and ring around white throat. Upperparts grey. White post-ocular round ear-coverts and down. Underparts buff. ♀: brown bill; toned-down browner version of ♂. Voice: loud and clear song 'pitytewp - towee' or 'wee too - toowheeew' with variations.

6 **BLACK-THROATED SALTATOR** *Saltator atricollis* Pepitero de corbata (Bol), Bico-de-pimenta (Br). L 20 cm. Habitat: scrub. Upperparts brown. Face and throat black. Grey post-ocular and ear-coverts. Below cinnamon-buff.

7 **RUFOUS-BELLIED SALTATOR** *Saltator rufiventris* Pepitero colorado (Arg, Bol). L 21 cm. Habitat: copses and agricultural areas in mountain valleys. Upperparts and breast all grey. Long white brow. Lower breast and belly rich rufous. Voice: sings 'fweet-fweet'.

8 **BLACK-THROATED GROSBEAK** *Pitylus fuliginosus* Pepitero negro (Arg), Pimentao (Br). L 22 cm. Habitat: at middle and upper levels of rainforests. Red bill. All blackish. Voice: melodious, slow song 'wheet-too-wheew… piriweep-poo-peew… teeroo-tew-toweet-you… turoowee-too-tew…tiroo-tee-too-t yeew…'.

9 **BLACK-BACKED GROSBEAK** *Pheucticus aureoventris* Rey del bosque (Arg, Bol), Rei-do-bosque (Br). L 22 cm. Habitat: open woods, usually in thick foliage, or under the canopy. Massive bill. ♂: head, breast and back black. Underparts yellow, spotted with black on flanks. Wings with white spotting. ♀: patterned like ♂ but dark brown instead of black, and speckled yellow breast. Voice: varied and melodious song 'piddly weep… piddly weep… too-reew…'.

10 **ULTRAMARINE GROSBEAK** *Passerina brissonii* Reina mora grande (Arg), Reina mora (Bol, Uru), Azulao or Azulao-verdadeiro (Br). L 16 cm. Habitat: savannahs, woods and forests, undergrowth, thickets. ♂ dark glossy blue with pale blue on forehead, face, eyebrow and shoulders. ♀: above reddish-brown, below cinnamon. Voice: a loud, fast song 'triddle tiddle deedle toodle-oo…', descending at the end.

11 **GLAUCOUS-BLUE GROSBEAK** *Cyanoloxia glaucocaerulea* Reina mora chica (Arg), Azulinho (Br). L 14 cm. Habitat: forest edges, woods, secondary growth. ♂ powdery blue. ♀: reddish-brown above, cinnamon below. Voice: a fast tiddly-trilling song, phrases lasting three to four seconds.

12 **PLUSHCAP** *Catambyrhynchus diadema* Diadema (Arg), Cabecipeludo or Tangará coronado (Bol). L 14 cm. Habitat: montane undergrowth, especially with cane. Forehead yellow and puffy. Hind-crown and nape dull black. Rest of upperparts dark grey. Face and underparts chestnut.

Note: The Plushcap is an aberrant species once considered a family of its own.

13 **RED-CRESTED CARDINAL** *Paroaria coronata* Cardenal común (Arg, Bol), Cardeal (Br), Cardenal de copete rojo (Uru). L 18 cm. Habitat: woods. Hood, including pointed crest, to throat and a point on upper breast, scarlet. Grey above. Underparts white. Voice: lovely, slow, melodious and phrased song 'pidiwheew…tewee…tereewheew…pureew…' on and on.

14 **YELLOW-BILLED CARDINAL** *Paroaria capitata* Cardenilla (Arg), Cavalaria (Br), Cardelina or Cardenal sin copete (Bol). L 17 cm. Habitat: bushy areas near water. Yellow bill. Red hood. Dark grey back. White breast and belly slightly buff, as also under tail-coverts. Voice: melodious and varied song 'chit chewee choo chirowee'.

▶

Plate 90

15 RED-CRESTED FINCH *Coryphospingus cucullatus* Brasita de fuego (Arg, Bol), Guyra pytâ'i (Par), Tico-tico-rei (Br). L 14 cm. Habitat: arid scrub, dry woods and semi-open farmland. ♂: scarlet crown bordered black forms slight crest. Whitish eye-ring. Above brownish-red. Crimson rump. Below plum red. ♀ lacks crown colours, otherwise a browner version of ♂. Voice: song is in march time: '*chirep - wheew - chidip - wheew - chirip - wheew…*'.

Plate 91

CARDINALS, GROSBEAKS AND ALLIES (SUBFAMILY CARDENALINAE)

1 YELLOW CARDINAL *Gubernatrix cristata* Cardenal amarillo (Arg), Cardeal-amarelo (Br). L 20 cm. Habitat: scrub, savannahs, steppes and open woods. ♂: forehead and pointed crest black, bordered bright yellow. Olive face and upperparts, latter streaked black. Central tail feathers olive, outers yellow. ♀ is a toned-down version with grey instead of yellow. Pairs. Voice: lovely and musical song.

EMBERIZINE FINCHES (SUBFAMILY EMBERIZINAE)

2 MANY-COLOURED CHACO-FINCH *Saltatricula multicolor* Pepitero chico (Arg, Bol), Manchadito (Uru). L 17 cm. Habitat: edge of dry Chaco woods, grass and bushes. Face and sides of throat black. Upperparts brownish. White brow. Neck and collar across breast grey. Pink sides of breast and flanks. White belly. Tail broadly tipped white. Voice: song '*piree-weeroo-weeroo*' repeated ten or more times.

3 BLACK-MASKED FINCH *Coryphaspiza melanotis* Cachilo de antifaz (Arg), Tico-tico-do-campo (Br). L 13 cm. Habitat: open tall grass with few shrubs. ♂: black head, white brow. Back streaked olive and darkish brown. Below white. Tail black, terminal half white. ♀: head and back streaked buff and dark. Buff brow, blackish forehead. Below, wings and tail like ♂. Voice: an insect-like '*tseelee*'.

4 COAL-CRESTED FINCH *Charitospiza eucosma* Afrechero canela (Arg), Mineirinho (Br). L 13 cm. Habitat: grass with bushes and trees. Long, floppy crest. ♂: crown, crest, chin, face, throat and breast black. Sides of head white. Upperparts pale grey. Flanks, belly cinnamon. Wings black, coverts grey. Tail black, outer feathers white at base, seen in flight. ♀: brown, greyer on back. White in tail as in ♂.

5 FULVOUS-HEADED BRUSH-FINCH *Atlapetes fulviceps* Afrechero cabeza castaña (Arg, Bol). L 17 cm. Habitat: undergrowth in montane forests. Chestnut head. Yellow spot before the eye. Yellow malar streak. Yellow throat and breast. Above olive. Voice: a thin, high-pitched song '*tsit - tsit - tsiddle tsoo tsoo tsoo*'.

6 YELLOW-STRIPED BRUSH-FINCH *Atlapetes citrinellus* Afrechero ceja amarilla (Arg). L 17 cm. Habitat: undergrowth of montane forests and alder woods. Back, wings and tail olivaceous. Eye-stripe, ear-coverts and mustachios black. Chin and long eyebrow yellow. Olive breast and flanks.

7 STRIPE-HEADED BRUSH-FINCH *Atlapetes torquatus* Afrechero vientre blanco (Arg), Afrechero grande or Corbatico (Bol). L 19 cm. Habitat: undergrowth and edges of montane forests. Black bill. Black head with grey crown stripe. White brow. Olive upperparts, tail and wings, these with yellow spot at bend. All white below. Grey flanks. Voice: a high-pitched, slow song '*tseewee…tseew…*' almost inaudible.

8 SAFFRON-BILLED SPARROW *Arremon flavirostris* Afrechero de collar (Arg, Bol), Tico-tico-de-mato-de-bico-amarelo (Br). L 15 cm. Habitat: undergrowth of woods and forests. Bill orange-yellow. Yellow spot at bend of wing. Below white with black band across breast, greyish flanks. Voice: song a thin, high-pitched series of '*tip-tsip-seeps*'.

9 SOOTY GRASSQUIT *Tiaris fuliginosa* Cigarra-do-coqueiro (Br). L 12.5 cm. Habitat: forest edges, woods and cleared areas with grass. Often congregates at seeding cane. ♂: dull brownish-black. ♀ overall olive-brown, brighter on underparts. Voice: said to be '*eezoodlee*'.

10 DULL-COLOURED GRASSQUIT *Tiaris obscura* Espiguero pardo (Arg). L 11 cm. Habitat: forest and wood edge, savannahs. Sexes alike. Resemble ♀ seedeaters (below). Above olive-brown. Below brownish-grey. Voice: a buzzing '*zeetig, zeezeezig*' song with variations.

11 BAND-TAILED SEEDEATER *Catamenia analis* Picodeoro chico (Arg), Semillero (Ch). L 13 cm. Habitat: grassy uplands, fields, hedges, between 1500 and 3000 m. Bill pale yellow. ♂ blue-grey, blackish on face. White belly. Undertail chestnut. Tail with white band seen in flight. Wings have white patch at base of primaries. ♀: above greyish-brown streaked blackish. Below buff, streaked darker. Tail: patterned like ♂'s. Buff wing-patch. Voice: fast, rolling '*diddle diddle diddle didee*' song.

12 PLAIN-COLOURED SEEDEATER *Catamenia inornata* Picodeoro grande (Arg), Semillero peruano (Ch). L 14.5 cm. Habitat: open, grassy uplands, fields and scattered shrubs. In the Andes between 3000 and 4000 m; lower in Cordoba and San Luis mountains in Central Argentina. Pinkish bill. ♂: lead grey, streaked on back. Whiter on belly. Chestnut undertail. ♀: greyish-brown streaked on back. Buff below.

13 BLACKISH-BLUE SEEDEATER *Amaurospiza moesta* Arrocero azul (Arg), Negrinho-do-mato (Br). L 12.5 cm. Habitat: low in thick undergrowth of forests and woods. ♂ slaty blue. Under wing-coverts white. ♀ rich brown. Under wing-coverts white. Voice: fast and varied song '*swee-swee-swi-swee-seeseeoo…*'.

▶

Plate 91

14 LESSER SEED-FINCH *Oryziborus angolensis* Arrocero castaño (Arg, Bol), Curió or Avinhado (Br). L 13 cm. Habitat: edge of forest in grassy or shrubby clearings. ♂: upperparts, breast, wings and tail black. Wings with white patch; white underwing coverts. Belly and flanks rich chestnut. Voice: song starts '*tiwee tiwee tiwee…*' then on through rolls and trills.

15 BUFF-FRONTED SEEDEATER *Sporophila frontalis* Corbatita oliváceo (Arg), Pichochó (Br). L 12.5 cm. Habitat: forest edges, cane, overgrown clearings. ♂: olive-brown. Forehead, post-ocular streak and throat buff-white. Below lighter. Two buff-white wing-bars. ♀ lacks post-ocular streak, wing-bars buff. Voice: a harsh grating song '*che-che-chew*'.

16 TEMMINCK'S SEEDEATER *Sporophila falcirostris* Corbatita picudo (Arg), Cigarra-verdadeira (Br). L 11 cm. Habitat: secondary woods and forest edge with cane. Bill yellow. Overall grey, whitish mid-belly. White wing-bar and white patch at base of primaries.

Plate 92

EMBERIZINE FINCHES (SUBFAMILY EMBERIZINAE)

1 PLUMBEOUS SEEDEATER *Sporophila plumbea* Corbatita plomizo (Arg), Patativa-verdadeira (Br), Espiguero plomizo or Pimpín plomizo (Bol). L 11 cm. Habitat: open savannahs and tall grasslands. ♂: grey. White chin and mid-belly. Wings have white spot on secondaries.

2 WING-BARRED SEEDEATER *Sporophila americana* Gola or Coleira-do-norte (Br). L 11.5 cm. Habitat: grassy areas with bushes. ♂: black above, grey rump. Wing-coverts white-tipped forming a line of dots. White base of primaries. White throat extending to form incomplete collar. Black breast-band, grey flanks.

3 RUSTY-COLLARED SEEDEATER *Sporophila collaris* Corbatita dominó (Arg), Kapi'i (Par), Coleiro-do-brejo (Br), Corbatita de collar (Bol), Gargantillo de collar (Uru). L 12 cm. Habitat: tall grasses and edge of reeds. ♂: cap, back and collar black. White spots below the eye. White throat. Hind-neck and rump chestnut. Flanks cinnamon. ♀: above olivaceous. Underparts cinnamon-buff. White throat. Two buff wing-bars. Voice: canary-like song, fast, varied and musical, goes on and on.

4 LINED SEEDEATER *Sporophila lineola* Corbatita overo (Arg), Bigodinho (Br), Espiguero bigotudo or Pimpín bigotudo (Bol). L 11.5 cm. Habitat: tall grass with some trees, gardens, edge of cultivated areas. ♂: black hood and upperparts. Crown, malar stripe, wing patch, rump and underparts white. ♀: olive-brown above, buff below, paler on belly. Voice: a loud and alarming song '*pipipipipi-pee*' from a conspicuous perch.

5 YELLOW-BELLIED SEEDEATER *Sporophila nigricollis* Corbatita vientre amarillo (Arg), Baiano (Br), Espiguero ventriamarillo or Pimpín ventriamarillo (Bol). L 11.5 cm. Habitat: clearings with bushes, savannahs, tall grass. ♂: black hood. Upperparts olive. Lower breast, flanks and belly pale yellow. Voice: musical and short song '*pseepseepseepseeoo - bzzi bzzee*'.

6 DOUBLE-COLLARED SEEDEATER *Sporophila caerulescens* Corbatita común (Arg, Bol), Guyra juru tu'i (Par), Gargantillo común (Uru), Coleirinho or Papa-capim (Br). L 11 cm. Habitat: grasslands with scrubby bush or small trees. ♂: above grey. White malar streak. Black chin-spot. White collar on throat, black collar across upper breast. Underparts white. Voice: rather measured song '*tootootootetoo– teetooterteep*'.

7 WHITE-BELLIED SEEDEATER *Sporophila leucoptera* Corbatita ala blanca (Arg), Chorao (Br), Corbatita pico grueso (Bol). L 12 cm. Habitat: tall grass with scattered shrubs. ♂: above grey; wings with large white patch at base of primaries. Below all white. ♀: white in the wing as in ♂. Voice: sings a clear '*kleeoo kleeoo kleeoo kleeoo kleeoo*'.

8 CAPPED SEEDEATER *Sporophila bouvreuil* Corbatita boina negra (Arg), Caboclinho (Br). L 10 cm. Habitat: tall grass savannahs. ♂: black cap, wings and tail. White base of primaries. Rest pale cinnamon.

9 RUDDY-BREASTED SEEDEATER *Sporophila hypoxantha* Capuchino canela (Arg), Espiguero canelillo (Bol), Caboclinho-de-barriga-vermelha (Br), Pimpincito (Bol). L 10 cm. Habitat: tall grass near water and marshes. ♂: dull brownish-grey back. Rufous-cinnamon rump and belly, paling on breast to buff ear-coverts. White patch at base of primaries. Voice: song a deliberate '*cheeoo cheeoo chiwee choo*'.

10 DARK-THROATED SEEDEATER *Sporophila ruficollis* Capuchino garganta café (Arg), Caboclinho-paraguai (Br), Corbatita castaña (Bol, Uru). L 11 cm. Habitat: tall grass with shrubs, near damper areas. ♂: crown and back grey. Chestnut rump. Ear-coverts, throat and upper breast blackish-brown. Underparts chestnut. Tail and wings blackish, all edged buff. White patch at base of primaries. White in the wing. ♀ same as many others. Voice: slow, high-pitched and varied song.

11 MARSH SEEDEATER *Sporophila palustris* Capuchino pecho blanco (Arg), Corbatita de bañados (Uru), Caboclinho-de-papo-branco (Br). L 10 cm. Tall grass around marshes. ♂: grey crown and back. Throat and upper breast white. Rump and rest of underparts chestnut. White wing-patch. ♀: olive-brown above, buffy below, paler on belly. White wing-patch.

12 WHITE-COLLARED SEEDEATER *Sporphila zelichi* Capuchino de collar (Arg). L 10 cm. Habitat: tall grass near water and low woods. ♂: grey crown. Throat, chest, nuchal collar white. Chestnut back and underparts. ♀ same as many others.

▶

Plate 92

13 RUFOUS-RUMPED SEEDEATER *Sporophila hypochroma* Capuchino castaño (Arg). L 10 cm. Habitat: tall grass near marshes. Bluish-grey crown and back. Bright chestnut rump and all underparts. White wing-patch. ♀ same as many others.

14 CHESTNUT SEEDEATER *Sporophila cinnamomea* Capuchino corona gris (Arg), Caboclinho-de-chapéu-cinzento (Br), Guyra juru tu'i pytâ (Par). L 10 cm. Habitat: tall grass in wetter areas near marshes. Grey crown, rest chestnut. White patch in wing. ♀ same as many others.

15 BLACK-BELLIED SEEDEATER *Sporophila melanogaster* Caboclinho-de-barriga-preta (Br). L 10 cm. Habitat: taller grass in wet areas. Above grey. Black chin, throat, breast, belly and under tail-coverts. Grey flanks.

16 CHESTNUT-THROATED SEEDEATER *Sporophila telasco* Corbatita (Ch). L 12 cm. Habitat: grass with bushes and small trees. ♂: above grey, streaked black. Tail white at the base. Chin rich chestnut. Below all white. ♀: above sandy brown streaked darker; below whitish, streaked on breast and flanks.

17 BLUE-BLACK GRASSQUIT *Volatinia jacarina* Volatinero (Arg), Jakarimi (Par), Semillero chirri or Saltapalito (Bol), Sierra-sierra (Uru), Negrillo (Ch), Tiziu (Br). L 11 cm. Habitat: open country, farms, towns. ♂ shiny blue-black. White under wing-coverts. ♀ brown; below buff, streaked on breast and flanks. Voice: song an explosive '*dzée-oo*'.

Plate 93

EMBERIZINE FINCHES (SUBFAMILY EMBERIZINAE)

1 GREAT PAMPA-FINCH *Embernagra platensis* Verdón (Arg, Bol), Sabiá-do-banhado (Br). Pajonalero (Uru), Havia kapi'i (Par). L 21 cm. Habitat: tall wet grasslands (eastern form) or scrubby hillsides (western form). Orange bill. Head, throat and breast grey, darker face. Above olive, streaked (eastern form) or plain (western form). Large tail olive. Voice: a sharp '*quit*' contact call; song starts high-pitched and thin, then becomes quite musical '*siddle siddle tweet teeweet…*'.

Note: The two forms may revert into two separate species, the western form becoming the Olivaceous Pampa-finch (*Embernagra olivascens*) (**1a**).

2 WEDGE-TAILED GRASS-FINCH *Emberizoides herbicola* Coludo grande (Arg), Canário-do-campo (Br), Sabanero coludo or Cachilo coludo grande (Bol). L 20 cm. Habitat: tall grass with scattered woody plants. Wedge tail long. Above buff, streaked dark. Below buff-grey. Voice: musical and varied song '*chip - chooheedledoo - chip -chooroo - chewcheedledoo…*'.

3 LESSER GRASS-FINCH *Emberizoides ypiranganus* Coludo chico (Arg), Canário-do-brejo (Br). L 18 cm. Habitat: tall grasslands prone to flooding. Whitish brow. Pale above, heavily streaked blackish. Cinnamon rump. Grey face, white throat. Voice: a raucous and rattling song '*bzzbzzbzz bzbz - bidziz een ch'p ch'p ch'p ch'p pzee pzee budoo budoo zhweeew*'.

4 STRIPE-TAILED YELLOWFINCH *Sicalis citrina* Jilguero cola blanca (Arg), Canarinho-rasteiro (Br). L 12 cm. Habitat: grasslands and open fields. ♂: dingy olive-yellow, striped. Brighter on throat. ♀: brownish streaked on upperparts, streaked more yellow on breast and flanks. Olive-yellow rump. Tail of both sexes has large white patch on outer feathers.

5 PUNA YELLOWFINCH *Sicalis lutea* Jilguero puneño (Arg), Jilguero puna (Bol). L 14 cm. Habitat: *puna* grasslands between 3500 and 4000 m. ♂ bright yellow, olive-washed crown. ♀ yellow, browner back, grey-washed on breast.

6 BRIGHT-RUMPED YELLOWFINCH *Sicalis uropygialis* Jilguero cara gris (Arg Bol), Chirigüe (Bol), Chirihue cordillerano (Ch). L 14 cm. Habitat: high *puna*, grasslands and settlements. Olive-yellow head and breast. Brighter belly. Grey face, ear-patch and back. ♀ similar, browner above and paler below. Voice: quiet and rattling song, preceded by '*k'weep k'weep…*'.

7 CITRON-HEADED YELLOWFINCH *Sicalis luteocephala* No local names. L 14 cm. Habitat: scattered open areas, agricultural land on scrubby slopes. Like Bright-rumped Yellowfinch, but with yellow face and ear-patch, grey crown.

8 GREATER YELLOWFINCH *Sicalis auriventris* Jilguero grande (Arg), Chirihue dorado (Ch). L 16 cm. Habitat: Andean slopes between 2000 and 3500 m. Yellow, olive on back, slightly streaked. Greyish-yellow breast, brightest on lower belly. ♀ duller, browner, more streaky.

9 GREENISH YELLOWFINCH *Sicalis olivascens* Jilguero olivaceo (Arg, Bol), Chirihue vedoso (Ch). L 14 cm. Habitat: shrubby areas and open fields between 2000 and 3000 m. ♂ overall olive-yellow. Brighter on rump. ♀ browner overall, streaky on back. Yellow throat and belly. Voice: song a rattling '*tiddly*' sequence, descending.

10 PATAGONIAN YELLOWFINCH *Sicalis lebruni* Jilguero austral (Arg), Chirihue austral (Ch). L 15 cm. Habitat: Patagonian steppes, near steep banks or washes, small cliffs where it nests in summer. ♂: light grey and yellow. ♀ grey with yellow belly.

▶

Plate 93

Plate 93 (continued)

11 SAFFRON FINCH *Sicalis flaveola* Jilguero común (Arg), Jilguero amarillo (Bol), Dorado (Uru), Guyra sa'yju'i (Par), Canário-da-terra-verdadeiro (Br). L 13.5 cm. Habitat: towns, parks, open areas with trees, farms. Mostly bright yellow. Streaked on back. Orange forehead on breeding ♂. ♀ and imm all streaky. Voice: song musical and varied, though rather squeaky.

12 GRASSLAND YELLOWFINCH *Sicalis luteola* Misto (Arg, Uru), Tipio (Br), Jilguero chico or Canario chirigüe (Bol), Chirihue (Ch). L 12 cm. Habitat: open grasslands, fields and farms. ♂: greenish, streaked dark brown. Underparts yellow, olive-grey on breast. ♀: streaked greyish above; throat, breast and flanks greyish, yellow on belly. Voice: contact call '*chip chip*'. Song is fast, long and buzzing, perched or in flight display: '*chipichiriptirip BZZZ BZZZ BZZZ - tee teeee...*' and variations.

13 BAY-CHESTED WARBLING-FINCH *Poospiza thoracica* Peito-pinhao (Br). L 14 cm. Habitat: forest edge. Upperparts grey, olive-washed on back. White crescent below the eye on grey face. Underparts white with broad breast band, sides and flanks rich rufous.

14 RUFOUS-SIDED WARBLING-FINCH *Poospiza hypochondria* Monterita pecho gris (Arg, Bol). L 16 cm. Habitat: arid mountains, hillsides with shrubs. Above brownish-grey. White brow. White throat and malar streak separated by dark moustache. Grey breast, rest of underparts buff. Flanks chestnut. Tail broadly tipped white on outer feathers.

15 RINGED WARBLING-FINCH *Poospiza torquata* Monterita de collar (Arg, Bol). L 13 cm. Habitat: woods and open scrub. Grey above. Black face framed by white brow and throat. Neat black band across breast. Rest of underparts white. Wings with whitish wing-bars.

16 BLACK-CAPPED WARBLING-FINCH *Poospiza cinerea* Monterita cabeza negra (Arg, Bol, Uru), Capacetinho (Br). L 13 cm. Habitat: woods and scrubby areas. Black cap. Grey above, white below. Tail blackish with outer corners white. ♀ has grey cap. Voice: high-pitched, thin song '*tsip, sleep, seep, tseep, tsileep, tsip, sileep*' at marching rhythm; also a contact '*squit*'.

Plate 94 (continued)

16 BLACK-THROATED FINCH *Melanodera melanodera* Yal austral (Arg, Ch). L 15 cm. Habitat: on the ground of open grasslands where not overgrazed. ♂: black throat, white brow which continues down and around to frame all. Grey crown and neck. Yellow-washed back and breast. Wings bright yellow. Lower breast yellow. Tail: yellow outers, dark central feathers. ♀: buff-grey streaked dark. Breast yellowish-buff streaked greyish. Tail similarly patterned. Voice: sings '*cheet wheedeet wheer*', repeated.

17 YELLOW-BRIDLED FINCH *Melanodera xanthogramma* Yal andino (Arg), Yal cordillerano (Ch). L 16 cm. Habitat: above tree-line in summer, descending to grassy steppes in flocks in winter. ♂: black throat bordered bright yellow. Grey above. Greyish-yellow below. Wings with yellow patch. Tail centrally dark, outer feathers yellow. ♀: buff-cinnamon, heavily streaked. Voice: sings '*fweeet - wheew*'.

Plate 94

1 BLACK-AND-RUFOUS WARBLING-FINCH *Poospiza nigrorufa* Sietevestidos (Arg, Uru), Quem-te-vestiu (Br). L 15 cm. Habitat: shrubs and trees, mostly near water, open woods. Black face. All white brow. Rufous breast and flanks. Narrow white central belly. Voice: a musical song '*whit-toweeé-tew, whi-toweeé-tew…*' five or so times, to slow waltz-time.

Note: The western form is now considered a separate species, the Black-and-chestnut Warbling-Finch, *Poospiza whitii* Monterita negra-castaña (Arg), Monterita común (Bol). Habitat: arid woods and brushland. Long brow white before, chestnut behind the eye. Imm is buff below, barely freckled. Voice: song is thin, in short phrases '*seewee-psewt*' or '*cheeooee-tsew*'.

2 RUSTY-BROWED WARBLING-FINCH *Poospiza erythrophrys* Monterita ceja castaña (Arg, Bol). L 14 cm. Habitat: montane forests and woods between 1000 and 2500 m. Above grey. Large eyebrow rich chestnut. Below all rufous. White wing-bar. Outer tail feathers white. Voice: a high-pitched, thin song '*tswee - chew - swee - chuchu…*'.

3 TUCUMAN MOUNTAIN-FINCH *Poospiza baeri* Monterita garganta castaña (Arg). L 18 cm. Habitat: grassy slopes and streamside bushes between 2000 and 3000 m. Grey. Rufous forehead, brow and throat.

4 CINNAMON WARBLING-FINCH *Poospiza ornata* Monterita canela (Arg). L 13 cm. Habitat: arid woods. Above grey with chestnut back. Buff-cinnamon eyebrow. Chestnut rump. Throat buff-cinnamon. Breast rich rufous. Two white wing-bars. Dark tail, white outer tail feathers. ♀: duller, buff underparts and wing-bars.

5 RED-RUMPED WARBLING-FINCH *Poospiza lateralis* Monterita rabadilla castaña (Arg), Quete (Br), Monterita de rabadilla roja (Uru). L 14 cm. Habitat: forest edge, open woods. Grey head, bright chestnut rump. Long white eyebrow and malar stripe. Pale breast. Cinnamon flanks. Voice: a thin, high-pitched '*tsip…tsip…*'.

6 SLENDER-BILLED FINCH *Xenospingus concolor* Pizarrita (Ch). L 14 cm. Habitat: trees, bushes and grass near water; cultivated and irrigated areas. Bill long, slender and yellow. Overall grey, darker foreface, paler below. ♀: darker above. Imm: olive-brown above. Two slight buff wing-bars. Below yellowish-buff with indistinct streaks.

7 SHORT-TAILED FINCH *Idiopsar brachyurus* Yal grande (Arg), Fringilo grande (Bol). L 18 cm. Habitat: high, grassy slopes with boulders, above 2000 m. Long bill. Overall lead-grey, paler below. Freckled face. Wings and tail darker grey.

8 WHITE-WINGED DIUCA-FINCH *Diuca speculifera* Diuca ala blanca (Arg, Ch), Diuca aliblanca (Bol). L 18 cm. Habitat: grassland and rocky slopes in the very high Andes at 4500 m and above. Above mid-grey. White spot below eye. Throat and belly white. Grey band across breast. Wings with large white patch at base of primaries. Tail with white outer edge.

9 COMMON DIUCA-FINCH *Diuca diuca* Diuca común (Arg), Diuca (Ch). L 17 cm. Habitat: steppes, arid woods and scrub. Grey, white throat. Breast with grey band. Flanks ruddy in ♂. Centre of belly white. Tail with large white corners. Voice: long, loud song '*whit, chit, chewit, chew, wit, wit, chew…*'.

10 LONG-TAILED REED-FINCH *Donacospiza albifrons* Cachilo canela (Arg), Pajerita de cabeza gris (Uru). L 15 cm. Habitat: tall grasses and reeds or sedges around marshes. Above cinnamon with streaks. Eyebrow whitish. Grey ear-patch. Darker face. Below cinnamon-buff. Long tail. Voice: sings '*chup puree chup puree chup chup puree…*'.

11 BLACK-CRESTED FINCH *Lophospingus pusillus* Soldadito (Arg), Afrechero copetón negro (Bol). L 13 cm. Habitat: semi-arid woodland. Long, pointed, upright crest black. ♂: sides of head and throat black. Broad brow and malar stripe white. Rest grey. Tail blackish with broad outer tips white. ♀: similarly patterned but browner and lacks black throat.

12 GREY-CRESTED FINCH *Lophospingus griseocristatus* Soldadito gris (Arg), Afrechero copetón gris (Bol). L 14 cm. Habitat: arid, bushy terrain in sub-Andean valleys. Sharp upright crest. Grey. Darker tail with broad white tips to outer feathers. ♀ paler. Imm browner.

13 UNIFORM FINCH *Haplospiza unicolor* Afrechero plomizo (Arg), Cigarra-bambu (Br). L 12.5 cm. Habitat: undergrowth of rainforests; seems to follow the seeding of canes. ♂ lead-grey, browner wings. ♀: above olive-brown. Below whitish, streaked olive.

14 GREY-BELLIED FLOWER-PIERCER *Diglossa carbonaria* Comesebo negro (Ch), Diglosa carbonaria (Bol). L 14 cm. Habitat: high cloud-forest edges to arid slopes. Black. Wing-coverts, lower breast and belly grey. Undertail chestnut.

15 RUSTY FLOWER-PIERCER *Diglossa sittoides* Payador (Arg), Diglosa payador (Bol). L 12.5 cm. Habitat: wood edge, gardens, arid areas. ♂: above greyish-blue. Below cinnamon. ♀: olive-grey. Buff below.

◀

Plate 94

Plate 95

EMBERIZINE FINCHES (SUBFAMILY EMBERIZINAE)

1 PATAGONIAN SIERRA-FINCH *Phrygilus patagonicus* Comesebo patagónico (Arg), Cometocino patagónico (Ch). L 15 cm. Habitat: edge of woods and forests. ♂: hood with bluish tinge. Russet back. All yellow below except white undertail. ♀ is toned-down version of ♂, with olive back. Voice: a thin song 'tee… teedle-ee… tee…'.

2 GREY-HOODED SIERRA-FINCH *Phrygilus gayi* Comesebo amarillo (Arg), Cometocino de Gay (Ch), Fringilo cordillerano (Bol). L 16.5 cm. Habitat: shrubby steppes. ♂ hood grey. Olive back. Yellow below. ♀ duller, pink below, greyish-brown above. Voice: a simple, repetitive song 'twee-éee twee-éee twee-éee…'.

3 BLACK-HOODED SIERRA-FINCH *Phrygilus atriceps* Comesebo cabeza negra (Arg), Cometocino del norte (Ch), Yal cabecinegro (Bol). L 17 cm. Habitat: brush-covered slopes. ♂: black hood. Rufous back. Yellow rump. Yellow underparts. ♀: head grey, streaked blackish. Back olivaceous. Below yellowish. Voice: sings a series of five or six 'wheerips'.

4 MOURNING SIERRA-FINCH *Phrygilus fruticeti* Yal negro (Arg), Yal negro (Bol), Yal (Ch,Uru). L 17 cm. Habitat: tall shrubby steppes. Bill yellow. ♂: above grey, streaked black on head and back. Face, throat and breast black, belly white. Black tail and wings, two white wing-bars. ♀: grey, streaked brown above and on breast. Ear-coverts and cheeks reddish-brown. Pale brow and malar stripe. Voice: sings 'tish-glue' perched or in display flight, loud.

5 PLUMBEOUS SIERRA-FINCH *Phrygilus unicolor* Yal plomizo (Arg), Pájaro plomo (Ch), Fringilo plomo (Bol). L 15 cm. Habitat: highland grass and steppe. All grey, paler below. ♀ streaky).

6 RED-BACKED SIERRA-FINCH *Phrygilus dorsalis* Comesebo puneño (Arg), Cometocino de dorso castaño (Ch). L 18 cm. Habitat: *puna* and rocky slopes at 4000 m and above. Head, hind-neck and rump grey. Rufous mantle. Face and ear-coverts speckled white. Breast grey. Rest of underparts whitish. Dark wings.

7 WHITE-THROATED SIERRA-FINCH *Phrygilus erythronotus* Cometocino de Arica (Ch), Fringilo boliviano (Bol). L 14 cm. Habitat: *puna* grass and rocky valleys, above 4000m. Above and breast grey. Dark brownish-grey wings and tail. Throat, belly and flanks white.

8 ASH-BREASTED SIERRA-FINCH *Phrygilus plebejus* Yal chico (Arg), Plebeyo (Ch), Fringilo plebeyo (Bol). L 12 cm. Habitat: high stony areas with some grass, between 3000 and 4000 m. Small and drab. ♂: above greyish, streaked darker and brownish. Pale eyebrow. Below ash-grey. ♀ brownish and more heavily streaked above. Voice: song is a high buzz followed by up to five or so 'seedoo's' or 'seetooroo's.

9 BAND-TAILED SIERRA-FINCH *Phrygilus alaudinus* Platero (Arg, Ch), Fringilo plateado (Bol). L 14 cm. Habitat: high mountain grass and stony slopes with scattered bushes. Yellow bill. ♂: head, throat and breast lead-grey, darker on face. Back streaked dark. Rump grey. Tail black with white band invading from sides seen in flight. ♀: brownish-grey streaked darker above. Below buff streaked brown. Tail patterned as in ♂ but earthy grey. Voice: a high-pitched 'seely seely seew' song, often in flight.

10 CARBONATED SIERRA-FINCH *Phrygilus carbonarius* Yal carbonero (Arg). L 14 cm. Habitat: tall steppe vegetation. Bill yellow. ♂: above grey, heavily streaked black. Below all black. ♀: brownish-grey above, streaked dark. Below whitish, finely streaked brownish. Voice: in flight on a high looping arc sings 'trreee trreee trreee…' ten or so times.

11 STRIPE-CAPPED SPARROW *Aimophila strigiceps* Cachilo corona castaña (Arg). L 15 cm. Habitat: open scrubby brushland and low woods. Grey head (with chestnut stripes on crown), and chestnut post-ocular line. Above buff-brown streaked darker. Black moustachial streak. Rest of underparts greyish, pinker on flanks, whiter on belly. Voice: varied song 'chip chip swee pswee psee…' plus trill; also a fast 'weepweepweepweepweepweep'.

12 GRASSLAND SPARROW *Myiospiza humeralis* Cachilo ceja amarilla (Arg), Manimbe (Par), Tico-tico-do-campo-verdadeiro (Br), Chingolo de tierra (Uru). L 12 cm. Habitat: tall grass. Above greyish, streaked brown. Below whitish. Buff flanks. Yellow lores and shoulders seen in flight. Voice: sings a thin but musical 'tip - titsee terreechee frrreee…' and trill, or variations of this.

13 RUFOUS-COLLARED SPARROW *Zonotrichia capensis* Chingolo (Arg, Bol), Chingolo común (Uru), Che sy hasy (Par), Gorrión americano or Pichisanka (Bol), Tico-tico (Br). L 15 cm. Habitat: ubiquitous, from arid scrub to forest edge, though not high *puna*. Slight crest. Grey cap and face with black stripes along sides of crown, post-ocular and malar. (Southern race (**13a**) has all grey cap and face). Rufous collar round hind-neck. Voice: musical song 'seetee - weteew…' followed by a trill, (or not, in the southern form).

Plate 95

Plate 96

BLACKBIRDS, COWBIRDS, CACIQUES AND ALLIES (SUBFAMILY ICTERINAE)

1 **SHINY COWBIRD** *Molothrus bonariensis* Tordo renegrido (Arg, Bol), Tordo común (Uru), Chopim, Gaudério or Maria-preta (Br), Mirlo (Ch), Guyraû (Par). L 20 cm. Habitat: open areas, woods, forest edge, farms. ♂: shiny black with purplish gloss. ♀ uniform brownish-grey. Voice: song a gurgling warble '*prr prr prr prr…*', then musical.

2 **SCREAMING COWBIRD** *Molothrus rufoaxillaris* Tordo pico corto (Arg, Uru, Bol), Chopim-azeviche (Br). L 18 cm. Habitat: pastures, scrubby land, wood edge, around cattle and larger herbivores. Sexes alike. Jet black. Fairly short bill. Imm very like **3**, its obligate parents. Voice: '*ping*' call. Sings snatches and phrases '*tsip, tseerup, tsureep, chup, (buzz), wooree…*'. Courtship '*choochoochoo pee*'.

3 **BAY-WINGED COWBIRD** *Molothrus badius* Tordo músico (Arg, Uru), Tordo mulato (Bol), Tordo bayo (Ch), Asa-de-telha (Br). L 19 cm. Habitat: open areas, edge of the woods, pastures. Sexes alike. Blackish mask. Overall brownish-grey. Wings russet. Tail dark. Mixes with Screaming Cowbird and is its host. Voice: sings a quiet, musical continuum of warbles and trills, often in chorus. Also a short contact '*trup*' or '*tr'p*'.

4 **GIANT COWBIRD** *Scaphidura oryzivora* Tordo Gigante (Arg), Iraúna-grande (Br), Tordo pirata or Seboí grande (Bol). L ♂ 36, ♀ 30 cm. Habitat: lawns, edge of forests, clearings. Pale iris. Bill appears down-curved. Black with purple sheen. Hind-neck seems puffed out. Characteristic undulant flight. Often around Cacique colonies which they parasitize.

5 **CRESTED OROPENDOLA** *Psarocolius decumanus* Yapú (Arg), Boyero cola amarilla (Bol), Japu or Rei-congo (Br). L ♂ 45, ♀ 35 cm. Habitat: forests. Shiny black. Back, rump and undertail chestnut. Central tail feathers black, outers yellow. Creamy bill. Voice: sings a wonderfully throaty, hollow musical 'improvisation' with a '*yapoo*' signature phrase.

6 **RED RUMPED CACIQUE** *Cacicus haemorrhous* Cacique (Arg), Guaxe or Japira (Br), Arrendajo común or Tojito silbador (Bol), Japu rái (Par). L ♂ 27, ♀ 22 cm. Habitat: rainforests with gaps. Glossy black with red rump. Bill ivory. Voice: calls include '*shushing*' scolds, descending trills, '*teeerrroo*', '*dishts*' and long '*feeeayohoo*'.

7 **GOLDEN-WINGED CACIQUE** *Cacicus chrysopterus* Boyero de alas amarillas (Arg, Bol, Uru), Soldado or Tecelao (Br). L 20 cm. Habitat: deciduous woods, gallery forests, forest edge. Black. Ivory-blue bill. Yellow rump and wing-coverts. Voice: unexpected and varied, musical song '*rrrreee - chiroo, whooo, tooweetooweetoowee - teeeeay* (very high-pitched) *whooweet, whooway, teeoo…*'.

8 **SOLITARY CACIQUE** *Cacicus solitarius* Boyero negro (Arg, Bol), Boyero (Uru), Arrendajo negro llanero (Bol), Iraúna-de-bico-branco (Br). L ♂ 26, ♀ 23 cm. Habitat: lower vegetation at forest edge and woods, gallery forests. All black. Bill creamy green. Voice: starts with '*woop woop woop*' then explodes into a startlingly '*teew tseew*' or '*towee, eew wah - weeeah*'.

9 **AUSTRAL BLACKBIRD** *Curaeus curaeus* Tordo patagónico (Arg), Tordo (Ch). L 27 cm. Habitat: Southern Andean woods and forest edge, bushy steppes. ♂: glossy black. Crown feathers as if combed with hair gel. ♀: duller. Voice: musical '*c'teew - rrrrreew*'.

10 **CHOPI BLACKBIRD** *Gnorimopsar chopi* Chopí (Arg, Bol), Tordo negro común (Bol), Graúna (Br), Mirlo or Charrúa (Uru). L 21 cm. Habitat: usually around palms, open areas, farmland, buildings. All shiny black. Crown and nape with pointed feathers, as if combed with hair gel. Voice: gurgling, warbled, varied, long song with '*chopee chopee*'.

11 **YELLOW-WINGED BLACKBIRD** *Agelaius thilius* Varillero ala amarilla (Arg), Trile (Ch), Tordo de ala amarilla (Bol), Chopî estero (Par), Alférez (Uru), Sargento (Br). L 18 cm. Habitat: marshes and reed-beds. ♂: black with bright yellow shoulders. ♀: streaked blackish on brown. Yellow shoulders. Voice: '*chip*' contact call. Long, complex song.

12 **CHESTNUT-CAPPED BLACKBIRD** *Agelaius ruficapillus* Varillero (Arg), Garibaldi (Br), Tordo de cabeza canela (Bol, Uru), Guyra tagua (Par). L 18 cm. Habitat: marshes, especially those with emerging broad-leaved vegetation. ♂ black with dark chestnut cap and throat. ♀: upperparts dark, streaked darker. Voice: '*quit…quit… tseetseetsee' tseeeew*' call, descending.

13 **UNICOLOURED BLACKBIRD** *Agelaius cyanopus* Varillero negro (Arg), Tordo negro chico (Bol), Carretao (Br). L 18 cm. Habitat: marshes. ♂: uniform black. ♀ and imm ♂s: above brown streaked black. Wings and tail black. Breast and belly dirty yellow.

14 **YELLOW-HOODED BLACKBIRD** *Agelaius icterocephalus* Iratauá-pequeno (Br). L 17 cm. Habitat: riverbanks, ricefields and marshes. ♂: black with yellow hood. ♀: crown, head and back olive-brown, streaked darker on back. Throat and upper breast olive-yellow. Belly dull brown.

15 **EPAULET ORIOLE** *Icterus cayennensis* Boyerito (Arg), Tordo de cobija canela (Bol, Uru), Inhapim or Encontro (Br), Guyraûmi (Par). L 21 cm. Habitat: woods, forest edge, gallery forests. Dull black with dark brown on shoulders (often hard to see). Voice: frequent nasal contact calls. Varied song – low-pitched, neighing, warbling, scolding and explosive.

▶

Plate 96

16 TROUPIAL *Icterus jamacaii* Matico (Arg), Trupial común (Bol). L 23 cm. Habitat: clearings and forest edge. Yellow-orange with face, forehead, throat, breast, upper back, tail and wings black.

17 SAFFRON-COWLED BLACKBIRD *Xanthopsar flavus* Tordo amarillo (Arg), Tordo de cabeza amarilla (Uru), Pássaro-preto-de-veste-amarela (Br). L 19 cm. Habitat: tall grasslands with copses, often wet. ♂ bright yellow; nape, back, wings and tail black. ♀: upperparts brown, rump and underparts dirty yellow. Now uncommon or absent over most of its former range; reasons unknown.

Plate 97

BLACKBIRDS, COWBIRDS, CACIQUES AND ALLIES (SUBFAMILY ICTERINAE)

1 SCARLET-HEADED BLACKBIRD *Amblyramphus holosericeus* Federal (Arg, Uru, Bol), Cardeal-do-banhado (Br), Tordo curichero (Bol). L 24 cm. Habitat: marshes. Black. Head flame-orange. Voice: melodious, far-carrying '*quit, cheeweeweeweeweewee*' song, or '*chipeeweeooweeooweeoowee*'.

2 YELLOW-RUMPED MARSHBIRD *Pseudoleistes guirahuro* Pecho amarillo grande (Arg), Chopim-do-brejo (Br), Pecho amarillo de la sierra (Uru), Guyraû chore (Par). L 24 cm. Habitat: waterside grasslands and wide grassy valley bottoms. Head and breast blackish-brown. Rump, shoulders and underparts yellow. Voice: a musical, loud song '*tooweet sitee…*' plus trills and warbles.

3 BROWN-AND-YELLOW MARSHBIRD *Pseudoleistes virescens* Pecho amarillo chico (Arg), Dragao (Br), Pecho amarillo común (Uru). L 22 cm. Habitat: grassland by marshes, dunes with tall pampas grass and wet areas. All upperparts brown. Lower breast, belly, shoulders and under wing-coverts yellow. Gregarious and noisy. Voice: song and flight call '*Trr…trrr…trriip… Trrreee… Trrreeee… trrreeeew*'.

4 WHITE-BROWED BLACKBIRD *Sturnella superciliaris* Pecho colorado chico (Arg, Uru), Loica argentina (Ch), Polícia-inglesa (Br). L 18 cm. Habitat: green grain fields, grasses. Pocket-sized meadowlark. ♂: black. White brow. Fore-neck and breast scarlet. ♀: streaked grey-brown. Breast tinged rosy. Voice: '*jewee*' call followed by buzzing, trilled flight song.

5 PAMPAS MEADOWLARK *Sturnella defilippi* Pecho colorado mediano (Arg), Peito-vermelho-grande (Br), Pecho colorado grande (Uru). L 20 cm. Habitat: grassy fields. ♂: upperparts and flanks black, feathers edged brownish-grey. Breast and shoulders red. Underwing black. ♀: above blackish, streaked. Centre of breast and belly pinkish. Black underwing. Now greatly reduced in distribution, probably to do with crop-spraying.

6 LONG-TAILED MEADOWLARK *Sturnella loyca* Pecho colorado grande (Arg), Loica (Ch). L 25 cm. Habitat: rough grassland, often with rocks. Grey-brown, streaked blackish above. Breast red. White under-wing. ♀: toned-down version of ♂. Voice: sings '*chup chup chup tchew ee chew chewee chweeeeew*', descending.

7 PERUVIAN MEADOWLARK *Sturnella bellicosa* Not illustrated. Loica peruana (Ch). L 21 cm. Habitat: grassy fields. Smaller version of Long-tailed Meadowlark, brighter red, blacker black. Voice: flight display song during breeding season.

8 BOBOLINK *Dolichonyx oryzivorus* Charlatán (Arg, Ch), Triste-pia (Br), Tordo arrocero or Seboí arrocero (Bol). L 15 cm. Habitat: rice fields and flooded grasslands. Winter plumage ♂s like ♀s: above streaked buff and blackish. Buff underparts. Dark crown streak. Pre-nuptial ♂s: white rump, yellowish hind-neck. Huge flocks. Voice: flight call '*pink*'. During heat of day, perch in bushes and small trees adjacent to feeding areas and sing together.

SISKINS (SUBFAMILY CARDUELINAE)

9 THICK-BILLED SISKIN *Carduelis crassirostris* Cabecita negra picudo (Arg, Bol), Jilguero grande (Ch). L 13.5 cm. Habitat: patches of woods and shrubs between 3000 and 4000 m. Bill pale and noticeably thick. ♂ black hood. Olive above, yellow below. Rump yellow. ♀: greyish, whitish belly.

10 HOODED SISKIN *Carduelis magellanica* Cabecitanegra común (Arg, Bol), Pintassilgo (Br), Cabecita negra (Uru), Jilguero peruano (Ch). L 12 cm. Habitat: open woods. ♂: black hood, olive back, yellow below. Black and yellow wings, yellow rump. Slightly notched tail. Voice: very fast, musical, varied song, containing imitations of other species.

11 BLACK SISKIN *Carduelis atrata* Cabecitanegra oscuro (Arg), Jilguero negro (Ch), Cabecita negra oscura or Negrillo (Bol). L 13 cm. Habitat: puna grasslands between 3500 and 4500 m. ♂: black with yellow belly, undertail, sides of tail and patch in wing. ♀ brownish-black and yellow, patterned as in ♂.

12 YELLOW-RUMPED SISKIN *Carduelis uropygialis* Cabecitanegro andino (Arg), Jilguero cordillerqano (Ch), Cabecita negra de capucho or Negrillo andino (Bol). L 12 cm. Habitat: shrubby ravines and slopes between 2000 and 4000 m. Appearance halfway between Hooded and Black Siskins. Hood to breast and back. Below bright yellow, as also rump. ♀ similarly patterned but duller.

13 BLACK-CHINNED SISKIN *Carduelis barbata* Cabecitanegra austral (Arg), Jilguero (Ch). L 13 cm. Habitat: forest edge. ♂: olive-yellow, black cap and chin. Whitish belly. ♀: olive, whiter on belly. Duller.

14 EUROPEAN GOLDFINCH *Carduelis carduelis* Jilguero europeo (Arg), Cardelino (Uru). L 12 cm. Habitat: forestry plantations, gardens and semi-open woods. Forehead, face and throat red. Black crown. Ear-patch white. Brown above, whitish rump. Below whitish. Sides brownish. Primaries with yellow patch and white tips. Introduced to Uruguay.

▶

15 EUROPEAN GREENFINCH *Carduelis chloris* Verderón (Arg, Uru). L 15 cm. Habitat: pine groves, plantations and gardens. Olive-green, yellow in wings and tail. ♀: greyer and duller. Voice: sings a buzzing '*tseeeeeh*' or a rapid '*plipliplipliplipli...*'. Introduced to Uruguay.

SPARROWS (SUBFAMILY PASSERINAE)

16 HOUSE SPARROW *Passer domesticus* Gorrión (Arg, Uru, Bol, Ch), Guyra tupao (Par). L 14 cm. Habitat: cities and towns, settlements and homesteads. ♂: crown and rump grey. Chestnut nuchal band. Back streaked. Throat and upper breast black. Underparts whitish. Brown wings and tail, chestnut lesser wing-coverts, rest black. ♀: brown, light line through the eye. Streaked darker on the back. Greyish below. Voice: '*shilip shilip...*' call. Introduced.

Plate A

19.1 BLACK VULTURE

19.2 TURKEY VULTURE

19.3 LESSER YELLOW-HEADED VULTURE

19.4 ANDEAN CONDOR

19.5 KING VULTURE

19.6 OSPREY

20.1 GREY-HEADED KITE

20.1 GREY-HEADED KITE (light form)

20.1 GREY-HEADED KITE (dark form)

20.2 HOOK-BILLED KITE

20.2 HOOK-BILLED KITE (imm)

20.2 HOOK-BILLED KITE (dark form)

20.3 SWALLOW-TAILED KITE

20.4 PEARL KITE

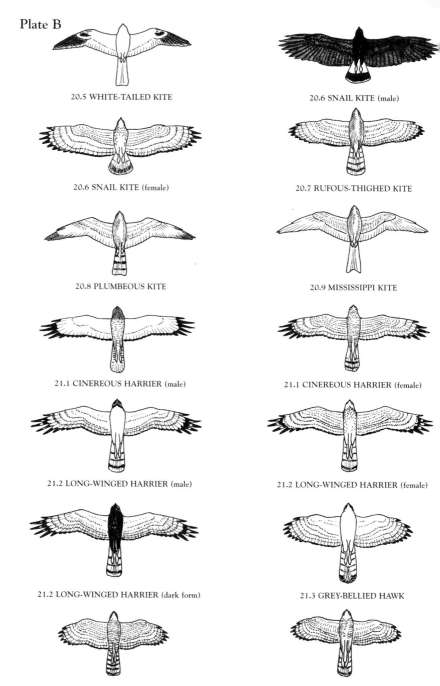

Plate B

20.5 WHITE-TAILED KITE

20.6 SNAIL KITE (male)

20.6 SNAIL KITE (female)

20.7 RUFOUS-THIGHED KITE

20.8 PLUMBEOUS KITE

20.9 MISSISSIPPI KITE

21.1 CINEREOUS HARRIER (male)

21.1 CINEREOUS HARRIER (female)

21.2 LONG-WINGED HARRIER (male)

21.2 LONG-WINGED HARRIER (female)

21.2 LONG-WINGED HARRIER (dark form)

21.3 GREY-BELLIED HAWK

21.4 TINY HAWK

21.5 SHARP-SHINNED HAWK

Plate C

21.6 BICOLOURED HAWK

21.7 CRANE HAWK

22.1 MANTLED HAWK

22.2 GREY HAWK

22.3 GREAT BLACK HAWK

22.3 GREAT BLACK HAWK (imm)

22.4 SAVANNAH HAWK

22.5 BAY-WINGED HAWK

22.5 BAY-WINGED HAWK (imm)

22.6 BLACK-COLLARED HAWK

22.7 BLACK-CHESTED BUZZARD-EAGLE

22.7 BLACK-CHESTED BUZZARD-EAGLE (imm)

22.8 SOLITARY EAGLE

22.9 CROWNED EAGLE

22.9 CROWNED EAGLE (imm)

Plate D

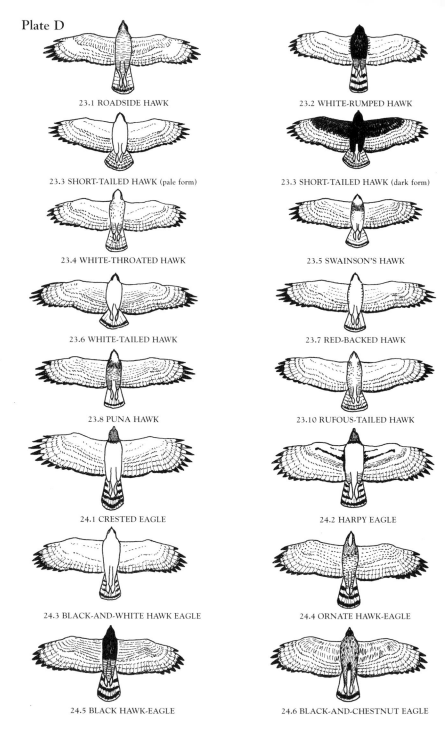

23.1 ROADSIDE HAWK

23.2 WHITE-RUMPED HAWK

23.3 SHORT-TAILED HAWK (pale form)

23.3 SHORT-TAILED HAWK (dark form)

23.4 WHITE-THROATED HAWK

23.5 SWAINSON'S HAWK

23.6 WHITE-TAILED HAWK

23.7 RED-BACKED HAWK

23.8 PUNA HAWK

23.10 RUFOUS-TAILED HAWK

24.1 CRESTED EAGLE

24.2 HARPY EAGLE

24.3 BLACK-AND-WHITE HAWK EAGLE

24.4 ORNATE HAWK-EAGLE

24.5 BLACK HAWK-EAGLE

24.6 BLACK-AND-CHESTNUT EAGLE

25.1 MOUNTAIN CARACARA

25.2 WHITE-THROATED CARACARA

25.3 STRIATED CARACARA

25.4 CRESTED CARACARA

25.5 YELLOW-HEADED CARACARA

25.6 CHIMANGO CARACARA

26.1 LAUGHING FALCON

26.2 BARRED FOREST-FALCON

26.3 COLLARED FOREST-FALCON

26.4 SPOT-WINGED FALCONET

26.5 AMERICAN KESTREL

26.6 APLOMADO FALCON

26.7 BAT FALCON

26.8 PEREGRINE FALCON

26.9 ORANGE-BREASTED FALCON

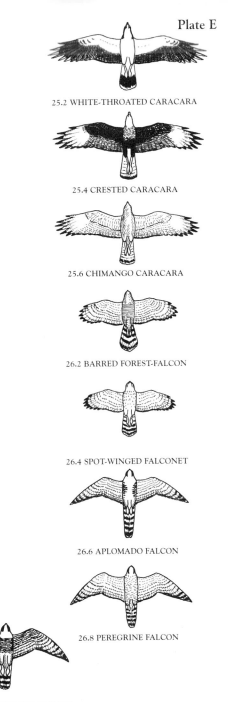

Plate E

DISTRIBUTION MAPS

The following 72 pages show distribution maps for all species. The number of the map refers to the relevant plate, followed by the number of the bird on that plate. The maps are by way of a final confirmation in the process of identification of any bird seen. Obviously the first step in identifying a bird is the consultation of the colour plates. However, for groups like some genera of the furnariids (horneos etc.), tyrannids and scolopacids (shorebirds) there are many birds which look so alike that the plates may not be decisive when you have only had a brief or poor look at the bird. The next recourse is the text facing the plate where a description mentions the salient physical features. If the bird has uttered any sound, proceed from there to the description of the voice or call (in forest and wood birding it was probably the sound which first attracted your attention). Then there is the habitat to be considered, and this is also mentioned in the text.

The area covered by the book, which is often referred to as the Southern Cone of South America, is so very vast, covering some 50 to 55° of latitude in a continent with tremendous physical contrasts, that habitat is a major consideration, going as it does with the biomes. There are rainforests, cloudforests, grasslands, scrublands, absolute deserts, woodlands of various kinds and latitudes, high mountain plateaux and even higher mountain peaks and more. But habitat is often patchy within the distribution, for example where forests grow on north-facing slopes and grasses on the south-facing, or stands of a particular sedge are sparsely distributed. Birds must get from one patch to another so may on rare occasions be found outside their preferred habitat, but are found generally within the distribution. The maps are useful where two similar species are distributionally separated, occurring in widely different areas, such as the Green-cheeked and Reddish-bellied Parakeets (44.2 & 44.3); the distribution map will give a clear indication of just which species is expected. So the distribution maps are a final step in the confirmation of any sighting.

The large-scale map of the total area covered (opposite) is for a better understanding of where places are relative to one another.

KEY TO MAP OPPOSITE: The letters refer to the countries (U - Uruguay, A - Argentina, Bo - Bolivia, P - Paraguay, Br - Brazil, C - Chile). The numbers refer to the following cities: 1 - Asunción, 2 - Buenos Aires, 3 - Montevideo, 4 - Santiago de Chile, 5 - Santa Cruz, 6 - La Paz, 7 - Puerto Montt.

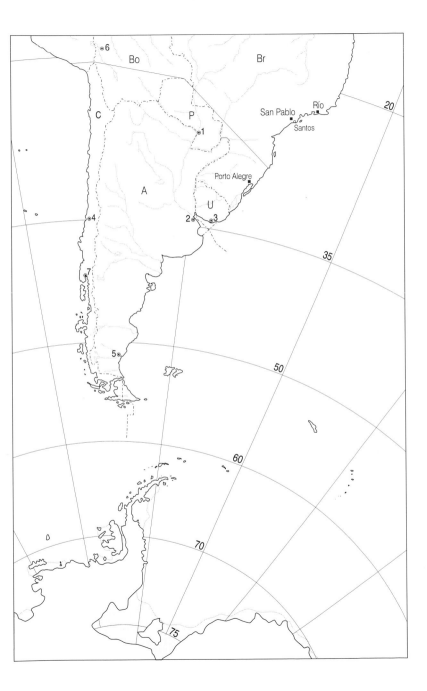

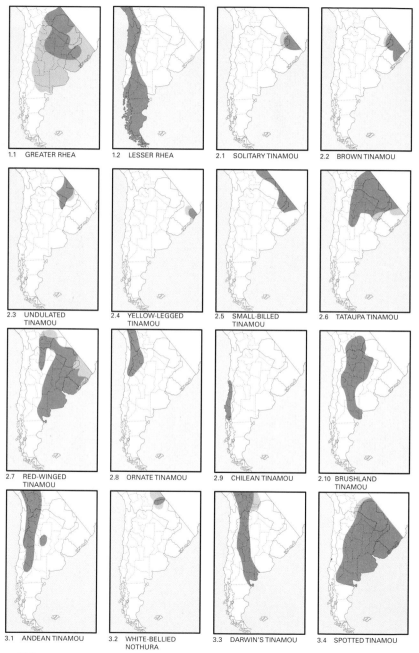

1.1 GREATER RHEA

1.2 LESSER RHEA

2.1 SOLITARY TINAMOU

2.2 BROWN TINAMOU

2.3 UNDULATED TINAMOU

2.4 YELLOW-LEGGED TINAMOU

2.5 SMALL-BILLED TINAMOU

2.6 TATAUPA TINAMOU

2.7 RED-WINGED TINAMOU

2.8 ORNATE TINAMOU

2.9 CHILEAN TINAMOU

2.10 BRUSHLAND TINAMOU

3.1 ANDEAN TINAMOU

3.2 WHITE-BELLIED NOTHURA

3.3 DARWIN'S TINAMOU

3.4 SPOTTED TINAMOU

220

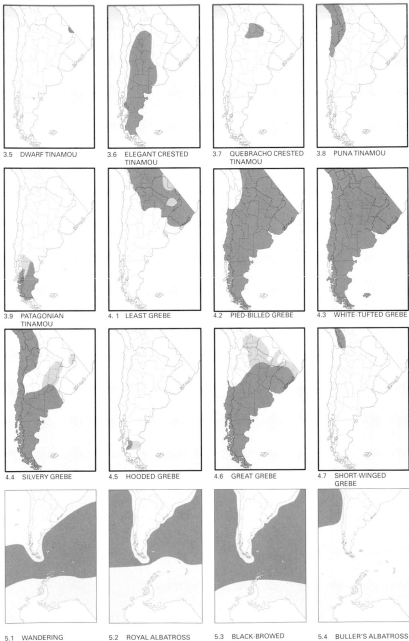

3.5 DWARF TINAMOU

3.6 ELEGANT CRESTED TINAMOU

3.7 QUEBRACHO CRESTED TINAMOU

3.8 PUNA TINAMOU

3.9 PATAGONIAN TINAMOU

4.1 LEAST GREBE

4.2 PIED-BILLED GREBE

4.3 WHITE-TUFTED GREBE

4.4 SILVERY GREBE

4.5 HOODED GREBE

4.6 GREAT GREBE

4.7 SHORT-WINGED GREBE

5.1 WANDERING ALBATROSS

5.2 ROYAL ALBATROSS

5.3 BLACK-BROWED ALBATROSS

5.4 BULLER'S ALBATROSS

221

5.5 WHITE-CAPPED
ALBATROSS

5.6 YELLOW-NOSED
ALBATROSS

5.7 GREY-HEADED
ALBATROSS

5.8 SOOTY ALBATROSS

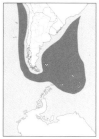

5.9 LIGHT-MANTLED
SOOTY ALBATROSS

6.1 GIANT PETREL

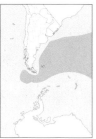

6.2 NORTHERN GIANT
PETREL

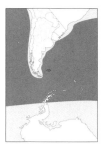

6.3 SOUTHERN FULMAR

6.4 ANTARCTIC PETREL

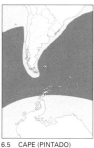

6.5 CAPE (PINTADO)
PETREL

7.1 GREAT-WINGED
PETREL

7.2 KERGUELEN PETREL

7.3 WHITE-HEADED
PETREL

7.4 ATLANTIC PETREL

7.5 KERMADEK PETREL

7.6 HERALD PETREL

222

7.7 MOTTLED PETREL

7.8 SOFT-PLUMAGED PETREL

7.9 PHOENIX PETREL

7.10 WHITE-NECKED PETREL

7.11 COOK'S PETREL

7.12 STEJNEGER'S PETREL

7.13 BLUE PETREL

7.14 BROAD-BILLED PRION

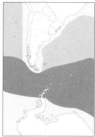

7.15 ANTARCTIC PRION

7.16 SALVIN'S PRION

8.1 FAIRY PRION

8.2 SLENDER-BILLED PRION

8.3 GREY PETREL

8.4 WHITE-CHINNED PETREL

8.5 WESTLAND PETREL

8.6 CORY'S SHEARWATER

223

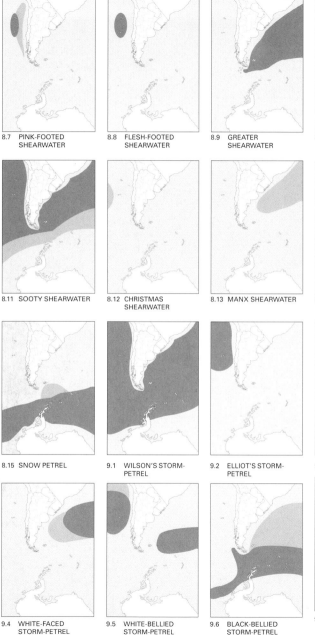

8.7 PINK-FOOTED SHEARWATER

8.8 FLESH-FOOTED SHEARWATER

8.9 GREATER SHEARWATER

8.10 GREY-BACKED SHEARWATER

8.11 SOOTY SHEARWATER

8.12 CHRISTMAS SHEARWATER

8.13 MANX SHEARWATER

8.14 LITTLE SHEARWATER

8.15 SNOW PETREL

9.1 WILSON'S STORM-PETREL

9.2 ELLIOT'S STORM-PETREL

9.3 GREY-BACKED STORM-PETREL

9.4 WHITE-FACED STORM-PETREL

9.5 WHITE-BELLIED STORM-PETREL

9.6 BLACK-BELLIED STORM-PETREL

9.7 WHITE-THROATED STORM-PETREL

224

9.9 SOOTY STORM-PETREL

9.10 RINGED STORM-PETREL

9.11 PERUVIAN DIVING-PETREL

9.12 MAGELLANIC DIVING-PETREL

9.13 COMMON DIVING-PETREL

9.14 GEORGIAN DIVING-PETREL

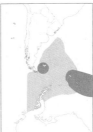

10. 1 KING PENGUIN

10.2 EMPEROR PENGUIN

10.3 GENTOO PENGUIN

10.4 CHINSTRAP PENGUIN

10.5 ADELIE PENGUIN

10.6 ROCKHOPPER PENGUIN

10.7 MACARONI PENGUIN

10.8 ERECT-CRESTED PENGUIN

10.9 PERUVIAN PENGUIN

10.10 MAGELLANIC PENGUIN

10.11 BLACK-FOOTED
PENGUIN

11.1 WHITE-TAILED
TROPICBIRD

11.2 RED-BILLED
TROPICBIRD

11.3 RED-TAILED
TROPICBIRD

11.4 MASKED BOOBY

11.5 BLUE-FOOTED BOOBY

11.6 PERUVIAN BOOBY

11.7 BROWN BOOBY

11.8 PERUVIAN PELICAN

12.1 OLIVACEOUS
CORMORANT

12.2 ROCK CORMORANT

12.3 GUANAY CORMORANT

2.4 RED-LEGGED
CORMORANT

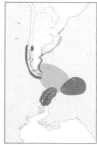

12.5 BLUE-EYED
CORMORANT

12.6 KING CORMORANT

12.7 AMERICAN ANHINGA

226

12.8 GREAT FRIGATEBIRD

12.9 MAGNIFICENT FRIGATEBIRD

13.1 PINNATED BITTERN

13.2 STRIPE BACKED BITTERN

13.3 LEAST BITTERN

13.4 RUFESCENT TIGER-HERON

13.5 FASCIATED TIGER-HERON

13.6 WHISTLING HERON

13.7 WHITE-NECKED HERON

13.8 GREAT EGRET

13.9 SNOWY EGRET

13.10 LITTLE BLUE HERON

13.11 CATTLE EGRET

13.12 STRIATED HERON

13.13 CAPPED HERON

13.14 BLACK-CROWNED NIGHT-HERON

227

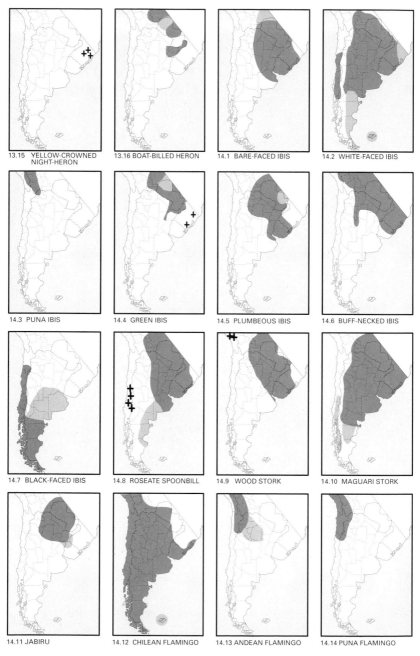

13.15 YELLOW-CROWNED NIGHT-HERON

13.16 BOAT-BILLED HERON

14.1 BARE-FACED IBIS

14.2 WHITE-FACED IBIS

14.3 PUNA IBIS

14.4 GREEN IBIS

14.5 PLUMBEOUS IBIS

14.6 BUFF-NECKED IBIS

14.7 BLACK-FACED IBIS

14.8 ROSEATE SPOONBILL

14.9 WOOD STORK

14.10 MAGUARI STORK

14.11 JABIRU

14.12 CHILEAN FLAMINGO

14.13 ANDEAN FLAMINGO

14.14 PUNA FLAMINGO

228

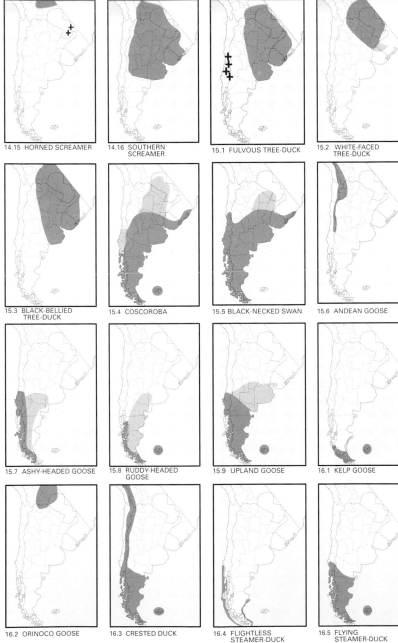

14.15 HORNED SCREAMER

14.16 SOUTHERN SCREAMER

15.1 FULVOUS TREE-DUCK

15.2 WHITE-FACED TREE-DUCK

15.3 BLACK-BELLIED TREE-DUCK

15.4 COSCOROBA

15.5 BLACK-NECKED SWAN

15.6 ANDEAN GOOSE

15.7 ASHY-HEADED GOOSE

15.8 RUDDY-HEADED GOOSE

15.9 UPLAND GOOSE

16.1 KELP GOOSE

16.2 ORINOCO GOOSE

16.3 CRESTED DUCK

16.4 FLIGHTLESS STEAMER-DUCK

16.5 FLYING STEAMER-DUCK

16.6 FALKLAND
STEAMER-DUCK

17.1 SPECTACLED DUCK

17.2 SPECKLED TEAL

17.3 SOUTHERN WIGEON

17.4 WHITE-CHEEKED
PINTAIL

17.5 BROWN PINTAIL

17.6 SILVER TEAL

17.7 PUNA TEAL

17.8 BLUE-WINGED TEAL

17.9 CINNAMON TEAL

18.1 RED SHOVELER

18.2 RINGED TEAL

18.3 TORRENT DUCK

18.4 ROSY-BILLED
POCHARD

18.5 SOUTHERN POCHARD

18.6 BRAZILIAN DUCK

230

18.7 COMB DUCK

18.8 MUSCOVY DUCK

18.9 BRAZILIAN MERGANSER

18.10 RUDDY DUCK

18.11 LAKE DUCK

18.12 MASKED DUCK

18.13 BLACK-HEADED DUCK

19.1 BLACK VULTURE

19.2 TURKEY VULTURE

19.3 LESSER YELLOW-HEADED VULTURE

19.4 ANDEAN CONDOR

19.5 KING VULTURE

19.6 OSPREY

20.1 GREY-HEADED KITE

20.2 HOOK-BILLED KITE

20.3 SWALLOW-TAILED KITE

231

20.4 PEARL KITE

20.5 WHITE-TAILED KITE

20.6 SNAIL KITE

20.7 RUFOUS-THIGHED KITE

20.8 PLUMBEOUS KITE

20.9 MISSISSIPPI KITE

21.1 CINEREOUS HARRIER

21.2 LONG-WINGED HARRIER

21.3 GREY-BELLIED HAWK

21.4 TINY HAWK

21.5 SHARP-SHINNED HAWK

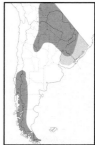
21.6 BICOLOURED HAWK

21.7 CRANE HAWK

22.1 MANTLED HAWK

22.2 GREY HAWK

22.3 GREAT BLACK HAWK

232

22.4 SAVANNAH HAWK

22.5 BAY-WINGED HAWK

22.6 BLACK-COLLARED HAWK

22.7 BLACK-CHESTED BUZZARD-EAGLE

22.8 SOLITARY EAGLE

22.9 CROWNED EAGLE

23.1 ROADSIDE HAWK

23.2 WHITE-RUMPED HAWK

23.3 SHORT-TAILED HAWK

23.4 WHITE-THROATED HAWK

23.5 SWAINSON'S HAWK

23.6 WHITE-TAILED HAWK

23.7 RED-BACKED HAWK

23.8 PUNA HAWK

23.9 ZONE-TAILED HAWK

23.10 RUFOUS-TAILED HAWK

24.1 CRESTED EAGLE

24.2 HARPY EAGLE

24.3 BLACK-AND-WHITE HAWK-EAGLE

24.4 ORNATE HAWK-EAGLE

24.5 BLACK HAWK-EAGLE

24.6 BLACK-AND-CHESTNUT EAGLE

25.1 MOUNTAIN CARACARA

25.2 WHITE-THROATED CARACARA

25.3 STRIATED CARACARA

25.4 CRESTED CARACARA

25.5 YELLOW-HEADED CARACARA

25.6 CHIMANGO CARACARA

26.1 LAUGHING FALCON

26.2 BARRED FOREST-FALCON

26.3 COLLARED FOREST-FALCON

26.4 SPOT-WINGED FALCONET

26.5 AMERICAN KESTREL

26.6 APLOMADO FALCON

26.7 BAT FALCON

26.8 PEREGRINE FALCON

26.9 ORANGE-BREASTED
FALCON

27.1 CHACO CHACHALACA

27.2 SPECKLED
CHACHALACA

27.3 ANDEAN GUAN

27.4 RUSTY-MARGINED
GUAN

27.5 RED-FACED GUAN

27.6 DUSKY-LEGGED GUAN

27.7 COMMON PIPING-
GUAN

27.8 BLACK-FRONTED
PIPING-GUAN

27.9 BARE-FACED
CURASSOW

28.1 SPOT-WINGED
WOOD-QUAIL

28.2 CALIFORNIA QUAIL

235

28.3 SPECKLED CRAKE

28.4 OSCELLATED CRAKE

28.5 RED-AND-WHITE CRAKE

28.6 RUFOUS-SIDED CRAKE

28.7 RUFOUS-FACED CRAKE

29.1 GREY-BREASTED CRAKE

29.2 BLACK CRAKE

29.3 DOT-WINGED CRAKE

29.4 AUSTRAL RAIL

29.5 GREY-NECKED WOOD-RAIL

29.6 GIANT WOOD-RAIL

29.7 SLATY-BREASTED WOOD-RAIL

29.8 ASH-THROATED CRAKE

29.9 YELLOW-BREASTED CRAKE

29.10 PAINT-BILLED CRAKE

29.11 SPOTTED RAIL

236

29.12 PLUMBEOUS RAIL

29.13 BLACKISH RAIL

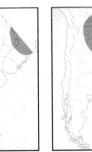
30.1 PURPLE GALLINULE

30.2 AZURE GALLINULE

30.3 SPOT-FLANKED GALLINULE

30.4 MOORHEN or COMMON GALLINULE

30.5 AMERICAN COOT

30.6 RED-GARTERED COOT

30.7 WHITE-WINGED COOT

30.8 RED-FRONTED COOT

30.9 GIANT COOT

30.10 HORNED COOT

31.1 SUNGREBE

31.2 LIMPKIN

31.3 RED-LEGGED SERIEMA

31.4 BLACK-LEGGED SERIEMA

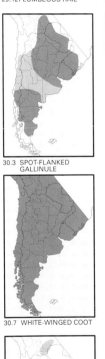

31.5 PERUVIAN THICK-KNEE

31.6 PIED LAPWING

31.7 SOUTHERN LAPWING

31.8 ANDEAN LAPWING

31.9 BLACK-BELLIED PLOVER

31.10 GOLDEN PLOVER

32.1 PACIFIC GOLDEN PLOVER

32.2 COLLARED PLOVER

32.3 TWO-BANDED PLOVER

32.4 PUNA PLOVER

32.5 SNOWY PLOVER

32.6 SEMIPALMATED PLOVER

32.7 KILLDEER

32.8 RUFOUS-CHESTED DOTTEREL

32.9 DIADEMED SANDPIPER-PLOVER

32.10 TAWNY-THROATED DOTTEREL

238

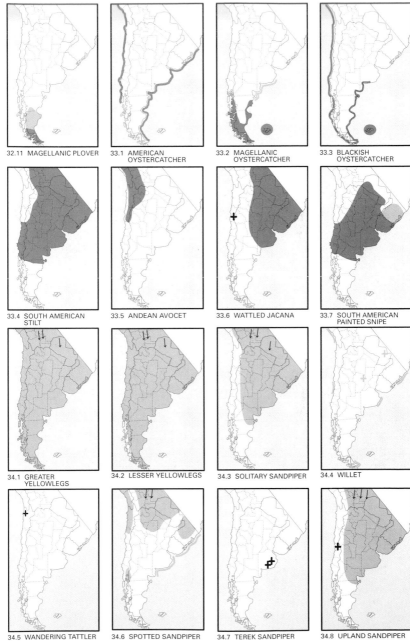

32.11 MAGELLANIC PLOVER

33.1 AMERICAN OYSTERCATCHER

33.2 MAGELLANIC OYSTERCATCHER

33.3 BLACKISH OYSTERCATCHER

33.4 SOUTH AMERICAN STILT

33.5 ANDEAN AVOCET

33.6 WATTLED JACANA

33.7 SOUTH AMERICAN PAINTED SNIPE

34.1 GREATER YELLOWLEGS

34.2 LESSER YELLOWLEGS

34.3 SOLITARY SANDPIPER

34.4 WILLET

34.5 WANDERING TATTLER

34.6 SPOTTED SANDPIPER

34.7 TEREK SANDPIPER

34.8 UPLAND SANDPIPER

239

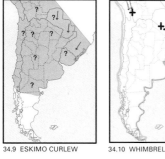

34.9 ESKIMO CURLEW

34.10 WHIMBREL

34.11 HUDSONIAN GODWIT

34.12 MARBLED GODWIT

34.13 RUDDY TURNSTONE

34.14 SURFBIRD

35.1 RED KNOT

35.2 LEAST SANDPIPER

35.3 SANDERLING

35.4 WHITE-RUMPED SANDPIPER

35.5 SEMIPALMATED SANDPIPER

35.6 WESTERN SANDPIPER

35.7 BAIRD'S SANDPIPER

35.8 PECTORAL SANDPIPER

35.9 CURLEW SANDPIPER

35.10 STILT SANDPIPER

240

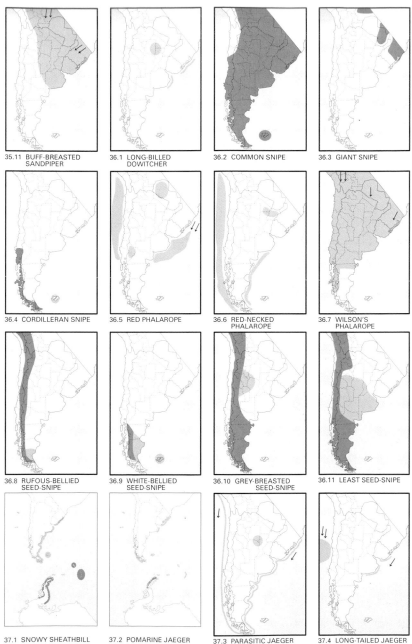

35.11 BUFF-BREASTED SANDPIPER

36.1 LONG-BILLED DOWITCHER

36.2 COMMON SNIPE

36.3 GIANT SNIPE

36.4 CORDILLERAN SNIPE

36.5 RED PHALAROPE

36.6 RED-NECKED PHALAROPE

36.7 WILSON'S PHALAROPE

36.8 RUFOUS-BELLIED SEED-SNIPE

36.9 WHITE-BELLIED SEED-SNIPE

36.10 GREY-BREASTED SEED-SNIPE

36.11 LEAST SEED-SNIPE

37.1 SNOWY SHEATHBILL

37.2 POMARINE JAEGER

37.3 PARASITIC JAEGER

37.4 LONG-TAILED JAEGER

241

37.5 GREAT SKUA

37.6 SOUTH POLAR SKUA

37.7 BLACK SKIMMER

38.1 DOLPHIN GULL

38.2 BAND-TAILED GULL

38.3 KELP GULL

38.4 GREY-HOODED GULL

38.5 ANDEAN GULL

38.6 FRANKLIN'S GULL

38.7 BROWN-HOODED GULL

38.8 SABINE'S GULL

38.9 SWALLOW-TAILED GULL

39.1 BLACK TERN

39.2 LARGE-BILLED TERN

39.3 GULL-BILLED TERN

39.4 SOUTH AMERICAN TERN

39.5 COMMON TERN

39.6 ARCTIC TERN

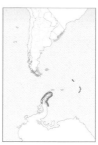
39.7 ANTARCTIC TERN

39.8 SNOWY-CROWNED TERN

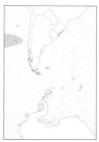
40.1 SOOTY TERN

40.2 SPECTACLED TERN

40.3 YELLOW-BILLED TERN

40.4 PERUVIAN TERN

40.5 LEAST TERN

40.6 ROYAL TERN

40.7 ELEGANT TERN

40.8 SANDWICH TERN

40.9 CAYENNE TERN

40.10 INCA TERN

40.11 BROWN NODDY

40.12 FAIRY TERN

243

41.1 ROCK DOVE

41.2 BAND-TAILED PIGEON

41.3 CHILEAN PIGEON

41.4 SCALED PIGEON

41.5 PICAZURO PIGEON

41.6 SPOT-WINGED PIGEON

41.7 PALE-VENTED PIGEON

41.8 PLUMBEOUS PIGEON

41.9 EARED DOVE

41.10 WHITE-WINGED DOVE

41.11 PLAIN-BREASTED
GROUND-DOVE

41.12 RUDDY
GROUND-DOVE

41.13 PICUI GROUND-DOVE

41.14 GOLDEN-BILLED
GROUND-DOVE

42.1 SCALY DOVE

42.2 BLUE GROUND-DOVE

244

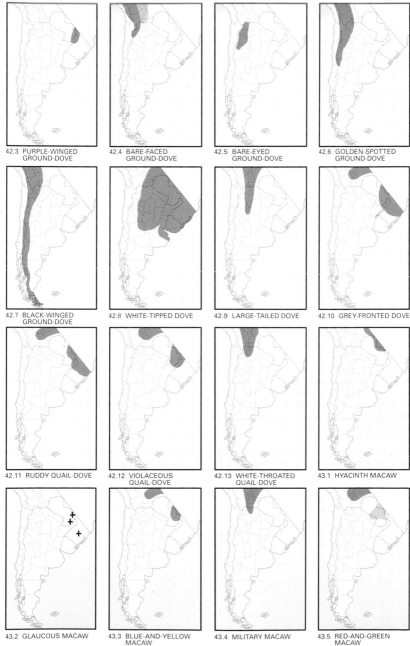

42.3 PURPLE-WINGED GROUND-DOVE

42.4 BARE-FACED GROUND-DOVE

42.5 BARE-EYED GROUND-DOVE

42.6 GOLDEN-SPOTTED GROUND-DOVE

42.7 BLACK-WINGED GROUND-DOVE

42.8 WHITE-TIPPED DOVE

42.9 LARGE-TAILED DOVE

42.10 GREY-FRONTED DOVE

42.11 RUDDY QUAIL-DOVE

42.12 VIOLACEOUS QUAIL-DOVE

42.13 WHITE-THROATED QUAIL-DOVE

43.1 HYACINTH MACAW

43.2 GLAUCOUS MACAW

43.3 BLUE-AND-YELLOW MACAW

43.4 MILITARY MACAW

43.5 RED-AND-GREEN MACAW

245

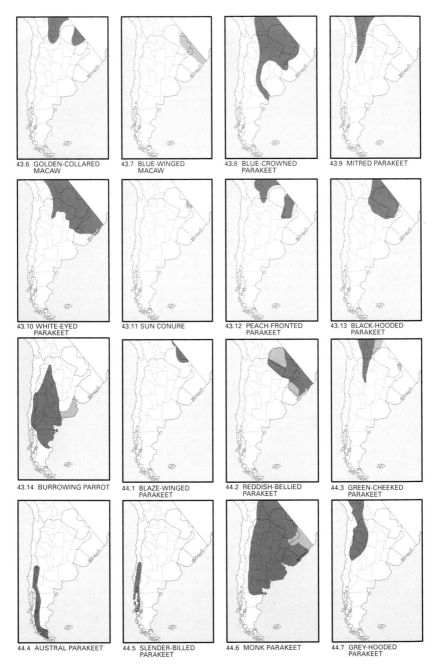

43.6 GOLDEN-COLLARED MACAW

43.7 BLUE-WINGED MACAW

43.8 BLUE-CROWNED PARAKEET

43.9 MITRED PARAKEET

43.10 WHITE-EYED PARAKEET

43.11 SUN CONURE

43.12 PEACH-FRONTED PARAKEET

43.13 BLACK-HOODED PARAKEET

43.14 BURROWING PARROT

44.1 BLAZE-WINGED PARAKEET

44.2 REDDISH-BELLIED PARAKEET

44.3 GREEN-CHEEKED PARAKEET

44.4 AUSTRAL PARAKEET

44.5 SLENDER-BILLED PARAKEET

44.6 MONK PARAKEET

44.7 GREY-HOODED PARAKEET

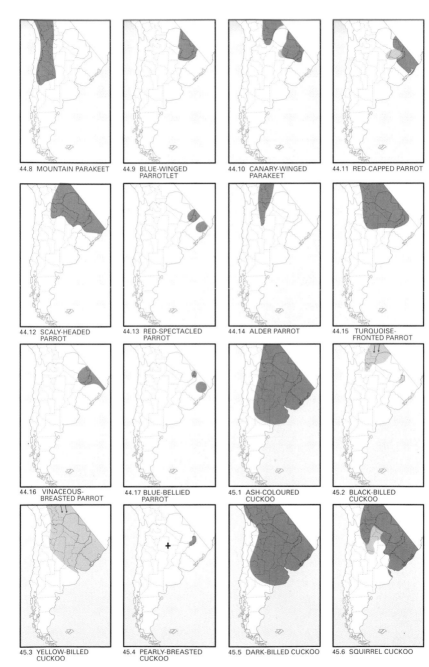

44.8 MOUNTAIN PARAKEET

44.9 BLUE-WINGED PARROTLET

44.10 CANARY-WINGED PARAKEET

44.11 RED-CAPPED PARROT

44.12 SCALY-HEADED PARROT

44.13 RED-SPECTACLED PARROT

44.14 ALDER PARROT

44.15 TURQUOISE-FRONTED PARROT

44.16 VINACEOUS-BREASTED PARROT

44.17 BLUE-BELLIED PARROT

45.1 ASH-COLOURED CUCKOO

45.2 BLACK-BILLED CUCKOO

45.3 YELLOW-BILLED CUCKOO

45.4 PEARLY-BREASTED CUCKOO

45.5 DARK-BILLED CUCKOO

45.6 SQUIRREL CUCKOO

45.7 STRIPED CUCKOO

45.8 PHEASANT CUCKOO

45.9 PAVONINE CUCKOO

45.10 GREATER ANI

45.11 SMOOTH-BILLED ANI

45.12 GROOVE-BILLED ANI

45.13 GUIRA CUCKOO

46.1 BARN OWL

46.2 TROPICAL
SCREECH-OWL

46.3 LONG-TUFTED
SCREECH-OWL

46.4 SPECTACLED OWL

46.5 TAWNY-BROWED OWL

46.6 GREAT HORNED OWL

46.7 MOTTLED OWL

46.8 BLACK-BANDED OWL

47.1 RUSTY-BARRED OWL

248

47.2 RUFOUS-LEGGED OWL

47.3 LEAST PYGMY-OWL

47.4 FERRUGINOUS PYGMY-OWL

47.5 AUSTRAL PYGMY-OWL

47.6 ANDEAN PYGMY-OWL

47.7 BURROWING OWL

47.8 BUFF-FRONTED OWL

47.9 STRIPED OWL

47.10 STYGIAN OWL

47.11 SHORT-EARED OWL

48.1 CHESTNUT-BANDED NIGHTHAWK

48.2 LESSER NIGHTHAWK

48.3 COMMON NIGHTHAWK

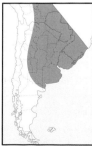

48.4 NACUNDA NIGHTHAWK

48.5 PAURAQUE

48.6 OCELLATED POORWILL

249

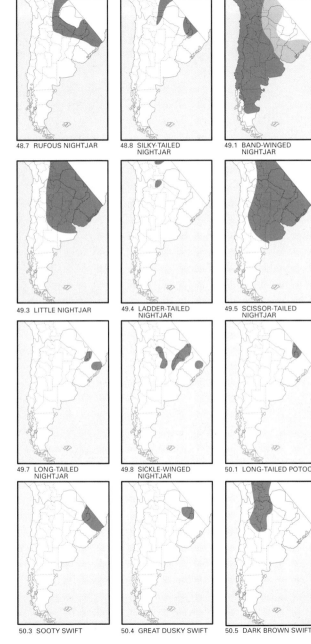

48.7 RUFOUS NIGHTJAR

48.8 SILKY-TAILED NIGHTJAR

49.1 BAND-WINGED NIGHTJAR

49.2 WHITE-WINGED NIGHTJAR

49.3 LITTLE NIGHTJAR

49.4 LADDER-TAILED NIGHTJAR

49.5 SCISSOR-TAILED NIGHTJAR

49.6 LYRE-TAILED NIGHTJAR

49.7 LONG-TAILED NIGHTJAR

49.8 SICKLE-WINGED NIGHTJAR

50.1 LONG-TAILED POTOO

50.2 COMMON POTOO

50.3 SOOTY SWIFT

50.4 GREAT DUSKY SWIFT

50.5 DARK BROWN SWIFT

50.6 WHITE-COLLARED SWIFT

50.7 BISCUTATE SWIFT

50.8 CHIMNEY SWIFT

50.9 ASHY-TAILED SWIFT

50.10 GREY-RUMPED SWIFT

50.11 WHITE-TIPPED SWIFT

50.12 ANDEAN SWIFT

51.1 SCALE-THROATED HERMIT

51.2 PLANALTO HERMIT

51.3 SWALLOW-TAILED HUMMINGBIRD

51.4 BLACK JACOBIN

51.5 GREEN VIOLETEAR

51.6 SPARKLING VIOLETEAR

51.7 WHITE-VENTED VIOLETEAR

51.8 BLACK-THROATED MANGO

51.9 BLACK-BREASTED PLOVERCREST

51.10 FESTIVE COQUETTE

251

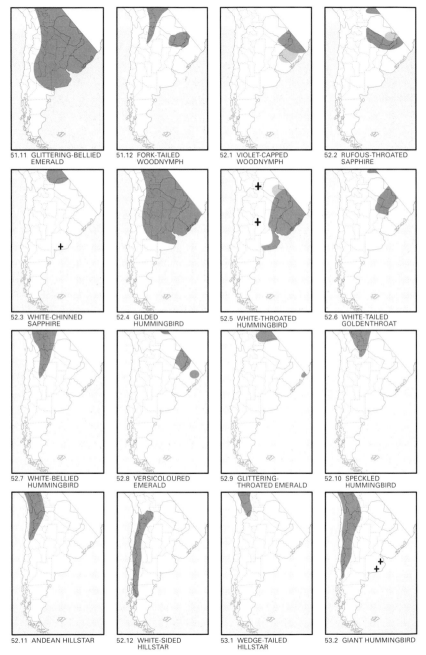

51.11 GLITTERING-BELLIED EMERALD

51.12 FORK-TAILED WOODNYMPH

52.1 VIOLET-CAPPED WOODNYMPH

52.2 RUFOUS-THROATED SAPPHIRE

52.3 WHITE-CHINNED SAPPHIRE

52.4 GILDED HUMMINGBIRD

52.5 WHITE-THROATED HUMMINGBIRD

52.6 WHITE-TAILED GOLDENTHROAT

52.7 WHITE-BELLIED HUMMINGBIRD

52.8 VERSICOLOURED EMERALD

52.9 GLITTERING-THROATED EMERALD

52.10 SPECKLED HUMMINGBIRD

52.11 ANDEAN HILLSTAR

52.12 WHITE-SIDED HILLSTAR

53.1 WEDGE-TAILED HILLSTAR

53.2 GIANT HUMMINGBIRD

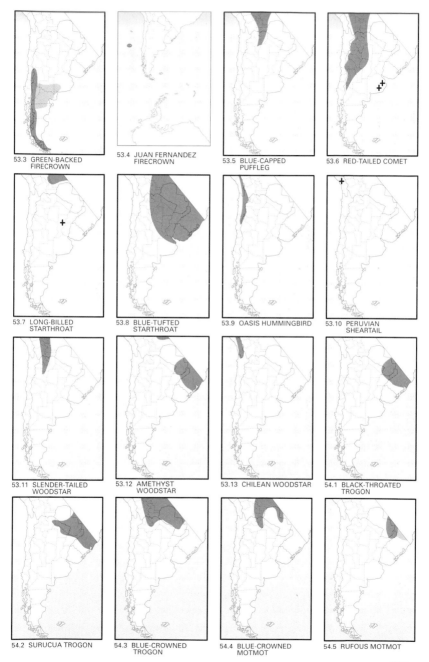

53.3 GREEN-BACKED FIRECROWN

53.4 JUAN FERNANDEZ FIRECROWN

53.5 BLUE-CAPPED PUFFLEG

53.6 RED-TAILED COMET

53.7 LONG-BILLED STARTHROAT

53.8 BLUE-TUFTED STARTHROAT

53.9 OASIS HUMMINGBIRD

53.10 PERUVIAN SHEARTAIL

53.11 SLENDER-TAILED WOODSTAR

53.12 AMETHYST WOODSTAR

53.13 CHILEAN WOODSTAR

54.1 BLACK-THROATED TROGON

54.2 SURUCUA TROGON

54.3 BLUE-CROWNED TROGON

54.4 BLUE-CROWNED MOTMOT

54.5 RUFOUS MOTMOT

54.6 RINGED KINGFISHER

54.7 AMAZON KINGFISHER

54.8 GREEN KINGFISHER

54.9 GREEN-AND-RUFOUS KINGFISHER

54.10 PYGMY KINGFISHER

54.11 WHITE-NECKED PUFFBIRD

54.12 WHITE-EARED PUFFBIRD

54.13 SPOT-BACKED PUFFBIRD

54.14 RUSTY-BREASTED NUNLET

54.15 RUFOUS-TAILED JACAMAR

55.1 CHESTNUT-EARED ARAÇARI

55.2 SPOT-BILLED TOUCANET

55.3 SAFFRON TOUCANET

55.4 RED-BREASTED TOUCAN

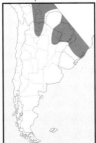

55.5 TOCO TOUCAN

56.1 ARROWHEAD PICULET

254

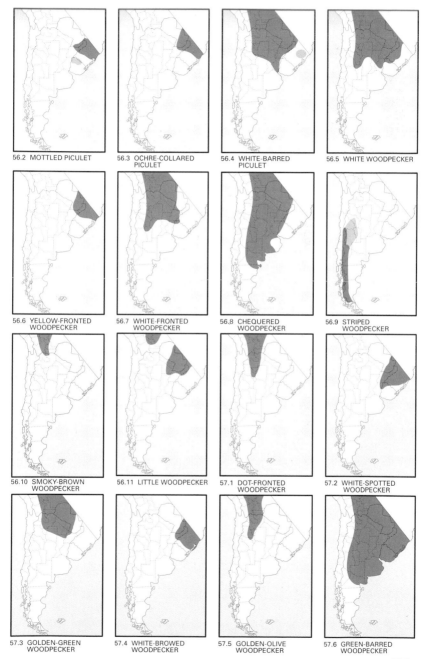

56.2 MOTTLED PICULET

56.3 OCHRE-COLLARED PICULET

56.4 WHITE-BARRED PICULET

56.5 WHITE WOODPECKER

56.6 YELLOW-FRONTED WOODPECKER

56.7 WHITE-FRONTED WOODPECKER

56.8 CHEQUERED WOODPECKER

56.9 STRIPED WOODPECKER

56.10 SMOKY-BROWN WOODPECKER

56.11 LITTLE WOODPECKER

57.1 DOT-FRONTED WOODPECKER

57.2 WHITE-SPOTTED WOODPECKER

57.3 GOLDEN-GREEN WOODPECKER

57.4 WHITE-BROWED WOODPECKER

57.5 GOLDEN-OLIVE WOODPECKER

57.6 GREEN-BARRED WOODPECKER

255

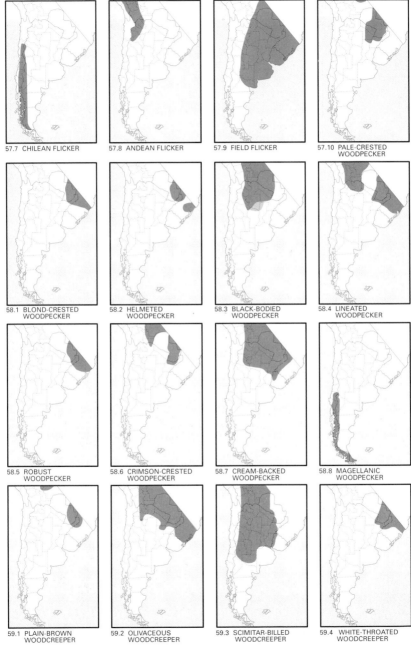

57.7 CHILEAN FLICKER

57.8 ANDEAN FLICKER

57.9 FIELD FLICKER

57.10 PALE-CRESTED WOODPECKER

58.1 BLOND-CRESTED WOODPECKER

58.2 HELMETED WOODPECKER

58.3 BLACK-BODIED WOODPECKER

58.4 LINEATED WOODPECKER

58.5 ROBUST WOODPECKER

58.6 CRIMSON-CRESTED WOODPECKER

58.7 CREAM-BACKED WOODPECKER

58.8 MAGELLANIC WOODPECKER

59.1 PLAIN-BROWN WOODCREEPER

59.2 OLIVACEOUS WOODCREEPER

59.3 SCIMITAR-BILLED WOODCREEPER

59.4 WHITE-THROATED WOODCREEPER

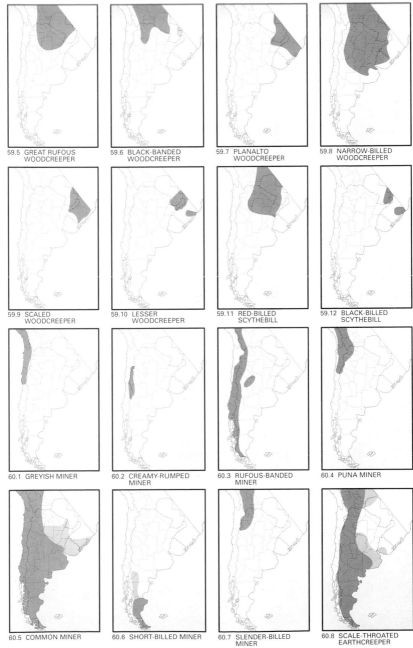

59.5 GREAT RUFOUS
WOODCREEPER

59.6 BLACK-BANDED
WOODCREEPER

59.7 PLANALTO
WOODCREEPER

59.8 NARROW-BILLED
WOODCREEPER

59.9 SCALED
WOODCREEPER

59.10 LESSER
WOODCREEPER

59.11 RED-BILLED
SCYTHEBILL

59.12 BLACK-BILLED
SCYTHEBILL

60.1 GREYISH MINER

60.2 CREAMY-RUMPED
MINER

60.3 RUFOUS-BANDED
MINER

60.4 PUNA MINER

60.5 COMMON MINER

60.6 SHORT-BILLED MINER

60.7 SLENDER-BILLED
MINER

60.8 SCALE-THROATED
EARTHCREEPER

257

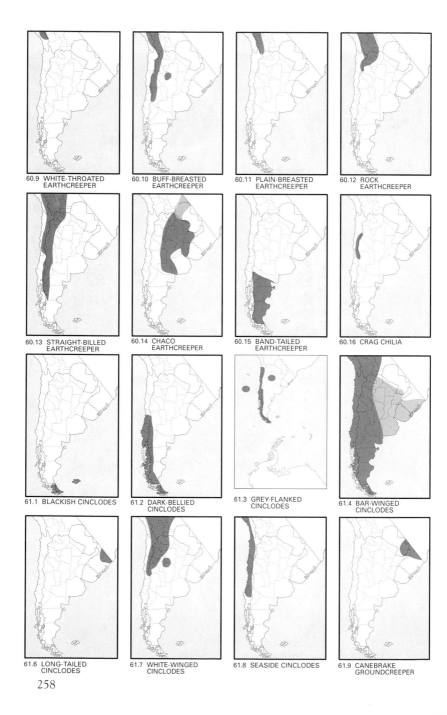

60.9 WHITE-THROATED EARTHCREEPER

60.10 BUFF-BREASTED EARTHCREEPER

60.11 PLAIN-BREASTED EARTHCREEPER

60.12 ROCK EARTHCREEPER

60.13 STRAIGHT-BILLED EARTHCREEPER

60.14 CHACO EARTHCREEPER

60.15 BAND-TAILED EARTHCREEPER

60.16 CRAG CHILIA

61.1 BLACKISH CINCLODES

61.2 DARK-BELLIED CINCLODES

61.3 GREY-FLANKED CINCLODES

61.4 BAR-WINGED CINCLODES

61.6 LONG-TAILED CINCLODES

61.7 WHITE-WINGED CINCLODES

61.8 SEASIDE CINCLODES

61.9 CANEBRAKE GROUNDCREEPER

258

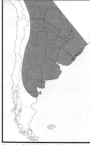

61.10 RUFOUS HORNERO

61.11 CRESTED HORNERO

61.12 CURVE-BILLED REEDHAUNTER

61.13 STRAIGHT-BILLED REEDHAUNTER

61.14 DES MUR'S WIRETAIL

61.15 THORN-TAILED RAYADITO

61.16 MASAFUERA RAYADITO

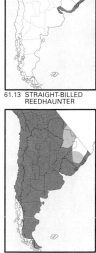

61.17 WREN-LIKE RUSHBIRD

61.18 STREAKED TIT-SPINETAIL

61.19 STRIOLATED TIT-SPINETAIL

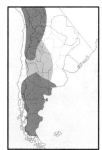

62.1 PLAIN-MANTLED TIT-SPINETAIL

62.2 TUFTED TIT-SPINETAIL

62.3 BROWN-CAPPED TIT-SPINETAIL

62.4 ARAUCARIA TIT-SPINETAIL

62.5 CHOTOY SPINETAIL

62.6 RUFOUS-CAPPED SPINETAIL

259

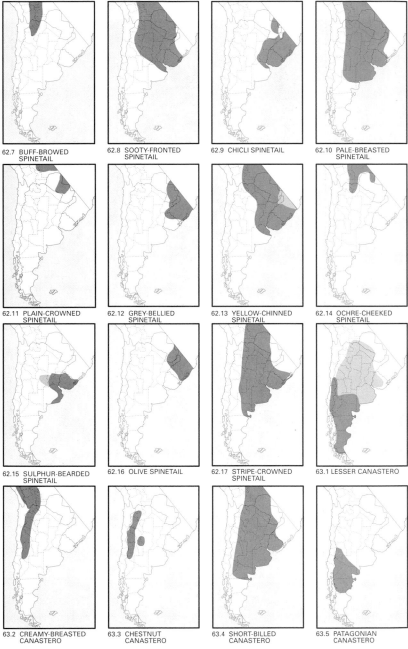

62.7 BUFF-BROWED SPINETAIL

62.8 SOOTY-FRONTED SPINETAIL

62.9 CHICLI SPINETAIL

62.10 PALE-BREASTED SPINETAIL

62.11 PLAIN-CROWNED SPINETAIL

62.12 GREY-BELLIED SPINETAIL

62.13 YELLOW-CHINNED SPINETAIL

62.14 OCHRE-CHEEKED SPINETAIL

62.15 SULPHUR-BEARDED SPINETAIL

62.16 OLIVE SPINETAIL

62.17 STRIPE-CROWNED SPINETAIL

63.1 LESSER CANASTERO

63.2 CREAMY-BREASTED CANASTERO

63.3 CHESTNUT CANASTERO

63.4 SHORT-BILLED CANASTERO

63.5 PATAGONIAN CANASTERO

260

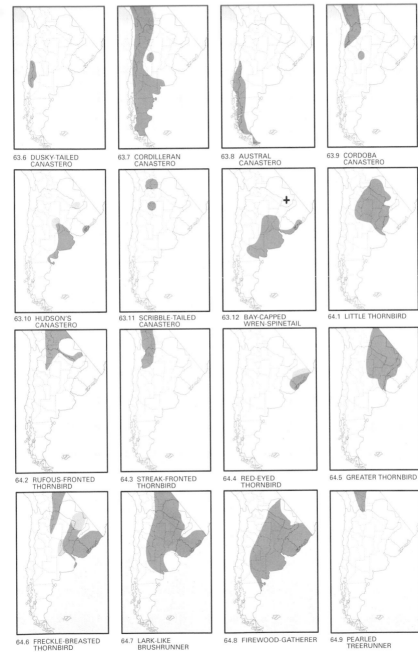

63.6 DUSKY-TAILED CANASTERO

63.7 CORDILLERAN CANASTERO

63.8 AUSTRAL CANASTERO

63.9 CORDOBA CANASTERO

63.10 HUDSON'S CANASTERO

63.11 SCRIBBLE-TAILED CANASTERO

63.12 BAY-CAPPED WREN-SPINETAIL

64.1 LITTLE THORNBIRD

64.2 RUFOUS-FRONTED THORNBIRD

64.3 STREAK-FRONTED THORNBIRD

64.4 RED-EYED THORNBIRD

64.5 GREATER THORNBIRD

64.6 FRECKLE-BREASTED THORNBIRD

64.7 LARK-LIKE BRUSHRUNNER

64.8 FIREWOOD-GATHERER

64.9 PEARLED TREERUNNER

261

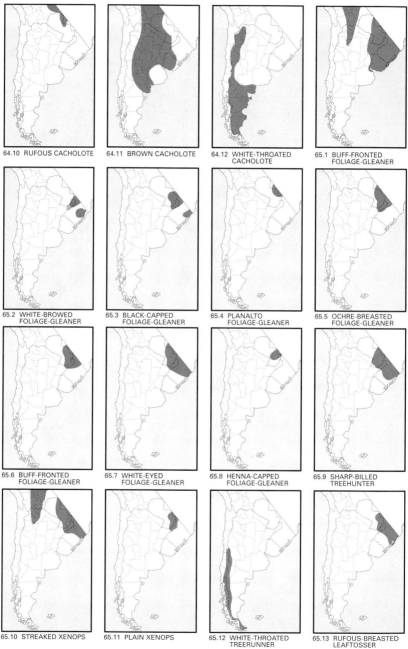

64.10 RUFOUS CACHOLOTE

64.11 BROWN CACHOLOTE

64.12 WHITE-THROATED CACHOLOTE

65.1 BUFF-FRONTED FOLIAGE-GLEANER

65.2 WHITE-BROWED FOLIAGE-GLEANER

65.3 BLACK-CAPPED FOLIAGE-GLEANER

65.4 PLANALTO FOLIAGE-GLEANER

65.5 OCHRE-BREASTED FOLIAGE-GLEANER

65.6 BUFF-FRONTED FOLIAGE-GLEANER

65.7 WHITE-EYED FOLIAGE-GLEANER

65.8 HENNA-CAPPED FOLIAGE-GLEANER

65.9 SHARP-BILLED TREEHUNTER

65.10 STREAKED XENOPS

65.11 PLAIN XENOPS

65.12 WHITE-THROATED TREERUNNER

65.13 RUFOUS-BREASTED LEAFTOSSER

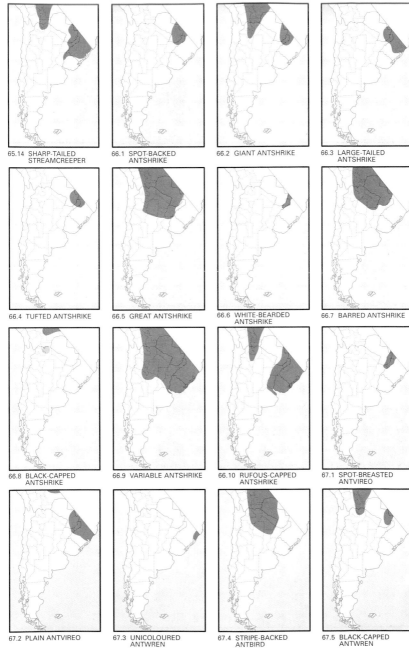

65.14 SHARP-TAILED
STREAMCREEPER

66.1 SPOT-BACKED
ANTSHRIKE

66.2 GIANT ANTSHRIKE

66.3 LARGE-TAILED
ANTSHRIKE

66.4 TUFTED ANTSHRIKE

66.5 GREAT ANTSHRIKE

66.6 WHITE-BEARDED
ANTSHRIKE

66.7 BARRED ANTSHRIKE

66.8 BLACK-CAPPED
ANTSHRIKE

66.9 VARIABLE ANTSHRIKE

66.10 RUFOUS-CAPPED
ANTSHRIKE

67.1 SPOT-BREASTED
ANTVIREO

67.2 PLAIN ANTVIREO

67.3 UNICOLOURED
ANTWREN

67.4 STRIPE-BACKED
ANTBIRD

67.5 BLACK-CAPPED
ANTWREN

263

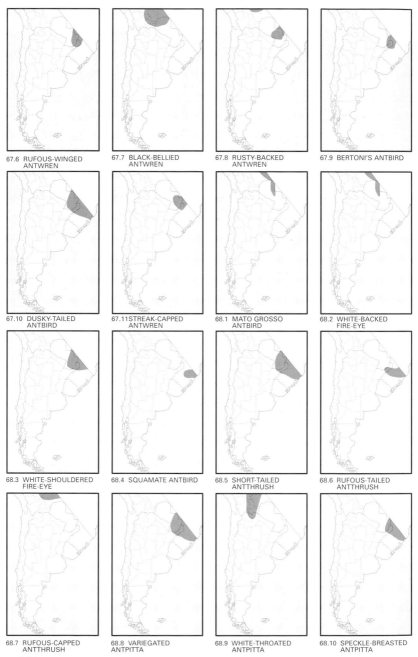

67.6 RUFOUS-WINGED ANTWREN

67.7 BLACK-BELLIED ANTWREN

67.8 RUSTY-BACKED ANTWREN

67.9 BERTONI'S ANTBIRD

67.10 DUSKY-TAILED ANTBIRD

67.11 STREAK-CAPPED ANTWREN

68.1 MATO GROSSO ANTBIRD

68.2 WHITE-BACKED FIRE-EYE

68.3 WHITE-SHOULDERED FIRE-EYE

68.4 SQUAMATE ANTBIRD

68.5 SHORT-TAILED ANTTHRUSH

68.6 RUFOUS-TAILED ANTTHRUSH

68.7 RUFOUS-CAPPED ANTTHRUSH

68.8 VARIEGATED ANTPITTA

68.9 WHITE-THROATED ANTPITTA

68.10 SPECKLE-BREASTED ANTPITTA

68.11 RUFOUS GNATEATER

69.1 CHESTNUT-THROATED
HUET-HUET

69.2 BLACK-THROATED
HUET-HUET

69.3 MOUSTACHED TURCA

69.4 WHITE-THROATED
TAPACULO

69.5 CHUCAO TAPACULO

69.6 CRESTED GALLITO

69.7 SANDY GALLITO

69.8 COLLARED
CRESCENT-CHEST

69.9 OLIVE-CROWNED
CRESCENT-CHEST

69.10 SPOTTED
BAMBOOWREN

69.11 OCHRE-FLANKED
TAPACULO

69.12 MOUSE-COLOURED
TAPACULO

69.13 MAGELLANIC
TAPACULO

69.14 WHITE-BROWED
TAPACULO

70.1 PLANALTO
TYRANNULET

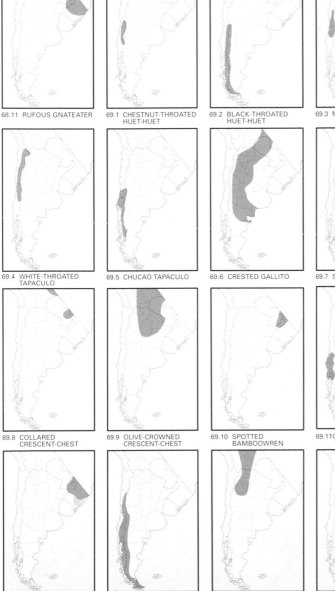

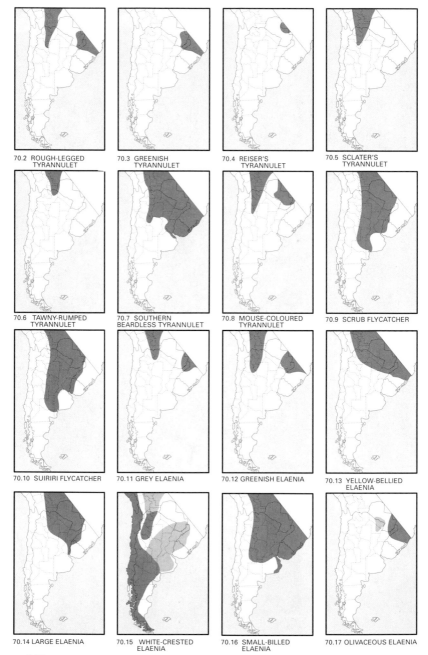

70.2 ROUGH-LEGGED TYRANNULET

70.3 GREENISH TYRANNULET

70.4 REISER'S TYRANNULET

70.5 SCLATER'S TYRANNULET

70.6 TAWNY-RUMPED TYRANNULET

70.7 SOUTHERN BEARDLESS TYRANNULET

70.8 MOUSE-COLOURED TYRANNULET

70.9 SCRUB FLYCATCHER

70.10 SUIRIRI FLYCATCHER

70.11 GREY ELAENIA

70.12 GREENISH ELAENIA

70.13 YELLOW-BELLIED ELAENIA

70.14 LARGE ELAENIA

70.15 WHITE-CRESTED ELAENIA

70.16 SMALL-BILLED ELAENIA

70.17 OLIVACEOUS ELAENIA

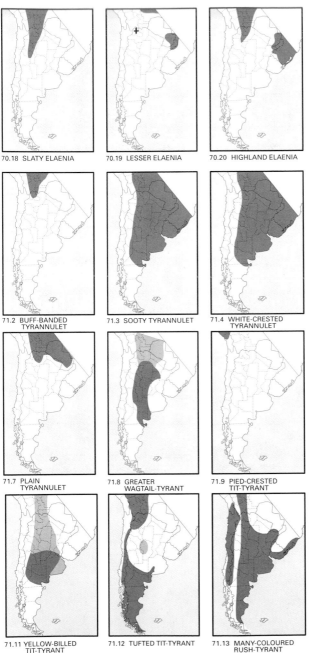

70.18 SLATY ELAENIA

70.19 LESSER ELAENIA

70.20 HIGHLAND ELAENIA

71.1 WHITE-THROATED
TYRANNULET

71.2 BUFF-BANDED
TYRANNULET

71.3 SOOTY TYRANNULET

71.4 WHITE-CRESTED
TYRANNULET

71. 6 GREY-CROWNED
TYRANNULET

71.7 PLAIN
TYRANNULET

71.8 GREATER
WAGTAIL-TYRANT

71.9 PIED-CRESTED
TIT-TYRANT

71.10 JUAN FERNANDEZ
TIT-TYRANT

71.11 YELLOW-BILLED
TIT-TYRANT

71.12 TUFTED TIT-TYRANT

71.13 MANY-COLOURED
RUSH-TYRANT

72.1 SHARP-TAILED
GRASS-TYRANT

267

72.2 BEARDED TACHURI

72.3 CRESTED DORADITO

72.4 DINELLI'S DORADITO

72.5 SUBTROPICAL
DORADITO

72.6 WARBLING DORADITO

72.7 TAWNY-CROWNED
PYGMY-TYRANT

72.8 RUFOUS-SIDED
PYGMY-TYRANT

72.9 GREY-HOODED
FLYCATCHER

72.10 SEPIA-CAPPED
FLYCATCHER

72.11 SOUTHERN
BRISTLE-TYRANT

72.12 YELLOW
TYRANNULET

72.13 MOTTLE-CHEEKED
TYRANNULET

72.14 SERRA DO MAR
TYRANNULET

72.15 SAO PAOLO
TYRANNULET

72.16 BAY-RINGED
TYRANNULET

73.1 SOUTHERN ANTPIPIT

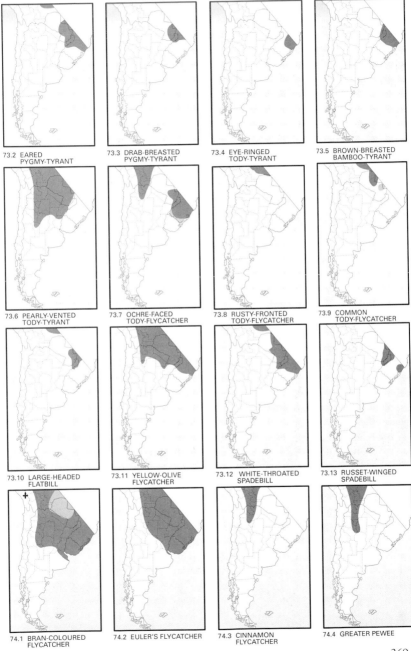

73.2 EARED PYGMY-TYRANT

73.3 DRAB-BREASTED PYGMY-TYRANT

73.4 EYE-RINGED TODY-TYRANT

73.5 BROWN-BREASTED BAMBOO-TYRANT

73.6 PEARLY-VENTED TODY-TYRANT

73.7 OCHRE-FACED TODY-FLYCATCHER

73.8 RUSTY-FRONTED TODY-FLYCATCHER

73.9 COMMON TODY-FLYCATCHER

73.10 LARGE-HEADED FLATBILL

73.11 YELLOW-OLIVE FLYCATCHER

73.12 WHITE-THROATED SPADEBILL

73.13 RUSSET-WINGED SPADEBILL

74.1 BRAN-COLOURED FLYCATCHER

74.2 EULER'S FLYCATCHER

74.3 CINNAMON FLYCATCHER

74.4 GREATER PEWEE

269

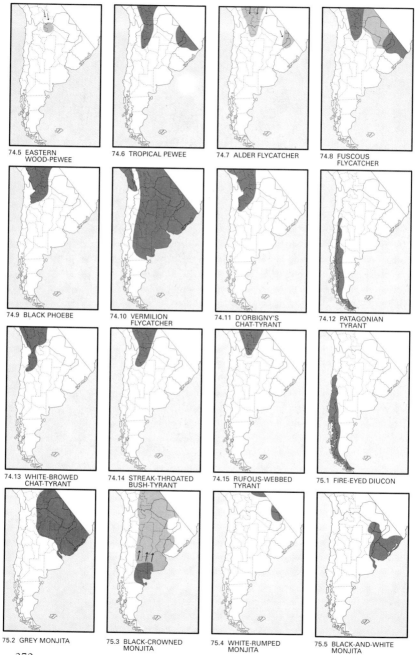

74.5 EASTERN WOOD-PEWEE

74.6 TROPICAL PEWEE

74.7 ALDER FLYCATCHER

74.8 FUSCOUS FLYCATCHER

74.9 BLACK PHOEBE

74.10 VERMILION FLYCATCHER

74.11 D'ORBIGNY'S CHAT-TYRANT

74.12 PATAGONIAN TYRANT

74.13 WHITE-BROWED CHAT-TYRANT

74.14 STREAK-THROATED BUSH-TYRANT

74.15 RUFOUS-WEBBED TYRANT

75.1 FIRE-EYED DIUCON

75.2 GREY MONJITA

75.3 BLACK-CROWNED MONJITA

75.4 WHITE-RUMPED MONJITA

75.5 BLACK-AND-WHITE MONJITA

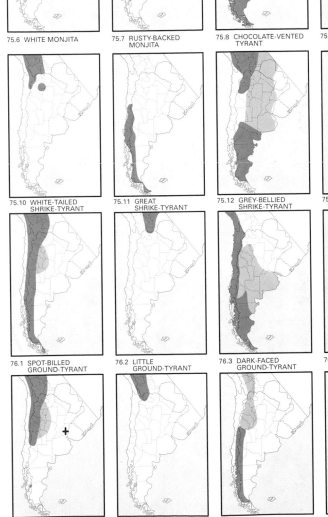

75.6 WHITE MONJITA

75.7 RUSTY-BACKED MONJITA

75.8 CHOCOLATE-VENTED TYRANT

75.9 BLACK-BILLED SHRIKE-TYRANT

75.10 WHITE-TAILED SHRIKE-TYRANT

75.11 GREAT SHRIKE-TYRANT

75.12 GREY-BELLIED SHRIKE-TYRANT

75.13 LESSER SHRIKE-TYRANT

76.1 SPOT-BILLED GROUND-TYRANT

76.2 LITTLE GROUND-TYRANT

76.3 DARK-FACED GROUND-TYRANT

76.4 CINNAMON-BELLIED GROUND-TYRANT

76.5 RUFOUS-NAPED GROUND-TYRANT

76.6 PUNA GROUND-TYRANT

76.7 WHITE-BROWED GROUND-TYRANT

76.8 CINEREOUS GROUND-TYRANT

271

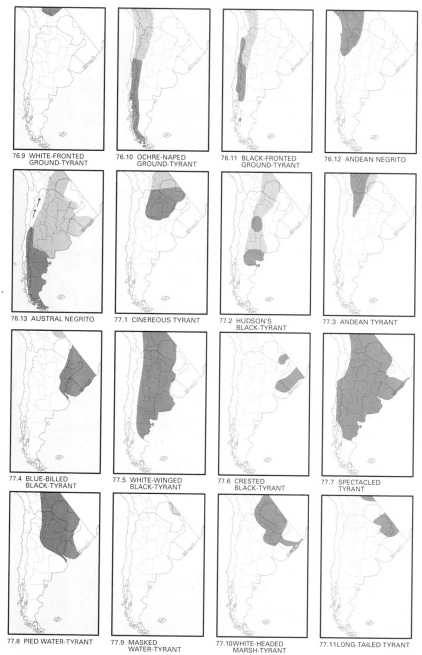

76.9 WHITE-FRONTED GROUND-TYRANT

76.10 OCHRE-NAPED GROUND-TYRANT

76.11 BLACK-FRONTED GROUND-TYRANT

76.12 ANDEAN NEGRITO

76.13 AUSTRAL NEGRITO

77.1 CINEREOUS TYRANT

77.2 HUDSON'S BLACK-TYRANT

77.3 ANDEAN TYRANT

77.4 BLUE-BILLED BLACK-TYRANT

77.5 WHITE-WINGED BLACK-TYRANT

77.6 CRESTED BLACK-TYRANT

77.7 SPECTACLED TYRANT

77.8 PIED WATER-TYRANT

77.9 MASKED WATER-TYRANT

77.10 WHITE-HEADED MARSH-TYRANT

77.11 LONG-TAILED TYRANT

77.12 COCK-TAILED TYRANT

77.13 STRANGE-TAILED TYRANT

77.14 STREAMER-TAILED TYRANT

78.1 YELLOW-BROWED TYRANT

78.2 SHORT-TAILED FIELD-TYRANT

78.3 CLIFF FLYCATCHER

78.4 CATTLE TYRANT

78.5 SHEAR-TAILED GREY-TYRANT

78.6 RUFOUS-TAILED ATTILA

78.7 RUFOUS CASIORNIS

78.8 SIRYSTES

78.9 DUSKY-CAPPED FLYCATCHER

78.10 SWAINSON'S FLYCATCHER

78.11 SHORT-CRESTED FLYCATCHER

78.12 BROWN-CRESTED FLYCATCHER

78.13 LESSER KISKADEE

273

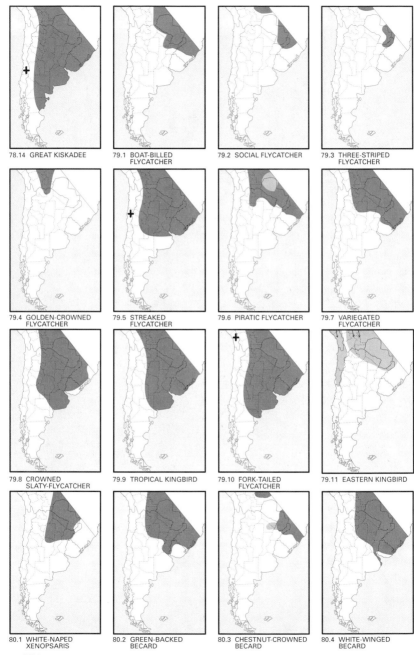

78.14 GREAT KISKADEE

79.1 BOAT-BILLED FLYCATCHER

79.2 SOCIAL FLYCATCHER

79.3 THREE-STRIPED FLYCATCHER

79.4 GOLDEN-CROWNED FLYCATCHER

79.5 STREAKED FLYCATCHER

79.6 PIRATIC FLYCATCHER

79.7 VARIEGATED FLYCATCHER

79.8 CROWNED SLATY-FLYCATCHER

79.9 TROPICAL KINGBIRD

79.10 FORK-TAILED FLYCATCHER

79.11 EASTERN KINGBIRD

80.1 WHITE-NAPED XENOPSARIS

80.2 GREEN-BACKED BECARD

80.3 CHESTNUT-CROWNED BECARD

80.4 WHITE-WINGED BECARD

274

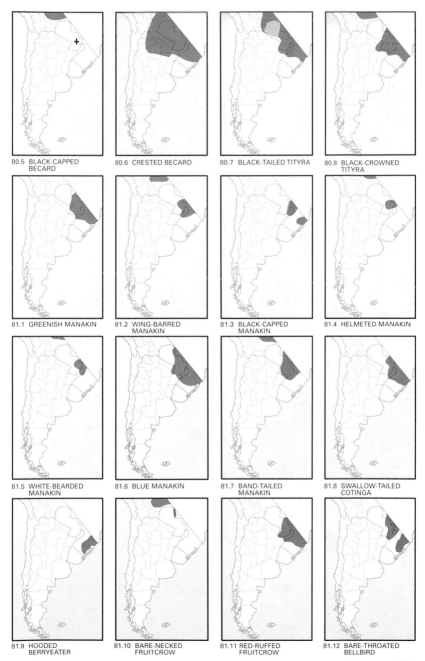

80.5 BLACK-CAPPED
BECARD

80.6 CRESTED BECARD

80.7 BLACK-TAILED TITYRA

80.8 BLACK-CROWNED
TITYRA

81.1 GREENISH MANAKIN

81.2 WING-BARRED
MANAKIN

81.3 BLACK-CAPPED
MANAKIN

81.4 HELMETED MANAKIN

81.5 WHITE-BEARDED
MANAKIN

81.6 BLUE MANAKIN

81.7 BAND-TAILED
MANAKIN

81.8 SWALLOW-TAILED
COTINGA

81.9 HOODED
BERRYEATER

81.10 BARE-NECKED
FRUITCROW

81.11 RED-RUFFED
FRUITCROW

81.12 BARE-THROATED
BELLBIRD

275

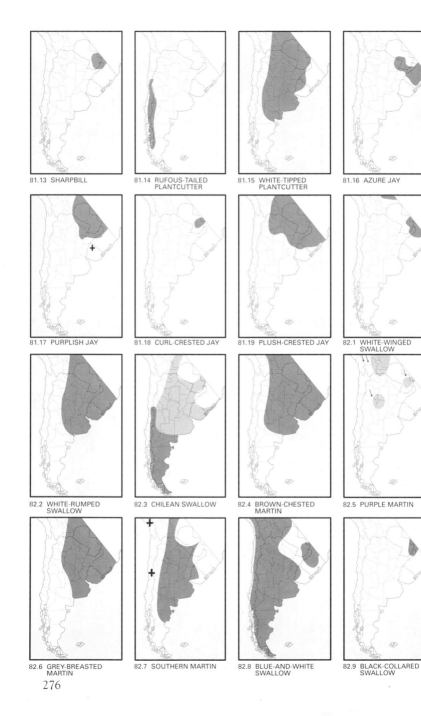

81.13 SHARPBILL

81.14 RUFOUS-TAILED PLANTCUTTER

81.15 WHITE-TIPPED PLANTCUTTER

81.16 AZURE JAY

81.17 PURPLISH JAY

81.18 CURL-CRESTED JAY

81.19 PLUSH-CRESTED JAY

82.1 WHITE-WINGED SWALLOW

82.2 WHITE-RUMPED SWALLOW

82.3 CHILEAN SWALLOW

82.4 BROWN-CHESTED MARTIN

82.5 PURPLE MARTIN

82.6 GREY-BREASTED MARTIN

82.7 SOUTHERN MARTIN

82.8 BLUE-AND-WHITE SWALLOW

82.9 BLACK-COLLARED SWALLOW

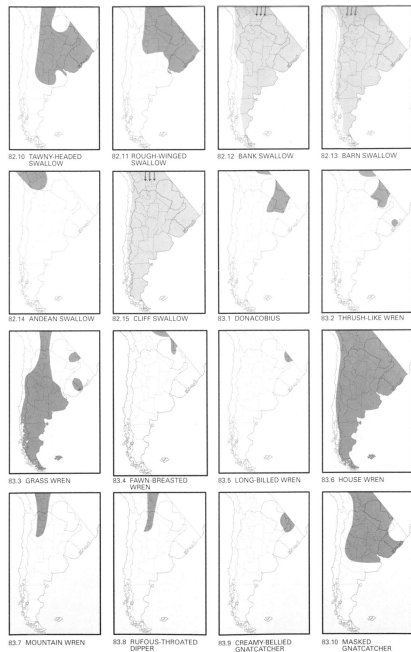

82.10 TAWNY-HEADED SWALLOW

82.11 ROUGH-WINGED SWALLOW

82.12 BANK SWALLOW

82.13 BARN SWALLOW

82.14 ANDEAN SWALLOW

82.15 CLIFF SWALLOW

83.1 DONACOBIUS

83.2 THRUSH-LIKE WREN

83.3 GRASS WREN

83.4 FAWN-BREASTED WREN

83.5 LONG-BILLED WREN

83.6 HOUSE WREN

83.7 MOUNTAIN WREN

83.8 RUFOUS-THROATED DIPPER

83.9 CREAMY-BELLIED GNATCATCHER

83.10 MASKED GNATCATCHER

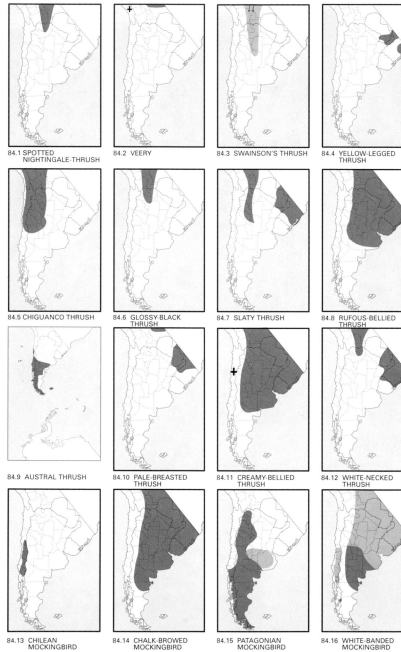

84.1 SPOTTED NIGHTINGALE-THRUSH

84.2 VEERY

84.3 SWAINSON'S THRUSH

84.4 YELLOW-LEGGED THRUSH

84.5 CHIGUANCO THRUSH

84.6 GLOSSY-BLACK THRUSH

84.7 SLATY THRUSH

84.8 RUFOUS-BELLIED THRUSH

84.9 AUSTRAL THRUSH

84.10 PALE-BREASTED THRUSH

84.11 CREAMY-BELLIED THRUSH

84.12 WHITE-NECKED THRUSH

84.13 CHILEAN MOCKINGBIRD

84.14 CHALK-BROWED MOCKINGBIRD

84.15 PATAGONIAN MOCKINGBIRD

84.16 WHITE-BANDED MOCKINGBIRD

278

84.17 BROWN-BACKED MOCKINGBIRD

85.1 SHORT-BILLED PIPIT

85.2 HELLMAYR'S PIPIT

85.3 YELLOWISH PIPIT

85.4 CHACO PIPIT

85.5 CORRENDERA PIPIT

85.6 OCHRE-BREASTED PIPIT

85.7 PARAMO PIPIT

85.8 SOUTH GEORGIA PIPIT

85.9 EUROPEAN STARLING

85.10 CRESTED MYNA

86.1 RED-EYED VIREO

86.2 RUFOUS-CROWNED GREENLET

86.3 RUFOUS-BROWED PEPPERSHRIKE

86.4 TROPICAL PARULA

86.5 BLACKPOLL WARBLER

279

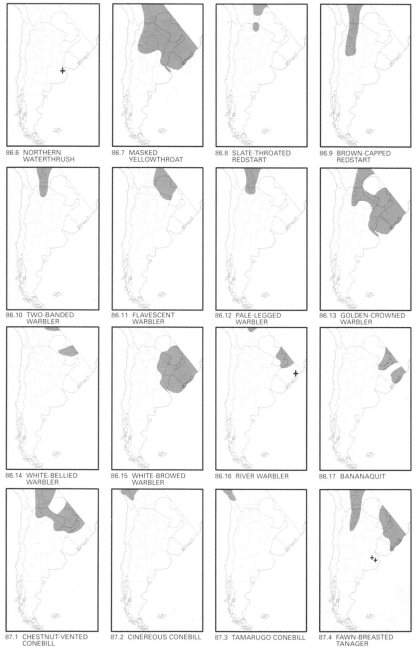

86.6 NORTHERN
WATERTHRUSH

86.7 MASKED
YELLOWTHROAT

86.8 SLATE-THROATED
REDSTART

86.9 BROWN-CAPPED
REDSTART

86.10 TWO-BANDED
WARBLER

86.11 FLAVESCENT
WARBLER

86.12 PALE-LEGGED
WARBLER

86.13 GOLDEN-CROWNED
WARBLER

86.14 WHITE-BELLIED
WARBLER

86.15 WHITE-BROWED
WARBLER

86.16 RIVER WARBLER

86.17 BANANAQUIT

87.1 CHESTNUT-VENTED
CONEBILL

87.2 CINEREOUS CONEBILL

87.3 TAMARUGO CONEBILL

87.4 FAWN-BREASTED
TANAGER

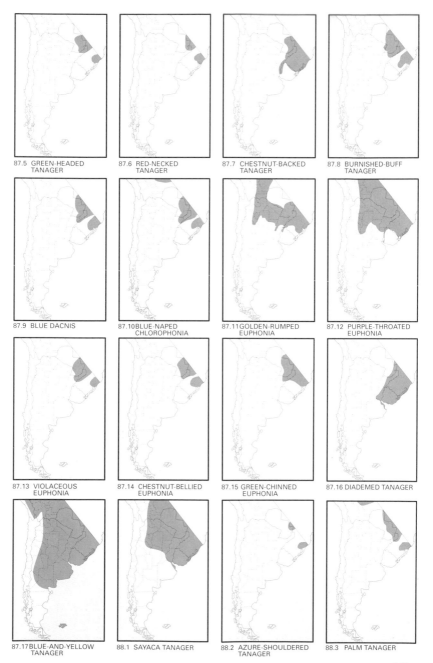

87.5 GREEN-HEADED
TANAGER

87.6 RED-NECKED
TANAGER

87.7 CHESTNUT-BACKED
TANAGER

87.8 BURNISHED-BUFF
TANAGER

87.9 BLUE DACNIS

87.10 BLUE-NAPED
CHLOROPHONIA

87.11 GOLDEN-RUMPED
EUPHONIA

87.12 PURPLE-THROATED
EUPHONIA

87.13 VIOLACEOUS
EUPHONIA

87.14 CHESTNUT-BELLIED
EUPHONIA

87.15 GREEN-CHINNED
EUPHONIA

87.16 DIADEMED TANAGER

87.17 BLUE-AND-YELLOW
TANAGER

88.1 SAYACA TANAGER

88.2 AZURE-SHOULDERED
TANAGER

88.3 PALM TANAGER

281

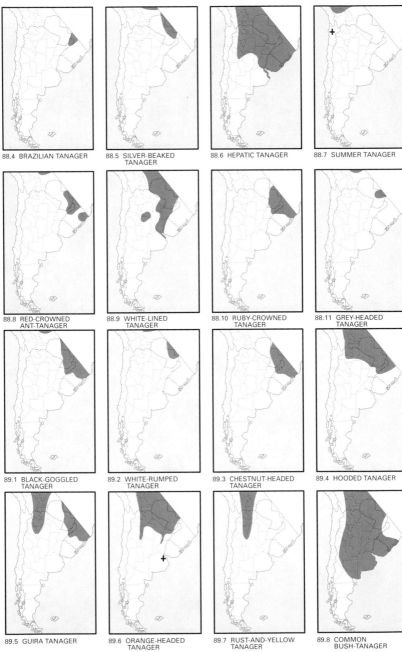

88.4 BRAZILIAN TANAGER

88.5 SILVER-BEAKED TANAGER

88.6 HEPATIC TANAGER

88.7 SUMMER TANAGER

88.8 RED-CROWNED ANT-TANAGER

88.9 WHITE-LINED TANAGER

88.10 RUBY-CROWNED TANAGER

88.11 GREY-HEADED TANAGER

89.1 BLACK-GOGGLED TANAGER

89.2 WHITE-RUMPED TANAGER

89.3 CHESTNUT-HEADED TANAGER

89.4 HOODED TANAGER

89.5 GUIRA TANAGER

89.6 ORANGE-HEADED TANAGER

89.7 RUST-AND-YELLOW TANAGER

89.8 COMMON BUSH-TANAGER

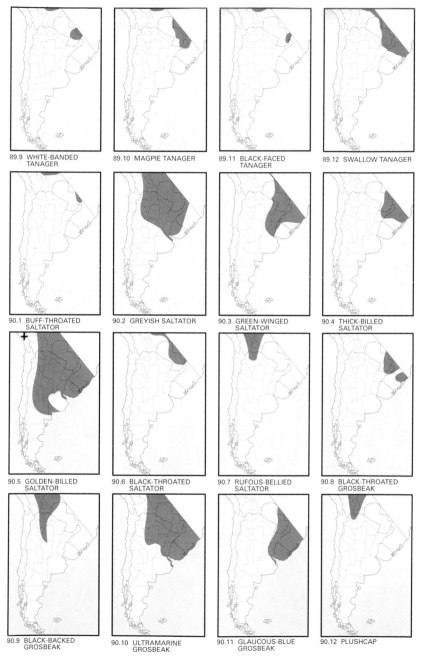

89.9 WHITE-BANDED TANAGER

89.10 MAGPIE TANAGER

89.11 BLACK-FACED TANAGER

89.12 SWALLOW TANAGER

90.1 BUFF-THROATED SALTATOR

90.2 GREYISH SALTATOR

90.3 GREEN-WINGED SALTATOR

90.4 THICK-BILLED SALTATOR

90.5 GOLDEN-BILLED SALTATOR

90.6 BLACK-THROATED SALTATOR

90.7 RUFOUS-BELLIED SALTATOR

90.8 BLACK-THROATED GROSBEAK

90.9 BLACK-BACKED GROSBEAK

90.10 ULTRAMARINE GROSBEAK

90.11 GLAUCOUS-BLUE GROSBEAK

90.12 PLUSHCAP

283

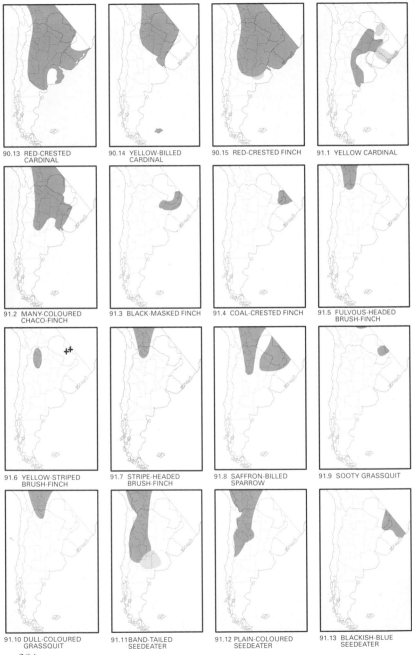

90.13 RED-CRESTED CARDINAL

90.14 YELLOW-BILLED CARDINAL

90.15 RED-CRESTED FINCH

91.1 YELLOW CARDINAL

91.2 MANY-COLOURED CHACO-FINCH

91.3 BLACK-MASKED FINCH

91.4 COAL-CRESTED FINCH

91.5 FULVOUS-HEADED BRUSH-FINCH

91.6 YELLOW-STRIPED BRUSH-FINCH

91.7 STRIPE-HEADED BRUSH-FINCH

91.8 SAFFRON-BILLED SPARROW

91.9 SOOTY GRASSQUIT

91.10 DULL-COLOURED GRASSQUIT

91.11 BAND-TAILED SEEDEATER

91.12 PLAIN-COLOURED SEEDEATER

91.13 BLACKISH-BLUE SEEDEATER

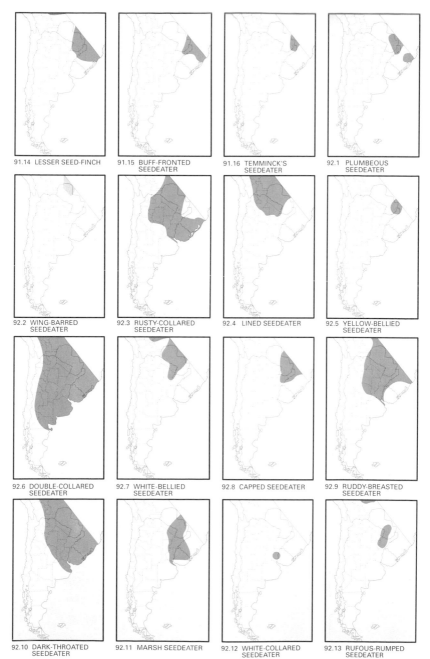

91.14 LESSER SEED-FINCH

91.15 BUFF-FRONTED
SEEDEATER

91.16 TEMMINCK'S
SEEDEATER

92.1 PLUMBEOUS
SEEDEATER

92.2 WING-BARRED
SEEDEATER

92.3 RUSTY-COLLARED
SEEDEATER

92.4 LINED SEEDEATER

92.5 YELLOW-BELLIED
SEEDEATER

92.6 DOUBLE-COLLARED
SEEDEATER

92.7 WHITE-BELLIED
SEEDEATER

92.8 CAPPED SEEDEATER

92.9 RUDDY-BREASTED
SEEDEATER

92.10 DARK-THROATED
SEEDEATER

92.11 MARSH SEEDEATER

92.12 WHITE-COLLARED
SEEDEATER

92.13 RUFOUS-RUMPED
SEEDEATER

285

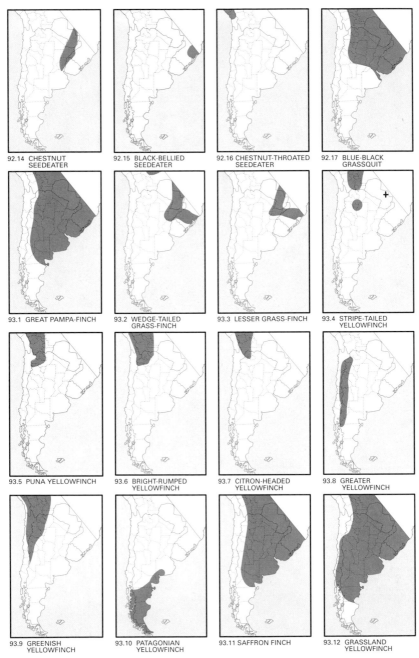

92.14 CHESTNUT
SEEDEATER

92.15 BLACK-BELLIED
SEEDEATER

92.16 CHESTNUT-THROATED
SEEDEATER

92.17 BLUE-BLACK
GRASSQUIT

93.1 GREAT PAMPA-FINCH

93.2 WEDGE-TAILED
GRASS-FINCH

93.3 LESSER GRASS-FINCH

93.4 STRIPE-TAILED
YELLOWFINCH

93.5 PUNA YELLOWFINCH

93.6 BRIGHT-RUMPED
YELLOWFINCH

93.7 CITRON-HEADED
YELLOWFINCH

93.8 GREATER
YELLOWFINCH

93.9 GREENISH
YELLOWFINCH

93.10 PATAGONIAN
YELLOWFINCH

93.11 SAFFRON FINCH

93.12 GRASSLAND
YELLOWFINCH

286

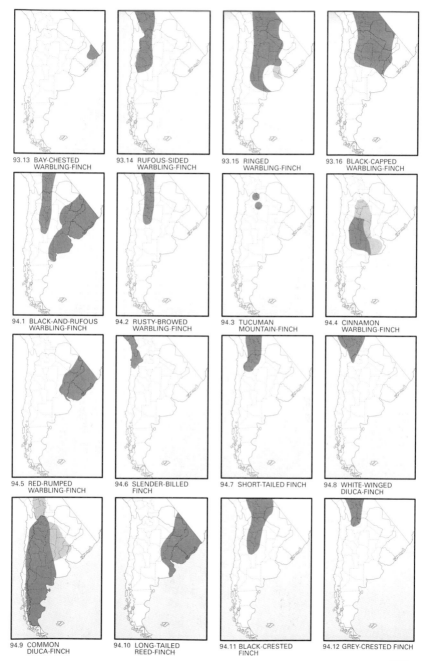

93.13 BAY-CHESTED
WARBLING-FINCH

93.14 RUFOUS-SIDED
WARBLING-FINCH

93.15 RINGED
WARBLING-FINCH

93.16 BLACK-CAPPED
WARBLING-FINCH

94.1 BLACK-AND-RUFOUS
WARBLING-FINCH

94.2 RUSTY-BROWED
WARBLING-FINCH

94.3 TUCUMAN
MOUNTAIN-FINCH

94.4 CINNAMON
WARBLING-FINCH

94.5 RED-RUMPED
WARBLING-FINCH

94.6 SLENDER-BILLED
FINCH

94.7 SHORT-TAILED FINCH

94.8 WHITE-WINGED
DIUCA-FINCH

94.9 COMMON
DIUCA-FINCH

94.10 LONG-TAILED
REED-FINCH

94.11 BLACK-CRESTED
FINCH

94.12 GREY-CRESTED FINCH

287

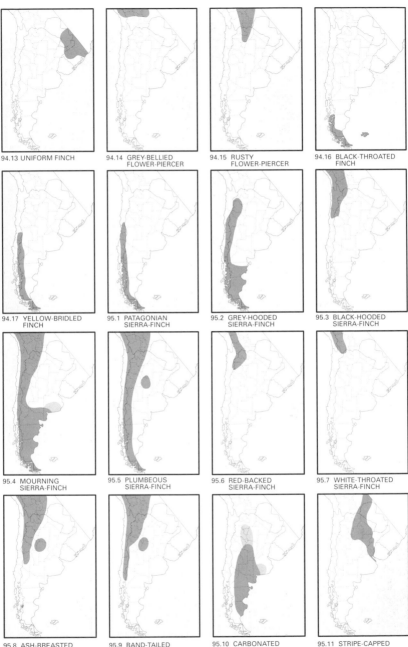

94.13 UNIFORM FINCH

94.14 GREY-BELLIED
FLOWER-PIERCER

94.15 RUSTY
FLOWER-PIERCER

94.16 BLACK-THROATED
FINCH

94.17 YELLOW-BRIDLED
FINCH

95.1 PATAGONIAN
SIERRA-FINCH

95.2 GREY-HOODED
SIERRA-FINCH

95.3 BLACK-HOODED
SIERRA-FINCH

95.4 MOURNING
SIERRA-FINCH

95.5 PLUMBEOUS
SIERRA-FINCH

95.6 RED-BACKED
SIERRA-FINCH

95.7 WHITE-THROATED
SIERRA-FINCH

95.8 ASH-BREASTED
SIERRA-FINCH

95.9 BAND-TAILED
SIERRA-FINCH

95.10 CARBONATED
SIERRA-FINCH

95.11 STRIPE-CAPPED
SPARROW

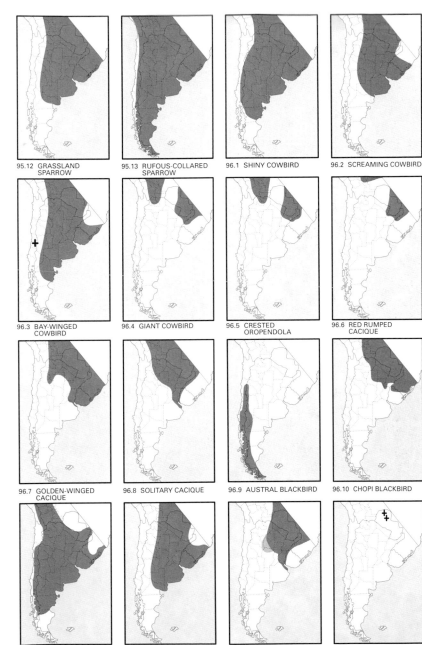

95.12 GRASSLAND SPARROW

95.13 RUFOUS-COLLARED SPARROW

96.1 SHINY COWBIRD

96.2 SCREAMING COWBIRD

96.3 BAY-WINGED COWBIRD

96.4 GIANT COWBIRD

96.5 CRESTED OROPENDOLA

96.6 RED RUMPED CACIQUE

96.7 GOLDEN-WINGED CACIQUE

96.8 SOLITARY CACIQUE

96.9 AUSTRAL BLACKBIRD

96.10 CHOPI BLACKBIRD

96.11 YELLOW-WINGED BLACKBIRD

96.12 CHESTNUT-CAPPED BLACKBIRD

96.13 UNICOLOURED BLACKBIRD

96.14 YELLOW-HOODED BLACKBIRD

289

96.15 EPAULET ORIOLE

96.16 TROUPIAL

96.17 SAFFRON-COWLED BLACKBIRD

97.1 SCARLET-HEADED BLACKBIRD

97.2 YELLOW-RUMPED MARSHBIRD

97.3 BROWN-AND-YELLOW MARSHBIRD

97.4 WHITE-BROWED BLACKBIRD

97.5 PAMPAS MEADOWLARK

97.6 LONG-TAILED MEADOWLARK

97.7 PERUVIAN MEADOWLARK

97.8 BOBOLINK

97.9 THICK-BILLED SISKIN

97.10 HOODED SISKIN

97.11 BLACK SISKIN

97.12 YELLOW-RUMPED SISKIN

97.13 BLACK-CHINNED SISKIN

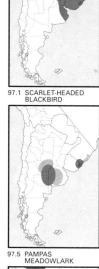

290

97.14 EUROPEAN
GOLDFINCH

97.15 EUROPEAN
GREENFINCH

97.16 HOUSE SPARROW

BIBLIOGRAPHY

ARAYA, M.B. and G.MILLIE HOLMAN.1986. *Guía de campo de las aves de Chile*. Ed.Universitaria. Santiago de Chile.

ARRIBAS, M.A. et al. 1995. *Lista de las aves de Bolivia*. Asoc. Armonia. S.C. de la Sierra. Bolivia.

BELTON, W.1984.1985. *Birds of Rio Grande do Sul*, Parts I & II Bull. Am. Mus. Nat. Hist., Vols 178 & 180, New York.

CANEVARI, M. et al.1991 *Nueva guía de las aves Argentinas*. Vols I & II. Fundación Acindar, Buenos Aires.

CLEMENTS, J.F.1981. *Birds of the world - a check list*. Ibis Vista. Cal.

DE LA PEÑA, M.R.1992.*Guía de las aves argentinas*, vols I to VI. L.O.L.A. Buenos Aires.

DE SCHAUENSEE, R.M. 1970. *A guide to the birds of South America*. The Acad. Nat. Sci. Philadelphia. Pennsylvania. USA.

FJELDSA, JON. & NEILS KRABBE. 1990. *Birds of the High Andes*. Apollo Books. Denmark.

HARRISON, P. 1987. *Seabirds of the world - a photographic guide*. Christopher Helm. London.

HAYES, F.E.1995. *Status, distribution and biogeography of the birds of Paraguay*. Am. Birding Assoc.

MERCADO, N.K. 1985. *Aves de Bolivia*. Ed. Gisbert y Cia. La Paz, Bolivia.

OLROG, C.C. 1979. *Nueva lista de la avifauna argentina*. Op. Lilloana 27. Tucuman, Argentina.

PARKER, T.A., S. ALLEN PARKER and M. PLENGE, 1982. *An annotated checklist of Peruvian birds*. Buteo Books, S.Dakota.

RIDGELY, R. and G. TUDOR, 1989 and 1994. *The birds of South America*. vols 1 & 2. Univ. of Texas Press, Austin, Texas, USA.

SICK. H, 1985. *Ornitologia brasileira, uma introduçao*. vols 1 & 2. Ed.Univ. de Brasilia.

STRANECK, R. 1990. *Canto de las aves ...* (argentinas) Vols I to VIII. Editorial L.O.L.A. Buenos Aires.

Index of scientific names

Numbers refer to the relevant plate, followed by the number of the bird on that plate.

Index of common names

Numbers refer to the relevant plate, followed by the number of the bird on that plate.